CHINA'S
MODERN ECONOMY
IN HISTORICAL
PERSPECTIVE

Contributors

KANG CHAO   RAMON H. MYERS

ROBERT F. DERNBERGER   DWIGHT H. PERKINS

MARK ELVIN   THOMAS G. RAWSKI

JOHN C. H. FEI   CARL RISKIN

PETER SCHRAN

CHINA'S MODERN ECONOMY IN HISTORICAL PERSPECTIVE

Edited by Dwight H. Perkins

Sponsored by the Social Science Research Council

STANFORD UNIVERSITY PRESS

Stanford, California

1975

Stanford University Press
Stanford, California
© 1975 by the Board of Trustees of the
Leland Stanford Junior University
Printed in the United States of America
ISBN 0-8047-0871-1
LC 74-82779

Preface

The papers in this volume were prepared originally for a conference in Bermuda in June 1973 under the sponsorship of the Subcommittee for Research on the Chinese Economy of the Joint Committee on Contemporary China of the Social Science Research Council and the American Council of Learned Societies, with support from the Ford Foundation. The papers presented were substantially revised and edited prior to their inclusion in this volume.

Participants in the conference who did not prepare papers for this volume played a particularly valuable role as discussants and rapporteurs. Those present, in addition to the authors, were Alexander Eckstein (University of Michigan), John Gurley (Stanford University), Robert Hartwell (University of Pennsylvania), Albert Keidel (Harvard University), Paul Kuznets (Indiana University), Simon Kuznets (Harvard University), Bruce Reynolds (University of Michigan), David L. Sills (Social Science Research Council), and Yeh-chien Wang (Kent State University).

The subcommittee is indebted to Mrs. Olive Holmes, who edited the conference papers, and to Miss Laura Hannan, who did much of the typing.

D.H.P.

Contents

Tables

Chao: Growth of a Modern Cotton Textile Industry

Rawski: Growth of Producer Industries

Contributors

KANG CHAO is Professor of Economics at the University of Wisconsin—Madison, and the author of *Agricultural Production in Communist China, 1949–1965* (1970), and *Capital Formation in Mainland China, 1952–1965* (1974).

ROBERT F. DERNBERGER is Professor of Economics and Associate Chairman of the Department of Economics at the University of Michigan. He has written numerous papers on the economy of the People's Republic of China and has published papers on that subject in several collections.

MARK ELVIN is Lecturer in Chinese History and a Fellow of St. Antony's College, Oxford. He is the author of *The Pattern of the Chinese Past* (1973) and the co-editor (with G. William Skinner) of *The Chinese City Between Two Worlds* (1974).

JOHN C. H. FEI received his Ph.D. in economics from the Massachusetts Institute of Technology in 1952. He formerly taught at Antioch College, the University of Washington, MIT, and Cornell University, and is currently Professor of Economics at Yale University.

RAMON H. MYERS is Professor of Economics and History at the University of Miami, Coral Gables, Florida, and the author of *The Chinese Peasant Economy: Agricultural Development in Hopei and Shantung, 1890–1949* (1970). He is currently writing a book on the transformation of the Chinese peasant economy.

DWIGHT H. PERKINS is Professor of Economics at Harvard University and Associate Director of the university's East Asian Research Center. He is the author (with M. H. Halperin) of *Communist China and Arms Control* (1965), *Market Control and Planning in Communist China* (1966), and *Agricultural Development in China, 1368–1968* (1969).

THOMAS G. RAWSKI is a member of the Department of Political Economy, University of Toronto. He has published several articles on the development of China's economy since 1949, and is completing a book on China's producer industries.

CARL RISKIN received his Ph.D. in economics from the University of California —Berkeley in 1969 and has taught at Columbia University and Queens College, City University of New York. The major part of his work has been on small-scale industrialization and work motivation in China.

PETER SCHRAN is Professor of Economics and Asian Studies at the University of Illinois. He is the author of *The Development of Chinese Agriculture, 1950–1959* (1969), and of a forthcoming volume, *Guerrilla Economy, 1937–1945: The Development of the Shensi-Kansu-Ninghsia Border Region.*

CHINA'S
MODERN ECONOMY
IN HISTORICAL
PERSPECTIVE

Dwight H. Perkins

Introduction: The Persistence of the Past

FOR TWO decades and more, economists and others interested in the People's Republic of China have thought of China after 1949 as a case apart. But throughout these two decades China's economic development has been the product of at least three parts of the Chinese experience: the revolution of 1949, the elements of the Chinese economy that were typical of many less-developed economies, and the unique features of China's own past. The latter two in particular have tended to be neglected.

Although much of the analysis in this volume sheds light on whether China was a "typical" less-developed country, the primary focus is on the degree to which China's post-1949 economy was a product of the nation's own past. In some essays the connections between the earlier and later periods are drawn explicitly, but even in those in which the author deals only with the prerevolutionary era, the issues discussed are not just interesting in their own right; they are essential to any understanding of what has happened since 1949. For example, one cannot really understand the effects on the economy of the Communist policy of excluding foreigner participation and limiting foreign trade unless one has a grasp of what the historical role of the foreigner in China has been. Thus, even in areas where the People's Republic has instituted radical change, one cannot comprehend the magnitude or significance of that change unless one can answer the question, change from what?

Tradition—Barrier or Aid to Growth

Much of the analysis of China's economy of the nineteenth and early twentieth centuries has centered on the issue of what prevented modern economic growth prior to the 1949 revolution. For economic historians in the People's Republic, this work has been devoted to explaining or defining the historical role of the Communist Party, i.e. what it was that

inhibited growth that only a Communist revolution could have removed. Our concern in this volume is much broader. In this introduction
and in the essays that follow, positive as well as negative elements in the
tradition are identified. It is simply not true that all features of China's
premodern economy and society acted as barriers to progress (or were
at best neutral). Many characteristics of the Chinese tradition played
an important role in facilitating developments under the People's Republic.

Some of the confusion surrounding the issue of whether China's past
was a help or a hindrance arises because scholars studying the issue
are often asking two different questions. To many the central problem is
whether China could have entered an era of modern economic growth
prior to and independent of any contact with Europe and America. To
others the major question is why it took China more than a century
after its defeat in the first Opium War to begin systematically acquiring the fruits of modern technology.

The focus of this volume is mainly on the second question, but a complete answer to that question is not possible without at least a general
outline of an answer to the first. For example, as Robert Dernberger
points out, foreign imperialism cannot be blamed for all of China's lack
of development in the nineteenth and twentieth centuries unless one
is also prepared to argue that China was on the verge of independently
entering into modern economic growth. But the *sine qua non* of such an
event would have been the prior or simultaneous development of modern science and technology. And Mark Elvin, in his essay, demonstrates
that there is little evidence that Chinese science and technology were
on the verge of major breakthroughs. In fact there were few changes
in technology of any kind in the five centuries prior to the Opium Wars,
and those that did occur were of marginal significance. Thus China's
economy expanded in size as population grew, but expansion took place
within a stagnant technology, and hence per capita income rose little
if at all.

Whatever else foreigners did in China, they removed this single most
important barrier to modern economic growth. From the latter half of
the nineteenth century on, China could import modern science and
technology. But for the next one hundred years few Chinese took advantage of this opportunity, and economic progress was modest at best.
At the same time, Japan, China's neighbor and a disciple of Chinese
civilization, almost immediately began an industrialization effort that
soon left its former teacher far behind.

It is not easy to sort out what happened in China that prevented development for so long. The most popular explanation in China, and among many non-Chinese as well, is that foreign imperialism stifled indigenous attempts to initiate industrial growth and quickly bought out those enterprises that did get off the ground. But as Dernberger shows, a systematic analysis of the direct economic impact of foreigners almost inevitably comes to the conclusion that their net *economic* effect, in spite of some negative features, was positive though not sufficient by itself to initiate modern economic growth.

When one turns to barriers within Chinese society, the problem of determining what was central is complicated by the fact that many features of that society differ radically from those in the societies of Western Europe and the United States. It has thus been common among scholars to argue that one or another feature of Western civilization was essential to progress in China, and that accordingly its absence there explains China's difficulties. The inevitable impression left by such analyses is that traditional Chinese society was riddled with characteristics that had to be swept away by revolution, education, or some other force before progress was possible.

But, if instead of comparing China with Europe one views China in the perspective of other less-developed countries, traditional Chinese society appears to have nurtured within itself certain values and traits more compatible with modern economic growth than those of many other less-developed states. That is, far from being negative barriers, several principal features of Chinese society were a vital positive force once other real barriers to economic development were removed.

The Prior Accumulation of Experience

The traits and values of relevance here had many facets, but all or most can be subsumed under the theme of *a prior accumulation of experience with complex organizations or institutions.* This accumulation of experience in turn came about as a result of a millennium or more of a particular kind of economic development, one that did not involve a rise in per capita income but did lead to an increasingly complex society and economy.

The historical origins of this premodern development go far back into antiquity, and most of its key features were firmly established by the seventeenth or eighteenth century if not before. These features included:

1. A high degree of commercialization, so that most farmers produced

in part for the market and some, particularly along the coast, produced primarily for the market.*

2. A bimetallic monetary system backed up by a nationwide network of premodern banks.

3. A number of cities (as many as ten) with populations of half a million to a million supplied by commercial networks and organizations of considerable size and complexity.[1]

4. A system of land tenure based on private ownership of land. Sale or rental of land was carried out by means of formal written contracts.

5. A high man-land ratio necessitating the use of a complex farm technology that in turn made possible a high yield per acre. Included in this high technology were complex arrangements for sharing the water necessary for irrigation and a tradition of writing down what was known about agricultural technology and distributing agricultural handbooks that summarized this information.

6. A political system in which most of the senior positions were filled by men who had passed a series of written examinations, usually after two or more decades of study of the Chinese classics.

7. A high value placed on education and literacy by most members of the society, partly because it was the route to political power, but also because of its uses in commerce and other fields. Although the available evidence is sparse, it is likely that this interest in education was accompanied by a high level of literacy (as much as a quarter of the male population)—high, that is, by premodern standards.†

Those who know Japanese economic history will find the above list familiar; most of the same characteristics could be found in eighteenth-century Japan.[2] The principal differences were that Japanese political positions were allocated on the basis of birth not education, and, paradoxically, the level of literacy was probably somewhat higher than in China.

* Throughout China, the percentage of agricultural produce marketed probably averaged between 30 and 40 percent (Dwight H. Perkins, *Agricultural Development in China, 1368–1968*, Chicago, 1969, p. 114), but in many regions, the marketed portion was above 50 and even 60 percent (John Lossing Buck, *China's Farm Economy*, Chicago, 1930, p. 84).

† According to John Lossing Buck, *Land Utilization in China* (Nanking, 1937), p. 373, 45 percent of all males over seven years of age had received some schooling (an average of four years) and 30 percent were literate in the 1930's. In the late nineteenth century the Imperial Maritime Customs included questions about literacy in its decennial questionnaires to its regional offices. Although the figures thus arrived at are subject to a wide margin of error, they do suggest that the level of literacy in the late nineteenth century was about the same as in the 1930's. (Imperial Maritime Customs, *Decennial Reports, 1882–1891*, Shanghai, 1893, pp. 20, 62, 105, 147–48, 182–83, 221, 264, 309, 376, 403, 422, 486, 514–15, 568–69, 657–58, 673.)

Were these developments characteristic of all premodern societies? The answer is clearly not. In much of precolonial Southeast Asia, for example, population was sparse. There were few cities of any size, and none that matched or came close to the imperial capitals of Peking and Edo. Villages were far apart and trade between them limited. When a substantial long distance trade did develop, it was largely in the hands of foreigners (Chinese and Europeans). In most of the region land was plentiful, agricultural techniques simple, and yields low. With abundant land and a bounteous sea, maintaining adequate supplies of food was ordinarily not very difficult. Adequate food, however, did not necessarily imply a stable long life. Tropical disease and the frequent warfare associated with a fragmented political structure probably made life more unpredictable than in the large, settled agricultural states to the north. Finally, literacy was low and in many areas nonexistent.

If one is prepared to grant that sharp differences existed between the premodern histories of these two groups of societies, there remains the question of how these histories created values and traits beneficial or harmful to modern economic growth. In part the answer to this question turns on whether or not China's premodern development produced persons who could play an entrepreneurial role once other necessary conditions (for example, the availability of modern technology) were met. But there is more to the human component of growth than entrepreneurship. An easily disciplined and trainable labor force is clearly desirable. So is the existence of managerial-level personnel who can work effectively within a large and complex organization. Albert Hirschman in this context speaks of the cooperative or human relations component of entrepreneurship as being critical to effective action.[3]

The key argument here is that China's premodern development created values and traits that made the Chinese people on the average effective entrepreneurs, workers, and organization men when given the opportunity. Certainly few Chinese today or as far back as information has been available have lacked a drive to get ahead materially (lacked high levels of need-achievement, in the terminology of David McClelland).[4] Furthermore, it is reasonable to suppose that this drive to achieve was a product of China's premodern economic and political system. Farmers who did not work hard seldom if ever prospered. Poverty as a result of limited resources was a hard taskmaster. Even many members of the well-to-do classes worked with equal purpose on their study of the classics in order to obtain high official position.

Poverty and limited resources of land, however, did not affect just the willingness to work. A farmer had to apply a considerable fund of knowledge of technology and market behavior in order to survive. He had to know how to raise different cash crops, and he had to be reasonably astute in guessing which to sow, and when, for the maximum profit. On the financial side, Chinese peasant farmers well understood mortgages, deeds to land, credit, and interest.

At high income levels and in urban areas, familiarity with market behavior was even more profound. Foreign merchants, for example, were never able to compete successfully with Chinese merchants on the Chinese domestic market. European goods were sold to Chinese, and Chinese tea and silk were shipped to Europe, but European traders handled these goods only as they left Chinese shores or up to the point of entry to those shores. As Chinese merchants increased their knowledge of the requirements of foreign markets and sources of supply, even foreign trade gradually passed into Chinese hands.[5]

The contrast with, say, the history of the Indonesian archipelago is striking. There most trade other than local exchange quickly passed into and largely remained in the hands of overseas Chinese and Dutch, i.e. outsiders. It is highly unlikely that this sharp difference in the responses of the Chinese and the Indonesians had anything to do with an inborn talent for commerce on the part of the one that was lacking in the other. It is far more likely that the differing responses merely reflected different heritages. The Chinese had vast experience in all kinds of commercial operations and hence could eventually compete with the Europeans. The Indonesians had no comparable experience at the time they had to face the Dutch-Chinese challenge and until after independence were given no opportunity to acquire it.

The Chinese emphasis on education is even more obviously a condition of value to a nation about to enter into a period of modern economic growth. Anyone who has lived and worked in Chinese communities knows how even the very poor are willing to make almost any sacrifice to educate their children, and there is ample evidence that this attitude has a long history. Equally important is the fact that prior to 1949 (or 1900) many Chinese did receive some education and a few received a great deal. If part of a good education is being raised in a well-educated family, there were perhaps hundreds of thousands of Chinese who had had that opportunity as of 1949.* In no way was China com-

---

* Nearly 200,000 persons in China graduated from universities in the 1928–47 period and, though some left for Taiwan or abroad, the great majority remained in China. See data in Leo A. Orleans, *Professional Manpower and Education in Communist China* (Washington, D.C., 1961), pp. 126–28. Though 200,000 is not a large number given China's size, it still dwarfs the situation as of 1949 in Indonesia, much of Africa, etc.

parable to, say, Indonesia or worse still the Belgian Congo, where only a handful of persons had even a high school education at the time of independence.

Thus China on the eve of its post-1949 push on the economic front had a hardworking, readily trainable population already experienced in the operation of or participation in a commerical economy. It does not follow that if left alone China would have entered automatically into a period of modern economic growth, any more than nineteenth-century Japan would have without the reforms of the Meiji Restoration. On the contrary, even though these characteristics had existed for hundreds of years, China had not built an industrial society; there were too many other ingredients usually associated with successful economic development missing. The point is that the Chinese people had many values and traits that prepared them for modern economic growth once it came. And these values and traits had in large part arisen out of the accumulated Chinese experience with a complex premodern society.

The Evidence

What evidence is there that these Chinese values and traits were in fact well suited to modern economic growth? Bits of the evidence have already been mentioned: the ability of Chinese merchants to compete with their European rivals in the late nineteenth century, for example; and the irrefutable fact that from the seventeenth century on, the Chinese economy was far more advanced than, say, that of Malaya or Indonesia. But none of this evidence really establishes the connection between the premodern situation and China's post-1949 economic growth.

Unfortunately there are no neat statistical tests one can apply to some existing body of data that will establish this relationship. Instead it is necessary to rely on two kinds of evidence, neither of which can be unambiguously interpreted. The first of these is the experience of China after 1949 with a variety of complex organizations, advanced technology, and the like. The second is the correlation between the regional pattern of economic growth in East and Southeast Asia and the location of ethnic Chinese. The features in China's own post-1949 experience of relevance here include China's willingness after 1960 to do without foreign technical assistance except in very small amounts, the decision in the early 1950's to socialize and centrally plan and control the entire modern sector of the economy, and, finally, the effort to develop a small-scale industrial technology suitable to China's factor proportions.

When the Soviet Union withdrew all of its technicians from China in 1960, Chinese industry appeared to be in deep trouble. Within five

years, however, most difficulties had disappeared, and plants were operating near capacity and without any significant infusion of technical
talent from abroad.

The simple conclusion that some observers draw from this experience
is that most less-developed nations could kick out their foreign technicians with only temporary economic loss. But other countries have
tried, and the results have often been near-disastrous. Indonesia under
Sukarno, for example, expelled many foreign technicians, and the facilities they operated deteriorated steadily thereafter. Burma went even
further and threw out its Indian minority as well as most other foreigners; more than a decade later the country had still to find effective
Burmese replacements, and the whole economy had gone downhill.
Few would predict any great success for Uganda, which began taking
similar measures in the early 1970's. Furthermore, the technology of the
modern sector of these countries was still relatively simple. None were
involved in the construction of nuclear weapons, missiles, ships, steel
mills, and numerous kinds of complex machinery, as China was in 1960.

The point is not that these countries will never be able to do without
foreign technical assistance or that China is unique among less-developed nations. The point is rather that it takes time to develop this
kind of talent. One cannot take a person who has been half-trained
in poor rural primary and secondary schools and then send him abroad
for a few years and turn him into a first-class nuclear physicist. One
must first upgrade those primary and secondary schools, and that requires, among other things, good teachers, who are in very short supply
in many less-developed countries. And it usually helps if the person
to be trained has been raised in an educated family. Thus the process of
creating a core of skilled technicians takes time, perhaps a generation
or more in nations with a weak or nonexistent educational heritage.
China even in the 1950's had such a heritage, as did India, several Latin
American states, and a few of the other less-developed countries around
the world. Indonesia, most of the African states, and many other less-
developed nations did not.

The Chinese decision in the early 1950's to introduce the Soviet system of planning and control of the modern sector is a second example
of a measure that would have been difficult, perhaps even impossible,
to carry out if China had not had a large number of skilled people
already experienced in running complex organizations. The accounting
and statistical reporting requirements of central planning alone would
have exhausted the limited pool of skilled personnel available in most
other less-developed countries. But central planning and the direction of

enterprises by means of physical controls involve much more than the presence of people who can calculate and balance books. Considerable managerial skills of all kinds are required at many levels in order to ensure that the plan is properly implemented. China, to be sure, ran into problems in this area and had to decentralize many planning functions as a result, but this decentralization was carried out within a framework that still allowed for a high degree of centralized control. Removing authority from Peking to a provincial planning and implementation group, for example, still leaves that agency with the problem of directing hundreds if not thousands of enterprises.*

The case of Indonesia provides a useful contrast with China. Indonesia at the time this is written (1974) has as able a group of economic ministers as any country in the world. But no serious observer would suggest that these ministers could, if they desired, introduce and operate highly centralized controls over the Indonesian economy. The implementation capacity simply does not exist and probably will not exist for some years to come. The difference between China and Indonesia in this respect is not that China had a revolution and Indonesia did not. The crucial difference is that the Indonesian colonial heritage effectively cut off virtually all Indonesians from formal education and from experience in the operation of their own economy except at very low levels, whereas the Western experience of China did not.

A final example of the importance of the pre-1949 Chinese heritage, and probably the most controversial, is the relationship between that heritage and China's small-scale industry campaign. The contemporary literature on economic development is filled with discussions of countries with industrial plants introduced from abroad that are as advanced and capital-intensive as any in the world (e.g., in petrochemicals). There are many reasons for this phenomenon, but one that is frequently mentioned is the difficulties plant managers in less-developed countries have with managing their labor force. The solution frequently resorted to is to reduce the size of that labor force as much as possible, hence the resort to capital-intensive technology.

China in the 1060's moved in precisely the opposite direction. Thousands of small-scale industrial enterprises using labor-intensive technologies were actively promoted throughout the countryside and by the early 1970's accounted for a significant portion of the output of several major commodities (e.g., cement and chemical fertilizer). As far as one can tell, at no time in that period, except at the height of major political

---

* A typical province in China has 30,000,000 to 40,000,000 people—or more than the great majority of the world's nations.

campaigns, did management or control of the labor force appear to have
been a major problem. Often workers lacked necessary skills and made
mistakes, but they learned quickly and were disciplined and hardworking. Some of this spirit can undoubtedly be attributed to the 1949 revolution, to the strength of the Communist Party, and to the Cultural Revolution, but this is not the whole story. Chinese workers did not begin to
learn quickly or become disciplined only after 1949 or only in the People's Republic. Chinese entrepreneurs in Hong Kong and Southeast
Asia are also noted for operating small-scale, labor-intensive enterprises,* and they too seem to look on their workers not as a problem,
but as their most valuable resource. The quality of these workers is
very much a product of the heritage of China's premodern economy and
society.

I have not presented any of these examples in order to deny the importance of the Chinese Revolution. Many, perhaps all, of the developments I have described would not have occurred if there had not been
a revolution that brought to power leaders who were determined to
promote socialism and self-reliance and to serve the people. The point
is that this same leadership could not have pursued these goals to anything like the degree they did if the people of China had lacked the
necessary skills and attitudes to fulfill them. The Chinese people in 1949
or even 1960 would not have had the necessary skills and attitudes if
it had not been for the complexity and sophistication of China's premodern society and the accumulation of experience with that society.

The second major body of evidence derives from the undisputed fact
that the Chinese populations of Southeast Asia and Taiwan succeeded in
engineering a rapid increase in their gross national product in the 1960's
and 1970's. The cases of Singapore and Hong Kong are well known. But
it is less well appreciated, perhaps, that the rapid growth of Thailand
in this period was concentrated in Bangkok, a heavily Chinese city, and
that growth in Malaysia was largely confined to the Chinese community.[6]
Nor would anyone seriously disagree that the other peoples of Southeast Asia fared less well in the same years, and generally much less well.
The Koreans alone are an exception, and Korea (North and South) is
the most sinicized non-Chinese state in Asia. The issue is the degree to
which this situation results from values and traits acquired from the
experience over centuries of premodern development.

If one hopes to draw conclusions about China from this pattern of

---

* Chinese, of course, were sent to Southeast Asia and elsewhere in the nineteenth
and twentieth centuries precisely because they were considered to be such good
workers.

development, one must begin by coming to grips with the argument that the overseas Chinese were somehow different from those that stayed behind. Undoubtedly, for example, the millions of Chinese who left their homeland were somewhat more adventurous than those who stayed behind, and hence this group may have had a higher percentage of people with entrepreneurial qualities. But one cannot carry this argument very far. The main thing that distinguished the Chinese who left from those who stayed was their desperate poverty. Even then many who went had to be forced to go through contracts obtained by coercive tactics and other less savory practices.

Furthermore, the Chinese who emigrated came from a few limited regions of China, regions distinguished mainly by the fact that they were located on the southeast coast near the countries toward which emigrants were going. To be sure, the counties from which these people came were also more commercialized than the Chinese average, but at least one hundred million Chinese who did not emigrate lived in equally commercialized areas. One reason people from a few counties left in disproportionate numbers was that when they arrived in a foreign and often hostile land, they could count on having friends, relatives, or friends of friends to help them through the first difficult period of adjustment (a clearly positive feature of strong family and quasi-family ties). In short, if geography, kinship, poverty, and other factors all figured in the decision to leave, there is no reason to believe that the Chinese who emigrated had substantially different traits from those who remained behind.

There is a still more serious barrier to any attempt to impute causality to the correlation between areas of Chinese culture and areas of high growth rates: the significant role that many elements besides culture played in these performances. Taiwan, for example, was a major recipient of economic aid and, probably more important, experienced several decades of Japanese colonial rule. Singapore benefited from large inflows of Chinese capital from all over Asia,* and both Singapore and Hong Kong had vast experience as major entrepôts. At the same time, these countries and Malaysia not only avoided the pitfalls of an overemphasis on import substitution, but indeed came to be among the most export-oriented nations of the world. This list of "advantages" could be extended.

---

* Singapore was the recipient of large inflows of capital because of the quality of its labor force, the efficiency of such services as banks, government planning efforts, and so on. Thus even if one could prove that most of its growth could be "explained" by these capital inflows, that would not negate my argument.

But not all the conditions facing these rapidly developing countries and territories were favorable. Only Malaysia and Thailand among the rapid developers were well endowed with natural resources. Indonesia, by contrast, is rich in natural resources. Taiwan had to resettle some two million refugees and maintain an army of 600,000, and this in a country with a population numbering some nine million in 1953. Furthermore, the political future of most of these nations was uncertain at best; prudent investors in Hong Kong and Taiwan all had short time horizons after 1949.

Finally, when one looks within nations possessing more than one cultural tradition rather than at comparisons between nations of differing cultures, the contrast in performance remains striking. In Malaysia, where Malays are to some degree favored by the state with preferential laws, special banks, and the like, economic growth was still almost exclusively confined to the Chinese community. Similar phenomena can be seen elsewhere in the region.

An essay on China, however, is not the place to attempt to explain the sources of economic growth in all of East and Southeast Asia.[7] My point in raising this subject has been twofold—to indicate the high correlation between Chinese culture and rapid growth in East and Southeast Asia, and to suggest that there is no obvious way of explaining the correlation by using conventional economic variables.

Traits Harmful to Growth

In view of all the evidence to the contrary, why is it that most analysts who have looked at China's pre-1949 society have concentrated on values and traits they considered inimical to growth? The lack of rapid industrialization prior to 1949 (or 1911) has been attributed to the low status of merchants in traditional China and to certain practices generated by the Chinese family system (e.g. nepotism), to name two of the most pervasive themes. The success of overseas Chinese entrepreneurs and workers is explained away as atypical of the Chinese population as a whole, either on the grounds that those who emigrated were the creative dynamic fringe or on the grounds that once overseas they became a minority group barred from other paths of advancement. The overseas Chinese, in fact, are frequently trotted out in support of theories attempting to explain entrepreneurship worldwide as arising primarily from such blocked minorities (samurai, Jews, Huguenots, and so on).[8]

It is true that traditional China formally placed a low value on commerce; merchants were at the bottom of the social scale, below scholars, farmers, and artisans. But evidence has accumulated in recent years that this formal ordering had little relationship to the reality of Chinese society. Whatever prestige farmers and artisans may have had, it was a poor substitute for the opportunity to increase one's income and wealth, an opportunity largely absent from agriculture or handicrafts but readily available to the successful merchant. Even if a man's ultimate goal was to make his sons and grandsons scholar-officials, he needed money to give them tutors and leisure time for study, and commerce was one of the few sources of such funds for people without other means.

There is also evidence that relations between scholars and merchants were often quite close.[9] Many commercial activities depended on a degree of official protection, and others (the salt monopoly, for example) were under the direct control of the government. Merchant families would sometimes train their sons in the classics precisely so they could become officials and protect the family interests. Even those sons who severed all connection with commerce when they entered the official class probably had some positive influence on the business activities of their relatives (by enhancing their prestige in the community, for instance). Certainly there are few grounds for the often-heard charge that the "loss" of these sons constituted a serious drain on the ability of Chinese society to supply itself with capable businessmen or entrepreneurs. There were fewer than 20,000 scholar-officials at any given time, and most of these were probably the sons of landlords and officials, not merchants. It could be more plausibly argued that the few thousand officials with a commercial family background provided a powerful additional incentive for men to become merchants.

Finally, we can note that the downgrading of commercial enterprise was far from unique to China. Few premodern societies placed merchants high on the formal social ladder. In Japan the order was samurai, farmers, artisans, merchants, and the barriers to entry into the samurai class were considerably stronger than the barriers to entry into the scholar-official class in Ch'ing China. Even in England, commerce was looked down on by the aristocracy, and the sons and daughters of merchants strove to leave their commercial past behind them. In neither Japan nor England, however, did this formal structure prove to be much of a hindrance to economic growth.

The alleged negative influences of the Chinese family system on economic or commercial development also do not stand up well under rigorous analysis. The argument that the system had a significant negative impact has two parts. One part proposes that because distant cousins could go to a rich relative for financial support in time of need, the rich relative had little incentive to accumulate wealth lest it be dissipated in this way.[10] This practice is carried on in parts of the world, among some American Indians, for example, and where it occurs it has a negative impact on economic growth. But China's family system, except in its most idealized form, did not work like this. A rich Chinese family might have assisted a financially distressed distant relative in a small way or allowed a relative to live with them while going to a nearby university, but the list of Chinese who dissipated large accumulations of wealth in this manner is certainly dwarfed by those who did not. Among persons who were not rich, the custom of giving money to less fortunate relations was even more restricted and in many villages did not exist at all.[11] If a man and wife did not have sons, for example, they were likely to have an impecunious and precarious old age.

The second part of the argument holds that owing to the concept of family obligations, nepotism dominated hiring practices. This in turn made it difficult or impossible to run an enterprise efficiently and is seen as a major cause of the failures of many early industrial firms in China. Part of the problem with this argument is that it does not distinguish between public and private employment. Chinese officials could appoint relatives to government positions at no cost and conceivably with some financial benefit to themselves. In privately owned firms, however, the motive behind hiring relatives is likely to be very different. In a society where the rule of law is weak or nonexistent, relatives, unlike outsiders, can be trusted, and the stronger the family ties the greater the basis for such trust. Furthermore, family employees can be expected to be more highly motivated than other employees since they will be working for the greater glory of the family and not just themselves. Family obligations are a two-way street.

There are those who would take the relationship between trust and the family system and turn it around, arguing that because trust could only be based on family ties, Chinese enterprises could not tap sources of capital beyond the family and so remained small. Thus, in Malaya, Chinese dominated tin mining when the technology was simple and required little capital, but lost out to the British when expensive dredges proved to be more efficient in the large mines. But in neither China nor Southeast Asia did Chinese businessmen receive much help from the law in the enforcement of contracts and the like. All they could rely on were family ties and quasi-family relations such as guilds and merchants associations. The alternatives were not family ties versus the rule of law but family ties versus anarchy.

The family system was probably a positive force in other ways as well. Ensuring the survival of one's family down through the generations, for example, can be a powerful reason for saving. Thus, although the argument is not conclusive, there is no good reason to believe that the direct impact of the Chinese family system on economic development was harmful. It is more likely that it was positive.

Government and Social Structure

The above discussion has dealt with the direct effect of China's premodern experience and values on the Chinese people. The principal questions asked were whether ingrained values and skills would be likely to continue even after other barriers to growth had been removed, and, if so, whether the effect of those values and skills that did continue would be positive or negative. On balance the conclusion reached was that these acquired traits were in many ways ideally suited to modern economic growth.

Although one has to pose the question in this way if one is to understand the nature of the human resources inherited by the People's Republic, this formulation of the question is rather artificial if one is interested instead in what actually prevented growth in the century preceding 1949. Chinese values not only influenced the behavior of entrepreneurs, managers, and workers; they also played a major role in shaping the attitudes and policies of government officials and in supporting the structure on which China's traditional government rested. And there is very little of a positive nature that can be said about the role of that government in the promotion of economic development.

Part of the problem was that nineteenth-century government officials, steeped in the Confucian tradition, were intensely conservative. Even the more progressive among them saw mainly the military aspects of Western technical superiority. In other areas, including most of the economy, Chinese ways were preferred. Defeat by the Japanese in 1895, the Boxer fiasco, and similar humiliations gradually eroded Chinese faith in traditional policies and governmental institutions, but the process was agonizingly slow.

Two other shortcomings of China's traditional government, however, were perhaps more important. The inability of Chinese governments of the late nineteenth and early twentieth centuries to maintain political stability requires little elaboration here. It is difficult to promote industry under either public or private auspices if warring armies and insatiable tax collectors are constantly marching up and down the country.

But even during periods of relative tranquillity when the government was led by comparatively progressive officials, its financial base was so

weak that major initiatives were never possible. Where the Meiji government of Japan financed half of the nation's capital formation and
subsidized entrepreneurs in many ways, the Ch'ing and early Republican governments were frequently a net drain on Chinese enterprises.

As Carl Riskin's essay demonstrates, China's pre-1949 lack of financial
resources was not the result of the country's population being so near
to a minimum level of subsistence that no one could afford to save and
invest. There was a "surplus" above subsistence, and this surplus was
largely in the hands of landlords and the urban well-to-do, neither of
whom appear to have done much saving. The problem was how to tap
these sources for economic development, a task not made easier by the
fact that these same groups were the main pillars of the traditional government. After 1949, of course, a very different government mobilized
these resources by means of a combination of taxes plus land reform.
These efforts, coupled with relative political stability, go a long way
toward explaining the difference between the performance of the economy before and after 1949.

What the Present Owes to the Past

But the heritage of the past was not just something that had to be
overcome before progress could begin. We have already identified important positive features of the premodern experience and of China's
century of humiliation by the West. And many other features of the pre-
1949 economy and society helped shape post-1949 developments as well.

As I indicate in my paper on the changing structure of China's national
product, the People's Republic was as much a land short–labor surplus
nation after the Revolution as before. And this factor endowment accounts in part for the large shares of industry and capital formation in
national product and expenditure. The great power of the Chinese Communist Party and the Soviet model of development also played a role
in shaping this pattern, but not as large a one as is commonly assumed.

The Chinese People's Republic also possessed a modern heritage as
well as a traditional heritage. The largest single modern industry was
the cotton textile industry, which is analyzed in the essay by Kang Chao.
To many contemporary observers, this was an industry that achieved
its remarkable growth only at a high cost in displaced handicraft workers. But Kang Chao shows that this picture is greatly overdrawn, and
that the real coup de grace to handicrafts was the result of post-1949
state purchase and sales policies.

There was also a small but significant machine-building industry in
Shanghai; and though there was little progress outside of Manchuria,

where the Japanese were involved, a start was made in the steel industry. Steel mills required large financial resources, and Chinese entrepreneurs did not have them. But as Thomas Rawski points out in his essay, machinery firms could be started up on a small scale with little capital. Rawski demonstrates that the Chinese industrialization program of the 1950's would have been very different in character without these modern producer-goods industrial bases in Manchuria and Shanghai.

The influence of the past on the agricultural sector was even more profound. John Fei, building on the work of G. William Skinner, theorizes that the village–market town structure of rural China was a product of two forces, transport costs and economies of scale in the production of commodities in the market town. Since neither the 1949 Revolution nor the formation of communes fundamentally altered these economic forces, at least in the short run, it presumably follows that they served to reinforce the continuance of older marketing patterns.

Even the cooperative way of work was not wholly new to rural China. Ramon Myers points out that market arrangements were frequently the preferred method of acquiring additional labor and capital, but there are numerous examples of cooperative efforts as well, particularly in the area of water control. And the Chinese family was itself a tiny cooperative.

Breaking with the Past

If China since the Revolution continues to be influenced and constrained by past values, practices, and factor endowments, it is obvious there have also been profound breaks with that past. Many essays in this volume are concerned with areas of continuity, but a knowledge of the past is also essential to an identification of areas of discontinuity.

We have already mentioned the unprecedented mobilization of China's "surplus" and the establishment of relative political stability. As I point out in my essay on the changing structure of Chinese product, it is the major redistribution of income in the early 1950's, not rising output and productivity, that accounts for the often observed profound changes in living conditions in the 1950's and 1960's. And there have been changes in economic institutions too numerous to mention, most of them connected with the massive application of cooperative methods to agriculture or state control to industry.

As these changes occur, the influence of the past on the present changes, at times becoming stronger, at other times disappearing altogether. And what is the present today will be the past tomorrow. Thus the Great Leap Forward and even the Cultural Revolution are already acquiring the aura of tradition and, as such, will continue to influence China's economic performance for years to come. And the intellectual origins of many of the ideas of the Great Leap Forward in turn owe much to the experience of China's leaders in the backward hinterland of Yenan, as Peter Schran so ably points out.

China's people, therefore, have never been free to create a completely new economic model, ideal or otherwise. In part, like the people of all countries, they have had to adjust to the demands of modern industrial technology. But these demands do not appear to be pulling China toward some carbon copy of every other nation that has entered into modern economic growth. If China has some features in common with other Asian or socialist countries, it also has features that are uniquely its own. These features plainly owe much to the goals and efforts of the current generation of Chinese leaders. But, as the essays in this volume demonstrate over and over again, they owe much to China's own past as well.

Robert F. Dernberger

The Role of the Foreigner in China's Economic Development, 1840-1949

CHINA's experience in the late-Ch'ing and Republican eras provides a classic example of the typical problems of economic development. With a per capita income considerably below U.S. $100, a savings ratio well below 10 percent, the inability to develop, produce, and work with modern industrial facilities on any significant scale, and a government unwilling or unable to subsidize and otherwise aid economic growth, China exhibited a wide range of the problems that are held to be the major causes of the failure of modernization in the "new states." Unfortunately, this rich example of the failure of modernization remains outside the mainstream of Western social science research.

Rather, China's failure to modernize is regarded as a special case, to be studied simply by China specialists. The reason for this distorted treatment is obvious: Western education produced a limited number of social scientists with the qualifications and the desire to study China's failure to modernize; and education in China produced a limited number of people who were trained in Western social science research and who could thus provide good secondary sources for Western scholars. It is because of this unhappy development that we find ourselves at this late date with an ambiguous and unclear picture of such an important question as the role of the foreigner in China's economic development.

For obvious reasons of space, this version of my paper is a greatly reduced summary of a research paper presented to the Conference on the Chinese Economy in Historical Perspective held in Bermuda in July 1973. I have benefited immensely from the generous editorial assistance of Dwight Perkins and Barbara Mnookin in summarizing the paper and from the comments and invaluable suggestions of many colleagues, who read various versions of the paper. Inasmuch as the original text of the research paper was at least four times as long as the essay published here, much of the detailed argumentation, statistical evidence, and citations of supporting research have been excluded. Those readers interested in reading the expanded version of the paper are invited to write to the author.

The Role of the Foreigner: The Broad Framework

As the carrier of modern technology to those countries that later became industrialized themselves, the foreigner has played a crucial role in the history of economic development throughout the world. Indeed, at the broadest level, all technology in the modern sector in every developing country can be said to have been transferred from abroad, and specifically from Western Europe, with England the original source of this technology. In the case of the other countries of the West, technology was successfully and peacefully transmitted by the "foreigner" via the normal channels of trade and investment, thanks in large part to the similar cultural, social, and political environment they shared; the foreigner came in peace and encountered limited resistance to his activities and eager acceptance of the technological innovations embodied in those activities.

But when the foreigner, i.e., the purveyor of modern technology, sought out trade and investment opportunities outside the pale of Western civilization, he encountered significant obstacles and resistance to his activities. In order to realize those opportunities for trade and investment, he had to rely on the economic and military superiority of his native country, employing "limited aggression" against the host countries. This served only to induce a reaction against the West in the undeveloped countries calling forth an even greater resistance to the foreigner. And increased resistance in turn often led to the outright colonization of the host country by a Western power.

China, of course, never became the colony of a single European power. Quite the contrary, for when the initial period of limited aggression failed to overcome the almost complete exclusion of foreigners by the Ch'ing Dynasty, China became the scene of open rivalry among the Western powers and Japan. They sought to open China to foreign trade and investment and, once this was accomplished, to establish a legal and institutional framework that would facilitate and protect the business interests of their nationals. The term hyper-colony is frequently used to describe the resulting pattern of concessions, spheres of influence, and special rights the Chinese were forced to grant to the various powers.

The antiforeign reaction to these developments became a decisive obstacle before the Revolution of 1911 and has remained a negative force ever since, due in large part to the severe cultural shock suffered by the Chinese. The intensity of this cultural shock stemmed from their idealization of and tremendous dedication to a long traditional history and their perception of contemporary problems as the consequence of the disruptive force of Western civilization unleashed on China by the foreigner.

One is prompted to ask why the pre-1949 reaction to the foreigner and his technology was so negative and so different from the reaction of Russia, Japan, and even the People's Republic. Comparing these different reactions reveals unmistakable distinguishing features.

First, it is unlikely that the antiforeign sentiment of the general population in China was so different from that in Russia and Japan, or varied so significantly in China before and after 1949, as to explain the differences that resulted from their relations with the foreigner. Rather, it appears to be the differing stances of the governments that is of key importance. Unlike the Ch'ing and Nationalist governments, the Chinese Communist, Russian, and Japanese governments actively pursued economic development by relying on and heavily borrowing the foreigner's technology, while at the same time effectively controlling and limiting his activities within their domestic economy.

Second, the ability of these governments to control both latent and open antiforeign sentiment, while at the same time engaging in large-scale adoption of foreign technology and limited, yet essential, foreign trade, worked to stave off the transition from limited aggression to open aggression. Thus, despite a good many hostile confrontations and some periods of military conflict, these governments were not forced to give up sovereignty over their domestic economy.

Third, the differing experiences with the foreigner have had markedly different results: at this writing (1974) the Soviet Union has the second-largest gross national product in the world, Japan the third-largest. Moreover, though it is premature to claim that the Chinese Communists' economic development effort has been successful, there is little doubt that present prospects for success are as good as those of any other underdeveloped country and contrast favorably with the efforts of the Nationalists before 1949.

It is not my purpose here to examine all the factors responsible for this fundamental difference in response to the spread of modern technology by the foreigner or to attempt to identify those factors that are common to the successful experiences. Rather, I want to examine the economic activity of the foreigner in China in the 100-odd years before the Communist Revolution and to determine whether that activity made a positive contribution, both direct and indirect, to China's economic development. Although restricted in scope, compared with the broad framework suggested in this introductory section, such an examination not only will shed light on a most important topic in modern China's economic history but should provide a necessary step in an analysis of the broader question as well.

The Received Picture of the Foreigner's Role

There are two widely accepted theories purporting to explain China's failure to modernize. The first, Lenin's theory of imperialism, gave Chinese intellectuals—both Marxist and non-Marxist—a general framework for understanding and interpreting China's modern historical experience. The Marxists on the whole simply bought the whole theory and forced Chinese history into its rigid structure. But China's Western-trained social scientists were influenced in a much more subtle and, for our purposes, more serious way. In reading the rich body of literature on China's rural economy produced during the 1930's by such leading Western-trained anthropologists, sociologists, and economists as Chen Han-seng, H. D. Fong, Fei Hsiao-t'ung, Franklin Ho, and members of the Institute of Pacific Relations, one is struck by the overwhelming acceptance of a single major theme: that Western industry, technology, and commerce entering China via the treaty ports and benefiting from the unequal treaties were detrimental to the development of China's economy and were rapidly destroying the economic and social fabric of China's countryside. As one reviewer of these studies has noted, "It is an understatement to say that many of these articles carry an ideological bias."[1]

The existence of a bias, something we can all be accused of, is not the real problem; what concerns me is the manner in which the uniformity of the bias has led to an accepted picture of the negative role of the foreigner in China's economic development. It is the picture Chi-ming Hou paints boldly in the introduction to his study of foreign investment and economic development in China:

First, it is argued that foreign economic intrusion—that is, foreign trade and investment in China—upset the economy by ruining the handicraft industries and disrupting agriculture. Second, foreign trade and investment are alleged to have drained the economy of its wealth because of the secularly unfavorable balance of trade and the large amount of income that was made or remitted to their home countries by Western enterprises. Third, it is maintained that foreign enterprises in China were so effective in their competitive power or enjoyed so many advantages secured by their respective governments that the Chinese-owned modern enterprises were utterly and hopelessly oppressed and had little, if any, chance to grow.[2]

But this analysis, singling out imperialism as the cause of China's difficulties, still does not explain why the governments of Russia and Japan, and of China after 1949, were able to control the activities of the foreigner and to protect and sponsor native enterprise, while the Chinese government before 1949 was not.

The second widely accepted explanation of why China did not achieve economic development ascribes the failure to unique characteristics of China's traditional economy and society. Prominent among the Western scholars who have searched for indigenous obstacles to growth are Marion J. Levy and Albert Feuerwerker. Levy argues that the family in "traditional" China and other aspects of the Chinese social system were remarkably stable in the face of pressures for modernization and, more important, generated a defensive and antidevelopment behavior pattern, so that "China has not made much headway with industrialization."[3] Feuerwerker goes beyond purely social institutions to identify four indigenous obstacles that (along with foreign competition) stood in the way of the development of modern industry "on even a limited scale": governmental weakness and lack of initiative; inadequate savings for significant capital accumulation; technical backwardness; and deficient motivation owing to the traditional cultural and social system.[4]

Unlike the Marxist analysis, this approach attaches secondary importance to the foreigner as a factor in China's failure to industrialize. Though its adherents may see the foreigner as a disruptive element, destroying the equilibrium of the traditional Chinese system, they insist that the Chinese were prevented from profiting from the Western influences because of their traditional system.

There are of course other studies of China's modern economic development that do not fall precisely into either of these general approaches. I have in mind, for example, the several case studies available on particular villages, areas, or industries, all of which contain promising and useful source material at the micro-level and explicitly or implicitly suggest the magnitude of the foreign impact on China's economic development.[5] But we need a good deal of additional evidence before accepting the conclusions reached in any one of these studies as typical for all of China; one observation can hardly serve as an adequate test of a hypothesis. Moreover, a careful reading of some of these studies reveals that the hypothesis advanced does not follow from the evidence presented or is only one of several hypotheses consistent with the evidence.

In recent years, several scholars have reopened and attempted to reassess the question of the foreigner's role in China's economic development.[6] Unfortunately, they have set out to disprove the accepted theories by citing contrary examples. But citing a few counter examples, admirable as this methodology is in mathematics and the natural sciences, cannot disprove a hypothesis in the social sciences. The most beneficial results of these studies have been in challenging the received arguments and pointing to possible positive contributions the foreigner made to China's economic development.

Givens

Ideally, any analysis of the impact of the foreigner on China's economic development in the modern era would begin with a unanimously agreed-to version of the facts. Since that seems clearly out of the question, I shall simply state in bold terms what I believe to be the major features of that development.

The existence of a "high-level equilibrium trap." By the end of the nineteenth century, China's agriculture was caught in what several writers have described as a high-level equilibrium trap.[7] For what is comprehended in that phrase, we refer to the accompanying diagram, which crystallizes the most important features of the problem. Total output of foodstuffs in physical terms (grain equivalent) is measured on the vertical axis, input bundles (land, labor, and capital) on the horizontal axis. Production *possibilities* with the given technology at the beginning of the period, the start of the Ming Dynasty, is portrayed by the curve AA. The ray from the origin, AB, shows the level of output necessary to maintain a socially determined minimum level of con-

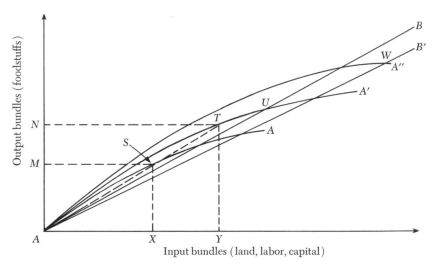

The high-level equilibrium trap in China's traditional agriculture. Shifts in the curves have been exaggerated for clarity's sake, but note that this distorts proportionate shifts along the axis.

sumption per labor input given in the input bundle measured along the horizontal axis. The particular shape of the production possibilities curve, with no change in the input *mix* per unit of land, is determined by the productivity of the marginal units of land. As the population increases, it is employed on less fertile units of land, and when the available land area is brought under cultivation, the input bundles can be increased by double cropping, but this does not increase the output proportionally. Following the arguments presented by Dwight Perkins in his excellent study of Chinese agriculture over this same period,[8] I have drawn the production possibilities curve so per capita foodstuffs, i.e., the marginal productivity of additional input bundles, remains relatively stable over a considerable range.

Simplified though this diagram is, considering the great variety of changes in Chinese agriculture over some five centuries, it reflects what I see as the fundamental dynamic mechanism that led to the observed results in the early decades of the twentieth century. Beginning with an input mix of X and an output of M, the growth in output between 1400 and 1800 can be broken down (1) into an upward shift of the production possibilities curve from AA to AA' due to the introduction and spread of new crops from America in the sixteenth century, the spread of large-scale irrigation projects, the steadily increasing reliance on better varieties of seed, and a host of innovations and improvements that made the existing land more productive per unit of input bundles; and (2) into an increase in the input bundles from X to Y due to the increases in population and cultivated land, the spread of double cropping, and the addition of new marginal areas of land. The relative stability in the input mix is consistent with the 141 percent increase in population and the 148 percent increase in cultivated land between 1600 and 1893; and with the relative stability in per capita consumption (expressed by the ray from the origin that intersects the relevant production possibilities curves at S and T). Thus, without major changes in technology, Chinese agriculture was able to achieve a relatively high level of output and support a relatively large population with constant but above-subsistence per capita levels of consumption.

At Y, however, further increases in population with no change in technology or available land would lead to increases in output but a decrease in per capita consumption. As the economy approached point U, per capita consumption would be at the subsistence level, unleashing the traditional Malthusian limits to population growth. Confronted with this situation, the Chinese took three major steps to maintain per capita consumption at a subsistence level as the population increased.

First, the input mix was changed by a rise in the ratio of labor to capital and land, thus increasing the production possibilities for the available land. The effect of this change, which cannot be shown on our two-dimensional diagram, would be an increase in the average output per unit of land but a decrease in the average output per unit of labor, i.e., a decline in per capita consumption.

Second, the production possibilities for the available land were further increased by changing the output mix in favor of higher yield but less preferred crops, such as potatoes and corn, which could be grown on more marginal units of land. The effect of this change, which also cannot be shown on our diagram, would be an increase in per capita consumption at *the given level of population* but a decrease in the quality of the diet.

Finally, the peasant household unable to raise enough food on the family farm to meet its total needs but unwilling to give up the land that provided security and social standing had two alternatives: to enter the growing network of commercial farming, turning to specialized crop production, or to send its unemployed or underemployed family members into subsidiary occupations (or both). The effect of this change was twofold and can be shown on our two-dimensional diagram. The increasing commercialization and specialization increased the production possibilities for the available land, but the farm family was also exposed to a far greater degree to the play of market forces. The greater use of unemployed or underemployed family members for subsidiary activities reduced the amount of foodcrops each family had to raise for its own consumption.

The net effect of these three changes when China's agriculture approached the intersection of the production possibilities curve and the subsistence per capita consumption ray at U would be an upward shift in the production possibilities curve to AA'' and a decrease in the subsistence per capita consumption ray to AB'.

By the end of the nineteenth century, however, China was no longer able to meet the newest of these crises, i.e., the equilibrium points represented by the intersections of the production possibilities curve and the minimum consumption line, by the methods described. What had worked in the past, increasing output to provide for an increasing population, was no longer possible without significant changes in technology or available land. Fifty years later, it would take nothing less than a major agrarian revolution in institutional organization and technology to free China from this high-level equilibrium trap. To look uncritically on the foreigner as the fundamental cause of the problems that brought Chinese agriculture to this impasse is thus clearly unwarranted.

TABLE 1

China's Exports, Imports, and Total Trade, 1871–1929

(Commodity trade only, annual averages in million current U.S. dollars)

Years	Exports	Imports	Total trade	Per capita	Pct. of world trade	Exports as pct. of GDP
1871–84	$102.5	$106.2	$208.7	$0.58	1.3%	2.5%
1885–1900	110.2	143.5	253.7	0.66	1.3	—
1901–14	201.0	293.8	494.8	1.19	1.5	—
1915–19	521.2	570.8	1,092.0	2.47	—	—
1920–29	619.6	799.0	1,418.6	3.01	2.4	7.3

Sources:

Trade. 1871–1928, Chinese Customs statistics, as converted into U.S. dollars, in C. Yang et al., *Statistics of China's Foreign Trade During the Last Sixty-five Years* (Shanghai, 1931), pp. 32–33; 1929 Chinese Customs statistics, as converted into U.S. dollars, in Yu-kwei Cheng, *Foreign Trade and Industrial Development of China* (Washington, D.C., 1956), pp. 258-59.

Population. Population at mid-point of period estimated by extrapolation, i.e., compounded annual rate of change, based on the estimates for 1873, 1893, 1913, and 1933 in Dwight Perkins, *Agricultural Development in China* (Chicago, 1969), p. 216.

World trade. League of Nations, *Industrialization and Foreign Trade* (Princeton, N.J., 1945), pp. 157-59.

National Income. 1871-1900, Chung-Li Chang's estimate of China's GNP in 1880's as adjusted by Albert Feuerwerker, *The Chinese Economy, ca. 1870-1911* (Ann Arbor, Mich., 1969), p. 2; 1920-29, 1931-36 average GNP estimate in T. C. Liu, *China's National Income, 1931-36* (Washington, D.C., 1946), p. 72.

The size and scope of the foreign sector. Despite continued attempts by China to restrict or control trade with the West, that trade increased steadily throughout the end of the nineteenth century and into the early twentieth century. A brief glance at the figures presented in Table 1 indicates that China's foreign trade was small over this period. Yet these magnitudes are consistent with the data Simon Kuznets presents for comparable countries in his detailed statistical analysis of economic development throughout the world.[9] No underdeveloped country has accounted for a large share of world trade in the modern era. Moreover, given China's low level of development, distance from the major maritime routes of trade, size, abundant and varied resources, and large domestic market, factors that according to Kuznets reduce a country's involvement in foreign trade, China's share of world trade was not "abnormally" low.* By the same token, given its low level of economic development and large population, the size of China's foreign sector and its per capita foreign trade relative to total domestic economic activity also were not "abnormally" low.

* For example, in 1925–29 China's share of world trade was 2.3 percent, against 3.0, 3.3, and 1.2 percent, respectively, for Japan, India, and the USSR; its per capita trade amounted to U.S. $3.3 against $6.3 and $5.4 for India and the USSR; and its foreign trade represented 17 percent of national income against 13 percent for the United States.

Much the same argument can be made concerning the size of foreign investment in China. The Chinese government, through local authorities, had borrowed relatively small amounts from foreigners between 1861 and 1894 to meet military needs, construct the Summer Palace, and repair the banks of the Yellow River at Chengchow. But large public loans were not negotiated and private foreign investment was not legal until after the Sino-Japanese War of 1894. Between 1861 and 1937, foreign loans totaling U.S. $1.25 billion were negotiated by the Chinese government, mostly borrowed for military, administrative, and railroad-building purposes.* What part of the annual flow of capital from abroad this represented is difficult to say. The figures in Table 2 indicate a gross private and public foreign investment of approximately U.S. $1.5 billion in 1902–30. But they are based entirely on estimates and are thus not very reliable. When reinvested profits and other private capital inflows are taken into account, the net flow of private foreign investment alone is estimated at close to U.S. $2 billion over the same period (see Table 3).

Chi-ming Hou argues, wrongly, I think, that foreign investment in China "was not large" in comparison with other underdeveloped countries.[10] For one thing, I think he is mistaken in using data on per capita foreign investment as a measure. His other measure has more force: as a percentage of national income and of gross domestic capital formation, foreign investment in China was small compared with other countries, especially Japan. Let us see how this evidence stands up. Kuznets estimates that international capital flows were a small proportion of national product for large, debtor, developed countries (the only countries for which systematic data are available), accounting for about 4 percent of national income and 30 percent of gross domestic capital formation in 1897–1906, the period of largest proportional inflow of foreign capital for those countries.[11] For Japan, the net inflow of foreign capital accounted for 2.3 percent of national income and 12 percent of net capital formation in 1896–1913.[12] Using our estimates of net private investment for 1928–30 and China's GNP in 1931–36, we find that net private foreign investment accounted for slightly less than 1 percent of China's GNP. This does seem to suggest China's foreign investment was small compared with Japan's.

However, the comparison breaks down on two counts. First, the data used are biased in favor of a relatively low percentage for China. Gross national product is larger than national income, and China's national

---

* The figures on the foreign loans to the Chinese government are as follows (in million current U.S. dollars): 1861–93, 63.3; 1894–98, 298.3; 1899–1911, 149.4; 1912–26, 574.2; 1927–37, 166.9. The precise 1861–1937 total is U.S. $1,252,100.

TABLE 2

Foreign Investment in China, 1902–1930

(Million current U.S. dollars)

Category	1902-13	1914-30	1902-30
Annual average:			
Public	27.98	12.39	18.84
Private	24.22	38.33	32.49
Total	52.20	50.72	51.33
Amount:			
Public	335.76	210.63	546.39
Private	290.64	651.61	942.25
Total	626.40	862.24	1,488.64

Source: C. F. Remer, *Foreign Investments in China* (New York, 1968), p. 170. Conversion from Chinese dollar data in this source to current U.S. dollars by means of average exchange rates presented in *ibid.*, p. 172.

TABLE 3

Estimated Balance of Payments, 1902–1930

(Million current U.S. dollars)

Category	1902-13	1914-30	1902-30
Total imports:			
Annual average	258.4	720.7	529.4
Total for period	3,100.6	12,252.1	15,352.7
Import surplus:			
Annual average	88.6	139.7	118.6
Total for period	1,063.3	2,375.5	3,438.8
Pct. of total imports	34.3%	19.4%	22.4%
Private foreign investment:			
Annual average	47.0	75.1	63.5
Total for period	563.6	1,276.7	1,840.3
Pct. of import surplus	53.0%	53.7%	53.5%
Remittances from overseas Chinese:			
Annual average	45.0	89.5	71.0
Total for period	539.6	1,502.7	2,060.3
Pct. of import surplus	50.7%	63.3%	59.9%

Sources:

Net flow of funds: trade data, same as in Table 1.

Private foreign investment and remittances from overseas Chinese: balance of payments estimates for 1903, from H. B. Morse, *An Inquiry into the Commercial Liabilities and Assets of China in International Trade* (Shanghai, 1904); for 1912, from R. S. Wagel, *Finance in China* (Shanghai, 1914), p. 473; for 1913 from C. S. See, *The Foreign Trade of China* (New York, 1919), p. 334; for 1920-23 (average), from A. G. Coons, *The Foreign Public Debts of China* (Philadelphia, 1930), pp. 181-84; for 1928-29, from C. F. Remer, *Foreign Investments of China* (New York, 1968), pp. 221-22; for 1930, K. T. Tsuchiya, in T. F. Kowh, *Fluctuation of Silver Prices and China* (Shanghai, 1935), p. 76. I have extrapolated the annual estimates for all the other years, assuming a constant compound annual rate of change between the years for which published estimates were available.

Note: Percentage for private foreign investment and remittances from overseas Chinese does not total 100 because these are not the only entries in the capital account and there are undoubtedly considerable margins of error in the estimates for these two categories of capital inflow.

income in 1914–25, when the inflow of foreign capital was at its peak, was undoubtedly lower than in 1931–36. Furthermore, private foreign investment is smaller than total foreign investment. The use of percentages for large, debtor, *developed* countries biases the comparison against China because, as is the case with foreign trade, which is significantly related to foreign capital flows, the largest share of those flows is between the developed countries. According to Kuznets, the developed countries received 79 percent of the total flow of foreign capital in 1921–38, and 93 percent of the total if Argentina is included in the group.[13]

Second, though the comparison of China with Japan has some relevance, Japan is an island economy, dependent on foreign trade for a relatively large portion of its raw materials and consumer goods, i.e., its foreign trade participation ratio is much larger than China's. In fact, the Japanese rate was double the Chinese rate in the 1920's and 1930's. In 1904–13, however, before Japan became a creditor nation and before China realized its peak flow of foreign capital, net foreign investment in China was almost double the amount invested in Japan. Finally, though the rate of investment in China was very low, about 5 percent in 1931–36, foreign investment represented about 20 percent of total investment in China at the end of the 1920's, compared with 12 percent in Japan in 1896–1913.

The presentation of these comparisons shows that the foreign sector in China, though small in the aggregate and certainly geographically limited, was by no means insignificant. But this says nothing about the impact of the foreign sector on China's economic development. For that, we must study the forward and backward linkages between the domestic and foreign sectors (which need not depend on the absolute size of the foreign sector itself) and we must make some judgment about the capacity of the domestic economy to achieve a more substantial rate of investment.

Nascent centers of growth in China. Before we can evaluate the foreign contribution to China's economic development, we need to know what the prospects of domestic development were. Did China's economy, with its high-level equilibrium trap, have sufficient resources in terms of potential surplus and entrepreneurial talent to make substantial headway on its own?

In his paper in this volume, Carl Riskin estimates that 31.2 percent of China's net domestic product was available for "nonessential" consumption in 1933. Granted that such an estimate depends on how one defines essential consumption and essential government expenditures, and that actual investment expenditures reduced the amount of potential surplus available for new investment opportunities, Riskin's findings indicate that the income flows in 1933 could provide for a rate of investment above 11 percent, cited by some economists as a threshold level for sustained economic development.

This brings us to the question of the availability of entrepreneurial talent, without which this potential could not be realized. There can be little doubt that there existed a host of conditions in the country that severely inhibited entrepreneurial activity in the modern sector. China had developed a different value system and different ways of doing business during its long period of isolation from the West, and so had to learn the pattern of Western entrepreneurial behavior from scratch when that isolation was broken. Still, the Chinese had a wealth of administrative and organizational experience, accumulated in their long history of bureaucratic rule in the largest country in the world; and once exposed to modern enterprise, they showed themselves apt students in those cases where the environment was favorable.

As the government's early rigid control of trade with the foreigner was relaxed and the treaty-port trade developed, the traditional merchants gave way to a new class of compradors. Where the old merchant class had clung to traditional values, used traditional methods, and invested in traditional forms of wealth, the compradors were willing to try new ways. Though they relied on existing institutions such as native banks and were not able to escape their traditional value system altogether, they learned and engaged in Western business activities quite successfully. Not only did they become the largest source of investment in modern Chinese industrial enterprises; they ultimately succeeded in replacing the Western trading firms in handling China's foreign trade in the treaty ports. In other words, with their knowledge of the Chinese mentality, language, and market conditions, they were able to beat the foreigner at his own game.

The same competitive superiority is found in many areas outside China. Though the bulk of Chinese emigrants were peasants seeking relief from poverty at home, numbers of Chinese who emigrated were energetic men seeking an environment more favorable to their entrepreneurial talents. The success of these Chinese entrepreneurs in commerce and modern industry, especially in Southeast Asia, is well known. Indeed, in many areas where they reside as a minority, the Chinese so dominate commerce that the host countries have made repeated attempts to restrict their activities.

Finally, there is the example of Chinese domestic industrial activity itself. According to the estimates of John Chang, the average annual rate of growth of Chinese modern industry in 1912–49 was 5.6 percent, with average annual rates of growth as high as 13.4 percent in the initial period, 1912–20, and 8.7 percent in 1923–36, after the post–World War I recession.[14]

We have begun the analysis of the foreign impact on China's economic development with the general conditions encountered by the foreigner when he arrived on the scene. And we have shown that after he did appear on the scene, the aggregate level of foreign investment was not abnormally small, which suggests that the foreigner was in a position to make what are generally held to be desirable contributions to the economic development of an underdeveloped country. Finally, despite the argument frequently advanced, that certain characteristics of the Chinese behavior and value system precluded modernization and economic development, the traditional economy was capable of generating a significant rate of savings and investment, and the country contained persons capable of learning the methods of Western enterprise. This in turn suggests that the Chinese were capable of taking advantage of any foreign contribution judged to be favorable.

The Role of the Foreigner: A Reevaluation

Our reevaluation of the role of the foreigner consists of nothing more than an attempt to work our way through a complete list of the possible ways his economic activity could have contributed to China's economic development. Given the very broad scope of the topic, we can but make a beginning in this analysis; its conclusions are mere hypotheses, to be tested by further research.

The foreign sector: trade. The direct effects of the foreigner's economic activities, of course, take place in the foreign sector itself: China's foreign trade and the commercial and manufacturing enterprises in China owned and operated by the foreigner. But any analysis of the contribution of foreign trade and investment to China's economic development must begin by recognizing the special political circumstances that served to isolate the relatively small foreign sector from the much larger domestic sector. Chief among these was the concerted effort to limit contact with the foreigner by confining his economic activities to specified treaty ports. The number of designated ports grew steadily, increasing from the original five named in the Treaty of Nanking at the end of the Opium War (Canton, Amoy, Foochow, Ningpo, and Shanghai) to 48 by 1913. The final number is deceiving, however, suggesting that the length and breadth of China were wide open to foreign trade. In fact, many of these treaty ports were only "ports of call," and the foreigner's movements were much more restricted than were his goods. Still, within most of these ports, he had virtually a free hand, with extraterritoriality and full trading rights. And in all of them, by the Treaty of Shimonoseki (1895), he had the right of direct investment.

Shanghai was far and away the most important of the treaty ports. Ideally located to provide access to the silk and cotton growing areas of China and to move important commodities to the major domestic consumption areas, it quickly became the largest city in China and the principal center for the foreign sector. By 1870, it handled almost two-thirds of China's foreign trade. It was also a focal point for foreign investment, accounting for more than a third of the foreign investment in China in 1931.*

This geographical concentration of foreign economic activity, along with legal restrictions on the foreigner's movements, severely limited the points of contact between the foreign sector and the large domestic economy. With a few notable exceptions to be discussed later, the foreigner conducted his business at the treaty port, with a Chinese merchant who was also located in the treaty port. Thus isolated from the Chinese producer and consumer, the foreigner was effectively prevented from directly inducing desirable innovations and technical changes in production; organizing the collection, dissemination, transportation, and merchandising of trade goods; and carrying out significant market research for new trade goods and investment opportunities. I believe this explains at least in part why producer goods remained only a small fraction of Chinese imports.

Granting that under these circumstances the foreign impact on China's economy was reduced, what were the effects of the trade and investment that did take place? On the positive side, the exchange of agricultural products and minerals for manufactured products obviously increased the net amount of goods available to the Chinese economy. In addition, thanks to a continuous inflow of foreign investment and remittances from overseas Chinese, China enjoyed a continuous import surplus. Finally, though the terms of trade did not move in China's favor, there is no evidence that they deteriorated between 1870 and 1930.† (See Table 4.)

Foreign demand for tea and silk, which together made up the bulk

---

* In terms of direct business investment alone, Shanghai accounted for almost half the total, most of the remainder being Japanese and Russian investment in Manchuria. C. F. Remer, *Foreign Investments in China* (New York, 1968), p. 97.

† Simple regression analysis indicates China's terms of trade—import prices divided by export prices—increased by two index points every five years. This result, however, is not statistically significant, i.e., is not statistically different from no change in the terms of trade over the entire period.

TABLE 4
China's Terms of Trade
(Index of import prices ÷ index of export prices; 1913 = 100)

Year	Average for 5-year period centered on year in adjacent column	Year	Average for 5-year period centered on year in adjacent column
1870	97.6	1905	90.1
1875	84.6	1910	108.6
1880	93.8	1915	107.2
1885	106.3	1920	135.6
1890	79.3	1925	105.0
1895	111.1	1930	108.1
1900	101.5		

Source: Nankai Institute of Economics, *Nankai Index Numbers, 1936* (Tientsin, 1937), pp. 37-38.

of China's exports at the start,[15] had both positive and negative effects. On the positive side, it encouraged the commercialization and speciali- zation of agriculture, and so enabled at least a segment of the peasantry to maintain an adequate standard of living. Less happily, the resulting structure of exports reduced the possible backward and forward link- ages with China's domestic economy. As Chenery and Clark point out, agriculture and mining (the other principal source of China's exports) do not rely to any appreciable extent on the products of other sectors and are used extensively as inputs in other sectors.[16] Thus, the foreign demand for Chinese agricultural and mineral products did not stimulate the production of other goods in China. In addition, as exports these products served as inputs in foreign industries, rather than being used as inputs in Chinese processing industries.

On the import side, the possible beneficial effects of foreign trade suffered from similar limitations. A major share of China's imports were final manufactured or processed products destined for consumption. Opium and cotton goods accounted for two-thirds of China's imports in 1880; opium, cotton goods, cereals, sugar, and kerosene for 53 per- cent in 1900, 45 percent in 1913, and some 33 percent in 1928.[17] Kero- sene was the first truly Western product, apart from opium, to capture the Chinese market. Opium, which can be described as a dead-weight loss in the Chinese economy, declined in importance after 1880 and accounted for less than 10 percent of China's imports after the turn of the century.

Imports such as cotton goods, cereals, and sugar could of course sup- plement domestic supplies of consumer goods, particularly in the coastal areas where distance from the producing regions combined with a poor transportation system made distribution problematical. On the other hand, if these imports merely replaced domestic production, they would serve to depress domestic employment and production. This is a question we shall take up later. For now, we are concerned only with the forward linkage effect of these imports, which is to say that most of these imports went to satisfy final demand and served neither as inputs in Chinese production nor as capital goods to increase China's productive capacity. Of the 29 sectors included in the input-output studies of Chenery and Clark, goods produced in the processed foods and apparel sectors had the relatively smallest demand for use as inputs in other sectors.[18] Thus, development of a cheap foreign source of such goods would benefit the consumers, but would not do much to reduce the costs of production in other sectors.

The import of producer goods does involve a significant linkage effect, but these goods represented only a small part of China's total import trade, even in the 1920's. Machinery (which was not even reported separately in the trade returns before 1886); iron, steel, and other metals; chemicals, dyes, and pigments; and transportation equipment together accounted for only 6 percent of the imports in 1880, 5 percent in 1900, 8 percent in 1913, and 17 percent in 1928.[19] Moreover, even this small amount could have had more impact on the Chinese economy than it did. Some of these goods were destined for projects either financed or owned and operated by the foreigner, i.e., were imported for use in the foreign sector itself. In addition, a large share of the machinery and equipment imports were for the textile industry, an industry producing consumer goods, not materials for use in other industries.

Two further aspects of China's foreign trade must be considered: the balance of trade and the state of the handicraft sector. Unlike most underdeveloped countries, China enjoyed a continuous inflow of capital from foreign investment and remittances from overseas Chinese. This available source of foreign exchange could have been used for significant capital accumulation, but the Chinese chose to use it for current consumption. Between 1871 and 1936, China had a cumulative import surplus of over U.S. $4.5 billion. The government might have effectively attacked the economic development problem by diverting some of this savings potential to the importation of producer goods, though its power to change the structure of imports was limited before the 1930's by lack of tariff autonomy, which gave the foreign seller of consumer goods free access to China's domestic market.

The destruction of the domestic handicraft market is probably the most common argument lodged against the foreign contribution to China's economic development. The rise of the Chinese handicraft industries in the nineteenth century was a fundamental outgrowth of China's high-level equilibrium trap: the use of a household's labor (low or zero cost labor) with limited capital to produce goods for use or for the market in order to supplement the family's income. But this worked only as long as these subsidiary occupations were sheltered from the competition of modern industry.

Unfortunately, smashing the modern machinery that can produce cheaper and better products and turning the clock back to some putative "golden age" are simply not options for the peasants of an underdeveloped and overpopulated country. Continuing further into the Malthusian dead end of the high-level equilibrium trap would in no way have improved the lot of the Chinese peasant. Admittedly, the forces of imperialism worked real and often unfair hardships on the Chinese peasantry. At the same time, to the extent that foreign exports and production weakened Chinese handicrafts, the foreigner served as the vital catalyst for the disruption of China's high-level equilibrium trap and the ensuing search for economic development. The long-run solution of a higher standard of living for the Chinese peasant lay not in the protection of the traditional economy from the forces of modernization, but in the industrial development of China.

In any case, the Chinese handicraft industries were not in fact destroyed. Handicrafts continued to occupy a considerable portion of the nonagricultural labor force and to provide a significant amount of China's manufactured goods, especially consumer goods.[20] Since the foreigner could not locate his factories outside the major coastal treaty ports, the craft activities of peasant households scattered throughout China's countryside still largely sustained the interior markets. To penetrate these markets, the foreigner had to bear the costs of transportation and distribution and still provide cheaper and better quality goods than his competitors.

Moreover, these markets also attracted Chinese entrepreneurs, and handicraft workshops sprang up in market towns all over China. The peasant household was hard put to compete with these small enterprises, which had more capital, better inputs, and full-time labor. Even more important was the steadily increasing output of Chinese-owned factories in the modern sector, especially in the textile and food-processing industries, which were the largest categories of handicraft production.

It is reasonable to assume, therefore, that the major damage done to the handicraft industries was due largely to the Chinese responses to the challenge of modernization and not to the competition of the foreigner; the foreign goods were of a different type and were sold in a different segment of the market from those issuing from the traditional handicraft sector. On the buyers' side of the market, the urban population and the young more readily adapted to the new products than did the older generation and the people of the countryside, who were prone to remain loyal to the traditional products. On the sellers' side of the market, the new Chinese handicraft workshops and factories tended to produce lower quality goods than the foreign products, and so directly competed with the products of the traditional handicraft sector.

The foreign sector: investment. As a major factor in the development of the modern sector in China, direct foreign investment obviously influenced the Chinese entrepreneurs who participated in that development. But when we look to its direct effects on the Chinese economy as a whole, we must repeat much of what we have said about foreign trade, namely, that the impact was seriously limited by the geographical location and structure of foreign investment. There are, however, several important exceptions to this somewhat negative conclusion.

The facts are well known. Most foreign investment was located in the foreign concessions of China's principal treaty port, Shanghai (almost one-half the total, mainly British and Japanese), and in Manchuria (more than one-third of the total, mainly Japanese and Russian).[21] The bulk of the real estate holdings acquired by the foreigner, mainly British, Japanese, Russian, American, French, and Belgian, accounting for 15 percent of total foreign investment in 1931, belonged to residents who bought it with income earned in China. Foreign businessmen in China were mainly associated with foreign trade and held large inventories of goods; the value of these inventories is estimated by Remer to account for better than a fifth of the total foreign investment in China.

Foreign trade itself was financed by foreign banks, inasmuch as any bill expressed in gold currency was financed abroad. However, the lack of modern credit and banking facilities in the domestic economy led to the creation of Western-owned banks operating on the basis of China's silver currency. The foreign investment in banking and finance, consisting of the physical facilities owned, the foreigners' net holdings of silver, and the outstanding advances to the Chinese sector of the economy, amounted to 10 percent of the total foreign investment in China in 1931. A similar derived demand for public utilities by the foreign residents of the treaty ports, especially electric power and light, induced about 5 percent of foreign investment in these industries. The total foreign investment directly related to the business activities and living accommodations of the foreign traders in the treaty ports thus made up half the total amount of foreign investment in China.

One-half of the remaining foreign investment was in transportation, the principal bottleneck to the development and integration of a modern economy in China. Outstandingly this meant the financing and operation of railroad lines, notably the Chinese Eastern Railway (Russian) and the South Manchurian Railroad (Japanese), which together accounted for 90 percent of the total investment in foreign-owned railroads in 1931. Though these railroads obviously were intended to serve the "imperialist" purposes of their foreign owners, they also provided the necessary transport facilities for Manchuria's industrial crops, which entered foreign trade. Thanks to these crops, Manchuria was the only area of China that enjoyed an export surplus. The failure to integrate this area into the Chinese economy, however, greatly reduced the spillover effects of its economic development on the rest of China. The remainder of the foreign direct investment in transportation was in shipping; in 1931 more than half the steamship traffic in Chinese waters was in foreign hands. Here, too, the effect was to facilitate the collection of Chinese export products and the distribution of imports in the absence of a well-developed domestic transportation network.

When denied the right of direct investment in railroads, the foreigner was instrumental in expanding China's railway network through loans to the Chinese government. According to estimates made by C. F. Remer, more than a third of the foreign obligations of the Chinese government in both 1914 and 1931 were associated with the construction and operation of government-owned railroads, which accounted for 70 percent of the total railway network in 1931. Despite the "imperialist," i.e., political, aspects of these foreign investments and loans, they must be considered one of the major direct contributions of the foreigner to China's economic development.

Direct foreign investment in the manufacturing sector accounted for only 17 percent of total foreign investment in 1931, and at roughly the same time (1933) the output of foreign-owned factories accounted for less than a third of the total output of China's modern manufacturers. Foreign participation was most important in terms of market shares in the tobacco industry (63.3 percent in 1933). The foreigner was also a dominant producer in two industries closely related to foreign trade, egg products (56.8 percent) and shipbuilding and repair, and in two very small industries, sawmills and tanneries. Though foreign textile enterprises were the largest recipient of foreign investment, they produced less than 50 percent of the country's yarn and only 3 percent of the cloth.

The forward and backward linkages of all these industries were very limited; their inputs were acquired directly from the agricultural producer, their output (except for cotton yarn) went directly to the consumer. The only place where the foreigner invested substantially in heavy industries that had important linkages with other segments of the industrial sector was the area he occupied outright—Manchuria. The smallest share of direct foreign investment was in the mining sector, based on concessions granted to foreigners. About 40 percent of China's coal was mined in these concessions. The largest by far was the complex of Japanese mines at Fushun, which alone produced almost a third of China's coal in 1928.[22]

As all these data demonstrate, the foreign sector—foreign trade and direct investment—clearly made a positive *direct* contribution to the Chinese domestic economy. Yet as I have tried to point out, it was also a limited contribution—limited not only by the narrow geographical location, but also by a structure that restricted the favorable backward and forward linkages between the foreign sector and the domestic economy. An estimate of the limits of these linkages can be made for the purpose of illustrating the argument. Defining a linkage index (L) as the sum of exports, imports, and direct foreign investment, each adjusted for the degree to which there is an induced demand for inputs from other sectors and to which it supplies inputs for another sector, *measured as a deviation from the average linkage for the products of all sectors in the economy*, divided by the sum of exports, imports, and direct foreign investments, the value of L for China's foreign sector is 0.86.[23] That our result is less than unity indicates the extent to which the foreign sector generated a smaller-than-average demand for inputs from other sectors and created a smaller-than-average supply of inputs to other sectors. Though this estimate is very crude, the result is consistent with both logic and my argument about the limited spillover effects of foreign economic activity in the Chinese economy.[*]

Domestic nascent centers of growth. Possibly the greatest significance of the foreign contribution lies in its indirect effects. The lessons of his

---

[*] The numerical estimate of L attempts to measure only the direct linkage effect of the trade good or the investment good itself, and therefore underestimates the true linkage effect of these goods on two accounts. First, trade and investment may have induced domestic economic activity in industries associated with those directly affected by the trade and investment activities. Second, the demonstration effect of these trade and investment activities may have induced innovations in both the modern sector *and* the traditional sector in China's domestic economy. Several cases could be cited where these indirect benefits occurred, but no attempt is made to estimate these important, though quantitatively immeasurable, results of foreign trade and investment in China.

tory clearly indicate that the crucial variable in the long-run success or failure of economic development in a country is to be found in the induced reactions to modernization within the domestic economy itself, the domestic nascent centers of growth. In China, these nascent centers of growth were located in cities and market towns throughout the country and were based not on the accumulated savings of the government or of those who acquired their wealth from their positions in the bureaucracy, but on the savings and enterprise of the landlord and merchant classes. The growth of handicraft workshops and subsidiary agricultural activities throughout China was simply a marriage between the surplus capital of the landlords (and the merchant class) and the surplus labor of the peasant household.

Whether or not the Chinese were capable of independently developing modern industrial techniques is of no concern; with a scarcity of capital that made moneylending a profitable enterprise and a surplus of labor that kept wages low, traditional labor-intensive methods were the rational choice. In addition, just as in the case of the peasant household's surplus labor, the strong pull of the land impelled the landlord to invest in subsidiary agricultural activities in the rural market towns rather than abandon the countryside for an urban life as the owner-operator of a modern industry.

Caught in a high-level equilibrium trap, dangerously close to the Malthusian checks on population growth, China needed an exogenous shock to induce modernization. The increased demand for export products and inputs for foreign-owned industry, the urbanization of the treaty ports, and the development of railroads made the further commercialization and specialization of agriculture possible. Meanwhile, with the supply of imports and the outputs of foreign-owned industry, the inefficient traditional products of subsidiary agricultural activities became unprofitable, even though the shadow price of labor may have been close to zero. In this situation, domestic entrepreneurs were forced to adopt new machinery in the handicraft industry and to compete with the foreigner in the modern industrial sector.

However, once we have given the foreigner his due for providing this shock to the traditional economy and inducing a change desired by a portion of the domestic entrepreneurial class, we must evaluate whether the foreigner helped or hindered those domestic entrepreneurs in their efforts to modernize their country.

Distortion effects of the foreign sector. The initial Chinese attempts to create a modern manufacturing sector resulted from a nationalistic reaction to the military superiority of the Western powers. Consequently, very few of the early projects involved the production of consumer goods or had any appreciable impact on the domestic economy. With the more than threefold increase in the volume of imports between the 1860's and 1890's, however, and the shift away from opium in favor of textiles, foodstuffs, chemicals, metals, and fuels, a Chinese consumer goods industry, using modern machinery and techniques, was inaugurated.

In the face of the rapid growth of the import trade and of direct foreign investment, the simultaneous growth of Chinese "factories" and their output after the turn of the century is quite remarkable. By 1912, there were 20,749 Chinese factories employing seven or more workers.[24] Even in 1933, after the peak of direct foreign investment, Chinese-owned factories in the modern manufacturing sector outnumbered foreign-owned factories by more than ten to one.[25] Three features of this development are relevant to our discussion of the distortion effects of the foreign sector: the Chinese-owned factories were much smaller, were much more widely dispersed, and were much more evenly distributed over the range of the various industries than the foreign-owned factories.

In 1912, apart from a few large enterprises (such as the Han-Yeh-P'ing Coal and Iron Corporation and the Ta-shing Cotton Mill) that used Western techniques on a small scale, China's modern sector consisted of countless small and nonmechanized workshops. There were fewer than 30 workers in 88 percent of the Chinese-owned factories in that year; by way of contrast, in 1913, 40 percent of the spindles in China were operated by the eight foreign-owned cotton mills.[26] This same picture holds true for the early 1930's, when about 90 percent of the factories were Chinese-owned, but accounted for less than 70 percent of the value of output and employment and less than 40 percent of the industrial capital in the country.[27] As in the earlier period, these factories were dominant in the production of textiles, flour, matches, edible vegetable oils, soap, and candles. Modern Chinese manufacturing, in short, did not develop along Western lines but took the form of small workshops devoted to the traditional products of the handicraft sector. The few Chinese factories that did attempt to follow the Western model and develop important substitutes "were isolated cases rather than an epidemic of industrialization."[28]

Nowhere is this pattern so well illustrated as in the cotton-spinning industry, which by 1925 had completely displaced domestic handicraft production and imports. The once-imported high count (or fine) and more valuable yarns, however, were produced in the foreign-owned mills, whereas the Chinese-owned factories turned out the cheaper low-count yarns. Thus, though 61 percent of the factory production of yarn in 1931 came from Chinese-owned mills,[29] their share of the industry replaced not imports but domestic handicraft production. Once set, the structure of the industry did not change significantly over time.

What all this suggests is that the domestic pattern of development was dictated by and based on competition with the existing pattern of handicraft production and not greatly distorted by foreign activity. The tendency toward small factories, a high labor-capital ratio, and the production of handicraft goods rather than import substitution products was the natural result of the Chinese beginning at the beginning before moving on to a full-scale duplication of the foreign model, not the result of unfair competition from the foreign sector. Moreover, what distortions there were did not prevent a significant and vigorous Chinese modern sector from taking root—one that because of its diversity and dispersion through the country had a much greater forward and backward linkage effect on the domestic economy than the foreign sector, and one that received valuable technological assistance in its development from the foreigner's presence.

Transfer of modern technology from the foreign sector. The social, economic, and political views molded by long years of tradition in China may have limited the adoption of Western business practices and technology, but many Chinese businessmen certainly relied on the services of the foreign community.[30] Though the native banks continued to be a significant source of funds for Chinese merchants, some Chinese enterprises borrowed heavily from Western banks and deposited their funds in them. Foreign banks were also an important supplier of foreign currencies and bills of exchange, as well as large importers of silver. Quantities of Chinese goods were moved by the foreign-owned shipping companies and railroads. And in the treaty ports, Chinese enterprises benefited from the economic "environment" created by the foreign sector. Finally, many Chinese enterprises employed foreign engineers and managers to improve their operations.

The foreign sector also set the pattern for a wave of new Chinese enterprises: modern banks and shipping firms, insurance companies, a Chinese stock market, joint-stock companies with limited liability, even a Chinese Chamber of Commerce. By the 1920's, Chinese import-export companies had replaced the comprador–Western commission trader and controlled the dominant share of China's foreign trade. All this was accomplished, moreover, despite the resistance to change of the Ch'ing government and the precarious authority of the central government during the ensuing warlord period, which precluded the adoption of the innovations that would have aided this development: a unified currency, standard weights and measures, a modern legal framework and educational system.

Imported producer goods were still another source of transferred technology, indeed a more important source than the figures suggest, since the largest share of these imports after 1900 were destined for Chinese enterprises, not foreign-owned enterprises. Here the record is one of complete foreign cooperation and help. In the hope of gaining access to the Chinese market and increasing the use of modern machinery in China, foreign corporations often gave equipment and machinery to Chinese research, educational, and trade associations and institutions. Foreign engineering firms trained Chinese technicians, and, after World War I, a number of Chinese were sent abroad to learn factory skills. Most of these arrangements were made by private agreement between Chinese and Western entrepreneurs, for unlike the exemplary case of Japan, the Chinese government made only sporadic attempts to foster the technical training of the Chinese labor force. Still, the government did play an indirect but no less important role in the transfer of technology by hiring Western experts and firms for projects the Chinese could not carry out themselves.

To be sure, the Western businessman did not transfer technology to the Chinese out of an unselfish desire to help them achieve modernization. Quite the opposite. He was in search of profit, and it was his competition for profit that led him to provide the Chinese with banking and transportation services, advisors, modern machinery and equipment on credit, and technical training, often to the detriment of one of his own countrymen with business interests in China.

Unfair competition from foreign enterprises in China. Many economists cite the political and economic concessions the foreigner extracted in his "imperialistic wars" against China as an important, if not the most important, obstacle to the country's economic development. What most have in mind are the unfair advantages granted by the "unequal treaties": China's lack of tariff autonomy, the foreigner's legal and tax haven in the foreign concessions, the spheres of influence giving him special rights in mining, railroad, and trade activities in certain areas of China, and his power to set discriminatory transportation rates. (Some go further, including in the list of things that gave the foreigner an "unfair" competitive edge his access to better financial facilities and to technical and managerial talent. But these factors ought to be considered "natural" economic advantages, not the "unfair" result of the unequal treaties.)

That the foreigner had competitive advantages cannot be denied. But neither can we dismiss the facts that we have already noted, namely, that a Chinese modern sector was formed, experienced vigorous growth, and held its own in the face of foreign competition. This is of course not to say that the foreigner's advantages did not limit that growth. Obviously, the inability to increase tariffs without the consent of the Western treaty partners (these were pegged at a general rate of 5 percent ad valorem on both imports and exports in 1843) prevented China from protecting "infant" domestic industries, and this undoubtedly slowed their growth in the pre-1930 period.* All the same, it is important to note that the government might have done something about the problem. We must bear in mind that the lack of a protective tariff does not subsidize the foreigner; it *fails* to subsidize the domestic producer. Accordingly, in the absence of a protective tariff, the same objective could be accomplished by taxing the consumer and subsidizing domestic production. This was a policy available to the Chinese government, in theory at least. That it failed to pursue this policy was due in large part, of course, to the severe constraints on its ability to raise revenue and the large demands on the revenue it did raise. But the failure can be ascribed as well to the government's general inability to introduce and carry out those policies necessary for China's economic development.

Another "unfair" advantage enjoyed by the foreigner should be examined more closely. This involves the likin tax, which was introduced in China during the Taiping Rebellion as a temporary tax to finance the government's military expenditures. As with many "temporary" taxes, the likin's life and scope were extended: it was collected at many spots along the major domestic trade routes, at production points, and at marketplaces throughout China and remained in effect until 1931. In the Treaty of Tientsin (1858) foreign-produced goods, which later included those produced in foreign factories in China, were exempted from this tax on payment of a sum equal to half the import duty, i.e., about 2.5 percent ad valorem. Precisely how much of an advantage this was, however, is open to question. Though rates as high as 10 percent were levied on some domestic goods in transit and were collected at several stages en route, the rate on a good many others was 1 or 2 percent and was collected only once. Furthermore, some domestically produced goods were exempted from the likin tax, and numbers of others were illegally shipped under a transit pass issued for foreign goods.

* In 1928 the United States and 11 other treaty powers finally restored China's tariff autonomy; the effective tariff was 8.5 percent in 1929, 10 percent in 1932, and 30 percent in 1935.

In any case, here again we must be careful in calling this competitive advantage an unfair one, since the likin tax was in effect a discriminatory "domestic" tax in favor of the foreigner enforced by the Chinese government, which could have lessened or ended the discrimination by reducing the tax on domestic producers or by subsidizing them. In fact, it was the foreigner who put an end to the likin tax by demanding that the Chinese government abolish it in exchange for tariff autonomy.

The full extent of the foreigner's competitive advantage, counting both "unfair" practices and natural economic forces, is difficult to determine. The claim is made that, with access to capital markets in their home countries or the financial backing of their parent companies, foreign enterprises in China paid lower rates for capital financing than Chinese competitors, who had to borrow at the higher local rates. But against this is the fact that some Chinese enterprises borrowed heavily from foreign banks in China at rates far below those in the traditional money market. Moreover, even if the foreigner did enjoy cheaper capital costs than the Chinese entrepreneur, this does not mean he also enjoyed higher profits. The cheaper capital costs would explain why the capital intensity and output per unit of capital were higher in foreign enterprises, but this advantage could be offset by cheaper labor costs and greater labor intensity in Chinese enterprises. In other words, facing different relative factor costs, the Chinese firm and the foreign firm would adopt production methods relying on different factor intensities, and the evidence, if any, of the foreign firm's aggregate competitive advantage should show up in higher profit rates.

The available data suggest otherwise. In a study of 50 foreign business firms in China in 1930, Remer found a rate of profit on investment of between 10 and 20 percent in "years of prosperity"; a Japanese study of 89 Japanese manufacturing concerns in China in 1927 reports an average rate of 5.5 percent; a study of 77 Japanese manufacturers in Manchuria in the years 1907–16 and 1921–26 puts the average annual rate at 9.4 percent; and Chi-ming Hou's study of 115 financial statements for foreign manufacturing firms in China in the period 1872–1932 shows an average annual rate of 9.6 percent.[31] Thus, 10 percent can be accepted as a crude approximation of the normal profit rate on foreign investment in the manufacturing sector. Inasmuch as Chinese moneylenders could earn between 30 and 50 percent on loans, and pawnshops and native banks 15 to 25 percent, many Chinese enterprises in the modern sector were forced to guarantee dividends of upwards of 8 percent in order to secure investment capital. To be sure, dividends are not the same thing as profits, but this fact taken together with what few data there are on profits and rates of return in Chinese enterprises indicates the Chinese firms also had a profit rate of approximately 10 percent.[32]

Though nothing can be proved by these scattered bits of evidence, they do not support the view that the foreign firm was more profitable than the Chinese enterprise. And this in turn suggests that the arguments concerning the absolute "unfair" advantage of the foreign sector are exaggerated.

Conclusion

In our attempt to assess the foreigner's role in China's economic development, we have had to investigate a host of interdependent factors and have ended up with a good many pluses and minuses that cannot be quantitatively evaluated. Yet our discussion has returned repeatedly to certain themes that implicitly provide an answer to our question.

First, given the existence of a high-level equilibrium trap in the Chinese economy and the need for an exogenous shock to break out of that trap, the foreigner served as a necessary agent to start the Chinese economy on the road to modernization.

Second, no matter what the terms of trade or what the extent of unfair advantages and special privileges associated with foreign loans and investment, the Chinese economy enjoyed significant absolute gains from trade and a gross transfer of *productive* capital and technology; this transfer of resources and technology, which would not have been possible without a foreign sector, was undoubtedly the foreigner's largest contribution to China's economic development.

Third, the structure of trade and foreign investment and the foreigner's unfair competitive advantages may well have had a negative impact on the development of a modern sector in China compared with a structure that had greater forward and backward linkages with the domestic economy and no unfair competitive advantages; but this negative impact was *on the margin*; it did not wipe out the absolute contribution of the foreigner.

Fourth, the observed and frequently cited impoverishment of certain sectors of the population or economy was due, on the one hand, to the forces of modernization and, on the other, to the continuation of the peasants' struggle for survival in the face of Malthusian checks to population growth; as the agent who unleashed the forces of modernization in China, the foreigner can be held responsible, but the Chinese modern sector ultimately was a much greater threat to the traditional sector than the foreigner.

Finally, blaming the foreigner for the failure of economic development in China before 1949 implicitly assumes it was his responsibility to secure that development for China. Not only was this not his basic objective, but where the attempt was made, his efforts were often frustrated by the many social, economic, and political obstacles placed in his path. In the one case where the foreigner had free reign, in Japanese-occupied Manchuria, the economic results were remarkable. In terms of human suffering and national humility, the costs were great, but Manchuria is still the industrial and transportation heartland of the Chinese economy.

In contrast to the Russian and Japanese reaction to the foreigner, the Chinese government itself was the greatest and most obvious obstacle to economic development: it failed to create a favorable legal, financial, and economic environment for the support of the emerging Chinese modern sector. One can list the many factors that limited the ability of the government to take positive action; some of those limits, but by no means all, were imposed by the West. But one can also list the many proposals made to the government for positive actions that would have favored the emerging Chinese modern sector, steps that could have been taken but were rejected. Quite simply, though some Chinese entrepreneurs were able to escape the inhibiting limits of their tradition and reacted favorably to the forces of modernization, the government did not.

Carl Riskin

Surplus and Stagnation in Modern China

D<small>ID</small> <small>CHINA</small>'s failure to parallel the Japanese industrial revolution of the late nineteenth and early twentieth centuries stem from the absence of an economic surplus comparable to that which had slowly accumulated during the Tokugawa era, or is it attributable instead to the misuse of a substantial surplus? Different answers to this question underlie divergent schools of thought regarding the reasons for China's continuing economic backwardness in the modern, pre-Communist era. Where the existence of a substantial surplus above subsistence is assumed, inquiry is naturally focused on the patterns of its expropriation and use; politics, social structure, and cultural values become legitimate and even necessary subjects of analysis. Where the absence or inadequacy of such a surplus is deemed the critical factor, technological considerations come to the fore to explain this circumstance, and sociopolitical considerations correspondingly fade into the background.

Despite the deliberately oversimplified nature of this formulation, I believe it is the crux of a major issue that has emerged in the study of the modern economic history of China. Moreover, there has been a clear shift in recent years from a "distributive" to a "technological" point of view in the literature, raising new kinds of problems that deserve atten-

I am indebted to Robert Dernberger, Alexander Eckstein, Michael Edelstein, and Dwight Perkins for valuable comments that led to substantial improvements in this essay. John Curley has my special gratitude for his detailed criticisms of an earlier draft. He suggested to me much of the algebraic formulation of the potential surplus used here, but must not be held responsible for any errors in my statement and development of it. I owe to the work of Victor Lippit the idea of attempting to estimate the potential surplus, as well as some of the estimates themselves. Other participants in the conference from which this volume derives also provided me with helpful discussion. Research for this paper was assisted by a grant from the Subcommittee on Research on the Chinese Economy of the Joint Committee on Contemporary China, SSRC-ACLS. Responsibility for errors and interpretations is mine alone.

tion. In particular, if an essentially technological paradigm is to be accepted, how do we explain the rapid attainment of very high levels of investment by the Chinese Communists immediately after their victory in 1949?

1. *The Potential Economic Surplus*

The concept of surplus here refers basically to the excess product a country either does or can produce above some specified measure of the subsistence needs of its population.* Paul Baran, whose work gave currency to the use of the concept, identifies several variants of surplus, stressing particularly the *potential* economic surplus, which consists of four components:

One is society's excess consumption . . . , the *second* is the output lost to society through the existence of unproductive workers, the *third* is the output lost because of the irrational and wasteful organization of the existing productive apparatus, and the *fourth* is the output forgone owing to the existence of unemployment caused primarily by the anarchy of capitalist production and the deficiency of effective demand.[1]

Although the potential economic surplus is defined nominally as the difference between potential total output and "what might be regarded as essential consumption," Baran excludes from it also investment, "essential outlays on government administration and the like," and the output of scientists, artists, and teachers. It is thus meant to encompass a quantity of resources that would be available for redistribution toward development-oriented ends under a differently ordered—specifically, socialist—society.[2] The measurement of such a quantity thus requires specifying not only the dividing line between essential and nonessential personal consumption, but also that between desirable and objectionable government activities, professional activities, scientific activities, and so on. Consistency requires, in addition, that the values that guide the separation of essential from nonessential be those of the (proposed or actually impending) new government. With respect to China, this suggests that a useful way of viewing the potential surplus in the Republican period is from the perspective of what the Chinese Communists regarded as available for mobilization. A rough attempt will be made

* This use of the concept must be clearly distinguished from the "economic surplus" in traditional microeconomic theory, which refers to the gain in total utility achieved by a buyer ("consumer's surplus") or a seller ("producer's surplus") by means of a transaction. For a review of the literature on the traditional concept of surplus, see John Martin Currie, John A. Murphy, and Andrew Schmitz, "The Concept of Economic Surplus and Its Use in Economic Analysis," *The Economic Journal*, 324: 741–89 (Dec. 1971).

in Section 3 of this paper to gauge the general magnitude of the potential surplus in the 1930's from this perspective.

But much of Section 3 will be devoted to estimating the size of a rather different sort of "potential economic surplus." This I refer to as the "potential surplus above mass consumption," and define as the difference between total potential current output and the *actual* level of labor and peasant income, assuming that those whose entire incomes take the form of returns to property (i.e., pure rentiers) are limited to the same consumption as wage and salary recipients (or peasants) in their sectors of the economy. This concept of potential surplus does not require the injection of values regarding what is essential and nonessential. If Baran's conception tells us what part of current potential output a new and reorganized society would regard as available to try to mobilize on behalf of development, the potential surplus above mass consumption tells us simply what proportion of the currently produced (or producible) national income lies above the current consumption of the laboring population and consumption at the same level for the non-laboring population under existing social conditions. How that society actually uses its surplus above mass consumption is of course an important subject of analysis. The degree to which the components of potential surplus above mass consumption currently contribute to development or other worthwhile goals is discussed once the surplus itself has been estimated. The estimate and discussion of its interpretation occupy most of Section 3 of this essay.

Both concepts of potential surplus are of historical interest. The Baranian surplus throws light on development policy after 1949 with respect to the size of consumption and investment and the loci of capital accumulation efforts. Surplus above mass consumption tells us something about the technological potential of the pre-Communist modern Chinese economy to "afford" a development program, and forces attention to the values, institutions, and conditions that affected the realization of that potential.

It is therefore useful to define the two concepts more precisely and to clarify the relationship between them. The variables are denoted as follows:

C_a = actual consumption
C_e = essential consumption
C_m = mass consumption
N = total labor force = employed workers (N_e) + unemployed workers (N_u)
R = total number of pure rentiers

S_e = potential surplus above essential consumption
S_m = potential surplus above mass consumption
w = average level of mass consumption per worker = average of wage
       and salary incomes in nonagricultural sectors and returns to labor
       and imputed returns to self-cultivated land in agriculture
Y_a = actual net domestic product (NDP)
Y_p = potential NDP = Y_a + potential output of unemployed factors

The potential surplus above mass consumption is defined as

(1) $S_m = Y_a - C_m + Y_p - Y_a$,

i.e., the difference between actual output and mass consumption, plus the potential additional output producible by unemployed factors (including rentiers; see Section 3). Mass consumption is given as

(2) $C_m = w(N + R)$.

The potential surplus above *essential* consumption (the Baran surplus) is defined as

(3) $S_e = Y_a - C_e + Y_p - Y_a$.

Clearly, if the socially determined *essential* consumption (C_e) is greater than the actual level of *mass* consumption [$C_m = w(N + R)$], then S_e will be smaller than S_m. For China in the decades before 1949, such a relation would mean that not all of the potential or actual income identified as surplus above mass consumption would have been treated by the Communist contenders as a valid target of mobilization for investment under a new revolutionary government. Only if C_m and C_e coincide exactly would the two concepts of surplus also coincide.

The relation between the two concepts is illustrated in the accompanying figure, in which total income is measured horizontally and its components are measured vertically.[3] Line C_a is a standard consumption function, showing actual total consumption as a function of total income. Line C_e illustrates a hypothetical relation between essential consumption and income. At very low levels of income (below Y_1 in the diagram), social standards of minimum decent livelihood may dictate an essential consumption higher than the actual level of total consumption, and C_e will exceed C_a. At higher incomes, however, actual consumption pulls above essential consumption as luxury consumption at the higher levels of the income distribution begins to outweigh sub-par consumption of the very poor. Line C_m indicates actual mass consumption, i.e., $w(N + R)$. It lies below the other two consumption schedules

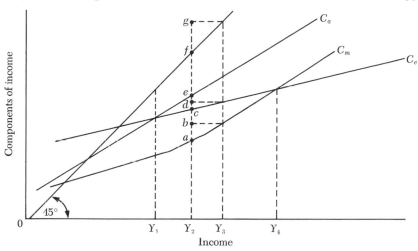

Relationship Between Two Kinds of Surplus

for low and medium levels of income. It may continue to fall short of essential consumption indefinitely, if social standards of minimum acceptable consumption rise faster than the average level of wages and salaries. Or, at some fairly high income (e.g., Y_4), mass consumption might exceed essential consumption, as drawn here.

From the perspective of the Chinese Communist Party, China in the several decades prior to final victory undoubtedly was situated in the range of incomes between Y_1 and Y_4. That is, essential consumption was less than actual total consumption but greater than mass consumption: $C_a > C_e > C_m$. That C_a exceeded C_e is implied by the fact that the new government rapidly and sharply raised the aggregate investment rate in the first three years of its existence, and must at least temporarily have thereby reduced *average* per capita consumption; it would have done this only if it believed essential consumption was lower than total consumption. That C_e exceeded C_m is implied not only by many statements of leading officials to the effect that land reform and the development of mutual aid practices were expected to make life a little easier for the masses of poor and middle peasants, but also by the government's action in permitting some of the benefits of land redistribution to remain with the beneficiaries, rather than extracting them all to beef up the investment rate; this suggests an effort to bring mass consumption levels up to minimum standards.*

* Since C_m is defined as total wage and salary incomes extended even to pure rentiers at the average levels of their sectors, plus the imputed returns to land farmed

If it is true that the CCP perspective put pre-Revolution China at a position such as that of Y_2 on the diagram, then the potential surplus above mass consumption, shown as ag (where fg represents output not produced because of factor unemployment), would overstate the potential surplus above *essential* consumption, cg, by the amount ac. However, since both C_e and C_m are taken to be rising functions of income, we must take account of the fact that if the unemployed factors were put to work and the extra output fg produced, higher levels of both types of consumption would result (Y_2d and Y_2b, respectively, on the diagram). The surpluses potentially available for nonconsumption uses should in principle, therefore, be measured above these new, higher consumption levels:

$$S_e = dg$$
$$S_m = bg$$

Composition of S_m and S_e. The surplus above mass consumption contains all income (consumed or invested) above mass consumption as calculated for the different sectors of the economy. The surplus above essential consumption contains all "nonessential consumption" as well as investment and government purchases. Both concepts of surplus also include the potential output of unutilized factors of production. The output of "unproductive workers," in Baran's terminology, must be included in these components of S_e. It cannot be significantly present in the value of essential consumption, C_e, because we estimate essential consumption on the basis of standards adopted in the early 1950's, when presumably such unproductive work had already been eliminated or at least vastly reduced (see Section 3). However, the value of mass consumption, C_m, as calculated on the basis of actual mass incomes in the 1930's, may contain an element of cost imparted by such unproductive activities as advertising and rent collecting. Thus, the actual level of mass consumption expenditures may overstate the minimum necessary expenditures that would be required in a different institutional framework to support the same physical level of livelihood. The same consid-

---

by its owners, it is possible that as the incomes of poor and lower-middle peasants rose, the imputed rents of better-off peasants and some extremely high managerial salaries in nonagricultural sectors fell more than correspondingly, so that C_m on balance fell. Since most of the gains of poorer peasants probably came out of what previously had been explicit property incomes (rents and interest actually paid and profits earned on land farmed by full-time hired laborers), I think this extremely unlikely. But even if C_m did fall, it would have done so only because of the peculiarity of its definition as including *all* incomes (even high ones) not explicitly paid to property. See Victor Lippit, "Land Reform in China: The Contribution of Institutional Change to Financing Economic Development" (unpublished manuscript, 1972).

erations apply to Baran's costs of "irrational and wasteful organization of the existing productive apparatus." Some of these costs, however, take the form of potential output not produced (on account of underutilization of capacity, monopoly restrictions on output, and so on). This component should be included in $Y_p - Y_a$, but no attempt is made here to estimate it, and S_e is accordingly somewhat understated.

Since essential income above which S_e is defined should in theory include not only essential personal consumption, but also essential investment, "essential outlays on government administration and the like," and the output of scientists, artists, and teachers, we should ideally distinguish between the essential and nonessential with respect to investment in physical and human capital, and to government consumption expenditures. Because an effort at quantifying such distinctions is beyond the scope of this essay, I limit myself to a brief discussion of the degree to which the relevant components of S_e as estimated here might have represented activities that the new, post-1949 values regarded as useful and not subject to redirection. This is done after the estimate of S_e is made in Section 3.

Although S_m, unlike S_e, is not based on social norms of adequate consumption and so is a relatively objective concept, its specification is not entirely free of such norms. Like S_e, it includes the element $Y_p - Y_a$, the potential output of unutilized factors. In an economically underdeveloped country with high population density on cultivable land and great underemployment in the countryside, it is difficult even in principle to measure the extent of unemployment of labor.[4] The problem of choice between leisure and income is inevitably involved. Moreover, different degrees of absorption of surplus labor might require different degrees of institutional change—from the provision of more adequate credit facilities to the organization of collectives under a socialist government. Since the essence of the concept of S_m is the idea of a quantity of income present or potentially present under existing institutional arrangements, it should not contain an element that could be realized only under radically different social conditions. For this reason, I adopt a very conservative approach to estimating $Y_p - Y_a$, but the results are conjectural in any case and therefore carefully separated from the other components of S_m.

Finally, neither concept of surplus implies that income inequalities do not provide incentives to private investment and entrepreneurship. Where the evidence shows such incentives to be effective and substantial, relatively large proportions of both surplus measures will be devoted to investment in human and physical capital, and the likelihood of still better performance by an institutionally reorganized society will be correspondingly small. On the other hand, if only negligible portions of the surpluses associated with income inequality are being devoted to entrepreneurial pursuits, it would be a fair guess that such incentives are minimal in importance, and the opportunity costs of institutional change are correspondingly slight. Similarly, neither concept of surplus ignores the possible work incentives associated with income inequality. S_m is defined net of actual (unequal) labor and peasant incomes. S_e is defined net of socially determined essential expenditures, and the social standard is perfectly capable of encompassing inequalities necessary to maintain work incentives.[5]

2. Two Schools of Thought

The two alternative approaches to explaining the relative weakness of China's economic modernization in the modern period were labeled distributional and technological, respectively, in the introduction to this paper. Despite the oversimplification involved in these terms, I shall retain them for convenience.

The distributional school encompasses a large number of writers with different interests and viewpoints. Many are conversant with the severe technological constraints placed upon the rural economy by population growth, limited cultivable land, and a stagnant technology. What justifies their being grouped together as distributionists here is their common reliance on social and political factors to explain the inability of the Chinese economy to break through these barriers and to bring modern science to the countryside. Thus, for example, Marion Levy argues that "differences in 'non-social' factors, such as raw material resources, do not account for" the contrast between Japan's rapid modernization and China's relative stagnation, and he attributes this contrast instead to elements in the social structures of the two countries.[6] Similarly, John K. Fairbank, Alexander Eckstein, and L. S. Yang suggest only two possible explanations for China's "record of retarded development," the first centered in the integration and vitality of Chinese culture, and the second in the peculiarities of China's political institutions. Although they treat population pressure as a serious problem and refer more than once to a "scarcity of capital," they do not ascribe China's "retarded development" simply to a "vicious circle of poverty"; on the contrary, they supply much evidence that would tend to refute such a thesis.[7] In arguing that only a "massive effort . . . involving large outlays on capital-intensive projects" by the state could have overcome the stagnation of nineteenth-century China, and that such efforts must have failed "because of the very nature of the state and its officialdom," they implicitly acknowledge that the surpluses required for such an effort were at least potentially available to a state and officialdom capable of properly raising and using them.

The views of some of the earlier distributionists, such as Chen Hanseng, L. Magyar, and Fei Hsiao-t'ung, are conveniently summarized by Ramon Myers.[8] In the paragraphs that follow, I shall try to describe—with reference to our concern with surplus and its use—a composite distributionist view, drawing on the works of these and other writers.

According to such a view, a major cause of continuing rural stagnation in the first third of the twentieth century was the siphoning off of income from the tiller of the soil and its unproductive expenditure by a variety of parasitic elements who lived on, but contributed nothing to, the rural surplus. Surplus extraction took several forms, of which the most important were rent, interest, taxation, and theft by bandits or warlord armies. In addition, certain outlays in the rural society that would appear to be costs were in fact part of the potential surplus in our terminology. Protection payment to local gangsters organized into "crop-watching associations" is one not very subtle example of surplus masquerading as cost. Another, more significant example is ceremonial expenses, which claimed a sizable share of rural family expenditures. Fei estimated that perhaps one-seventh of the average annual expenditures in Kai-hsien-kung was devoted to birthdays, weddings, and funerals, and John Lossing Buck found such expenditures to be not only substantial but responsible in large degree for rural indebtedness. In addition to major life-cycle ceremonies, there were several other observances (e.g., festivals at the New Year, Ch'ing Ming) that claimed considerable resources.*

Unemployment and underemployment were still another source of potential surplus in that they signified a potential for increased output

---

* Fei Hsiao-t'ung, *Peasant Life in China* (London, 1939), p. 132; John Lossing Buck, *Land Utilization in China* (Shanghai, 1937), pp. 467–68. This treatment regards such ceremonies not as involving direct expenditures for social security purposes (which would be essential consumption rather than surplus expenditures), but as a means of strengthening family bonds so that family help could be called on when needed. From the viewpoint of a set of institutions that would provide directly for social security needs, such as that which evolved in the 1950's, these ceremonies are legitimately part of the potential surplus. This treatment is clouded by the fact that some degree of reliance on family support has continued to exist in China. Also, it can be argued that direct means of providing for health, education, and welfare (i.e., via state or collective institutions) involve costs of their own that must be taken into account in estimating the potential surplus above *essential* consumption. Finally, Myron Cohen in his Introduction to Arthur H. Smith, *Village Life in China* (Boston, 1970), p. xx, has argued that ceremonies played an important role in providing meat protein and other nutrients not otherwise available to some of the celebrants. To the extent that this was true, expenditures on ceremonies were part of subsistence rather than of potential surplus.

from given factor supplies.[9] Bandits, warlord armies, and other such elements can be counted among the unemployed in this respect, and thus represented not only a means of siphoning income away from its producers,* but also a latent source of expanded production.

Labor was not the only underutilized resource. Rural institutions imposed various inefficiencies on the use of land and capital as well. Land used for graves or for boundaries between parcels was lost to production; and parcelling made farm management, labor use, and irrigation unduly difficult. To this we may add output lost because of differences between large farms and small farms as measured by capital and labor per mou and the degree of crop specialization.†

The distributionist position seeks not only to identify and describe ways in which substantial amounts of income were extracted from the primary producers; it also investigates the uses to which the extracted income was put. Insofar as this income constituted potential surplus, its use is relevant to the question of the effectiveness with which this surplus was employed in the service of development, and in particular, for investment purposes. The distributionists specify a number of ways in which rent, interest, and profit income were used other than for investment in agriculture or industry. First, of course, was luxury consumption. Increasingly in modern times, those with sufficient wealth took up residence in towns and cities, which became "the center of landlord power," and lived as lavishly as they could manage off the rural surplus. "The markets for modern manufactured goods are among city and town dwellers, and the purchasing power of these people depends largely on income derived from the countryside in the form of rent and interest."[10] This was true not only of modern manufactured consumer goods but of traditional luxury crafts as well:

The greater the concentration of landowners as well as of wealth, the greater the development of craftsmen and the more skilled and varied the types of things produced.   · · ·

Economic activity in these fortified centers of administration, then, was based not on an exchange of goods between producers but on the purchasing power

---

* But that part extracted from property incomes in the countryside constitutes a transfer from one form of surplus to another, not a net addition to total surplus.

† To the extent that this last phenomenon is due to the desire of better-off farmers to keep down the risk of reliance on an unpredictable market by devoting a greater share of their land to subsistence crop production (a luxury poorer peasants could not afford), it constitutes underspecialization that greater market stability would remedy. See Dwight H. Perkins, *Agricultural Development in China, 1368–1968* (Chicago, 1969), p. 107; and Ramon H. Myers, "The Commercialization of Agriculture in Modern China," in W. E. Willmott, ed., *Economic Organization in Chinese Society* (Stanford, Calif., 1972), p. 174.

of consumers who gained their wealth largely from exploitative relationships with the country.[11]

In the same category as luxury consumption might be placed such "non-productive investment" as the construction and maintenance of extravagant residences and ancestral halls.[12]

Certain other direct methods of disposition of property incomes are less straightforward in their economic significance. The investment of rent, interest, and profit incomes in agricultural land and urban real estate, though not constituting "investment" in the economist's sense, either financed dissaving on the part of the seller (typical in the case of rural land sales and at least partly occasioned by the unequal distribution of wealth and income in the first place) or represented a transfer of surplus of which the disposition by the recipient must then be studied. The effect of gold and silver hoarding depended on the nature of the suppliers of these metals. Where the assets were imported, their opportunity cost was the capital goods imports forgone.[13] Where purchased from domestic stocks, the effect depended on the sellers' use of the proceeds.* A net increase in the demand for precious metals for hoarding purposes will tend to stimulate increased imports and production of such items, both of which claim resources that otherwise might be available for expanding consumption or investment. Payments to rent collectors, runners, personal servants, personal armies, and other unproductive retainers, though appearing in form to be wage and salary income, are from a Baranian viewpoint payments out of surplus. Their recipients are maintained without contributing to the output of essential consumption goods.

Taxes (which, to the extent that they were paid out of rent, did not constitute additions to surplus) were spent in a variety of ways. Some expenditures were beneficial to society, e.g., those for social overhead facilities and essential administrative services, but many were not. In some areas, "a large proportion of the tax collected by the Hsien Governments from the farmers is not used for purposes which are of any value to the farmers, but goes for the support of the local politicians and private armies."[14] In the 1930's the rural tax situation was notable for the piling up of requisitions and surtaxes by various competing authorities, the proceeds of which "satisfy the rapacity of the local gentry, but

---

* From 1943 on, the Nationalist government sold gold in order to raise revenue, decrease reliance upon the printing press, and "attract the funds of those who otherwise would engage in hoarding rice or other important goods and speculate in them —in other words to divert them from that harmful activity, and thus add to the supply of goods available in the market" (Arthur N. Young, *China's Wartime Finance and Inflation, 1937–1945*, Cambridge, Mass., 1965, p. 190).

hardly at all contribute toward the cost of public works."[15] A large and probably major portion of central government expenditures (the revenue for which did not come from rural areas) for the years 1928–35 was allocated to military uses, and approximately half of the nonmilitary portion paid for tax collection. "Expenditures for public works were small and welfare expenditures almost nonexistent."[16] Although this is not the place for an extended discussion of the role of government in the economy of the 1930's, it is evident that a very large proportion of resources claimed by government was not used in a manner conducive to promoting economic development.

In sum, then, the distributionist position sees the peasant as a "helpless prey to the evil gentry, the tax collector, and any man with a gun —soldier or bandit," as the victim of a "rural triple alliance between the gentry, village usurers . . . and local government underlings"[17] that milked the surplus of the rural economy and used it for personal aggrandizement and familial fortune.

It should be recognized that the distributionist school does not deny the severe constraints to development posed by population pressure on arable land and by technological stagnation. On the contrary, the position of many writers who emphasize distributional constraints is rather that nothing could be done about the technical problems until social and political reforms were undertaken. Thus R. H. Tawney, in his introduction to the profoundly distributionist collection *Agrarian China*, explains: "The need for the modernization of agricultural methods is recognized; but the extensive introduction of technical improvements is regarded as improbable, until the social fabric within which they must function has been drastically modified."[18] In this respect the distributionists are eclectic, though they assign orders of priority to their variables.

The distributionist position has been subject to criticism on two counts that concern us here.* First, it is argued that the image of pre-Communist modern China as a landlord-dominated society characterized by gross inequalities of wealth is false. The Chinese countryside on the eve of the Communist conquest was "*not* a landlord society" but a "relatively egalitarian, competitive and fragmented" one.[19] For China as a whole, "the importance of land concentration and tenancy as the fundamental problem in the rural economy has been vastly overestimated by Chinese writers."[20] The fundamental empirical basis for this refu-

---

* An additional criticism relates to the distributionist view of the role of the treaty ports in contributing to rural decline. This subject will be touched on briefly in the conclusion to this paper.

tation is the work of Buck and, for those to whom it is accessible, of Muramatsu Yuji.[21]

Although conditions differed markedly by region, Buck found that for China as a whole, a third of all farmers were full tenants, almost a quarter rented part of their land, and the rest (44 percent) were full owners of their holdings. On the basis of land rather than population, he found that some 71 percent of farm area was cultivated by the owner, and 29 percent rented.[22] These figures are of course subject to different interpretations: witness one writer's observation that "about 50 percent of the peasantry were involved in the landlord-tenant relationship," and the contrary perception of another that the amount of land held by non-farming landlords was insufficient to make them a socially dominant class.[23]

The second focus of criticism concerns the distributionist stress on exploitative rural socioeconomic relations as impediments to agricultural development. On the contrary, according to the critique, landlord-tenant relations were not a significant obstacle, not only because of the relative unimportance of tenancy, but also because conditions of tenure preserved incentives for land improvement by the peasant where tenancy was widespread. Moreover, for those landlords who did possess large accumulations of wealth, land was generally not a major source. As for the moneylender, he played a role in enabling poor households to survive until the next harvest, as well as in financing purchases of farm animals, tools, and commodities for weddings and funerals.[24]

If, as the technologists hold, rural stagnation cannot be ascribed to exploitative socioeconomic relations and the institutions supporting them, what alternative explanations suggest themselves? In the work of several scholars, the outlines of an alternative causal hypothesis can be perceived which, because of its emphasis on the man–land ratio and stagnating techniques, I have called here the technological view. Central to the position of this school is the argument that by the late nineteenth and early twentieth centuries there was no longer any significant economic surplus above subsistence being produced by the overwhelming rural component of the Chinese economy. Therefore, questions of distribution in that part of the economy are largely irrelevant. Whatever surpluses were produced were located rather in the small modern enclaves, mainly the treaty ports. These aided the economy of the hinterland to some degree by stimulating commercialization and providing employment opportunities for surplus agricultural labor, thus stemming the otherwise inevitable decline in rural living standards that increasing population pressure would have caused. But because of the ultimate insignificance of the treaty-port economy when measured against that of the vast rural interior, these effects were sadly inadequate to the need of the rural economy for technological modernization. Thus, the suggested cause of rural stagnation is that "agriculture could not develop more rapidly than it did because the treaty-port economy failed to industrialize rapidly and introduce technological change to the peasant economy."*

The "high-level equilibrium trap." The basic model of surplus reduction behind this paradigm has been described both by Dwight Perkins and by Mark Elvin (who has dubbed it the "high-level equilibrium trap"). It is basically an application to China of the model of traditional agriculture suggested by Theodore Schultz.[25]

In this view, the relative stagnation of Chinese agriculture—and by extension, of the rest of the economy as well—was due to the exhaustion of opportunities for increasing farm productivity within the framework of the traditional technology. As population migrated over the centuries into the relatively underpopulated parts of the country and the land filled up with people, the most productive, labor-intensive techniques diffused throughout China. By the early nineteenth century, Chinese agriculture had already entered the phase of severe diminishing returns to additional labor inputs. Only the turmoil of the great rebellions of the mid-century and migration to Manchuria from the beginning of the twentieth century afforded temporary relief, by eliminating population in the one case, and by increasing the supply of land in the other. As Perkins sees it, the situation became critical by the middle of the twentieth century, when Manchuria had been substantially populated and the rate of population growth increased to well above the long-term growth potential of traditional agriculture. Elvin focuses on an earlier period, arguing that improvements in traditional agricultural technology, increases in investment, and the use of new resources "had all reached a point of sharply diminishing returns by the later eighteenth century,"[26] but his explanatory framework is essentially the same as that of Perkins.

* Ramon H. Myers, *The Chinese Peasant Economy: Agricultural Development in Hopei and Shantung, 1890–1949* (Cambridge, Mass., 1970), p. 293. Although Myers uses this argument to rebut as "simply false" the converse statement that the rural economy was a drag on development of the treaty ports, he almost immediately contradicts this position by arguing that "the growth of agriculture determined the rate and character of urban growth and the size of the nonfarm population that could be supported." It would seem that the way out of this apparent contradiction is to assert the mutual interaction between the treaty-port and peasant economies. Similarly, it could be argued that lagging agricultural growth in the 1950's was a drag on industrialization, and that inadequate industrial investment in agriculture in turn hindered agricultural growth.

Elvin, moreover, provides a link between agricultural stagnation and the behavior of the nonagricultural economy, as well as a hypothesis to explain why agriculture failed to break out of its "trap" with a technological revolution of its own. He argues that Chinese agriculture had reached a point of discontinuity at which "only inputs created by a fairly advanced stage of an industrial-scientific revolution . . . could have saved it from sharply diminishing returns to new methods, new investment, extra inputs and new use of resources."[27] Hence, an industrial revolution would have had to *precede* an agricultural revolution. But an industrial revolution was itself inhibited by the falling per capita surplus of agricultural goods imposed by the situation of diminishing returns, since this gave rise to "a reduction in effective demand per person for goods other than those needed for bare survival."[28] In other words, although capital was not inadequate and the surplus was substantial,* the constellation of falling surpluses over time and highly developed traditional technology in late-traditional China made it increasingly difficult for those surpluses to be used for productivity-enhancing innovations.

A comprehensive and sophisticated argument, with adumbrations of supplementary explanations brought to bear from a wide-ranging examination of traditional Chinese culture, the "high level equilibrium trap" hypothesis is nevertheless explicitly technological in its emphasis. Like other writers of a technological bent, Elvin specifically rejects the gamut of sociopolitical explanations for late-traditional Chinese economic stagnation.[29] His conclusions are fully consistent with the dictum that "the basic difficulty in rural China during the past century was that too many people were trying to make a living off too little land using a primitive technology."[30]

Yet, whatever the validity of this formulation for the analysis of China's economic history before the advent of substantial contacts with the West,† such contacts offered China the possibility of skipping historical

---

* Elvin makes these arguments on pp. 286–89 of *The Pattern of the Chinese Past* (Stanford, Calif., 1973), and on p. 314 he refers to "huge but static markets," which again suggests a sizable surplus. He thus implies that not only a substantial surplus but a rising one is a prerequisite for stimulating technical progress in the nonagricultural economy. In an earlier version of the "high-level equilibrium trap" formulation, he does appear to emphasize the absolute size of the surplus, arguing that its smallness by 1800 explains the lack of impetus to innovation. See Mark Elvin, "The High-Level Equilibrium Trap: The Causes of the Decline of Invention in the Traditional Chinese Textile Industries," in W. E. Willmott, ed., *Economic Organization in Chinese Society* (Stanford, Calif., 1972), pp. 171–72.

† Perkins's study indicates that agricultural output per capita remained constant over the long period from the fourteenth to the early twentieth centuries. Although such a finding is not necessarily inconsistent with the diminishing returns hypothesis (for example, if constant returns resulted only from frequent famines, plagues

stages in the technological revolution and created an essentially new situation. It was no longer technologically impossible for existing surpluses to be used innovatively once the spectrum of technical possibilities was broadened to include equipment, methods, and ideas available in the advanced countries. Such internationally inspired innovation did indeed occur on a very modest scale from the late nineteenth century on, and it gathered great momentum in the years after 1949. It is of course still possible to argue that diminishing per capita surpluses created poor incentives for modernizing innovation under existing institutional conditions, even given the technical possibilities for such innovation to occur. But then it is necessary to direct attention as much to the characteristics of the institutional setting as to the technological features, since both cooperated to inhibit the desired incentives. In short, for the period after the Opium Wars, a purely technological position seems to require demonstrating not only that diminishing returns put long-term pressures on the surplus, but that the absolute size of the surplus was so small as to render the question of its distribution and use inconsequential. It is for this reason that we turn our attention next to trying to gauge in a broad and general way the size of the potential economic surplus in China's pre-Communist economy.

3. *Estimating the Surplus, 1933*

The underlying meaning adopted here of economic surplus as the use of available resources for nonessential purposes (including undesired idleness) indicates that the criterion for identifying surplus is how income is spent rather than who receives it. A millionaire who lives frugally and spends most of his income to build machinery or improve farm productivity contributes little or nothing to surplus. But the same millionaire, spending his income on luxury articles, imported automobiles, and domestic servants, generates substantial surplus.*

Nevertheless, the method adopted here for estimating S_m—the economic surplus above mass consumption—is based on who receives the income, not how it is used. That is, S_m is treated as consisting of rent, interest, and profit incomes, estimated with varying degrees of crudeness and approximation for different sectors of the economy. Peasant

---

and wars, which relieved population pressure periodically), it nevertheless raises problems for a hypothesis that puts great weight on the existence of diminishing surplus per capita.

* This is true even though the servants and luxury goods producers are supported by him, because their activities generate nonessential goods and services. They do not themselves consume these goods and services, but subsist on the necessities (essential goods and services) produced elsewhere in the economy.

incomes, including the imputed returns to land and capital owned and used by the independent proprietor, are excluded from S_m. Labor incomes in nonagricultural sectors, including the returns to human capital (skills acquired from education or experience), are also excluded.

The reason for doing it this way is that the available data do not permit a breakdown of national product by sector of origin with which to separate activities supporting mass livelihoods from those constituting surplus. On the other hand, sufficient data do exist about rents, interest, and profits in the countryside, wages in nonagricultural activities, and occupational distribution of the labor force to permit a crude and illustrative breakdown of national income by (explicit) property and labor (plus implicit property) shares. Furthermore, since the great bulk of surplus product was undoubtedly associated with upper-income groups whose earnings largely took the form of returns to property, there is bound to be a fairly close relationship between surplus calculated our way and surplus calculated the ideal way.

Insofar as property incomes were used to finance investment, however, such incomes clearly overstate surplus as meant here. The extent of such overstatement is briefly investigated at the end of this section. Property incomes used to subsidize the consumption of unemployed persons is part of surplus if such persons are capable of productive employment. Some property income was no doubt used to support old and infirm relatives and retainers, and such income transferred to welfare purposes is not properly part of surplus. I know of no way to estimate this portion, however. On the other hand, the high salaries of managerial personnel and technical workers undoubtedly contain an element of surplus in that they are partly used to acquire luxuries, but this element is ignored here as well.

Although we are interested in the general order of magnitude of the potential economic surplus in pre-1949 China, and would therefore ideally like to have a substantial time series of data so as to be able to eliminate the influence of short-term fluctuations in economic conditions, such series do not exist. The estimates are based chiefly on the detailed national income statistics compiled for 1933 by T. C. Liu and K. C. Yeh, though some wage data from the late 1920's and early 1930's are also used. For agriculture, I rely heavily on the work of Victor Lippit, whose estimates also pertain to 1933.

Let us recall the definition of the potential surplus above mass consumption, combining equations (1) and (2) of Section 1:

$$(4) \qquad S_m = Y_a - w(N + R) + Y_p - Y_a.$$

The component $Y_a - w(N + R)$ is the potential surplus in actually produced output. It is estimated sector by sector, either directly (as in agriculture, following Lippit) or by subtracting estimates of sectoral wage bills from Liu-Yeh estimates of sectoral values-added. The second component of equation (4), $Y_p - Y_a$, is the potential output of unemployed workers and possibly of pure rentiers (those persons capable of working but who live entirely on the returns to their property) as well.

The potential output of unemployed workers can be written as

$$(5) \qquad\qquad Y_u = \frac{Y_a}{N_e} k (N - N_e) \, ,$$

where

    $Y_u =$ the potential output of unemployed workers,
    $N_e =$ the number of employed workers, and
    $k =$ the ratio of the potential productivity of unemployed workers to the productivity of employed workers, or

$$\frac{Y_p - Y_a}{N - N_e} \Big/ \frac{Y_a}{N_e} .$$

Equation (5), which expresses the potential productivity of unemployed workers as the product of their number $(N - N_e)$, the ratio of their productivity to that of employed workers (k), and the productivity of employed workers (Y_a/N_e), can also be written somewhat differently:

$$(6) \qquad\qquad Y_u = \frac{N}{N_e} Y_a k u \, ,$$

    where $u = 1 - \dfrac{N_e}{N}$, the rate of unemployment.

The ratio of potential output of unemployed workers to current NDP is, therefore,

$$(7) \qquad\qquad \frac{Y_u}{Y_a} = \frac{N}{N_e} k u \, .$$

This is the form in which the potential contribution of unemployed workers is estimated below.

Neither the potential contribution to output of pure rentiers nor their consumption is initially taken into account because of the difficulty of estimating their numbers. Consumption at the mass consumption level for pure rentiers is wR, and we may express their potential productivity as Y_r. Substituting the second term in the definition of S_m (equation (4) as amended by equation (6)), we get

$$(8) \qquad\qquad S_m = Y_a - wN - wR + \frac{N}{N_e} k u + Y_r \, .$$

Clearly, if the omissions of rentier consumption and rentier potential output are to compensate each other, then wR must $= Y_r$, or w must $= Y_r/R$. In other words, the average mass consumption level allowed to rentiers, w, must exactly equal their average potential productivity. If rentiers are capable of producing more than their mass consumption, the surplus will be underestimated, whereas if they produce less, it will be overestimated. Since as a group the pure rentiers probably average far more education per capita than the labor income recipients and peasants, it is probable that the potential productivity of those rentiers capable of working will exceed w. However, the rentier group also contains some elderly and disabled individuals whose potential productivity is nil or negligible.

The assumption that rentiers will begin to work and produce a labor income might legitimately be thought to violate the property of S_m that it not require radical institutional change to produce. If that assumption is therefore rejected, rentier consumption must be added to the consumption of peasants and labor income recipients in calculating C_m. In the absence of direct information on the number of pure rentiers, the best expedient would seem to be to add some 3 percent to C_m as calculated above.*

Because of the very different method of estimating the surplus above essential consumption, S_v, the problem of rentiers does not arise.

In the estimate of $Y_p - Y_a$, not only unemployed and underemployed labor is taken into account, but also unutilized land capable of profitable cultivation. As equation (8) indicates, however, the potential output of unutilized land does not enter explicitly into the estimate. Rather, it influences the surplus indirectly through its effect on the parameter k, which expresses the degree of diminishing returns to be encountered by the employment of unemployed labor. The manner in which this is done is indicated below.

Agriculture. Lippit finds the share of rural property income in net domestic product (Y_a/Y) as the sum of three component shares: rent

---

* The standard Chinese Communist analysis of pre-Communist class structure in the countryside puts the number of landlords and rich peasants at less than 10 percent of the rural population. (See, for example, Hsüeh Mu-ch'iao, Su Hsing, and Lin Tse-li, *The Socialist Transformation of the National Economy in China*, Peking, 1960, p. 2.) Well under half of this group must have been landlords, and of these, a substantial proportion must have farmed some land themselves. Thus, for the rural population, 3 percent would seem to be a generous estimate of the proportion of the total population that lived by returns to property alone. Similarly, in the nonagricultural sectors, the number of those who received property income but played no production or managerial role could hardly have been greater than 3 percent of the labor force.

(ρ/Y), profits on farming done by full-time hired labor (σ/Y),[*] and interest (i/Y). With considerable resourcefulness, he develops the following estimates:

$$\frac{\rho}{Y} + \frac{\sigma}{Y} + \frac{i}{Y} = \frac{Y_a}{Y}$$

$$.107 + .034 + .028 = .169$$

Thus, Lippit finds that about 17 percent of NDP in 1933 was accounted for by rural property incomes. In addition, he estimates that another 2.1 percent of NDP was absorbed by land taxes paid by owner-cultivators and net of those paid by landlords and already included in ρ/Y. It should be realized that the land tax figures do not include "miscellaneous sales, transit, animal slaughter and other local taxes of every variety and description which proliferated during this period,"[31] and that furthermore, a large portion of the payments concerned never reached government coffers but were siphoned off by tax farmers and into the pockets of officials. Adding estimated taxes net of property income payment to property incomes yields a total rural surplus from these sources equal to 19 percent of NDP.

Ideally, any transfers from the surplus to shore up mass consumption should be subtracted from S_m, and transfers to the surplus from peasant incomes should be added to S_m. An example of the first would be a net surplus of new consumption loans over payments or of land purchases by landlords from peasants over land sales to peasants (i.e., dissaving by peasants). On the other hand, a surplus of repayments over new consumption loans and of peasant land purchases over sales would be examples of transfers to S_m. I know of no way to estimate the quantitative significance, or even the direction, of such possible transfers with any degree of confidence.[†]

[*] While σ includes imputed managerial wages of owners, and is thus more than property income, Lippit deliberately chooses a low value of σ/Y to compensate for this. (Victor Lippit, "Land Reform in China: The Contribution of Institutional Change to Financing Economic Development," unpublished manuscript, 1972, pp. 72–73.) However, ρ includes only rent explicitly paid to landlords. The imputed returns to land cultivated by its owners are not included in ρ and hence in surplus. To avoid confusion with other variables discussed in this essay, I have changed Lippit's symbols.

[†] Rural instability and peasant agitation in the 1920's and 1930's "reduced the demand for land and encouraged landlords to sell their property" (John Lossing Buck, *Land Utilization in China*, Shanghai, 1937, p. 333). However, the severe price deflation of 1931–33 hurt the peasantry and may have forced numbers of them to sell their land and become tenant farmers (Ramon H. Myers, "The Commercialization of Agriculture in Modern China," in W. E. Willmott, ed., *Economic Organization in China*, Stanford, Calif., 1972, p. 191). Deflation may also have

Of the various components of rural potential surplus not estimated by Lippit, the most important were probably (a) income claimed by depredations of bandits and military units; (b) income claimed by local surtaxes, insofar as these did not come out of surplus already accounted for by property incomes; (c) output lost through rural underemployment; and (d) output lost through underutilization of land. Only for elements (c) and (d) can an attempt be made here to arrive at rough estimates of size.

Buck found that rural idleness, almost entirely seasonal in nature, averaged 1.7 months per able-bodied man, or 14 percent of the year. He advised making use of such idle labor to expand subsidiary production in fruit growing, animal raising, handicraft production, and the like.[32] He also found a significant amount of cultivable land, amounting to some 9 percent of the total cultivated area of 252.6 million acres, to be unutilized because of certain tenure conditions and social practices.[33]

Having obtained estimates of the underutilization of land and labor, we must next estimate the resulting shortfall of actual output below potential output. One way to make such an estimate would be to construct a production function for the agricultural sector and then calculate the increase in output associated with a 14 percent increase in labor and a 9 percent increase in land; but the only practical way of doing this embodies highly restrictive and unrealistic assumptions about factor markets and underlying technology,[34] and also improperly assumes that the unemployed labor would be put to work on the unutilized land even though such unemployment occurred almost entirely in the winter months. Therefore, I instead adopt the expedient of applying to 1933 the actual results of increased utilization of labor and land in the 1950's.

Cultivated land in 1956 was given as 1.677 billion mou, some 9.3 percent greater than the 1.533 billion mou estimated for 1933 by Liu and Yeh. This is almost exactly equal to Buck's estimate of the underutilization of land in the early 1930's. Between 1952 and 1956, according to Peter Schran's calculations, the total annual number of labor days in agriculture increased by some 40 percent, and the net value of peasant production increased by 24 percent,* or by 60 percent of the increase in

---

forced a net increase in peasant indebtedness in 1933. It should be remembered, however, that most borrowing was by middle-income or wealthy farmers with the collateral and credit ratings to make them good risks. The ability to borrow must have declined substantially during the deflation, and many activities (e.g., ceremonial) must have been postponed to avoid the need to incur new debt.

* T. C. Liu and K. C. Yeh, *The Economy of the Chinese Mainland* (Princeton, N.J., 1965), pp. 128–29; Peter Schran, *The Development of Chinese Agriculture, 1950–1959* (Urbana, Ill., 1969), pp. 75, 119. The year 1952 is taken as the starting

labor inputs. Assuming that the same discount must be applied to the 14 percent potential increase in labor in 1933 to account for diminishing returns, we come out with an estimate of output forgone in that year of .6 × 14 = 8.4 percent of agricultural output, or 5.5 percent of net domestic product.*

In summary, the shares in NDP of potential surplus originating or latent in the agricultural sector are 16.9 percent (luxury consumption, other unproductive expenditures, and some investment out of explicit property incomes) plus 2.1 percent (land tax) plus 5.5 percent (under-utilized land and labor), or a total of 24.5 percent. This excludes local surtaxes, extractions by military units and bandits, potential output of unutilized land outside of Buck's 22 provinces, net above-par consumption out of implicit property incomes of owner-cultivators, and, possibly, output lost on account of inefficiencies due to uneconomic land division and differences in factor ratios between farms of different sizes.

The nonagricultural sector. For factories, mining and utilities, construction, and modern transportation and communications, surplus was calculated by subtracting estimated labor income from sectoral value-added. The wage data and sources are given in Table 1, and the calculations and their results are shown in Table 2. The estimates for the other nonagricultural sectors are given, along with all the other sectoral estimates, in Table 4. It is evident that, all together, surplus above mass consumption for income actually produced outside of agriculture came to over 8 percent of NDP.

To estimate the potential surplus represented by output lost because of unemployment in nonagricultural sectors, we must multiply the amount of unemployment by an estimate of potential value-added per unemployed worker. Liu and Yeh state that of 53 million males (aged 12 to 65, excluding students) in the labor force in 1933, 12 million (or more than 20 percent) were unemployed.[35] Adopting the procedure of allocating this unemployment to the various nonagricultural sectors according to their share of total nonagricultural employment, and then calculating the potential addition to output in each sector by multiply-

point because the average number of annual labor days per employed person seems to have been about the same as in 1933 (Schran, pp. 67–69). The year 1956 is taken as the endpoint in order to avoid including the extreme intensification of labor inputs during the winter of 1957–58, when the Great Leap Forward began.

* Given the same (9 percent) increase in cultivated land, it is plausible to assume that a 14 percent increase in labor would encounter a lower rate of diminishing returns than a 40 percent increase. However, some increase in capital and current inputs occurred in the 1953–56 period, without which diminishing returns would have been even greater. By ignoring both factors, I implicitly assume that they balance out.

TABLE 1

Wages for Samples of Jobs in Factories, Mining, and Utilities, and Construction, 1933

Sector and type of job	Wage per month (Yuan)	
Factories, mining, and utilities		
Textiles		
Chungking cotton textile workers[a]	8	
Kwangtung weavers (machine)[b]	11	
Ho'pei cotton spinners[c]	12	
Wuhsing silk weavers (machine)[d]	31	
Other		
Chemical industry workers[e]	11	
3,156 factory workers[f]	19	
3,317 Ningpo factory workers[g]	22	
Boiler room workers[h]	20–60	
Machine industry workers[e]	32	
Printing workers[e]	36	
Engine room workers[h]	45–100	
Average Annual Wage		324
Construction		
Carpenters[i]	14	
Masons[i]	14	
Masons and carpenters[j]	15	
Average Annual Wage		168

Sources:

[a]P'eng Tse-i, *Chung-kuo chin-tai shou-kung-yeh shih tzu-liao, 1840-1949* (Materials on the history of the handicraft industry in modern China, 1840-1949), vol. 3 (Peking, 1957), p. 572. Data refer to average wage for iron loom workers, 1934 or 1935.

[b]*Ibid.*, p. 572. Assumes 26 workdays per month. Data are for 1934 or 1935.

[c]*Ibid.*, p. 571. Assumes 26 workdays per month. Data are for women factory spinners, 1932.

[d]*Ibid.*, p. 574. Data are for 1932.

[e]*Ibid.*, p. 566. Data are for Peiping, 1933. Highest and lowest wages are given, from which I have calculated the average.

[f]L. K. Tao, "The Standard of Living Among Chinese Workers" (Shanghai, 1931), pp. 31-34. I have taken a weighted average of the wages for factory workers in Tao's sample. The weights are the proportions of the different sub-samples in the total sample of factory workers. Tao's figures are for family expenditures. I have assumed (a) 1.5 wage earners per family (see Sidney D. Gamble, *How Chinese Families Live in Peiping*, New York, 1933, pp. 29-30), and (b) that all wages are spent.

[g]P'eng Tse-i, p. 570. Assumes 26 workdays per month. Data are for 1932. Highest and lowest wages per day are given, from which I have calculated the monthly average.

[h]Gamble, p. 317. An average of the range given is used in computing the overall average for this sector.

[i]*Ibid.* Average taken for range of 12-16 yuan for masons.

[j]L. K. Tao, pp. 31-33. Refers to 1927-28, and assumes 1.5 wage earners per family (see note f above).

Note: The obvious likelihood of bias in the use of such small samples should be kept in mind. However, Gamble, pp. 30-31, observes that in Peiping the wages of most unskilled and some semi-skilled workers began at 12 yuan per month, and that some men educated enough to teach or do clerical work were paid 14 yuan per month. The average wage for factory work that I am using, 27 yuan, is considerably above these figures. That for construction work, 14 yuan, is equal to the higher figure. It is thus not very likely that our estimates err in being too small, causing the resulting surplus to be too large.

TABLE 2

Estimates of the Potential Surplus in Factories, Mining, and Utilities,
Construction, and Modern Transportation and Communications, 1933

Category	Factories, mining, and utilities	Construction	Modern transportation and communications	Total
Net value-added (Million yuan)	980	340	430	
Employment (Millions)	1.94	1.55	44	
Net value-added per worker (Yuan)	505	219	977	
Average annual wage (Yuan)	324	168	486	
Surplus per worker (Yuan)	181	51	491	
Total surplus (Million yuan)	351	79	216	646
Total surplus as pct. of NDP				2.2%

Sources:
Net value-added. T. C. Liu and K. C. Yeh, *The Economy of the Chinese Mainland* (Princeton, N.J., 1965), p. 66.
Employment. *Ibid.,* p. 69.
Average annual wage. Factories, mining, and utilities, and construction: see Table 1. Modern transportation and communications: Insufficient wage data were available to provide a reasonable sample; I have therefore assumed the average wage in this sector to be 1.5 times that in factories, mining, and utilities.

ing its unemployment by 60 percent of its average labor productivity,[*] we derive a total income forgone of 1.206 billion yuan, or 4.1 percent of NDP (Table 3).[†]

These estimates, which are conservative and incomplete, indicate that the economy of 1933 produced or was capable of producing a total surplus above mass consumption equal to almost 37 percent of NDP (Table 4). If pure rentier consumption must be subtracted from this surplus (see above), the surplus above mass consumption is reduced slightly, to 35 percent.[‡] If output forgone because of underutilization of available resources is excluded, the surplus actually produced comes to over one-quarter (27.2 percent) of NDP.

[*] This last procedure is to make maximum possible allowance for possible diminishing returns to additional labor inputs. The rate of diminishing returns used is the same as for agricultural labor, and therefore constitutes a most generous allowance for diminishing returns in the nonagricultural sectors.

[†] This procedure makes no allowance for unemployed female workers, and so seriously understates the potential gains from full employment.

[‡] Assuming pure rentiers to constitute 3 percent of the population (see p. 67), C_m, which is equal to 63.2 percent $(100 - 36.8)$ of NDP, must be increased by 3.1 percent, which is equivalent to reducing S_m by 5.4 percent.

TABLE 3

Potential Output of Unemployed Workers, Nonagricultural Sectors, 1933

Sector	(1) Net value-added (Million yuan)	(2) Employment (Millions)	(3) Pct. of nonagricultural employment (2) ÷ 54.3 million × 100	(4) Labor productivity (Yuan) (1) ÷ (2)	(5) Unemployment (Millions) (3) × 12 million	(6) Potential output of unemployed workers (Million yuan) .6 × (4) × (5)
Factories, mining, and utilities	980	1.94	3.6%	505	.432	131
Handicrafts	2,040	15.74	29.0	130	3.480	271
Construction	340	1.55	2.9	219	.348	46
Modern transportation and communications	430	0.44	0.8	977	.096	56
Traditional transportation and communications	1,200	10.86	20.0	110	2.400	158
Trade	2,710	14.88	27.4	182	3.288	359
Government	820	5.12	9.4	160	1.128	108
Finance	210	0.14	0.3	1,500	.036	32
Personal Services	340	3.63	6.7	94	.804	45
Total	54.30		100.1%		12.012	1,206

Source: T. C. Liu and K. C. Yeh, The Economy of the Chinese Mainland (Princeton, N.J., 1965), pp. 66, 69.

TABLE 4
Sources of Surplus and Percent of Surplus in Net Domestic Product, 1933

Sector and source of surplus	Pct. in NDP	
Agriculture	24.5	
Rent		10.7
Interest		2.8
Profits		3.4
Land taxes paid by owner-cultivator		2.1
Underutilization of labor and land		5.5
Nonagricultural sectors	12.3	
Factories, mining, and utilities		1.2
Handicrafts		1.8
Construction		_a
Modern transportation and communications		0.7
Traditional transportation and communications		0.5
Trade		2.6
Finance		0.5
Residential rent		0.9
Unemployment of labor		4.1
All sectors	36.8	
Surplus due to unemployed and unutilized resources	9.6	
All sectors, excluding surplus due to unemployed and unutilized resources	27.2	

Sources:

Agriculture. See text.

Factories, mining, and utilities, construction, modern transportation and communications. See Tables 1 and 2.

Handicrafts. Surplus estimated by multiplying the Liu-Yeh estimate of net value added by handicrafts (see Table 3) by the Lippit estimate of the combined percentage of explicit rent, interest, and profit income in agricultural net value-added (26 percent). This operation leaves an implied consumption per worker 40 percent higher than in agriculture (96 yuan compared with 68 yuan). A gap of this nature is to be expected because (a) the cost of living was higher in towns and cities where much handicraft production occurred, (b) the standard of living of handicrafts workers was probably higher on the average than that of peasants, and (c) some income in kind in agriculture probably escaped tabulation.

Traditional transportation and communications. Surplus is calculated as the difference between value added by this sector (see Table 3) and the product of its labor force (Table 3) and the implied per capita consumption of handicraft workers (see above). This procedure yields a much smaller ratio of surplus to value-added than in agriculture.

Finance. Per worker income is assumed to be as high as in modern transportation and communications (see above), and is multiplied by employment in finance (Liu and Yeh, p. 69) to derive sectoral "mass consumption." This figure (68 million yuan) is then subtracted from net value added by finance (Liu and Yeh, p. 68) to get sectoral surplus.

Trade. Profits of trading stores and restaurants are put by Liu and Yeh (p. 600) at 629 million yuan, some 36 percent of value added by stores and restaurants. The rest of this sector consists of peddlers. I have calculated their surplus assuming the same ratio of surplus to net value-added as in traditional transportation.

Residential rent. Liu and Yeh (p. 610) put the value of residential rent paid by the nonagricultural population, net of depreciation, at 456 million yuan. One-half is here assumed to have been paid explicitly (not imputed to owner-occupiers).

Potential output of unemployed labor, nonagricultural sectors. See Table 3 and text.

Note: Value added by the government administration sector consists of the wages and salaries of government employees and the subsistence of members of the military. It thus excludes surplus by definition, when surplus is calculated as here according to national income by factor payments rather than by end use. Since value added by the personal services sector consists entirely of labor incomes, it excludes surplus for the same reason. Note that if we were estimating surplus according to domestic expenditure by end use, both of these sectors would be significant sources of surplus. Their exclusion is thus definitional and should not be read to imply that their services were all "essential."

[a]Negligible

TABLE 5
*Distribution of Actually Produced Surplus Between
Modern and Traditional Sectors, 1933*

Sector	Net value-added as pct. of NDP		Surplus as pct. of NDP	Surplus net value-added
Traditional	84.4		22.6	.27
Agriculture		65.0	19.0	
Handicrafts		7.1	1.8	
Transportation and communications		4.2	0.5	
Peddlers		3.3	0.4[a]	
Personal services		1.2	—	
Residential rents		3.6	0.9	
Modern	12.9		4.6	.36
Factories, mining, and utilities		3.4	1.2	
Trading stores and restaurants		6.1	2.2[a]	
Finance		0.7	0.5	
Transportation and communications		1.5	0.7	
Construction		1.2	— [b]	

Note: The modern and traditional sectors are differentiated according to the practice of Liu and Yeh.
[a]See Table 4, source note on trade.
[b]Negligible

Of the total potential surplus, some two-thirds (or a quarter of NDP) originated or was latent in the agricultural sector, and one-third (or 12.3 percent of NDP) originated or was latent in the nonagricultural sectors. Of the actually produced potential surplus (excluding potential output not produced), about 70 percent (or 19 percent of NDP) originated in agriculture and 30 percent (8 percent of NDP) in the nonagricultural sectors. Table 5 shows the distribution of the actually produced surplus (totaling 27.2 percent of NDP) between the modern and traditional sectors. It indicates that the traditional sectors were responsible for 83 percent and the modern sectors only 17 percent of this total. However, the ratio of surplus to value-added was higher in the modern than in the traditional sector, reflecting the much higher labor productivity of the former.

The surplus above essential consumption. I have interpreted this concept of surplus, it will be recalled, as measuring the nonessential components of the national income from the Chinese Communists' view of what is and what is not essential. S_e thus identifies the portion of the national income that would have been available for redistribution toward different uses, including the promotion of economic development, in a revolutionized China led by the Chinese Communist Party. In practice, however, as in the estimate of S_m, S_e is calculated above essential personal consumption only, and no attempt is made here to separate "essential" from "nonessential" government purchases or private net investment. This important question is reserved for discussion at the end of this section.

To estimate S_e it is necessary to adopt a standard for "essential consumption." For the purpose of analyzing how the Chinese Communists used the income flows in the economy they inherited to stimulate economic development, their standard of essential consumption is the relevant one. National product per capita was very similar in 1933 and the early 1950's, so that we can treat Chinese Communist standards for the latter period as applying to the earlier one as well. I have adopted two alternative procedures to derive such a standard. One is to peg it to estimates of actual average peasant consumption in the post–Land Reform period, the other is to relate it to estimates of "new middle peasant" consumption for the same period.[36] In both cases, the standard for essential consumption for the nonagricultural population is assumed to vary by sector in relation to labor productivity—an assumption that accords with the principle followed in China of payment "according to work."

The results are shown for three alternative estimates of peasant consumption in Table 6.[37] It is important to note that, because of uncertainty about the exact meaning and coverage of the underlying data as well as the great sensitivity of the estimates to small changes in estimated peasant consumption, these figures should be taken as illustrative only of broad orders of magnitude. Ranging from 12.5 percent to 17 percent of NDP, all three estimates of actually produced surplus above essential consumption fall considerably short of our estimate of S_m (27 percent). This result is consistent with the argument presented in Section 1—that C_m probably lay below C_e in the pre-1949 decades. However, it is also evident that the S_e ratios all imply considerable leeway for expanding investment beyond the limits actually reached in the 1920's and 1930's, an observation that is reinforced if surplus in the form of output forgone because of underutilized factors is added to the surplus out of actually produced income.*

---

* In Section 1, I pointed out that since both C_m and C_e are assumed to be rising functions of income, S_m and S_e should in principle be estimated with reference to the higher consumption levels associated with Y_p rather than the lower ones associated with Y_a. To do so requires estimating the functional relations between income on the one hand and C_m and C_e on the other—a refinement well beyond the crude objectives of this discussion. It should be pointed out, however, that our

TABLE 6

Alternative Rates of Surplus Above Essential Consumption, 1933

Sample	Peasant essential consumption per capita *(Yuan)*	Ratio of produced S_e to NDP[a]	Ratio of potential S_e to NDP[a]
All peasant classes, 1954[b]	94.6	.17	.27
Middle peasants, 1954[c]	99.9	.13	.23
All peasant classes, 1955[d]	97.0	.15	.25

[a]Estimates are pegged to those of peasant consumption in the mid-1950's (Col. 1). The latter are reduced to 1933 yuan and multiplied by the Liu-Yeh estimate of 1933 agricultural population, to get essential consumption of the agricultural population. That of the nonagricultural population is estimated by multiplying the per capita figure in agriculture by the ratio of net value-added per head of population in nonagricultural sectors, to that in agriculture, and then multiplying the product by the nonagricultural population. (T. C. Liu and K. C. Yeh, *The Economy of the Chinese Mainland*, Princeton, N.J., 1965, p. 102.) C_e in agriculture and C_e in nonagriculture are then added together and subtracted from NDP in 1933 to get the actually produced surplus, whose ratio to NDP is provided in Column 2. The rate of potential S_e, given in Column 3, is calculated simply by adding .096 (the rate of surplus due to unemployed and unutilized resources given in Table 4) to the Column 2 estimates.

[b]*T'ung-chi kung-tso* Data Office, "1954 nien nung-chia shou-chih tiao-ch'a chien-yao tzu-liao" (Highlight materials on an investigation of the incomes and expenditures of farm families in 1954), *T'ung chi kung-tso*, 10: 31-32 (1957). The figure for average expenditure on means of livelihood per household (454 yuan) is divided by the given average household size (4.8) to get the per capita figure used. Data given in 1954 prices.

[c]*Ibid.* The figure for average expenditure on means of livelihood of middle peasant households (499.6 yuan) is divided by average household size of middle peasants (5.0).

[d]*T'ung-chi kung-tso* Data Office, "Kuan-yü kung-nung sheng-huo shui-p'ing wen-t'i" (On the question of standard of living of workers and peasants), *T'ung-chi kung-tso*, 13: 4-5 (1957). Data are for 1955 in current yuan. Figure used is for average per capita peasant expenditures, including subsistence income calculated at retail prices.

Uses of the surplus. The potential surplus is of interest with respect to economic development because its use is potentially an object of policy. According to the interpretation adopted here, S_e is entirely a latent force that the CCP might have harnessed to the job of generating economic growth. However, the method of estimating S_e did not exclude from it certain nonconsumption items that the Chinese Communists might have regarded as essential nevertheless, and excluded from the surplus. Some private investment and government expenditures are in this category. Moreover, the concept of the surplus above mass consumption (S_m) by definition includes such expenditures out of property income and government revenue. S_m thus overstates what the Chinese Communists, or any other development-oriented authority, might have found potentially available for redistribution in the difference between potential output and actual mass consumption.

It is therefore instructive to investigate in a general way how much of our estimates of China's pre-Communist surplus was already mort-

method of basing the estimate of C_e on peasant income at a time when at least part of the gap between Y_a and Y_p had been realized partly implements the principle in question. But by the same token, it overstates C_e (and understates S_e) for actually produced income.

TABLE 7

Selected Indicators of Modern Industrial Growth, 1920's and 1930's

Year	Average railroad mileage constructed per year (Km)	Tonnage shipped by railroad (1917 = 100)			Machinery imports (Million taels)	Annual growth rates, net value-added indexes of selected producer goods			
		Manufactured goods	Mining products	Agricultural goods		Coal	Ferrous metals	Mining products	Electric power
1921	⎫				57.3				
1925	⎬ 228^a	152.5	132.6	97.0					
1926					19.7				
1927	⎭								
1928	⎫					.016	.167	-.115	.142
1929						.049	.098	-.029	.153
1930	⎬ 339				47.5	.055	.068	.004	.094
1931						.057	-.038	.109	.157
1932	⎭					-.042	.134	-.205	.392
1933	⎫	200.9	192.4	94.6		.088	.122	.176	.158
1934	⎬ 1,359					.174	.148	.037	.116
1935						.166	.630	.246	.147
1936		268.3	282.6	132.9	53.9	.123	.196	.221	.159
1937	⎭								

Sources: Railroad mileage: John K. Chang, Industrial Development in Pre-Communist China (Chicago, 1969), p. 110; I have calculated the annual averages from Chang's figures on mileage constructed over the periods listed. Tonnage shipped: ibid., p. 111. Machinery imports: ibid., p. 108; no figure is provided for 1933. Growth rates: ibid., pp. 78-79, gives the indexes, from which I have calculated year-to-year changes (where y is the year) according to the formula $(Index_y/Index_{y-1}) - 1$.

^{a} Average for the years 1912-27

gaged and thus not available for redistribution—or how much was already employed in modernizing roles and thus not available for creating net additions to such roles.

The first striking fact, in this regard, is that personal consumption expenditures claimed over 94 percent of net domestic expenditure in 1933, leaving less than 6 percent for government consumption, "communal services" (public health, education, and cultural activities), and investment.[38] Net domestic investment was less than 2 percent of net domestic expenditures. It can of course be argued that the year 1933, near the height of the world depression, was a particularly poor one for investment, and that the surplus might have been utilized much more productively in other years.* Although in no other year during the period 1931–36 (for which estimates are available) did net investment exceed 3 percent of total product,[39] these too were depression years, and thus possibly unrepresentative.

Available data from the 1920's, however, when prices were rising and economic conditions were generally better, do not indicate an investment picture significantly different from that of the 1930's. Data for the 1920's are poor, and only impressions can be offered in support of this conclusion. For example, the entire modern sector in factories, mining, utilities, construction, modern transportation and communications, trading stores, restaurants, and modern financial institutions, provided less than 13 percent of NDP in 1933.[40] Even on the generous assumptions that the modern sector was equally large in the 1920's and that (by John Chang's estimate) it was growing by 7.7 percent per year,[41] reasonable capital-output ratios would yield a total investment for this sector of between 1 percent and 3 percent of NDP. In fact, Chang's index of production by modern industries grows much faster in 1933 than the average rate for the 1920's,[42] and the number of factories with 30 or more workers was over one-third greater in that year than in 1929. Table 7 brings together some data on railroad mileage constructed, tonnage shipped by railroad, and growth rates of selected producer goods industries for various years in the 1920's and 1930's. These series are all relevant to the growth of the modern sector of industry, and on the whole they seem consistent with a more rapid pace of development in 1933 than in the 1920's.

Similarly, there is no evidence that agriculture saw substantially heavier investments in the 1920's than in the 1930's. It has been estimated that farm output increased an average of 1 percent per year

* Against this, though, one might argue that the surplus itself may have been abnormally small in the depression years.

from 1911 through 1957.[43] Buck, in his 1921–25 study of Chinese agriculture, found that average capital per farm in the form of farm equipment, supplies, and livestock came to 145 yuan, or 0.61 times average farm earnings of 239.6 yuan.[44] Let us assume that farm output in the 1920's was growing by 1.5 percent per year (50 percent faster than the 1911–57 average), and that the incremental capital-output ratio was 1.2 (double the above 0.61 figure to allow for capital in the form of land improvements and buildings related to production). Such figures would imply an investment rate of 1.8 percent out of agricultural income, or 1.2 percent of NDP.

Other observations of Buck support the picture of a very low investment rate in agriculture. Since our estimate of S_m in this sector consists largely of explicitly paid rent and interest, the investment behavior of landlords has a major bearing on the degree to which S_m was used for investment purposes. Buck found that the landlord's capital on tenant farms was "chiefly confined to investment in land and buildings, which constitute 98 percent of his total,"[45] and that livestock, supplies, and farm equipment together came to only 1.6 percent of total landlord capital. For landlords of part-owner–cultivators, the average percentage of total capital taking the form of "land owned" was no less than 99.5 percent.[46] Thus, it seems highly unlikely that much of the 10.7 percent of NDP extracted from the countryside in the form of rent, and of that portion which landlords earned of the additional 2.8 percent extracted as interest, was reinvested in agriculture.

Data on the overall performance of handicrafts in the 1920's are extremely rare, but one study estimates that the total value of exports of 67 handicraft products grew by an average rate of 1.1 percent per year from 1912 to 1931.[47] If this rate is at all reflective of the growth of output, the implied contribution to the national investment rate, at any reasonable incremental capital-output ratio, is less than 1 percent of NDP.

Although such arguments certainly do not prove the case, they do make it seem very unlikely that the rate of net investment in the Chinese economy of the 1920's was substantially higher than in 1933. If this conclusion is valid, it implies that in a pre–World War II economy with a potential surplus above mass consumption of more than one-third of total product there was bound to be much room for expanding the investment rate.

Part of the surplus as estimated here went to the government in the form of taxes out of property incomes and peasant incomes. Government administration is of course a necessary activity under any circumstances;

and indeed, in size and proportion of national income, this sector increased after 1949.[48] But it can be fairly argued that the value added by this sector in 1933 was not growth-inducing. Even the limited resources at the government's disposal during this period were "largely dissipated in maintaining a hypertrophic military establishment and financing continual civil war, or hypothecated to service the foreign and domestic debt."[49]

In sum, even under the most charitable of interpretations of how the potential surplus was actually used in the 1930's, the conclusion seems inescapable that the diversion of much of that surplus to investment and other growth-related activities would have involved very little opportunity cost, aside from the sacrifice of privileged consumption habits on the part of a relatively small portion of the population.

4. Conclusion

Any simple argument tying China's abortive pre-Communist modernization experience to the alleged insufficiency of the surplus above subsistence would seem to be contradicted by the results of our inquiry into the relative magnitude of the surplus. If it is plausible that even in the midst of world depression and toward the end of a century of war, civil war, governmental decline, and recurrent famine, the potential surplus occupied a share of national product that dwarfed the highest investment rates in the panoply of now-industrialized countries, absolute shortage of wherewithal for savings could hardly have been a crucial problem. Yet if China, an indubitably poor country, could in this sense afford to save a substantial portion of its national income, it seems that we are obliged to look with some skepticism on a vicious-circle-of-poverty explanation for the economic backwardness of any country. No matter how poor, given motivation and opportunity, cannot any nation find within itself the capacity to save and invest in the service of economic development? Such a conclusion would not have surprised a historian like Mary Wright, who wrote this about early twentieth-century China:

Money poured in for reform and revolutionary groups. It was not uncommon for a member of an organization whose salary might be $25 per month, to live on one quarter and to contribute the other three quarters to the cause. Westerners in far corners of the world could hardly believe it, but their Chinese houseboys were sending most of their salaries to patriotic organizations.[50]

Comparison of nineteenth-century China's economic situation with Meiji Japan's indicates that at least with respect to per capita agricultural product, and possibly even total income per capita, the Chinese were not worse off. The Japanese peasant was perhaps even closer to the margin of subsistence, yet through taxation and voluntary saving he contributed appreciably to economic growth.[51] In fact, James Nakamura has concluded that a "substantial surplus above subsistence" already existed in agriculture at the beginning of the Meiji era, and that institutional changes at that time made possible a "radical redistribution of income," which in turn led to a sharp rise in savings and investment.[52] The similarity between Nakamura's view and the argument of this essay is obvious.

The picture of a substantial surplus is also consistent with evidence reported by Ping-ti Ho and others of thriving domestic trade, the rise of merchant guilds, expanded agricultural commercialization, and "numerous accounts of a rising standard of living and of unprecedented levels of affluence and conspicuous consumption among the elite"[53] in the eighteenth and early nineteenth centuries. And it squares with Chung-li Chang's estimate of a gentry class constituting some 2 percent of the population and enjoying a per capita income 16 times that of commoners at the end of the nineteenth century.[54] In short, this is not as surprising and unexpected a result as it might at first appear. And it would seem to underscore the validity of the fundamental questions— if not of all the detailed answers—supplied by the "distributionists": why was the surplus not used for developmental purposes, and how in fact was it used?

Yet it is precisely in addressing such questions that the undeniably significant evidence of the "technologists" must be considered. For if the Chinese economy was characterized by technological stagnation, high and ever-increasing population pressure on cultivable land, and the consequent slow but inexorable operation of the law of diminishing returns, it is quite likely that by the early twentieth century the surplus itself was under pressure. Ping-ti Ho has said, of the nineteenth century: "At the point where the margin above bare subsistence became much smaller than the traditional or customary living standard, the effect of irrational land tenure on the marginal segments of the population presumably became disproportionately greater."[55] However large the surplus that survived into the 1930's might have been relative to national income, it could not have supported a standard of living among the privileged that was high by contemporary international lights, except for a very small number of people. Attempts to defend that standard by shifting the burden imposed by diminishing returns onto "the marginal segments of the population" were bound to be quickly resisted, and the ensuing strife to bring into sharp relief the "effect of irrational land tenure." Here we have a plausible explanation for the apparent paradox that so many competent and informed observers in the 1930's believed the socioeconomic institutions in the countryside were growing even more exploitative and burdensome to the peasants when by all available direct evidence there was in fact no consistent trend toward increasing concentration of landownership or levels of land rent.

The obvious place to look for the source of investment embodying the technological change capable of transforming this situation is the treaty ports, where virtually all modern industry developed. There was no physical barrier preventing economic interaction between port city and hinterland; indeed, where economic conditions warranted and political conditions permitted, the two were closely linked. Yet on the whole, as Rhoads Murphey points out, the ports did not play the modernizing role they were technologically equipped to play. Rather, they were "economically . . . extraneous and tiny outposts of a system which remained foreign to China and made little impact on it."[56] In part, this was due to the resiliency of the traditional economy and its continuing ability to compete successfully with the modern enterprise outside of the special conditions of the treaty ports themselves. But it was also due to the insecurity of long-term productive investment in the unstable and war-torn conditions of the early twentieth century; to the drain of resources associated with a continuing net outflow of capital over the period 1902–31; to the denial of tariff autonomy until 1930; and to what Albert Feuerwerker calls "the ideological and political disequilibrium which was the most profound consequence of the impact of the West."[57]

In the late Tokugawa era, as investment in land became increasingly profitable owing to urbanization and improved transportation and commercial organization, Japan witnessed a steady concentration of landownership.[58] Such an effect would seem to be normal in the face of rapidly increasing demand for food and raw materials. If it did not occur generally in response to commercialization and treaty-port industrialization in China, as the "technological" position holds, then this in itself is evidence of the limited impact that these phenomena had on the rural economy in "using up" the potential surplus and demanding still more.

Although the potential surplus in early twentieth-century China may have been large in comparison with historical investment rates of rapidly growing countries, this is not at all to say that it was also large in comparison with their *surplus* rates. The relationship between potential surplus and investment in the development experiences of advanced countries is not a subject that has been explicitly investigated. It can be surmised, however, that the process of corralling and concentrating the available potential surplus in the hands of those willing to invest it productively in risky and path-breaking enterprises was a clumsy and inefficient one at best. In the absence of a powerful state, possessing either formidable coercive means or an overwhelming aura of legitimacy, the generation of a given rate of productive investment may have required a surplus rate many times as large. Owing in part to the sharpening class antagonism noted above, in part to the corrosive effects of imperialist incursions, and in part to the historical juxtaposition of all this with the cyclical occurrence of dynastic decline, early-twentieth-century China was particularly notable for its lack of either of these characteristics. Only with the victory of Chinese communism were they established, thus making possible a closer alignment of investment and surplus.

Mark Elvin

Skills and Resources in Late Traditional China

By THE later Middle Ages both Europe and China had mechanized manufacture. By this I mean they had machines that could be substituted for a complex operation by the human hand and perform many such operations simultaneously, using inanimate power if appropriate. In both areas these machines were approximately identical. They were devices with multiple spindles for twisting and doubling silk and other thread. The European version is the *filatorium* or *torcitorium* of Lucca, invented in the thirteenth century.[1] Its Chinese contemporaries were the water-powered machines for twisting hemp and silk described in Wang Chen's *Treatise on Agriculture* of 1313.[2]

They were destined for very different careers. The filatorium was the direct ancestor of Arkwright's spinning-frame and the textile machinery of the first Industrial Revolution. The Chinese machines were without direct progeny, except perhaps the hand-operated silk-doubling and twisting machines of a somewhat different design that were used in the nineteenth century and are discussed below.

These contrasting fates are the key to the central concern of this paper. In Europe there was a period of several centuries of increasingly active technical experimentation and innovation, such that the advances embodied in the characteristic triumphs of the first Industrial Revolution were, in purely technical terms, relatively slight. This was even true of the railway and the steam engine.[3] It was the economic aspects that were revolutionary. In their impact on supply, and indirectly on demand, these advances brought the new technology across some sort of qualitative threshold.

My warmest thanks are due to E-tu Zen Sun of Pennsylvania State University, William Jenner of the University of Leeds, Andrew Watson and Nicholas Fisher of the University of Glasgow, and the participants in the Bermuda Conference for helpful comments on this paper and, in many cases, for bibliographical material and references.

During the same period, from the fourteenth to the eighteenth century, China did not remain inactive in the field of technology, though creating nothing to compare in world-historical significance with earlier contributions like printing and gunpowder. What is puzzling is why this activity added up to so little in terms of qualitative change. The problem is approached here in three steps.

The factual picture is still so hazy that our first concern must be to establish at least the outlines of technological progress in China during Ming and Ch'ing times. This is really too big a task for so short a paper, and the reader is cautioned that every conclusion in this poorly documented area is more than usually provisional. Since a technical evaluation of a machine or a process is necessary before we can test any economic hypothesis about its use, diffusion, or neglect, many of the arguments advanced below rest perforce on insecure foundations.

Our second concern will be to try to find a way of accounting for the pattern of changes that emerges from the preceding survey. Here I shall argue that much of what happened, and much of what did not happen, may be explained by a greater interest on the part of the Chinese in improving the return from already accessible natural resources than in making labor or capital more productive. But there is at least one major obstacle to such a simple approach. This is the almost unchanging state of hydraulic technology. Given the enormous pressures that were almost certainly operating for better methods of pumping both in agriculture and in mining, sectors where advances could have yielded a spectacular payoff in food, metals, and fuels, it is astonishing that nothing was accomplished. What is more, inhibition due to restraints associated with the high-level equilibrium trap[4] seems to have only the most limited relevance here. There *were* better methods that did not involve science-based inputs.[5] Cultural factors would seem, by a process of elimination, to have played an important part in retarding invention and diffusion.

The third objective is to evaluate what impact the technical advances made in the late traditional period had on output. Except for restricted localities and periods, the nonhomogeneity of resources across both space and time renders misleading any attempt to estimate the impact of improvements from the scattered statistics that exist. The fertility of land varies from place to place; as exploitation progresses, deposits of metallic ore become harder to mine. We have therefore to rely in good part on the evidence of our impressions, and this suggests that technological change was just about sufficient to stabilize the standard of living as the population grew and the average quality of resources suffered a long-term Ricardian decline. Looking at the question from the standpoint recently made familiar by Richard Wilkinson,[6] we might equally hypothesize that population growth stimulated only sufficient technological growth to preserve a familiar equilibrium.

Progress: Certain, Probable, and Possible

In our analysis of technological change we need to make two sets of distinctions. The first is tripartite: between Chinese inventions and improvements, the adoption of new methods from abroad, and the diffusion of superior practices already well known in one region during the preceding age. The second is along a sliding scale: estimating the differing degrees of probability that a given technique was adopted in the late traditional period. Only rarely is it possible to be confident that we know when something was done for the first time; and many of the machines and methods listed below may eventually turn out to have a more venerable ancestry than they are credited here with having.

Perhaps the most spectacular addition to the post-Mongol countryside was the Chinese type of windmill, which resembled a cross between a small sailing-ship and a merry-go-round. The earliest surviving description comes from the first half of the seventeenth century:

In some cases [pallet-] pumps are turned not by men but by an ox. A [horizontal] wooden plate, like a cartwheel but with a larger circumference, is fitted with cogs that turn the driveshaft of the pump. This economizes on the [human] energy needed to make the pump go round, and is twice as effective. In some cases not even an ox is employed; rather the wind is used to turn the pump. The method of construction resembles the ox-powered pump, but the sails are set on the wheel [on masts mounted vertically around the rim], and advantage is taken of the wind to make it rotate. This is the most ingenious of all the machines used in farming. It is not suited to common use, however, for when great winds blow the pump is liable to be smashed.[7]

In central Kiangsu in the present century, wind-pumps of this sort were said to be able to irrigate 50 mou in a day, given a good wind.[8]

Another advance in pneumatic technology was the adaptation of the closed-in rotary fan to the ventilation of mineshafts. This machine, used until this innovation for winnowing grain, consisted of a paddle-wheel turning in a circular box with an air intake at its hub and a peripheral vent. The earliest illustration and description seem to be those in Wu Ch'i-chün's *Illustrated Summary of the Mines of Yunnan*, published in 1845, so this may be a Ch'ing development.[9]

Progress was made in various forms in the control of heat and humidity: in incubators for poultry eggs, the killing of silkworm pupae for the temporary preservation of the cocoons, greenhouses and the

forcing of plants, and cellars for the spinning of cotton yarn in a suitably
moist atmosphere. Only the last of these, however, can be indubitably
dated as late traditional.

According to Pao Shih-ch'en, writing in the first half of the nineteenth
century:

If one puts [eggs] in a basket, places it high up and covers it with grass, so
causing them to incubate, they will hatch out of the basket in 15 days. (The
present-day method is for everyone to use heating by fire. . . . The old method
is as I have described. It is definitely not unfounded gossip, so I have preserved a record of the theory to facilitate its experimental use.)[10]

How old was the "old method"? The earliest reference to incubation by
fire that I have found is in a Ming miscellany compiled by T'ien I-heng
and quoted in Ch'en Yüan-lung's early-eighteenth-century *Reflected
Sources on the Sciences*: "In Kwangtung they hatch ducklings by warming ducks' eggs in hot water. In Chekiang they hatch them in a different
fashion, by warming ducks' eggs over a fire."[11] The first proper description of an incubator seems to be in Ch'ü Ta-chün's *New Discourses on
Kwangtung*, published in 1700:

Many of the people of Kwangtung are skilled at incubating ducks. They take
five or six hundred ducks' eggs to each basket and put them in a clay hut,
cover them with coverlets, and encircle them with woodchips in which they
kindle both slow and quick fire [probably fire smothered with ashes for controlled burning]. Once the eggs are slightly warm, they switch the positions
of the high and low baskets and continue to change them back and forth
about six or seven times in every day-and-night period. On the eleventh day
they put them up onto a rack, the slats of this rack likewise being covered
with coverlets, which are reduced according to time. After a month has
elapsed, the ducklings diligently peck through their shells and emerge.[12]

From this we can establish that there was probably a diffusion of advanced incubation technique from Chekiang to Kwangtung in the late
traditional period. But it is not clear when the Chekiang poultrymen
abandoned the haybox for the charcoal-fired double-shelled earthenware incubators described by Franklin King and other modern observers.[13] On the strength of Pao Shih-ch'en's observations and the general timing of the somewhat analogous methods described in the following passages, we may guess that it was in Yüan or Ming times.

Only about ten days are available for reeling the silk off live cocoons.
After this point the moths emerge and tear the filaments. When modern
filatures were introduced late in the nineteenth century, it became essential to preserve the cocoons so that the machinery could be operated
round the year. But even before this, killing some of the pupae before

reeling could usefully take pressure off the reelers. The two major agricultural compendia of the Yüan dynasty, Wang Chen's *Treatise* and the
officially sponsored *Essentials of Farming and Sericulture*, describe three
ways of doing this: steaming, sunning, and soaking in brine.[14] During
late traditional times, two more methods were added to the repertoire:
packing with salt in an air-tight jar and killing by heat-drying. The first
of these is mentioned in Pao Shih-ch'en's *Four Arts for the Governance
of the Common People* from the early nineteenth century and also, with
some minor variations, in Wei Chieh's *Collected Notes on Sericulture*
of 1898(?).[15] Wei recommends the Yüan steaming technique except in
humid weather, when drying is a problem. Then the following practice
is preferred:

Drying Cocoons. When there is not the time to reel many of the cocoons, and
so reason to fear that moths will break out, drying the cocoons on a brick bed
warmed by fire will ensure that no moths emerge. If the brick bed has an extensive surface, it is possible to dry several hundred catties of cocoons in a
day. In the north, where the brick beds are kept very warm, it is necessary
for the heat to be evenly distributed and for the cocoons to be turned over
from time to time so that they are dried through to the appropriate degree
and do not become too scorched. Smoky fuel should not be used. The best way
of drying cocoons is that found in eastern Szechwan: hot air is brought into
the brick bed from outside, so there is no trouble from damp heat and no
anxiety that they will be dried up. But when silk filaments undergo drying by
heat, the color and sheen inevitably suffer.[16]

It was probably the concern with quality apparent in this last sentence
that limited the use of these techniques before the coming of the modern
filature. Even with modern steam-killing the silk is easily damaged.

I have made no systematic inquiry into the origins of the Chinese
type of greenhouse, but its association with the luxury horticultural
market generated by the new northern capital at Peking suggests that it
may have been a Yüan or Ming development. Hsieh Ch'ao-che, writing
in late Ming times, disapproved of the uses to which it was put:

Out-of-season flowers are regularly among the items presented these days at
Court. All of them, however, have been produced in earthen cellars where
they have been forced by fires placed around them. Thus peonies can blossom
in the depths of the winter. It is reckoned that this work costs a dozen ounces
of silver or more per plant. This is merely esteeming what is hard to obtain;
and, in truth, things out of season are proper neither to Heaven nor to Earth.[17]

There is a full description of these "cellars" in the *Mémoires concernant
les Chinois*, written by missionaries in eighteenth-century Peking. They
were partially underground structures, sunk to a depth of seven to
twelve feet, with stepped floors so that all the plants had equal access

to the sunlight, and thick walls on three sides rising to ten or twelve feet above ground. The fourth side, which was always the one facing south, was entirely covered with paper windows backed by heavy matting blinds that could be raised or lowered as desired. Heating was provided by brick stoves or charcoal braziers; and humidity was maintained by distributing vases of water about the interior. The growth of plants could be forced by filling the houses with steam, and there were special techniques (whose efficacy awaits trial by experiment) for opening the buds. One such method was to place the plants on racks over a trench full of compost blended with ox or goat urine and pour boiling water onto this mixture.[18]

One by-product of this sort of expertise was the use by northern Chinese of cellars to create the humid atmosphere needed for the spinning of cotton yarn. This was fairly certainly a Ming development, since cotton was hardly spun at all in the north under the Yüan. According to Hsu Kuang-ch'i's *Encyclopedia of Agricultural Policy* of 1639.

In recent times much cotton has been grown in the north; but it is not convenient to spin or weave it there, the north having an arid climate such that the cotton fibers snap and it is impossible to get a continuous filament. . . . The south is low-lying and humid. Therefore the filaments are tight and fine, and the cloth likewise strong and substantial. These days many people in Hsien-ning [in Ho-chien county, central Hopei] make underground cellars several feet deep and build houses over the top of them, the eaves being only two feet or so above ground. They pierce windows to let in the sunlight. People live in them and make use of the humidity to spin and weave. . . . It would be unusually interesting to know who began this.[19]

Some useful existing machines were improved. Thus a treadle was added to the Yüan cotton gin. This made it necessary to have a flywheel (or bobs on spokes serving the same purpose), which in turn imposed such a torque on the upper roller that it had now to be made of metal rather than wood.[20] A more complicated case is that of the silk-spinning machine, which Wang Chen, writing in 1313, said had been "recently" created on the same lines as the hemp-spinning machine, being "particularly saving of effort as compared to doubling filaments by means of the horizontal board on the open ground."[21] The hemp-spinning machine subsequently went out of use altogether, and a silk-spinning machine does not surface again in the literature until more than 500 years later, in Wei Chieh's book on sericulture written at the end of the nineteenth century. Moreover, Wei's machine differs substantially from Wang's.[22] In place of vertical spindles surmounted by bobbin-rollers (rotating hollow cylinders halfway between fliers and the rings used in ring-spinning), it has simple horizontal pirns (cone-shaped spindles) and draws the threads either around a horizontal roller through a trough of water or across pads of moistened felt.[23] In structural terms, we have here a development analogous to the seventeenth-century European flax-retwisting mills (which also had horizontal pirns and no fliers), unless we are dealing with a fresh start or an unacknowledged borrowing.

There were probably one or two advances in metallurgy. The extraction of pure zinc may have been one of these. Analysis of the content of Chinese coins shows that the first virtually pure zinc specimens date from the fifteenth century, and the percentage of zinc in alloy coins rises sharply after this time.[24] It is known that coal was used in China for iron smelting by means of a crucible process long before Sung times, and some scholars believe that coke, invented during the T'ang dynasty for cooking food, was not long afterward also employed in ferrous metallurgy.[25] If so, the practice seems not to have survived into late traditional times, although anthracite continued to be used in the ironworks of Shansi and Szechwan.[26] This is a curious development, since coke, in a variety of grades and large quantities, was used for smelting silver and copper in the Ch'ing period.[27] Presumably the use of crucibles, whose successful manufacture eluded Europeans trying to smelt iron with coal in the seventeenth century,[28] made it unnecessary to use a refined fuel, except perhaps for extra heat.

Agriculture is the most difficult sector to evaluate. The Ming and Ch'ing periods saw the introduction of new crops, new fertilizers, and new varieties of familiar food plants, but it is possible that the biggest economic impact came from refinements in the application of long-known basic principles regarding rotations, intercropping, and soil preservation. There seems to have been a slow shift from a mixture of monoculture and polyculture toward a symbiotic farming in which every plant was a part of a deliberately designed interlocking whole. A further contribution was made by the diffusion of superior local methods, sometimes the length and breadth of the empire, and often through official or semiofficial initiative.

The new food plants introduced from the Americas were maize, peanuts, and sweet and white potatoes.[29] At the same time tobacco, also from the New World, and opium, long known as a medicine, became widely cultivated cash crops.[30] Here, as an illustration of this process, is the seventeenth-century scholar Yeh Meng-chu describing how tobacco came to his native Shanghai:

Smoke leaves. These . . . originally came from Fukien. When I was young I heard my elders say that in Fukien there were some who smoked them by inhaling, and that doing this made people drunk. They were called "dry wine." But there were none in this locality. At the end of the Ch'ung-chen reign [1628–44] a man surnamed P'eng in the county capital got some seeds from I know not where, and grew them here. He picked the leaves and dried them in the dark. Then those who worked at this business cut them into fine shreds, and they were sold to merchants from places far away. The local people still did not dare to try them. Later a severe prohibition was issued by the authorities. . . . People were not allowed to grow them or merchants to traffic in them. Those who disobeyed were to be punished in the same way as those who had dealings with foreigners. . . . Tobacco cultivation therefore came to an end. At the beginning of the Shun-chih reign all the soldiers smoked tobacco; and in next to no time dealers gathered and cultivators multiplied, obtaining redoubled profits.[31]

The new fertilizers were oilseed cakes (made from soya, rape, and cotton) and green fertilizers such as clover that were turned over and spaded into the soil or worked into a mud-and-clover compost.[32] Pao Shih-ch'en describes the benefits of planting some acreage in rape:

When growing wheat or barley [as a winter crop] would use up too much fertilizer and labor, one should divide one's land into three sections. Plant two of these with wheat or barley, and the other with rape. Rape is harvested for use as a vegetable in the late winter and early spring. Much of it can be sold. One mou yields two piculs of seeds from which 80 catties of oil may be pressed and 120 oilcakes obtained. These will fertilize three mou of land and their [fertilizing] power will safeguard the harvests. Rape is as profitable as wheat or barley; the fertilizer and labor needed are similar; and the stalks will serve as fuel just as wheat-stalks do. But the fertilizer obtained can revitalize the exhausted wheat-fields.[33]

An example of a new strain of a known grain developed in late traditional times is the salt-resistant rice of Ch'üan-chou.[34]

The late traditional concern with the design of rotations and combinations of crops is evident in Pao Shih-ch'en's *Four Arts for the Governance of the Common People.* Turnips and cabbages should be used to restore the fertility of fields where cereals had been grown. In shallow-pit cultivation, "one grows in sequence beans, millet, taro, and potatoes." "Growing beans beneath mulberry trees is also of benefit to the mulberries." "Barley and broadbeans make a suitable base for a rice-seedling field."[35] In other sources one finds a sharp awareness that cotton and sugarcane should be alternated with rice or other grains.[36] A sort of inverted rotation involved moving the soil rather than the crops. King noted that the Chekiang farmers periodically exchanged the soil of their mulberry orchards with that of their paddy-fields.[37] As Pao Shih-ch'en observed, in discussing the "recent" adoption of transplanting for taro: "Plants all like a change of soil and receive fertility [from the move]."[38]

Intercropping was also intensified in this period, and Pao describes a characteristic system of double-cropping with intercropping for either the first or second harvest:

Two harvests [of rice] are common in the southern regions. For the first harvest [the farmers] transplant the rice-shoots just as for early-ripening rice elsewhere. In the middle of the sixth moon, ten days before reaping, they broadcast seed beneath the stalks of grain. When the first crop is cut, the sprouts of the second are four to five inches high. They are weeded with a hoe as in dry farming. At the end of the eighth moon they are harvested and barley planted as usual. . . . After the early-ripening rice has been harvested it is [also] possible to plant buckwheat for reaping in the eighth moon, and before this harvest to scatter-sow mud-beans beneath the grain-stalks in the same way as the second rice crop is sown. So long as there is plenty of fertilizing power, the fields are not damaged.[39]

Other possibilities were planting cotton under millet or mud-beans under rice, mixing garden peas with wheat, and sowing early- and late-ripening rice at the same time for two separate crops, at the cost presumably of doing without transplanting.[40] There were also some minor changes in the ways of growing indigo, sorghum, and hemp.[41]

The most impressive example of late traditional skill in soil preservation is to be found in Pao's account of how to open up marginal hill lands and prevent erosion:

From the summit of the hill downward divide [the land] into seven levels. The fifth level and those below it may be opened up for cultivation. One begins with the lowest level. (In general, hills shaped like mounds are opened up like upland fields. Stony hills that are opened up are 70 to 80 percent rocks, and 20 to 30 percent soil. Whenever there is a heavy rain the mountain streams break forth in torrents and sweep the rich topsoil away downstream. Therefore [the land] becomes unusable after three years. Furthermore, the richness of the hills adheres to the surface; once streams have been opened up to flow through them, the richness dries up within and one is constantly afraid of drought.) One starts by cutting down the undergrowth and grasses on the spot, and burning them. Then one opens up [the soil] with a heavy wedge-shaped hoe, using one chopping blow to every two pounding blows.

When one first opens up land, no matter whether in summer or winter, one begins by planting a crop of turnips everywhere. These plants are good at loosening the soil and at guaranteeing a harvest. Their roots serve as vegetables, and the leaves can be fed to pigs or used as fertilizer. . . . Next one plants maize and darnel mixed together with sweet sorghum. Where the topsoil is relatively heavy one may also grow cotton. In every case one must [also] choose some moderately level ground and dig ten or more pits in which to grow taro, yams, melons, and greens to serve as vegetables, and to prepare [the soil] for grains. (If there are many people in the mountain hut there will be no shortage of manure. Therefore one should prepare lots of pits for growing crops.) After every two years one changes one level, proceeding gradually upward. What is more, the fertility of the soil moves downward from above. If the upper half of the land is not opened up, the fertility will flow from its surface and be retained by the lower levels, making it fertile everywhere. Furthermore, one should estimate the point at which the mountain streams are at about the same height as the ground that has been opened up, and excavate winding [contour-line] ditches to these streams, using stones and mud to dam the water. . . . When the fifth level has been reached, the richness from the top four levels will flow down every day to the lower levels, and one can start the cycle again from the beginning, reaping harvests without end.[42]

The effect of such skills must have been greatly to extend the area accessible to cultivation.

The interregional diffusion of agricultural techniques had analogous consequences. An example of a very long-distance transmission may be found in a Ch'ing dynasty poem written by Ch'i Chung. It describes his feelings on seeing wet-field paddy growing in Tz'u-chou, in what is now southern Hopei:

> Some people say the lands of the northeast
> Have soil so porous that water easily runs short.
> Flooded in the morning, they are parched by nightfall.
> How then can one lightly talk of irrigation?
> Success in farming—according to my view—
> Lies in weeding and hoeing to the limit.
> If mud's well blended, cracks won't open in the tilth;
> With plenty of manure, soil becomes like an alluvial deposit.

He adds the following explanatory note:

Some time ago I helped Ch'iu Wen-ta manage water-conservancy in Chihli [Hopei]. Our talk turned to the farmers' fields, and this is what he told me: "When Kao An-hsiang was managing fields he thought the soil [here] too porous to retain water, and this matter [of wet-field paddy] was neglected. Recently I was reading the section on double plowing in Chou Shih-hsun's gazetteer of Lien-chou prefecture [Ho-p'u, Kwangtung]. He says: 'At the beginning of spring, plow for the first time and then, when the time has come for transplanting, plow and hoe again. The reason for this is that the first plowing is only capable of making the soil open and scatter. It is therefore necessary to plow and hoe again, after which the cracks and leaky crevices in the fields will be filled up and blocked, and they will be resistant to drought.' I tried this out with [two] fields that were as close as the upper and lower lip. The one that had been plowed and hoed only once was the first to dry out when there was a period of drought. The field plowed twice was easily kept from drying up. The appearance of the paddy, flourishing in the one and withered in the other, was quite different in each case."[43]

Two points are worthy of note in this passage. One is that literary sources served to spread technical knowledge. The other is that Kao An-hsiang understood the principle of the controlled experiment.

Presumably, technology usually traveled by means of the movements of skilled workers. This emerges from the proposals made in the fourteenth and fifteenth centuries to bring southeastern methods of water-control in coastal areas to the northeastern seaboard:

During the T'ai-ting reign-period [1324–27] of the Yüan dynasty, when Yü Chi was an Auxiliary Han-lin Academician, he made the following proposal: "There are reed-swamps to the east of the capital along several thousand li of coastline, reaching northward to the gulf of Liao-yang, and southward bordering on Ch'ing and Ch'i [Shantung]. The tides that come in every day from the sea have silted them up, so that they are now rich land. We should use the technique of the men of Che [southern Kiangsu and Chekiang] to build dikes to keep the water out, and turn them into fields. We should allow rich persons who want to obtain official rank to gather their followers together and be allocated land. . . . Those able to farm with ten thousand men should be given land for this number, and be the leaders of ten thousand. Similar measures should be adopted for those with a thousand or a hundred. . . . If for five years they have accumulated reserves of grain, they should be given official rank . . . and if they show no failing for ten years, this rank should be made hereditary, as with the system for military officials."[44]

Yü's proposals were not taken up at the time, but in 1352 the Mongol Chancellor Toqto revived them with an added suggestion. Farmers, he said, should be recruited from Kiangnan together with "one thousand each of those able to farm wet-field paddy, and those able to build and repair polders and embankments, who will serve as agricultural instructors."[45] Once again, nothing happened. About a hundred years later, the idea was taken up again, this time by Ch'iu Chün, who also thought that official rank should be bestowed on those leading the enterprise. He advised that people from Chekiang and Fukien with a good knowledge of farming should investigate the possibilities before anything was done on a large scale.[46] Hsü Kuang-ch'i, writing in the first half of the seventeenth century, noted that no progress had been made until the Wan-li reign (1573–1619), and then only on a modest scale. He urged further efforts, but was opposed to people "acquiring official rank by contributing funds for the opening up of land."[47] This phrasing of the last point was a misrepresentation of the original scheme, and together with Hsü's attitude throws an interesting light on the changed nature of land tenure by the late Ming.

The Wan-li breakthrough was inspired by a certain Wang Ying-chiao and accomplished in the military colony lands near Tientsin.

When I saw the region around Tientsin and Ko-hu [Wang wrote], everyone told me that this land had hitherto been saline and unfarmed. Here and there, near the rivers, where it was fertile, there were people growing beans but getting only two piculs a mou. It was my opinion that it was alkaline where there was no [fresh] water, but fertile where there was [fresh] water. If one used the methods of Fukien and Chekiang for dealing with the land along the coast, dug canals, and irrigated with water, it would no doubt be fit to become paddy-fields. For a time, however, neither the civil nor the military authorities were willing to respond. This year they bought cattle and built machinery, cut ditches and constructed embankments, everything being done at one and the same time. . . . Where plenty of manure was used and the men worked hard, yields were from four to five piculs a mou. . . . The dry-field rice, however, withered at once because of the alkalinity. . . . With this the local soldiers and civilians have for the first time learned to trust the methods of land-management of Fukien and Chekiang.[48]

Unfortunately, neither Wang nor Hsü gives any indication of where the know-how came from.

It was probably in late traditional times, too, that animal and human manures were used to fertilize fish ponds.[49] The carp, the foundation of traditional pisciculture, was also to some extent replaced by the pai-lien and the ts'ao, fish that fed off grasses tossed into their pool.[50]

Although Katō Shigeshi argues that there were improvements in the organization of locust-control in late traditional times,[51] there is no evidence that these amounted to much. In the summer of 1269, for example, we already find the relief administrator Ch'en Yun-kung mobilizing more than 2,000 men for locust-catching in Pao-ti county (Hopei). The method they used was the following: "The edge of the field was plowed by an ox to form an extended moat, and in the middle of the moat a small well was dug; one side of the moat was walled with rush matting, and the locusts were driven into it, killed, and buried."[52] This is virtually identical with the late traditional method described in a long poem by Ch'iu Yueh-hsiu in the eighteenth century.[53] Another argument against Katō's hypothesis of better organization in later times is that official incompetence often resulted in any grain spared by the insects being trampled down by the locust-catchers; and official help was often made the pretext for all sorts of exactions on the peasants.[54] Possibly, though, the use of ducks to eat up unfledged locusts was new.[55] Flocks of these birds were also relied on to control the land crabs that infested the newly opened polders of Kiangnan and Kwangtung.[56]

Finally, in regard to our list of improvements originating in China, it seems likely that there was some progress in the art of seafaring north of the mouth of the Yangtze. It is not possible to prove this, but a tentative argument may be constructed on the following lines: (1) Up to and including early Ming times the northern seas were regarded as more dangerous than they were later; (2) there is no obvious reason for the improvement in the safety of navigation in later times; (3) in addition, some fragmentary collateral evidence suggests that the type of boat mainly used, the *sha-ch'uan*, or "sand junk," was either a new creation or greatly improved. These points are developed below.

(1) Sung writers such as Lu I-hao emphasized the dangers of the northern seas.[57] The frequency of disasters was one of the reasons the sea transport of grain from Kiangnan to Peking was discontinued by the Ming government early in the fifteenth century.[58] It is possible that the institutional arrangements increased the hazards. Fleets set off too early in the year to avoid the bad weather; government ships may have been less sturdily built than private ones, if warships are to be taken as a guide.[59] Yet by the eighteenth century there was an enormous maritime trade between Shanghai and Manchuria; the junks routinely sailed through the icy fogs and the gales of the northern waters in winter; and in spite of occasional major disasters the annual loss of vessels did not exceed 1 percent.[60]

(2) The *Record of the Sea Transport of the Great Yüan Dynasty* indicates that the mariner's compass was used early in the North China sea.[61] Unless its early use was restricted to government ships, greater knowledge of the compass would not seem to be the key to the safer navigation of late Ming and Ch'ing times. One possibility, though, is the official system of inspection and licensing. Boats had to be seaworthy and carry adequate crews for their size, and a record was kept of the number of voyages made.[62] But this is a thin explanation for a major change.

(3) The most important type of ship on the run from Shanghai to Manchuria was the sand-junk. Its tumble-home construction, with gunwales that curved back in toward each other, gave it the strength to resist the undertows and currents off the North China coast.[63] Lee-boards gave it an exceptional maneuverability, as a seventeenth-century gazetteer for Sung-chiang prefecture indicated:

Only the sand-junk's system of maneuvering on the water is such that it can, by adjusting its lee-boards, advance when it wants, go back when it wants, hover and wheel as if flying, and sail with the wind on the quarter or ahead. Next best are ships like the *ts'ang-chung*, which uses both sails and oars, and is also able to maneuver. Ships like those from Kwangtung and Fukien do not have oars, relying entirely on sails. These ships are large and go with the wind abaft. They are unable to go back in the face of a contrary wind or an opposing tide, and are not convenient for advancing, retiring, or turning.[64]

This is part of a discussion of naval warfare, and a little later it is noted that the sand-junk's lee-boards allowed it to move upwind of larger Japanese pirate vessels—the smaller ones were simply rammed—before attacking with firearms.

Assuming that the sha-ch'uan was the key to safe sailing in the northern seas, what reason is there to think that it was new? Previous scholarly opinion—not lightly to be dismissed—has held that the hull embodied one of the oldest designs in China.[65] Lee-boards were also being used on warships, though with a different hull design, in the late T'ang and Sung.[66] Three points offer a basis for a revisionist hypothesis, though not for any firm conclusion. First, the sand-junk, which never held more than 3,000 piculs of cargo, was much smaller than many of the ships used for the Yüan dynasty sea-transport, which often held up to 9,000 piculs.[67] This in itself hints at some change in design. Second, Nishikawa Jōken, a Japanese astronomer and geographer who was a native of Nagasaki, a regular port of call for these ships, thought that the sand-junks, which he called "Nanking junks," were derived from the flat-bottomed boats that plied the Grand Canal from Nanking to Peking.[68] Since any name containing the word Nanking must be of Ming vintage or later, and this particular canal, whose most elevated reaches were shallower than those of the quite differently aligned T'ang and Sung canals, was of early-fifteenth-century origin (with brief Yüan antecedents), our suspicion of a late date is strengthened. Third, there is clear evidence that new types of junks were produced in late traditional China. One such was the Chekiangese vessel called "Unlike the Three Others," first built in 1699 and used mainly in northern waters.[69] So far as I know, the term sha-ch'uan does not appear until Ming times, which is at least consistent with our hypothesis.

Last of all, we have to look at techniques imported from abroad, concentrating for the moment only on those that found widespread practical use. Outstanding among these were corrective lenses for defective vision. Ming accounts mention only spectacles for farsightedness and middle-aged sight, but Yeh Meng-chu in the early Ch'ing also refers to those for nearsightedness:

Spectacles. When I was young I sometimes chanced to see old people wearing them. I had no idea, however, how much they cost. Later on I heard that those made in the West were the best, and cost from four to five ounces of silver the pair. Glass was used for the body and elephant hide for the stems. Only the very rich could afford them. After the Shun-chih reign [1644–61] the price gradually fell, and a pair cost no more than .5 or .6 of an ounce of silver. Recently many people in Soochow and Hangchow have been making them. They are on sale everywhere, and everyone can get them. At the most expensive a pair is only .007 or .008 of an ounce of silver, or even .002 or .003. All of these are suitable for the general purpose of brightening vision. There is another kind in the West, however, with lenses thicker than leather [presumably convex], which enable the nearsighted to see clearly the minutest details. Farsighted and elderly persons who wear them will, on the contrary, find their vision blurred. There is still no one selling them in the markets, but I suspect that in a few more years the cunning artisans of this region will be making them in large numbers.[70]

John Larner has suggested that spectacles were a major factor in the growth of textual scholarship in Italy after the beginning of the fourteenth century.[71] It is intriguing, in this comparative perspective, that the rise of the school of "empirical research" in China, with its delight in the minutiae of textual criticism, should have coincided with the spread of spectacles in the seventeenth century.

The use of the cylinder-and-piston pump with inlet and outlet valves for projecting a jet of water for fighting fires was probably, but not certainly, introduced by the Jesuits. There is the following description in the *Illustrated Account of Remarkable Machines from the Distant West*, dictated by Schreck (Terrentius) to Wang Cheng in 1627:

This water-gun puts out fires. . . . Its merit lies in [alone being of any use when] the power of a conflagration rapidly becomes overwhelming and people cannot get near it. What is more, it does not waste a drop of water and it can reach anywhere, no matter how high or far away. . . . It is neither difficult to make nor very expensive. Every city and village should install two or three of these machines, which are advantageous for warding off disasters. We have already made a small version and tried it out with great success.[72]

A century later Chu Hua, who wrote a poem on the use of these "water-dragons" against a fire in his native Shanghai, gave a different version:

In times past we had only water-bags and tubes for carrying water to fight fires. The present-day method of using the water-dragon was obtained at the beginning of the dynasty from the Japanese by a certain T'ang who lived in Ch'iao-nan in the county capital. After a time it gradually spread to other areas. . . . Its fire-fighting power is a hundred times greater than that of any other device.[73]

Whichever version we adopt, the device was clearly of foreign origin.

The case of the "pulling dragon," the only type of cylinder-and-piston pump used in premodern Chinese mines, is more doubtful. Since it resembles the pumps used in sixteenth-century German mines,[74] and a comparable pump was not introduced into Japan until 1618,[75] presumably as the result of Western contacts, it may well have been imported.

But there are other considerations that suggest it may have been an indigenous development. It was of the most rudimentary description, consisting of a circular valved shoe fixed to a long handle working up and down a short travel inside the lower end of a cylinder, into the bottom of which the water could flow freely. The operator kept the shoe below the level of the water in the channel from which it was being pumped; he forced water in through the shoe-valve on the downstroke and pulled it up with the upstroke, hence the Chinese name.

Wu Ch'i-chün provided this description in his mid-nineteenth-century book on the mines of Yunnan: "It is from eight to sixteen feet long, hollow inside, and with a diameter of four to five inches. There is also a wooden or iron rod *of the same length* [sliding inside] and tipped with a piece of leather cut to make a base. It is used to draw up the water."[76] In other words, it was only a little more than a reversed form of the piston air-blower used in the Yunnan mines,* and embodied a principle long known to the Chinese in the buckets with flap-valves on their lower ends used in the brine-wells of Szechwan, a source of inspiration much nearer to Yunnan than the southeastern seacoast. On the other hand, Joseph Needham mentions "piston pumps" employed to drain the bilge-water from junks after the late sixteenth century.[77] It would be interesting to know if they were also of this very simple type.

The Pattern of Technical Change

It is not easy to characterize the trend of technological advance described in the preceding section in terms both appropriate to the subject and acceptable to the modern economist. Broadly speaking, the kind of progress that was best understood, and the only one that was more or less consciously aimed at, was a more effective adaptation to the natural environment, an extension of the range of useful resources. Two minor "improvements" on existing practice epitomize this approach. In Fukien, the Ming dynasty saw the abandoning of salt-boiling in caldrons in favor of solar evaporation, with economies in expenditure on increasingly costly fuel.[78] Sometime in the seventeenth century a Shantung peasant discovered that spirit could be distilled from moldy grain that was useless for any other purpose.[79] Such instances are a reminder that a useful definition of "technical advance" is possible only with reference to the relative cost of resources.

And late traditional China was caught in a severe shortage of re-

---

* There is no reference to a valve halfway up the cylinder, such as was found on German pumps; and the statement that the rod was "of the same length" as the cylinder tends to argue against the existence of such a valve. Thus no use was made of the partial vacuum created beneath the piston on the upstroke.

sources for its enormous and growing population. The desperate eco-
logical adaptation described by the Ch'ing writer Chou Hsi-p'u was an
extreme case but one that dramatized widespread pressures and hazards:

I was returning to Ning-hsia from Chung-wei in Lan-chou, when I received
orders from the prefect to inspect a disaster caused by hail in the Hsiang
mountains. These are 80 li south of Chung-wei city, but it was a journey of
several hundred li to the site of the disaster, and a weary tramp over huge
sand dunes. When I brought out cash to exchange for grain and fodder, none
was forthcoming. On asking the reason for this I learned that it was because
the people who lived in the mountains ate *p'eng* grasses, some of which were
shown to me. There were three kinds: sand p'eng, water p'eng, and soft
p'eng. They are prepared for eating by boiling them once in water, straining
them out, putting them in water again, and cooking them into a broth. This
serves as breakfast and supper, morning and night. Large quantities are dried
in readiness for the winter. . . . I ordered some to be boiled and presented to
me. So rank and acrid was the taste that I almost could not swallow them. Yet
these frontier people eat them all year round.

Behind this there was a story, which Chou disclosed in a poem:[80]

> Their forebears in times past built terraces for farming;
> Ten thousand hoes chopped at the hills till the hills' pulses shifted
> Saline flakes appeared on the sprouts and early stems,
> And they speak of mosquito larvae as big as silk cocoons.
> Onto the ground like rushes they tossed the state-provided hoes;
> And now the sons and grandsons live by chewing grass.

Failure to maintain adequate moisture deep in the soil to prevent salt
being drawn to the surface by evaporation had made the land unfit for
farming. The colonists had to eat grasses, and to rely on raising the cattle
and sheep that were mentioned later in the poem as having suffered from
hail. This story reminds us of an important fact about development projects in the late traditional period: they sometimes damaged as much
as they developed. The overly dense building of lake-polders could increase the danger of floods by reducing the size of the intervening
channels. New irrigation schemes sometimes robbed existing schemes of
much of their water.[81]

Understandably, experiment in agriculture was directed at increasing
yields per acre. An example of this is the adaptation by P'an Tseng-i,
early in the nineteenth century, of the old technique of cultivation in
shallow pits to wet-rice paddy. The idea was to do away with the transplanting of rice seedlings, which he held was apt to harm the sprouts,
especially in a multiple-crop system which imposed a timing that was
less than ideal, and also to do away with the usual secondary wheat
crop in such a system, compensating for its loss with heavier yields.
Trials by P'an and by Ch'i Yen-huai in the Soochow area reportedly

produced exceptional results in the range of 180 to 200 bushels of rice per acre.[82]

Why, then, was this practice not widely adopted? There are two possible technical reasons, and one probable social one. The basic objective of shallow pits, which had been known and used since antiquity, was to conserve moisture. They were found in Yüan and Ming times for growing dry-land crops in areas without adequate well or river water, and sometimes for cotton in years of drought elsewhere.[83] It is not clear what advantage they would have had in wet-rice cultivation in the Yangtze delta; and one wonders if the good results were not due to unusually good soil or especially intensive care. Further, the absence of a supplementary crop reduced the safety margin of the ordinary peasant in the face of bad weather. Finally, tenants in Kiangnan were charged rent only on their rice crop and not on their wheat crop;[84] switching to the exclusive cultivation of rice would have been disastrous for them.

This concern to squeeze the utmost out of resources was combined in the Chinese with a well-developed appreciation of economy of effort. A characteristic illustration of this may be found in the comments of P'eng T'ing-mei on the revival in Ch'ing times of the long-neglected Sung technique known as the "wooden dragon." This was a sausage-shaped raft that could be moored against an embankment on the outer bend of a river to protect it from erosion, and to retain a fill of earth and stones placed between it and the bank.[85] According to P'eng: "The wooden dragon is able to deflect the water so as to protect the dike on one side of a river, and by deflecting the water cause it to cleanse away the silt on the other bank. Compared with installing [temporary] embankments and [draining and] dredging, it is half as much trouble and twice as effective. It is a good method of river protection and should not be forgotten again."[86]

The Chinese appreciation of labor-saving practices was not limited to cases like this, where nature was, with a little art, persuaded to do man's work for him, but also extended to machinery. An example of this is Wei Chieh's praise of the multi-spindle silk-spinning machines:

Only Kiangsu, Chekiang, and Szechwan have sophisticated methods of spinning. In northeast China they use the technique of "striking the thread," and this is also employed in Shansi, Shensi, Yunnan, and Kweichow, one person drawing the filament and another walking away from him using a small turning device to twist it in such a way that five to eight filaments are joined to form one thread. This costs much energy and yields little thread. The method of spinning used in Chekiang requires one person to work the horizontal bar at the front of the machine. . . . With one session at this machine a single person can obtain fifty threads, and a hundred threads from two sessions. Compared with the method of twisting silk used in the various [other] provinces, one person does the work of a hundred.[87]

It is notable that this sort of economy is virtually always discussed in terms of energy or effort, not of costs, that is to say, from the point of view of the operator rather than of the entrepreneur. One is inclined to associate this with the fragmented nature of the productive structure of late traditional Chinese industry, in which merchants coordinated a multiplicity of small producers but rarely organized production directly themselves. One of the few exceptions I know of to this generalization is Wu Ch'i-chün's observation on the use of "pulling dragon" pumps in series to drain the government's Yunnan mines. When there were more than 10 to 12 pumping stations "it is always the case that the cost of the workers' upkeep is too great for one to recover one's outlay, and the only long-term solution is to select a place to cut a drainage channel."[88]

It is thus easy to point to a strong trend toward making the land yield more and to a much weaker one toward slight reductions in the labor needed for a given output or operation. (The flywheel cotton gin, for example, could be worked by one person if necessary, whereas the older version required at least two.) What is difficult is to contrive a satisfactory conceptual scheme for the analysis of the advances described in the first section of this paper. One or two, such as the greenhouses for forcing out-of-season plants, provided new capabilities that had not existed before, but cannot be shown to have economized on any factor of production. Others, such as the humid cellars used in the north for cotton spinning, may have been valuable because they used labor that would otherwise have been subject to seasonal unemployment. (Of course, we should not overlook the savings on the labor previously used to transport the cotton to other spinning centers.) Spectacles were somewhat comparable; by allowing people with defective vision to do work that they could not otherwise have done they enhanced the quality of the labor supply. Firefighting pumps and better navigation in the northern seas reduced the loss of houses, ships, and human life, which I suppose must be defined as economizing on both labor and capital. Mineshaft ventilators and "pulling dragon" pumps made ores accessible that could not otherwise have been mined. What was saved, here, ultimately, were the capital and labor that *would have had to be* used to prospect and open new mines; but in practical terms these innovations are best compared to the new fertilizers that, at the cost of some extra labor and expense, increased the output of the fields. I am therefore inclined to believe that a straightforward approach on the basis of factors of production is likely to contain so much artificiality and to require so many arbitrary decisions as to which categories are appropriate for which data that it will lead to nothing useful.

We have also to account for what did *not* happen. As we have just seen, silk-spinning machinery was not used in several parts of China. Similarly, the three- and four-spindle treadle-operated wheels of the Sung-chiang cotton region seem to have been confined to this area.[89] Iron wire, which required a special technique of repeated annealing, was produced only in Fo-shan, where in its heyday it provided work for more than 1,000 men.[90] There were obviously barriers to diffusion, though their nature is by no means clear. But the most important problem concerns water technology. There should have been enormous benefits from more efficient pumping devices both in irrigated agriculture and in mining, which was beset by drainage problems. Yet for half a millennium almost nothing was done to improve on the methods inherited from the past.

The need for better techniques was perceived, if only by an imaginative minority. Early in the nineteenth century, Ch'i Yen-huai experimented with the Archimedean water-screw, which had been known in the literature at least since the *Western Hydraulics* dictated by the Jesuit De Ursis to Hsu Kuang-ch'i some 200 years earlier.[91] In spite of a method of manufacture adapted to materials available in China, it seems to have been hardly used. Here are some lines from a poem written by Ch'i on his efforts:[92]

> Kiangnan farmers have few reserves in store.
> Ten days they can pedal the pumps and still fear shortage.
> They brush the grime away and piteously sigh,
> For the springs are dry, the moisture gone, and in due course there will
>   be famine.

> Now see how this dragon's tail* goes down into the stream,
> Producing a flooded expanse from a mere foot of water!
> Within, it never runs backwards; outside, it never leaks.
> By early morning a hundred mou will look as if heavy rain had fallen.

> Five to ten people may be served by one machine,
> And the smallest effort yields very great results.
> Eight families who share a well and one of these pumps
> Need never fear drought or flood will rob their fields of grain.

>   .   .   .

> The high officials and provincial governor are worthy men
> Who study water control and make plans for farming.
> Having heard my account of this pump, they urgently wanted to see it.
> So two were set up in a boat on the Ching-ch'i River.†

---

* The "dragon's tail pump" was the Chinese name for the screw.
† Probably the river of this name in south Kiangsu.

When we tested them by the Hay Bridge at noon,
We were watched by a throng of entrancing ladies
Who came, their excitement all bubbling over
And the ground trembling like thunder with their calls of welcome.

The pool covered ten mou and was two feet deep.
In three-quarters of an hour the pumps drained seven inches.
With a laugh the provincial governor said to me:
"This will help more than just fields and gardens.
The lakes are rising just now and lap the skies.
Long have Huai and Huang been a burden to our people;
If we drained with a thousand [ordinary] pumps and dredged the yellow
    stream,
The two haulovers and three rivers might be closed for a long time.

"The Liu River is choked with silt; I have long wanted to clear it.
But pumping out water is slow, and I have feared to squander funds.
If we used a hundred of these instead, installed by the rivers and marshes,
We could mobilize workers with baskets and spades, and finish the job
    in days."

An equally clear indication of an awareness of need is the passage of the *Western Hydraulics* (reprinted both in Hsü Kuang-ch'i's *Encyclopedia of Agricultural Policy* of 1639 and in the *Comprehensive Examination of Seasonal Practices* of 1742) on a more developed type of cylinder-and-piston pump. In this pump the upstroke of the piston creates a partial vacuum in a chamber and so draws in water through a flap-valve from below; the downstroke expels it from the chamber by pressure and through another valve up a pipe. It is a more sophisticated and efficient mechanism than the "pulling dragon":

The cylinder-and-piston pump is a machine for raising water from wells and springs. When one is far away from rivers it is necessary to depend on wells for sustenance. Drawing water from wells is mostly done by means of a rope and an earthenware container. From breakfast until supper, from dawn till dusk, people [will do this], unaware of how troublesome it is. In upland areas that I have seen, where wells are used to irrigate the fields, the people use either the windlass and bucket or the well-sweep. Although these appear to be convenient, one may look up and down all day without managing to water all of a mou of land. I have heard that in Shansi and Honan the people work extremely hard to irrigate fields with water drawn from wells. In a year of drought, eight people toiling night and day can manage only several mou. In other areas it is the custom to be lazier. Having seen the difficulties involved, people no longer inquire into the method of watering the fields from wells. . . . If the machine shown here is made, there is no need for a well-rope and an earthenware container, or for a windlass or a well-sweep; and one man using it can do the work of several men. Used for irrigating fields, it can save about four-fifths of the labor needed.[93]

It can hardly be argued in the light of this that "cheap" labor was an

obstacle to all sorts of technical progress. Yet, so far as I know, this type
of pump was never used by farmers in premodern China. Since we have
already shown, in the simpler case of double plowing for water reten-
tion, that farm techniques were sometimes successfully taken from books
(and P'an Tseng-i was another technologist who delved into old writ-
ings), it is permissible to be surprised.

We conclude this demonstration of economic pressure on hydraulic
technology with an account of the problems that beset mining. The accumulation of water as shafts grew deeper drove up the price of coal in
eighteenth-century Peking.[94] Wu Chen-yü, governor-general of Yunnan
and Kweichow in the first half of the nineteenth century, spoke of the
"hundreds of stratagems" tried to drain the copper mines, and of the
"limitless expense" of the work.[95] Wang Tsai-yo observed that "what in
times past could be obtained in a morning now needs ten days" as ores
grew less accessible.[96] As the Reverend Williamson observed in the
course of a journey through Shantung in 1867: "The Chinese system of
mining misses the lower and better strata. . . . A pit is dug down, or a
hole is made, at a more or less acute angle in the side of a hill, and they
work until the water rises; they then leave that place, and open another
pit."[97] Yet pumping equipment remained rudimentary. Lu Shih, who
investigated the Shantung mines in 1720, mentions in a poem that "in
deep shafts they have installed well-sweeps."[98] Chao Lei-sheng noted
of the Chien-yang lead mines that "the springs flow in the deep pits, so
they smash an opening from above and lower in a water pump," but he
did not specify what kind.[99] The "pulling dragon" was the only innovation, and we know from a competition arranged in Japan in the seventeenth century between this kind of pump and the Archimedean screw
that the latter was more efficient.[100] Yet Chinese at the level of Wu Chen-
yü and Wu Ch'i-chün had easy access to information about the screw.

There was another simple pump that could have helped the Chinese.
This was the paternoster pump, in which circular pallets or balls fixed
at intervals along a continuous chain pull the water up through a pipe.
Needham has pointed out that this pump, more than any other, has
ousted the traditional square-pallet chain pump from the fields of China
in recent decades, a tribute to its efficiency and economy.[101] This pump
figures prominently in such Western works as Agricola's *De Re Metallica*
of 1556,[102] but it is not mentioned in either the *Western Hydraulics* of
De Ursis and Hsü or the *Illustrated Account of Remarkable Machines
from the Distant West* of Schreck and Wang Cheng. There was thus
no need here for inputs based on modern science or industry to break
through the sort of ceiling that late traditional technology had reached

in agriculture and inland water transport. In other words, in the case of hydraulic techniques there was a situation in which there were relatively few constraints imposed by the high-level equilibrium trap; a strong and perceived need for progress existed; and yet there was minimal advance. We are thus inescapably drawn to ask if this could have been due to cultural factors.

Any explanation based on cultural factors, however, will have to be a subtle one. Inventions were appreciated in China. Shrines were even put up to innovators, as may be seen from Chu Hua's eighteenth-century *Cotton Manual*:

The Taoist nun Huang was a native of this county [Shang-hai] but went to live on the rocky islands off the coast of Yai-chou. During the Yüan-cheng reign-period [1295–96] of the Yüan dynasty she returned home with spinning and weaving equipment and taught the techniques to the people of Wu-ni-ching. Everyone profited greatly thereby. When she died a shrine was erected at which sacrifices could be made to her spirit and a statue of her displayed. An image of her was also made for the Ning-kuo Temple. At the present time there is also a small temple for sacrifices to her on a little street to the northwest of the Tu-ho-lou in the county capital. The women workers of the county gather here in crowds at harvest time to pay her their respects, and call her "Mother Huang."[103]

Evidence of another kind for the appreciation of technology may be found in the anthology of Ch'ing poetry about everyday life entitled *The Bell of Poesy of the Present Dynasty*, which contains numerous poems on machines and techniques. Ch'i Yen-huai's lines on the paradoxical mechanism of the water-screw is characteristic of the delight in useful ingenuity shown by many of the authors:[104]

> Eight bands spiral about a central post.
> Winding back and forth, they form a revolving streambed
> Like a bottomless bucket open at both ends.
> The waist is slightly constricted and girt with a ring.
> The stream flies thirty thousand feet straight down,
> Quite unaware of having been lifted up!

Poems were written to propagandize better methods. Thus P'eng K'ai-yü, a native of Kiangsu who lived in the K'ang-hsi reign (1662–1722), tried by this means to popularize a bizarre but apparently effective two-man reaping combine he had seen in the wheatfields round Tsinan in Shantung.[105] Nor were the lower levels of society rigidly conservative in their ways. A late Ch'ing gazetteer for Nan-hui county tells how aquatic grasses had recently become popular as a fertilizer for cotton because the use of pig manure tended to give rise to weevils, and concludes that this change had taken place "because the farmers seek out the principles to be derived from their experience over many years and gradually introduce improvements."[106]

One criticism that might perhaps be leveled against popular Chinese attitudes toward technology is that they were, if anything, *too* practical. There was intense competition between artisans, and the tastes of their customers were uncompromisingly utilitarian, with the result described by one of the French missionary-authors of the *Reports on the Chinese*: "Since no one here looks for anything in necessities except what is necessary, or for anything in objects of use except what is useful, no one ever pays—or hardly ever—for additional charm. For this reason, fortune never favors the arts of taste, imagination, and fantasy, which is just as the government would wish."[107] He speaks of how the continually increasing population "puts merit ceaselessly in competition with merit, diligence with diligence, and work with work, in a manner that prevents great fortunes."[108] It is easy to imagine how, under such circumstances, experiment with its attendant errors and reflection with its consumption of time to little apparent profit were luxuries that were not easily afforded.

Artisans may also have disapproved of cheaper methods of production, understanding that their adoption could lead to the loss of jobs. It is not possible to show this at present for the period before the Opium War, but there is evidence for it afterward. Ch'en Ch'i-yüan, who pioneered modern silk-reeling in Kwangtung in the 1870's, would have had his factory destroyed by a Luddite mob but for official intervention.[109] An even more interesting case, though complicated by the interweaving of antiforeign sentiment, was recounted in the *North-China Herald* of July 22, 1867:

Beancake Manufacture. An experiment is about to be made in the north of China, the progress of which will be watched with great interest. A New-chwang firm has conceived the project of establishing at that port machinery for crushing beans, and making the cake and oil which form so important a staple of local trade. . . . A similar experiment was tried, some years ago, in Hong Kong, but resulted in complete failure, through native combination against it. A slight spurt at the commencement led to the conception of gorgeous hopes. Good oil was manufactured and profitably disposed of. But as soon as the importance of the innovation was appreciated by the Chinese hitches of every kind began to arise. The machinery was good, and in San Francisco, where it was purchased, had worked well; yet it was always getting out of order. Precisely as in the case of the beans imported here in foreign vessels, the oil could not be sold. There was no more rational objection to oil turned out of a foreign mill than to cake imported in a foreign ship. But influence was successfully exerted to bring about the rejection of both. Another experiment in machinery, once tried in Shanghai, had a very similar result. An adverse combination was got up, and the enterprise had to be abandoned. The washermen, here, established such a terrorism that the Steam Washing Company could get no workmen. . . . A like opposition to the new experiment will, we fear, be met in Newchwang. . . . With all their readiness to adopt mechanical contrivances, the Chinese seem to dread the higher appliances of European science, as tending to subvert and ruin their own slow process of labour.[110]

Where such attitudes prevailed, probably only an innovator with official backing would have had much chance of long surviving the jealous egalitarianism and organized obstruction of those whom he had put at a disadvantage in his chosen line of business.

When the Chinese gift for practical invention reappeared in the early modern period, the entrepreneurs pioneering the practical use of new machines regularly sought official backing and rights of exclusive usage equivalent to a patent. This was the case, for example, with the three major Chinese inventions of 1904: a new type of wooden loom in Fukien, the use of crushed sugarcane pulp for paper manufacture in Szechwan, and Yen Chung-lun's method of extracting gas, oil, and tar from coal in conjunction with the brine-boiling traditionally practiced for the recovery of salt. It is interesting to note in passing that the gas container used in Yen Chung-lun's invention needed good quality foreign iron imported through Shanghai, an illustration of how international trade helped technical advance in a multitude of small ways.[111]

Superstition seems to have had no inhibiting effect on economic enterprise, with the exception of geomantic objections to mining. Even here it is hard to be sure how far the fear that cutting the veins of the earth would bring misfortune was the real reason for opposition. In northern Taiwan in the eighteenth century the chief opponents of coal mines were gentry; the local commoners had no hesitation in digging as the market for the fuel expanded.[112] Moreover, we know of at least one case where geomantic pretexts were used as a smokescreen: the campaign mounted in the fifteenth century against the extension of the Grand Canal from T'ung-chou to Peking by those who had vested interests in carting and porterage.[113]

Government policy is harder to evaluate. Some measures did substantial damage. Obvious examples are the early Ming paper money policy and the ban on the raising of horses by commoners, which was lifted only in 1690.[114] Possibly the most disastrous was the interdict placed on coastal shipping during the Yung-lo reign (1403–24). Al-

though this ban was relaxed in 1567, it was reimposed at the end of the
Ming with renewed unfortunate consequences for the coastal economy.
An already bad situation became still worse under the Ch'ing with the
forcible removal of much of the coastal population inland until the war
with Coxinga was over.[115]

In regard to mining, policy fluctuated. Ever since the miners' rising
fomented by Yeh Tsung-liu in the 1440's, there was a fear that as ores
ran out unemployed miners would turn to brigandage or worse. At the
same time there was a genuine if intermittent concern with the people's
welfare, exemplified by a decree in 1740 encouraging private coal mining
throughout the empire—a relaxed attitude that had disappeared again
by the beginning of the nineteenth century.[116] The positive effects of
state action were most often at a local level. Thus in 1629 Lu Chen-fei,
county magistrate of Ching-yang in Shensi, opened up a water route
previously thought too dangerous for continuous navigation in order
to provide the inhabitants with cheaper coal.[117] But attitudes were generally benign toward anything that had a positive effect on the people's
welfare. Pao Shih-ch'en spoke for a long tradition of physiocratic concern when he justified his own contribution to the study of technology:
"The most important matters in ruling the prefectures and counties are
agriculture and sericulture."[118]

Certain Chinese criticisms of Europe point up the most significant
cultural aspects of our problem. Here is Ch'eng T'ing-tso, writing around
the middle of the eighteenth century: "Far-off Europe! . . . Its people are
known for their many-sided cleverness, excelling particularly at mathematics. Apart from this, *everything else is excessive ingenuity*, enough
to amaze those of little knowledge. Often to play around with things is
to bring myriad burdens on oneself. They have investigated to the utmost such cruel things as firearms.[119]

His phrase was echoed some 100 years later by Hsüeh Shih-yü in his
poem on "The Fire-Wheel Ship," or Western paddle-steamer:[120]

> When the ancient sages fashioned tools they forbade excessive ingenuity.
> Boats and carts were everywhere the same.
> In the hills and marshes exploitation was not unrestrained.
> In each skilled art men obeyed the Supervisor of Works.
> In handling fire they did not give it dominion over water.
> How could they ever have put wheels upon a warship?*
> Their intelligence was in no way inferior,
> But they would not pit their human skill against the gods' achievements.

---

* Forgetting that this is what his fellow countrymen had done in Sung times,
though without the benefit of the steam engine.

Both comments have an element of justice. As one can see from the treatises of men like Besson (1573), Ramelli (1588), and Böckler (1662), enthusiasts for the new technology in early modern Europe were sometimes carried away by the prospect of the seemingly impossible feats that could be accomplished by gears, pulleys, and levers.[121] And as Hsüeh noted—though he used a different mythology—there was an element of Promethean striving and Promethean impiety in the Western quest for power over nature.

With hindsight we can see that the exuberant European imagination served a useful long-run purpose even if it was (perhaps almost because it was) intermittently impractical in its pursuit of perpetual-motion machines and other follies. But Ch'eng T'ing-tso missed something more important than the payoff of "excessive ingenuity," for all that he appreciated Western mathematics. By the eighteenth century it was already evident that the spirit of analytical calculation inspired by Euclid and Archimedes had permeated the work of practical engineers. In a sense, the new machinery was geometry set in motion. When the French hydraulics expert De Bélidor was confronted with a startling variation in efficiency in two square-pallet chain pumps used at Strasbourg—typically Chinese machines, and borrowed from China—he reacted in a way that was quintessentially un-Chinese:

It would appear that so far no one has followed any exact rule for the construction of pallet chain pumps, judging by the variety of proportions that has been given to their parts, two such machines that were perfectly similar having never perhaps existed. Yet there is no doubt that there must be a perfect construction. The example of the two pumps that I have just been discussing is a most convincing proof of this, since the one that drains twice as much as the other in the same time, and holds this advantage very likely from luck rather than reasoning, must approach this perfection more closely. Let us try to find out whence it comes, so as to derive a general rule therefrom that will leave nothing to be desired so far as this matter is concerned.[122]

He then showed that the pallets should be at least as close to each other as a distance equal to their height, calculated the theoretical flows of the pumps on the basis of their proportions, and found that the ratio between them agreed closely with the reality (actual flow, of course, depending on how hard the cranks were turned).

It was this capacity to see ghosts in machines, those abstracted skeletons of lines and angles that appear increasingly as diagrams in technical books from the seventeenth century on, that differentiated modern Europeans from Chinese. Chinese pumps were subtly varied to suit different conditions. In Sung-chiang, for example, pallets 1.3 to 1.5 feet wide but only .5 feet high were used for low-angle lifts, and pallets .7 feet wide and .8 feet high for steep angle lifts.[123] Yet so far as I know the Chinese never sought a quantified rationale for what they were doing.

The Economic Effects

Estimating the economic contribution made by late traditional technical advances is close to impossible. At best we can hazard a few informed guesses. Thus humid cellars made possible a new regional cotton-textile industry. Better navigation in the northern seas brought cheap Manchurian beancake to fertilize the cotton fields of Kiangnan, and so helped keep down the price of raw cotton. The improved gin halved the labor needed to remove the seeds from the same material. Incubators made a helpful contribution to the supply of protein. Spectacles extended the useful life of the elderly and the scholarly. Slightly better drainage and ventilation of mines restrained the rising prices of minerals. A new power source—the wind—was of great importance locally, but limited in its use to the coastal belt from Chekiang to Hopei.

But the main problem concerns agriculture. It may well be that over the centuries a number of individually slight improvements added up cumulatively to a significant advance. What makes it hard to tell is that technology is here so intermixed with other inputs, such as land and labor, that its effect cannot be isolated, given the simple materials at our disposal. As the quantity of land in cultivation grew,[124] its average quality must have fallen. Thus a considerable number of technical refinements may have been needed just to maintain existing yields per acre. In fact, yields improved in late traditional times.[125] But this may have been due to increased inputs of labor using time-honored methods. It is my impression that farm work, as opposed to small-scale trading, was not often done by women in Sung times. It was certainly quite common in many regions by the Ming and Ch'ing. The poet Wang Mien wrote of Kiangsu women who "follow their husbands to work in the fields during the day, and spin hemp at night without going to bed."[126] Chi Ch'i-kuang tells of women in the Huai region who "work at their looms by night and exert themselves in the fields by day . . . with sickles and hoes at their waists and babies on their backs."[127] Such instances can easily be multiplied, and no evaluation of the contribution of technology to farming can be made until such questions as the possible long-term increase in female participation in the agricultural labor force have been resolved.

Broadly speaking, it seems likely that technological change in late traditional China was a stabilizing factor. As population grew and pressure on resources became sharper, it helped to keep output per person from sinking or sinking too rapidly. A lesser or a greater measure of change would probably have provoked a social and political crisis. This conclusion, if it is correct, is a significant one, for it helps to explain both the immobility and the resilience of the last few centuries of the empire.

Dwight H. Perkins

Growth and Changing Structure of China's Twentieth-Century Economy

SUCH TERMS AS "entering into modern economic growth" or "taking off" have often been used to describe what happens to a nation when it discovers and begins to apply the lessons of modern science and technology to its economy. The term "take-off" in particular implies an abrupt break with the past, a past dominated by a "traditional" economy and society that suddenly begins growing and undergoing structural change. China's economy analyzed in such terms is seen as "traditional" and stagnant prior to 1949 and as having "taken off" thereafter. The post-1949 period, however, is not seen as a typical case of "take-off" like that experienced in Europe, Japan, and more recently, parts of Asia and Latin America. It is instead thought to be an example of the "forced-draft" growth of a Communist authoritarian state.

But these images of China's twentieth-century economic performance are at best only half-truths. Before 1949 it is likely, as will be demonstrated below, that China's per capita gross domestic product rose little if at all. It is also the case, however, that from the late nineteenth century on, China experienced long periods of sustained development of modern industry and transport. Although this development did not much affect per capita GDP at the time, it did have a considerable impact on the kind of growth that was to occur after 1949.

And it was not just the small modern sector that influenced Chinese developments in this period. The dominant "traditional" sector inherited by the People's Republic of China continues to shape profoundly the pattern of Chinese economic growth to this day. China did not acquire in 1949 an all-powerful government capable of creating in a few short

I am indebted to Simon Kuznets for comments on both the original and a revised version of this paper. Other participants at the conference or in follow-up letters also made helpful comments.

years a copy of the Soviet Union or some other completely new economy and society unrelated to China's own past. The simple fact that China had a great many people and very little arable land, for example, has had a major influence on the rate of change in the shares of industry and agriculture in national product and on the division between investment and consumption. In this important respect China's experience has had more in common with other labor-surplus, land-short less-developed economies than it has with the Communist states of Eastern Europe or even the Soviet Union.

The analysis of these issues that follows is limited in large part to what can be discerned from estimates of certain aggregates, such as national product and investment. Confining the analysis to these aggregates, of course, limits what can be said about many of the questions raised. But this approach is an important part of any attempt to deal with these questions, and other parts of the answers to them can be found elsewhere in this volume.

A more serious problem is that aggregates can often be misleading if not handled with care. For example, much of the controversy over whether or not living standards in China were higher in, say, 1957 than in the 1930's arises from confusing average per capita income with the average income of the majority of the people. Given a substantial redistribution of income, one can rise while the other is stagnant or even falling. These problems will be developed at greater length below.

1. *Limited Economic Modernization Before 1949*

Chinese economic statistics for the 1952–57 period are both plentiful and generally reliable, at least by the standards prevailing in most less-developed countries. For the years after 1957 (except for 1958–60), the figures available outside China also appear to be reliable, but they are sketchy at best. Before 1949, in contrast, great quantities of data were published, but their quality more often than not is suspect. Nevertheless, certain trends in the pre-1949 period are sufficiently clear to make meaningful discussion possible.

Estimates of China's GDP for selected years are presented in Table 1. The post-1949 estimates will be discussed in a subsequent section. Here we are concerned only with the period before 1949. Save for the farm output figure, which I have taken from my study of agriculture, the 1933 estimates are those of T. C. Liu and K. C. Yeh converted into 1957 prices.[1] Their figure on farm output is about 9 percent higher than mine, largely because they use a higher grain-yield figure. Indeed, their grain-yield estimates are even higher than those reported for 1957, and yet

TABLE 1
China's Gross Domestic Product for Selected Years
(1957 prices)

Sector	1914-18	1933	1952	1957	1962	1965	1970	1971
	(Billion 1957 yuan)							
Manufacturing+	8.5^a	11.77^b	17.23^c	30.47	40.74	57.63	86.52	94.76
modern	1.3^c	4.54^d	11.11^c	—	—	—	—	—
Agriculture	29.9^e	35.23^e	31.58^f	43.93	34.68	48.23	58.90	60.37
Services	10.0	12.52^g	17.07^g	21.31	22.33	28.29	36.31	38.23
Depreciation	—	2.19^h	—	—	—	—	—	—
GDP	48.4	61.71	65.88	95.71	97.75	134.15	181.73	193.36
	(Ratio to GDP)							
Manufacturing+	.176	.198	.262	.318	.417	.430	.476	.490
Agriculture	.618	.592	.479	.459	.355	.360	.324	.312
Services	.207	.210	.259	.223	.228	.211	.200	.198
GDP	1.000	1.000	1.000	1.000	1.000	1.000	1.000	1.000

Note:

The M+ sector estimate has been obtained by adding the transportation estimate in Table A.12 to the industry estimate in Table A.13 (see Appendix A). The italicized figures are based on a few simple assumptions and are subject to a particularly wide margin of potential error.

[a] Estimated by assuming that the nonmodern portion of this sector was the same as in 1933 and adding this total to the modern sector estimate.

[b] The figure is that of T. C. Liu and K. C. Yeh, *The Economy of the Chinese Mainland* (Princeton, N.J., 1965), p. 66, converted from 1952 to 1957 prices by multiplying by .898 (the price decline implied by dividing 1957 industrial output in 1957 prices by 1957 output in 1952 prices).

[c] Essentially "official" figures converted into 1957 prices by multiplying by .898. The modern sector figure excludes handicrafts and rural manufacturing activities whereas the total figure includes both. The 1914-18 figure was obtained by dividing by the modern industry index for the period estimated by John K. Chang, *Industrial Development in Pre-Communist China* (Chicago, 1969), pp. 60-61. The most commonly seen official figures for 1952 include rural manufacturing activities in the agriculture sector, but this practice was changed in 1957 when they were shifted to the industrial sector. For a discussion of the sources and methodology behind estimating these figures, see Shigeru Ishikawa, *National Income and Capital Formation in Mainland China* (Tokyo, 1965), pp. 56, 64.

[d] The figure is Liu and Yeh's, p. 66, converted from 1952 prices, and includes factory output, mining, utilities, and modern transport. The coverage may not be precisely identical to that of the 1952 modern sector figure.

[e] The gross value of agricultural output in 1933 prices for these years (and for 1957) has been estimated by Dwight H. Perkins, *Agricultural Development in China, 1368-1968* (Chicago, 1969), p. 30. These figures were converted into value-added and then into 1957 prices by ratios obtained by comparing the 1957 figure in 1933 prices with that same figure in 1957 prices.

[f] This figure is made up of two components. 1. The official net value agricultural output figure converted into 1957 prices by the ratio (1.088) obtained from dividing 1957 farm output (minus rural manufacturing activities) in 1957 prices by that same output in 1952 prices. For the data and sources, see Ishikawa, p. 56. 2. To this official figure was added 1.918 billion yuan to take into account the underreporting of grain output in 1952 as estimated by Kang Chao, *Agricultural Production in Communist China, 1949-1965* (Madison, Wis., 1970), p. 227.

[g] The 1933 and 1952 figures are those of Liu and Yeh, p. 66, in 1952 prices. Because there was no reliable way of converting these figures to 1957 prices and because they are subject to a particularly wide margin of error in any case, it was assumed for simplicity that the 1952 and 1957 prices in this sector were the same. The same procedure was followed with the 1957-71 services sector estimates.

[h] Converted from the estimate of Liu and Yeh, p. 66, in 1952 prices. For other years, depreciation has not been netted out of the individual sectors as it was in the Liu-Yeh estimates. For purposes of calculating the ratios in the lower half of the table, depreciation was distributed among the various sectors in proportion to their net product.

there is no reason to believe that yields fell between 1933 and 1957.[2] It seems more plausible to assume that yields in the two years were about the same, and the 1933 farm output figure in Table 1 has been estimated on that basis.

Agricultural product for 1914–18 was estimated in much the same way as the figure for 1933, but the raw data underlying this estimate are of much poorer quality than those of the 1930's. The 1914–18 services sector and nonmodern manufacturing figures are more in the nature of plausible guesses than true estimates. Only the modern manufacturing sector estimate is based on reasonably reliable series for individual products, and even those series are subject to considerable potential error. Whether or not the resulting GDP figure is useful can best be judged by seeing whether the trends it portrays are consistent with other kinds of information about the period.

There is little question that certain modern sectors of China's economy exhibited almost uninterrupted growth in the first four decades of the twentieth century. The leading modern industry throughout the period was cotton textiles, and the course of its development has been carefully documented.[3] But as early as the 1860's, well ahead of the first modern textile mills, Chinese officials had begun establishing arsenals and shipyards to supply a slowly modernizing army. The modern Kaiping coal mine began turning out coal in 1881 and by the late 1880's and early 1890's there were numerous steam silk filatures. A key turning point was China's 1895 defeat by Japan, which opened up China to foreign investors and resulted in a considerable inflow of foreign capital.[4]

By 1913 roughly 700 more or less modern manufacturing and mining enterprises had been started with a total capitalization of over Ch. $200 million[5] (several times that figure if converted into 1957 prices). Most of these enterprises were small, and many used only limited amounts of power-driven machinery, but by the time World War I was under way in Europe they had managed to produce output worth 2.5 to 3 billion yuan* (more than one billion U.S. dollars in U.S. 1957 prices). From 1913 until the Japanese attack in 1937, industrial growth continued unabated, with an average annual rate of increase of over 9 percent.

After 1937 growth continued and even accelerated in one important area of the country, Manchuria. Mining and manufacturing in Manchuria grew at a rate of only 4.4 percent a year between 1924 and 1936, but rose to 9.9 percent between 1936 and 1941 as part of the Japanese

---

* This is in terms of gross output, which in this period was about double value-added (John K. Chang, *Industrial Development in Pre-Communist China*, Chicago, 1969, p. 60).

war effort. Total GDP in the same periods rose from a yearly rate of 2.8 percent to 7.3 percent.[6]

Two other modern sectors that began to develop in the first decades of the twentieth century were transport and banking. In 1895 there were no railroads in China, but between 1902 and 1912 some of China's most important rail lines were built. By 1913 some 6,000 miles of track were open to traffic.[7] Although railroad development slowed after 1912 and existing lines were often diverted to unproductive military uses, these new facilities opened North China and Manchuria to development. The introduction of steamships in the late nineteenth century also improved transport, though the impact of a change from junks to steamships was bound to be less significant than a shift from portage by humans and mules to railroads. Similarly, the growth of modern banks probably brought essentially marginal benefits, since existing traditional banks were already performing many of the same functions.

Having remarked the fact of growth in the modern sector in this period, we are confronted with the problem of assessing the importance of this growth for the economy as a whole. One way of making such an assessment is to compare the size of China's modern sector with that of other countries and with China's own GDP.

A comparison with Japan of a few selected industries is presented in Table 2. Figures for 1952 as well as 1936 are used because 1952 is the year when most of China's modern industries reached their prewar peaks (in Japan full recovery was achieved three years later). As the table indicates, though China's industrial output was generally smaller than Japan's, the differences are not striking except in the important case of electric power. And Japan in 1936 (or 1952) was considered an industrialized nation. The essential difference, of course, is that Japan in the 1930's had only 70 million people against China's 500 million. Thus Chinese industrial output was not only substantially smaller in absolute terms, but miniscule when compared in per capita terms.

The same basic point can be made with reference to the data in Table 1. The entire modern sector in 1933 (exclusive of a few modern services) constituted only 7 percent of GDP. Some 93 percent of GDP and an even higher percentage of the population and work force* were still entirely dependent on traditional technology.

Any growth that occurred in Chinese GDP between 1914–18 and 1933 (or 1952), therefore, had to come in part from the traditional sector.

---

* Since per capita output in the modern sector, particularly industry, was much higher than in the traditional sector, it follows that the modern sector's share of the work force was smaller than its share of the national product.

TABLE 2
Selected Industrial Output Figures, China and Japan, 1936 and 1952

Product	China		Japan	
	1936	1952	1936	1952
Pig iron (1,000 MT)	672	1,929	2,022	1,074
Steel (1,000 MT)	414	1,349	4,249	4,513
Cement (1,000 MT)	1,243	2,860	4,876	6,983
Coal (1,000 MT)	33,918	66,490	41,803	43,359
Electric power (1,000,000 kwh)	3,075	7,260	27,315	51,647
Cotton yarn (1,000 t)	506	656	673	297

Sources:
China, 1936. John K. Chang, *Industrial Development in Pre-Communist China* (Chicago, 1969), p. 100, except for the 1936 cotton yarn figure, which has been converted from bales to tons at the rate of 181.4 kg per bale from the estimates of Richard Kraus, as reported by Kang Chao in this volume.
China, 1952. Official Chinese government figures, from Nai-ruenn Chen, *Chinese Economic Statistics* (Chicago, 1967), pp. 186-88. The yarn figure has been converted from bales to tons at the rate of 181.4 kg per bale.
Japan, 1936, 1952. The Japan Statistical Research Office, *Nihon keizai tokei shu.*

Growth of the traditional service sector is of limited interest because large segments of that sector in an economy like China's (for example, commerce) are essentially a function of the goods-producing sectors. The real issue is what happened to agriculture and handicrafts.

There is little doubt that agricultural output (in years when average weather prevailed) grew steadily if slowly during the first decades of the twentieth century. In the terminology used elsewhere in this volume, China's traditional agriculture did not reach the complete stagnation of a "high-level equilibrium trap" until after the mid-point of the twentieth century. Before that, both the acreage under cultivation and the rural work force in China were increasing, albeit slowly. Since there is ample evidence to indicate that the marginal productivity of rural labor, though low, was not zero, increased inputs, *ceteris paribus*, should have raised output.[8] The most rapid increases were in newly opened areas such as Manchuria and parts of the southwest. In Manchuria, for example, agricultural output between 1924 and 1941 rose at an annual rate of 1.9 percent even though the region's major export crop, soybeans, was hard hit in the early years of the world depression of the 1930's.[9] The value of agricultural output also increased as a result of the increased output of cash crops elsewhere in the country.[10]

Whether or not the handicraft sector also made gains in this period is a matter of considerable controversy, as Kang Chao points out elsewhere in this volume. The key issue is whether foreign imports and domestic modern industry destroyed or severely crippled Chinese handicrafts. For the largest handicraft sector of all, cotton textiles, Chao shows that one part, spinning, declined under the impact of competition from imports and domestic factory output, but that the other part, weaving, maintained its position and may well have grown.

A careful study of the rest of the handicraft sector is a task for the future, but several indirect arguments can be used to establish a *prima facie* case that other handicrafts could not have been badly hurt by imports and probably were not much hurt by domestic modern factories either. If one analyzes Chinese imports for a reasonably average year like 1923, for example, one quickly discovers that only half of all imports (51 percent) could in any way be considered to have been competitive with handicrafts. The remaining 49 percent consisted of such items as machinery, fuel oil, metals, and unprocessed foods. Of those products that were competitive, 60 percent (31 percent of total imports) were cotton textiles. The next largest categories were dyes, colors, and similar chemicals (7 percent), most of which were probably not really competitive with handicrafts, and cigarettes and tobacco (4.5 percent).[11] Since domestic production of tobacco increased between the 1910's and the 1930's,[12] imports clearly could not have led to a reduction in the size of the domestic tobacco processing industry. The other potentially competitive imports were so small in amount (a few million dollars in most cases) that substantial damage to domestic handicrafts from this source is inconceivable. Total imports in the 1930's, for example, were only between 2 and 3 percent of GDP, and hence imports even potentially competitive with handicrafts (exclusive of textiles) amounted to less than .5 percent of GDP. Domestic handicraft output in the 1930's, in contrast, was over 10 percent of GDP.

Similar arguments can be made with respect to competition between domestic modern industries and handicrafts. Can anyone seriously argue that modern factories processing food and tobacco (one-third of all modern industry in 1933) badly damaged handicraft processing when the total gross value output of these modern industries was only 2.5 billion yuan (in 1957 prices), 70 percent or more of which was the value of agricultural raw material inputs?[13] No more than 5 or 6 percent of farm

TABLE 3
Per Capita Gross Domestic Product
(1957 prices)

Period	GDP (Billion yuan)	Population (Millions)	Per capita GDP (Yuan)
1914–18	48.40	430	112.6
1933	61.71	500	123.4
1952	65.88	572	115.2
1957	95.71	647	147.9

Sources: Table 1; Dwight H. Perkins, *Agricultural Development in China, 1368-1968* (Chicago, 1969), p. 216. I have estimated the 1952 population from the official census figure for 1953 of 583 million, assuming this reflected a 2 percent increase over 1952.

output could have been processed in modern factories in the 1930's,[*] or less than half the percentage of *increase* in farm output between the 1910's and 1930's.

Of the other modern industrial products, only in the already discussed case of cotton textiles (also about one-third of the gross value output of modern industry) was the growth large enough to affect handicrafts seriously. Thus, given that farm output, and particularly cash crops, many of which involve substantial processing, was increasing during the early decades of the twentieth century, and that imports and domestic modern industry remained small, the assumption in Table 1 that handicrafts output was the same in 1933 as in 1914–18 can be considered conservative. At a somewhat comparable stage of development in Japan in the late nineteenth century, Japanese handicrafts increased in value.[†]

If my analysis is generally correct, then, there are many reasons for believing that China's GDP was rising slowly during the first decades of the twentieth century at a rate roughly indicated by the estimates in Table 1. But more interesting than total GDP is what was happening to per capita product in a period when China's population was also rising slowly. Estimates of per capita GDP are presented in Table 3. These figures indicate that per capita output rose slightly between 1914–18 and 1933, fell back sharply during the war with Japan, and had only recovered to the 1914–18 level by 1952. Given the potential error in both the GDP and population estimates, however, all one can really say with confidence is that there was no pronounced downward trend in per

[*] Since modern food-processing factories often relied heavily on imported farm products, even this 5 to 6 percent figure is too high.

[†] Non-factory manufacturing output in Japan nearly doubled between 1890 and 1914 (Kazushi Ohkawa and Henry Rosovsky, *Japanese Economic Growth*, Stanford, Calif., 1973, p. 81).

capita GDP in the first half of the twentieth century, and that there may have been a slight increase in the decades prior to the Japanese attack.

Why, then, is it so commonly believed that China's per capita income was declining during the first half of the twentieth century? There are several possible explanations.

To many people, an increase in goods and services means that they have become better off and not just in material terms. Conversely, if they feel worse off, the general assumption is that they have experienced a decline in real income. Thus in the late 1960's American magazines carried articles about a decade of stagnating or declining income for the American family. The logic of such articles seemed to be that since so many Americans felt worse off in the late 1960's, as compared with the early 1960's, it must be that their real income had fallen. In fact, the decade witnessed a rapid growth in real per capita income, but this did not stop some journalists from attempting to demonstrate the opposite.

In truth, there were many periods in the 1920's, 1930's, and 1940's when large numbers of Chinese were worse off in many respects than they had been at the beginning of the century. But this situation had little to do with economics. A 10 percent rise in per capita income is poor compensation for the heightened personal dangers attendant on political turmoil and warfare. Few people would consider themselves better off under such circumstances, even if no one close to them actually perished. Hundreds of millions of Chinese faced precisely this kind of trade-off during many of the years before 1949. Like people elsewhere, Chinese tended to conclude that their material income as well as their general welfare must have fallen.

Warfare, moreover, was not the only source of instability and insecurity. The economy itself was subject to wide fluctuations. The figures in Table 1 basically reflect long-term trends of production in average years or in years when there were few major natural or man-made calamities. But major economic calamities were frequent before 1949.

There has been no single year in Chinese history either before or after 1949 when all of China was free of flood, drought, or other forms of disaster, but some years in our period were particularly bad. The great drought of 1920–21 in North China and the Yangtze River flood of 1931 are two cases in point. Both destroyed crops over vast areas and left hundreds of thousands and even millions of deaths in their wake.[14] During the early stages of the Japanese invasion, the Chinese government's decision to breach the Yellow River dikes in order to slow the Japanese advance also caused widespread death and destruction.

Yet for all the natural and man-made disasters that struck China between 1900 and 1949, it is hard to make a case that the rate or severity of these disasters was increasing except for the periods of large-scale warfare between 1937 and 1949. To the contrary, there is evidence that the impact of such disasters was somewhat less severe in the twentieth century than in the late nineteenth century. The great northern drought of 1920–21, for example, appears to have killed far fewer people than a comparable drought in 1876–79, owing to the advent of the railroad, which made it possible to move large amounts of grain in from surplus areas. Human and animal carriers, the main forms of northern transport before the railroad, ate as much as they could carry after traveling relatively short distances.[15]

Finally, mention should be made of the possibility that the income of large portions of the population was declining even though average per capita GDP was stagnant or rising. To make a definitive statement about changes in the distribution of income in pre-1949 China requires much more substantial research than is possible. But the few pieces of available evidence do not suggest that the poor were getting poorer and the rich richer. Some groups, to be sure, did fare particularly poorly during certain periods. University teachers, for example, saw their relative as well as absolute incomes decline when they joined the government in retreat to the southwest in the late 1930's and early 1940's, and teachers are an articulate group. But most people lived in the countryside, and there is no convincing evidence that landlords were garnering an increasing share of the product during the first half of the twentieth century. The limited available data, in fact, suggest that the rate of tenancy might even have declined slightly, and that in periods of political turmoil landlords often had difficulty collecting their rents.[16]

Thus the view that the incomes of all or of the vast majority of the people were declining during the first half of the twentieth century is not supported by currently available evidence. Impressions to the contrary must be seen in part as a response to a worsening of conditions in noneconomic areas. In addition, many groups may have become increasingly aware of their own poverty through their contact with wealthier foreigners (the "demonstration effect") or exposure to the educational activities of the Communist Party. Corruption and great wealth among a small elite of the Kuomintang government may have had a similar effect.

The fact that per capita incomes were neither rising nor falling dramatically prior to 1949, however, should not lead to the conclusion that China's economy was stagnant in all respects or that no important changes occurred. By the late 1930's and early 1940's China had an established modern industrial and transport sector on which the Communist government could and did build. In fact most increases in Chinese output prior to 1958 were achieved through the recovery and expansion of existing enterprises.*

What the Communists inherited in 1949 was not so much machinery and equipment. There was some, to be sure, but great amounts had been destroyed by war or carted off by the Russian army. More important were such other resources as trained workers, experienced managers, and established organizations. Although, as I pointed out in the Introduction, Chinese traditional society imparted to its people values and experience of direct relevance to modern economic growth, there was still a gap between traditional experience and the requirements of modern factories. These modern-trained people and organizations became a vehicle for rehabilitating existing enterprises. Supplemented by Soviet advisors and schools, they also provided essential training and experience to millions of workers and managers, who went on to staff the new enterprises that began to appear rapidly in the latter half of the 1950's. Without this base, Chinese industrial development in the 1950's and 1960's would have been significantly slower or would have had to rely more heavily on foreign technicians, or both.

2. The Transition from the 1930's to the 1950's

Confusion surrounds just what it was that the People's Republic of China accomplished with the economy in its first decade. Much has been said that leaves the impression the Chinese economy was transformed beyond recognition by 1957 or 1958.

It comes as a surprise to most observers of the Chinese scene to discover that the average per capita GDP in 1957 was only about 20 percent above the level of 1933 (see Table 3), and that 1952 per capita output was actually below 1933. Converted into 1960 U.S. dollars, Chinese per capita product rose from a 1933 level of a bit over $60 to a 1957 level of between $70 and $80, hardly enough to transform the Chinese economic scene. Either figure placed China in the middle of the poorest category of less-developed nations.

The mystery of why impressions should be so divergent from the evidence of "hard data" is deepened when one adds the fact that average per capita consumption in 1957 was about the same as in 1933. If per

---

* Expanded output in old plants is estimated to have accounted for over two-thirds of the increase in industrial output in the 1952–57 period (K. C. Yeh, "Capital Formation," in Alexander Eckstein, Walter Galenson, and Ta-chung Liu, eds., *Economic Trends in Communist China*, Chicago, 1968, p. 528).

capita GDP was up only 20 percent, and the rate of investment also rose
from 5 percent to 18.2 percent of GDP between 1931–36 and 1952–57
(in 1933 prices), or from 7.5 percent to 24 percent of GDP (in 1952
prices),[17] it follows that consumption expenditures (personal and government) either rose only slightly (by perhaps 3 percent in 1933 prices)
or fell (by 1.4 percent in 1952 prices). However the estimates are made,
there is no way one can make them show a substantial rise in average
per capita consumption expenditures between the 1930's and the 1950's.

To this apparent mystery, however, there is a ready solution. Many
of the most fundamental changes brought about by the People's Republic during its first decade were not of a type to be reflected in aggregate statistics such as estimates of GDP. By the 1950's the Communists had succeeded in raising the per capita output and consumption
of many people above the 1930's levels and in increasing the security
and stability of the great majority.

Per capita output and consumption of the poor, of course, were raised
by confiscating the property and income of the small minority at the
top of the income ladder. Landlords and a few other individuals were
reduced to the level of ordinary peasants, and their land and other valu-
ables were given to poor and middle peasants (or retained by the state).
To use hypothetical but reasonably realistic figures, if the top 5 percent
of the population receives 25 to 30 percent of the national income and
the bottom half receives only 15 to 20 percent, one can reduce the top
5 percent to the national average and have enough left over to raise both
investment and consumption. The consumption of the poorest 50 percent of the population, for example, could be raised by 50 percent and
enough would still be left over to raise investment from 5 percent to
over 15 percent of GDP. Such calculations, to be sure, are based on a
number of implicit assumptions including the assumption that a redistribution of this magnitude will not itself reduce the national product.
Carl Riskin discusses these assumptions elsewhere in this volume. Here
we need merely note that a redistribution of income did take place in
China between the 1930's and the 1950's, and on a large enough scale
to raise substantially the consumption levels of a large portion of the
population together with the investment levels of the state.

A change of equal if not greater importance to the individual than
the redistribution of income was the increased security of the post-1949
decade. There were three principal reasons for this rise in personal security.

First and most important, the mere ending of thirteen years of war and civil war obviously increased the probability of living to an old age for the great majority of the population.

Second, the Chinese government in the mid-1950's took vigorous steps to ensure that everyone received adequate amounts of certain basic necessities (grain, edible oils, and cotton cloth) in good times and bad. This measure was achieved not by ironing out fluctuations in farm output (the 1959–61 farm output decline was probably as severe as the worst of the past), but by effective rationing. Food stores to protect against bad harvests were also built up. In 1970, for example, grain storage amounted to about 40 million tons, against roughly two to three million tons during the peak period of effectiveness of the imperial granary system (in the eighteenth and early nineteenth centuries).*

Finally, the Chinese government made a major effort to improve public health. Unlike the redistribution measures discussed above, the production and distribution of increased quantities of medicine and medical services are reflected in estimates of GDP. But the difference between the market value of these medicines and services and the "true social" value is so great that a major change in health in a poor country may be accomplished with a tiny fraction of GDP.† Such was the case in China in the 1950's.

The widespread belief that most Chinese were materially better off in the 1950's is thus not really in conflict with the fact that average per capita GDP was only slightly above the levels of the 1930's. The improvements that took place in the 1950's, however, were largely one-shot affairs. Future changes for the better in economic life could not be achieved readily (if at all) by similar measures.

There is a major barrier to continued reliance on redistribution as a method of raising the incomes of some in that such efforts can themselves reduce the product available for distribution. It does seem likely, however, that the degree of inequality existing in China in the 1930's and 1940's, given the nature of Chinese society, was dysfunctional even from the narrow standpoint of increasing national product as rapidly as pos-

---

* The figures for the imperial granaries are not entirely comparable to those for the post-1949 period because they exclude private stores of grain, but then these private stores were not really available for distribution in times of famine.

† In formal terms medical expenditures of this type do not include very large consumer surpluses and external economies, particularly when a country is moving from a situation where no medical services were available to a large part of the population to a point where they are generally available. We may note also that medical services in China (like services in general) are cheap even when government subsidies are included in costs owing to the relatively low wages of doctors.

sible. Chinese rural poverty was not the sole cause of the political turmoil that did so much to hamper growth, but it was a major cause. It
is also the case that a large portion of China's wealth was in the hands
of landlords and others who consumed most of it and invested very
little.

However, a truly rigorous defense of the proposition that the distribution of income in China in the 1930's was dysfunctional, and that redistribution in the 1950's may actually have promoted economic growth
is beyond the scope of this essay. It is sufficient here to state that a
plausible case can be made for that point of view.

3. *Changing Economic Structure, 1952–1971*

If there is confusion surrounding the changes that occurred between
the 1930's and 1950's, few challenge the proposition that beginning in
the 1950's China entered into a process of sustained economic growth
and structural change. Such debate as exists is over the rate of change,
not that it took place.

Disagreements over the rate of change arise out of the difficulties involved in using Chinese statistics. It is not a question of the Chinese
deliberately falsifying data or lacking the facilities for collecting reasonably accurate figures. On the contrary, considerable evidence has accumulated over the years to suggest that China's published official data,
except for the years 1958–60, are at least as reliable as those promulgated by the governments of many other less-developed nations and
considerably better than those of a number of them.

The problems with Chinese data lie elsewhere. First is the fact that
during the decade of the 1960's the Chinese government published or
leaked few national figures. In the early 1970's this policy of extreme
secrecy was relaxed, but not to a degree approaching the openness of
the 1950's. Nevertheless, far more can be done with officially released
Chinese statistics than has been accomplished to date.

An attempt has been made in Appendix A to estimate Chinese GDP
in 1957 prices for the years 1957–71. Except for the services sector, these
estimates are based almost exclusively on official data. For reasons
argued in part in the appendix, it is my opinion that these officially
based estimates are a generally accurate reflection of real trends in the
Chinese economy during this period.

Some official releases of data, however, have been rather imprecise,
and others have been difficult to interpret. Beyond that, these official
series often differ significantly from estimates made by observers outside of China. For reasons that have been argued at length in numerous

TABLE 4
Alternative Industrial Output Indexes
(1957 = 100)

Year	"Official"	Field
1952	62[a]	51
1957	100	100
1965	201	148–61
1970	307	199–230

Sources: Table A.13; R. M. Field, "Chinese Industrial Development, 1949-1970," in *People's Republic of China: An Economic Assessment* (Washington, D.C., 1972), p. 63.
[a]Includes an estimate of rural manufacturing, a category that was excluded from the actual official figure for 1952 but was probably included from 1957 on.

journal articles and are briefly discussed in Appendix A, differences between the official and outside estimates of farm output can almost always be resolved in favor of the official series. The differences in the outsiders' estimates of industrial output, however, cannot be so easily resolved until the Chinese government publishes more disaggregated data against which one can check their figures for gross value of industrial output. For this reason, the procedure followed here is to use a range for industrial output consisting of the most prominent outsider's (R. M. Field) estimate of industrial output as the lower end and the "official" figures as the upper end. Summaries of these two indexes are presented in Table 4. Subsequent analysis makes use of only the upper end of Field's range.

Estimates of the services sector were derived by assuming that the various components of that sector were correlated with growth of other sectors or population. Only Subramanian Swamy, among the various estimators of Chinese GDP, uses a significantly different procedure, and his results for the services sector are plausible only for highly atypical years, such as during the height of the Cultural Revolution in 1967–68.

The second problem with Chinese data is related to the prices that are used to convert output figures for individual products into national product totals. Because much of the analysis that follows involves comparisons of China with other nations, the ideal situation would be to work with estimates of the national product of each country in the prices of every other being compared. Since that is not practical, I instead present my Chinese data measured in three sets of prices: Chinese prices in 1957, Chinese prices in 1933 as estimated by T. C. Liu and K. C. Yeh, and Indian prices as estimated by Subramanian Swamy.

Most economists believe, with good reason, that post-1949 Chinese prices grossly overvalue industrial products relative to agricultural products. This is particularly true of the widely used 1952 prices, which reflect the demands of the Korean War together with some of the remaining effects of the dislocations of the pre-1949 period, when industry was more seriously disrupted than agriculture. By 1957, prices were largely administered by the government, and industrial prices were adjusted downward while those of agriculture were raised, but the relative valuation of industry was still high. Indian prices, in contrast, apparently place a very low valuation on producer goods as a result of deliberate government policy.[18] Chinese 1933 prices fall somewhere in between. Unlike either Indian prices or Chinese 1957 prices, the 1933 prices reflect market conditions of the period and not government policy, but conditions in China were very different in the two periods. Thus no one of the three sets of prices is ideal. Nevertheless, the use of all three together in the international comparisons made below should be adequate for most purposes.

Most comparative studies of changes in the structure of national product exclude all data from Communist countries, probably for no better reason than that the statistics for these countries are difficult to obtain or use; as is apparent from the preceding discussion, one cannot simply pull out a statistical handbook and key-punch the data onto cards. But Simon Kuznets explicitly excludes Communist nations from most of his work because of basic differences in the institutional and political structure of these nations, such as authoritarian management by a minority party of forced economic growth, the sharp restriction of the individual freedom of producers and consumers, and an emphasis on autarky.[19] Implicit in his analysis is the belief that government policymakers, if they have sufficient political power, have a wide range of choice of differing patterns of economic growth, particularly in the early stages of development. Similar views are implicit in the arguments of all those who hold that highly authoritarian states have significant advantages in promoting growth over their more democratic or loosely organized neighbors (for example, Gunnar Myrdal's concept of "soft" societies).[20] By and large, this point of view has been derived from the experience of the Soviet Union in the 1930's, where dramatic changes in economic structure were achieved in a brief period of time as a result of government action, both deliberate and inadvertent. But the question here is whether China after 1949 was in a comparable position to the Soviet Union in the 1930's. Certainly many of the initial conditions China were different. Soviet per capita income in 1928, for example, was three or four times that of China in the 1950's,* the Soviet level of grain output per capita in 1937 was two and a half times that of China in 1957,[21] and the differences in the amount of available cultivable land per head between the two countries was even more pronounced.

In the analysis that follows, I shall try to show that trends in the development of China's domestic product and its structure can often be explained by underlying economic conditions that existed long before the Communists took over the government in 1949. The fact that China has little cultivable land relative to the size of its population, for example, accounts for patterns of development that have more in common with certain other less-developed countries than with the Communist states of the Soviet Union and Eastern Europe. Even where the nature of Chinese growth can be attributed to deliberate actions by a powerful Chinese government and Communist Party, these actions often differ significantly from those of other Communist states. There are also similarities, of course, and I shall point these out as well.

Growth rates, 1952–71. As I have indicated, almost no one disputes the fact that the rate of growth of Chinese GDP rose markedly after 1949 and has continued to rise more rapidly than during the pre-1949 decades ever since. Summaries of the estimates used here and their derived growth rates are presented in Tables 1 and 5. The years 1952, 1957, and 1970, between which growth rates were calculated, are all more or less "average" years. That is, they are at neither a peak nor a trough of the pronounced cyclical movements that have characterized Chinese growth since 1949.

It is apparent from the figures in these tables that Chinese growth has been respectable but not remarkable by post–World War II standards. Although the use of alternative sets of prices affects the results, they do so only to a limited degree. For the entire two decades since 1952, when postwar recovery was largely achieved, Chinese GDP has

* One careful calculation puts Soviet per capita GNP in 1955 at U.S. $921.5 (Abram Bergson, "The Comparative National Income of the USSR and the United States," in D. J. Daly, ed., *International Comparisons of Prices and Output*, New York, 1972, p. 149). Elsewhere Bergson has estimated that per capita GNP grew between 2.7 and 4.4 times from 1928 to 1955 (Abram Bergson, *The Real National Income of the Soviet Union Since 1928*, Cambridge, Mass., 1961, p. 225). Since these growth rates were calculated from data in ruble factor costs, they provide only a very rough guide to the growth rate in terms of U.S. prices. Still, it is probably not too far off to say that Soviet national product per capita in 1928 was roughly $200 to $300 (in 1955 prices). The figure for China in the early 1950's would be under U.S. $70.

TABLE 5
Effect of Prices on Gross Domestic Product Growth Rates
(Percent per annum)

GDP	1933-52	1952-57	1957-70
1957 prices	0.3%	7.8%	4.2–5.6%
1933 prices	0.05	6.9	3.9–4.6
Indian prices	0.3	7.1	3.9–4.5

Note: For the methodology used, see the notes to Table 1. The lower end of the range for 1957-70 was obtained by using the Field industrial index ("high" estimate) in place of the "official" index.

grown at an average rate of from 4.5 to just under 6 percent a year, depending on which prices or industrial output index one prefers.

This level of development was well above the rate of population increase. In the 1950's, the number of people in China was growing at a bit above 2 percent a year. No reliable official population figures have been published since 1957, but most of the evidence collected by recent visitors indicates that, except for a few major cities, China's population is still growing at about 2 percent a year, though major efforts are under way to lower this rate.[22] Thus, in per capita terms, Chinese GDP was growing at about 3 percent a year, a rate that would double per capita income roughly every quarter of a century.

The data in Table 1 also show that Chinese growth was very uneven. There was rapid growth between 1952 and 1957, and this continued on into the first two years of the Great Leap Forward, 1958 and 1959. By 1962, however, as a result of the intervening crises of 1959–61, Chinese GDP had barely recovered to the level of 1957. Recovery and Growth were again rapid through 1966, when the Cultural Revolution halted development for two years, at least in the industrial sector. With the end of political turmoil, rapid growth again ensued though slowed temporarily by the poor harvest of 1972.

Thus the pace of Chinese development has been limited by poor harvests (in 1959–61 and 1972), by domestic political instability (1967–68), by international instability affecting China (the Soviet pull-out in 1960), and by a variety of mistakes in planning (mainly in 1958 and 1959). Although the specific form of these interruptions was peculiar to China, limitations of this type are typical of nations in the early stages of economic development. A very similar list, for example, could be readily drawn up for India and numerous other less-developed nations. Where China differs from these countries is in the causes of at least some of the disruptions. The Cultural Revolution and to a lesser degree the Great Leap Forward involved a deliberate attempt to make fundamental changes in Chinese society even at the price of temporary economic disruption.

A rising rate of capital formation. One of the most striking features of China's post-1949 economic performance has been the marked increase in the rate of gross domestic capital formation. Although the precise figures vary depending on the prices used, there is no significant controversy surrounding the estimate that the rate of capital formation tripled between the 1930's and the 1950's as shown in Table 6. Much more controversy surrounds the estimate that the rate of capital formation in 1970 was significantly higher than in 1957. But if producer goods output was growing much faster than GDP throughout the 1957–70 period, as was clearly the case, then capital formation rates must have risen unless huge proportions of this output were diverted to the military or used to substitute for declining imports. There were such diversions, but as argued in Appendix B, it is unlikely these were so large as to wipe out all the increase in capital formation. Other evidence attesting to a rising rate of capital formation in the 1960's and early 1970's is also presented in Appendix B.

This investment performance seems to set China apart from other less-developed countries. Where the "average" less-developed nation accumulated capital at a rate of 15 percent to 17 percent of GNP until per capita income reached the level of several hundred dollars, China's rate appears to have passed 20 percent even in 1933 prices with a per capita income in the neighborhood of only U.S. $100.

One is tempted to attribute this rise to China's adoption of forced-draft methods of Stalinist Russia. Between 1928 and 1937, for example, Soviet gross investment as a percentage of GNP rose from 12.5 percent to 25.9 percent at a time when per capita national product rose by less than 50 percent.[23] In this period, the Soviet government made a concerted effort to reduce personal income and consumption by sharply increasing compulsory delivery quotas for farmers, introducing high turnover taxes on most consumer goods, and other measures. After 1937, Soviet investment rates fell as military expenditures increased, then rose again after the war, but to a level only slightly above that of 1937 (28.1 percent in 1955) in spite of an 82 percent increase in per capita national product[24] and a sharp reduction in armaments spending.

The rise in the Chinese rate of capital formation between the 1930's and 1952 was the result of the introduction of Soviet-type measures, most notably high sales and profits taxes on consumer goods much like the Soviet turnover tax. There was also a period in the early 1960's when the investment rate dropped sharply, in part because of a need to expand

TABLE 6
Capital Formation and Per Capita Gross Domestic Product in Selected Countries

China in the years:	1933	1952	1957	1970
(1) Per capita GDP (U.S. 1957 $)	62	58	74	109
(2) $\frac{GDCF}{GDP}$ (percent)				
1933 prices	5%	16%	17%	23–24%
1957 prices	–	–	21%	28–29%
1952 prices	7%	19.5%	23.5%	31–32%
Japan in the years:	1886	1905	1930	1938
(3) Per capita GDP (U.S. 1960 $)	63	98	264	333
(4) $\frac{GDCF}{GNP}$ (percent)	11.1%	13.9%	18.8%	21.7%
South Korea in the years:	1960	1963	1967	1970
(5) Per capita GDP (U.S. 1960 $)	99	107	139	190
(6a) $\frac{GDCF}{GNP}$ (percent)	10.5%	15.3%	23.3%	27.3%
(6b) $\frac{GDI - Foreign\ Saving}{GNP}$	2.2%	6.9%	11.8%	15.4%
Taiwan in the years:	1953	1958	1966	1969
(7) Per capita GDP (U.S. 1960 $)	84	98	152	185
(8) $\frac{GDCF}{GNP}$ (percent)	14.0%	18.0%	23.2%	25.3%
Average of less-developed nations	Per capita GDP ranges			
(9) Per capita GDP (U.S. 1958 $)	under $100	100–199	200–349	350–574
(10) $\frac{GDCF}{GNP}$ (percent)	15.2%	16.4%	16.9%	20.9%

Sources and Methodology:

(1) Per capita GDP figures in yuan appear in Table 3 except for the year 1970, where the figure would be 218 yuan (assuming a population of 835 million, based on a 2 percent average growth since 1957). The official Chinese exchange rate of 2.36 yuan = U.S. $1.00 clearly understates purchasing power parity value of the 1957 yuan. I have used an exchange rate of 2.00 yuan = U.S. $1.00.

(2) Appendix B, Table B.1; K. C. Yeh, "Capital Formation," in A. Eckstein, W. Galenson, and T. C. Liu, *Economic Trends in Communist China* (Chicago, 1968), pp. 510-11.

(3) When one converts Japanese prices in 1934-36 yen into 1960 U.S. dollars, the exchange rate is close to 1:1, so the figures here are in fact the per capita figures in yen as calculated by Kazushi Ohkawa and Henry Rosovsky, "A Century of Japanese Economic Growth," in William W. Lockwood, ed., *The State and Economic Enterprise in Japan* (Princeton, N.J., 1965), p. 89.

(4) *Ibid.,* p. 90.

(5) For South Korea one not surprisingly gets rather different results for per capita income in U.S. dollars depending on the order in which one makes the necessary conversions. I started with the 1967 figure in current dollar prices, converted it into U.S. 1960 prices, and then derived the figures for the other years from an index of per capita GNP in constant 1965 won prices. The data were from Bank of Korea, *Economic Statistics Yearbook, 1971* (Seoul, 1971).

(6a) *Ibid.,* pp. 10-11; (6b) Foreign borrowing and transfer payments played such a large role in Korean capital formation in the 1960's that it is necessary to separate them out in order to establish that the rising trend did not simply result from increased borrowing. *Ibid.,* pp. 46-47.

armaments expenditures, but mostly because of a marked decline in per capita output in all sectors of the economy. Since the early 1960's, however, the rate not only has been recovered, but has apparently continued to rise to levels well above 20 percent of GNP.

As far as one can tell from skimpy data, this post-1957 rise in the Chinese rate of capital formation was achieved without any new taxes or a rise in tax rates and without severe inflationary pressure. The absence of rapid increases in prices was in turn due in part to a lack of vigorous competition between firms for the services of a limited pool of workers. Such competition in the Soviet Union led to a steady rise in real wages (after an initial drop in the early 1930's) and a much more rapid rise in money wages.[25]

In China, what evidence we have indicates almost no increase in real or money wages since the mid 1950's. As the indexes in Table 7 indicate, real wages in 1971 were virtually the same as in 1957, though some account needs to be taken of changes in housing and health care, both of which are heavily subsidized. Even in the 1950's wage rate increases were not so much the result of competition between firms as they were of central government administrative directives.[26]

One possible explanation for this lack of pressure on wages is simply that the political power of the government and the Chinese Communist Party enabled the leadership to freeze wages through administrative fiat. But a more plausible explanation is that pressures to raise wages were not great. There are several reasons why this might have been the case. First, China is a closed society and not subject to the pressures to raise consumption provoked by what is often termed the demonstration effect. Large numbers of high-spending tourists and foreign residents, images of higher standards of living elsewhere transmitted through movies, television, and advertising, none of these exist in China today. Nor are there many Chinese with high incomes to provide an example of the benefits of higher consumption to their neighbors. Not only are incomes more equal than in most other less-developed nations, but "conspicuous consumption" is severely discouraged. Thus Chinese planners are probably not under great pressure to raise the wage rates so more people can enjoy new consumer durables.

Still another and more important possibility has already been men-

---

(7) The per capita figure for 1958 was converted into 1960 U.S. dollar prices, and an index of per capita GDP in constant Taiwan prices was then applied to the 1958 figure. Source: United Nations, *Statistical Yearbook, 1970* (New York, 1971), pp. 571, 599.

(8) Based on data in *ibid.,* p. 581; and United Nations, *Statistical Yearbook for Asia and the Far East* (Hong Kong, 1971), p. 78. Subtracting the deficit on current account from the Taiwan data would make the percentages in this row rise even more dramatically because it would lower the figures for the 1950's without much affecting those for the 1960's.

(9) (10) Simon Kuznets, *Modern Economic Growth* (New Haven, Conn., 1966), p. 406. The U.S. wholesale price indexes of 1958 and 1960 were virtually the same, so that the presentation of data in 1958 prices in no way makes these figures less comparable to those for the individual countries.

TABLE 7
Wages and Prices
(1952 = 100)

Year	Money wages	Retail prices	Real wages
1952	100	100	100
1957	142.8	109.1	130.9
1963	—	118.4	—
1971	150+	115.6	130+

Sources:
   Money wages. 1952, 1957, State Statistical Bureau, *Ten Great Years* (Peking, 1960), p. 216; 1971, *Liang-chung she-hui, liang-chung kung-tsu* (Two kinds of societies, two kinds of wages; Shanghai, 1973), p. 15.
   Retail prices. See Appendix A, sources for Table A.4.
   Real wages. Obtained by dividing the money-wage index by the retail-price index.

tioned. The lack of competition for workers might well explain the lack of pressure on wage rates. The principal reason for this phenomenon seems to be that businesses have no need to so act in order to meet planned targets. Except in a few skill categories, there is more than enough labor to go around. Unlike the Soviet Union, China is a labor-surplus economy in the sense that the modern sector faces an almost infinitely elastic supply curve for labor. And it is in this sense that China is much like other less-developed countries.

But it is not just the failure of wage *rates* to rise that accounts for the increase in the percentage of national product devoted to capital formation and the declining share devoted to personal consumption. Average per capita personal consumption expenditures for the nation as a whole rose by roughly 30 percent between 1952 and 1957 but by only a little over 20 percent between 1957 and 1970.* The latter figure amounts to about 1.5 percent a year, or roughly half the rate of increase in national product.

In addition to stagnant urban wages, this relatively slow rise in consumption since 1957 can be ascribed to the fact that the Chinese managed to slow down the rate of urbanization. Because of the higher cost of urban services, the stronger pull of the demonstration effect in cities and towns, and other urban-rural differences, per capita consumption is generally markedly higher in urban areas than in the countryside. Thus the transfer of labor from rural to urban areas raises national average consumption considerably even when average consumption in each of the areas separately remains unchanged.

* These figures were obtained by subtracting per capita gross domestic capital formation (Table 6) and plausible guesses of Chinese military and other government expenditures not related to personal consumption from per capita product.

In spite of the Chinese leaders' determined efforts to squeeze this differential, it continues to exist. But they have plainly had some success in slowing the rate of urbanization. No precise figures are available, but what evidence we have indicates that 20 percent or less of China's population resides in cities of more than 2,000 people.* Thus, though industry has risen four- or five-fold since 1952, the urban population has only doubled. Without the Chinese government's elaborate efforts to slow rural migration and to press urban residents into projects in the countryside, it is likely that China's urban population would have been much larger (and consumption would also have been higher while capital formation would have grown by a lesser amount).

A recent study by Gur Ofer indicates that a relatively slow pace of urbanization may be typical of socialist countries in general.[27] Certainly, it is not typical of such "labor-surplus" countries as South Korea, where the nonfarm population passed 50 percent by 1969 (when per capita income was about U.S. $150).[28] But Korea is an extreme case. As late as 1920, for example, only 12 percent of Japan's population resided in cities of over 100,000[29] (when per capita income was over U.S. $200). Clearly, more research on the quantitative aspects of this topic is in order, but such a study is beyond the scope of this essay.

Even if urbanization did proceed faster in nonsocialist Asian labor-surplus economies, some of the effect of this process on consumption may have been reduced by the failure of the governments in many of these countries to provide what people elsewhere consider "necessary" urban services. That is, socialist countries have avoided these service expenses in part by slowing urbanization while many Asian economies have avoided them by simply ignoring them.† But one cannot carry this argument too far, because a number of important urban services are unavoidable (for example, commerce), though many of them can be provided very cheaply in a poor labor-surplus economy (for example, retail trade).

Whatever the reason, it is clear there are other labor-surplus economies whose rate of capital formation, like China's, has risen much faster

---

* The percentage in 1956 was 14 percent, but this appears to have risen sharply in 1958–59, and scattered statements indicate the percentage was above 14 percent in the 1960's.

† In European socialist countries the slow pace of urbanization can also be explained in good part by the difficulties in raising agricultural productivity, which has forced them to keep a large number of workers on the farm to maintain output (Gur Ofer, "Industrial Structure, Urbanization and Growth Strategy of Socialist Countries," unpublished paper). But this argument does not seem to be applicable to labor-surplus, land-short Asia, where the marginal product of labor is very low and hence where many workers can be removed without significantly reducing farm output.

than in the "typical" less-developed economy (see Table 6). The funds
that made this rise possible came in part from government revenues,
with the remainder (generally over half) coming from private savings,
company-retained profits, and the like. In China government revenues
alone accounted for over 90 percent of such funds. But the difference is
more apparent than real, since enterprise profits accounted for nearly
half of these revenues.

In both China and the other nations appearing in Table 6, it is likely
that the lack of wage pressures accounts at least in part for this rapid
rise in profits, a large portion of which was saved and invested by either
the government or wealthy individuals. To what degree the rapid increase in capital formation and the slow rise in consumption in China
were also the result of such socialist features as retarded urbanization,
if this is in fact a peculiarly socialist phenomenon, must await further
research. It is reasonable to assume, however, that China's massive
efforts to slow urbanization have played some role in holding down
personal consumption.

The structure of national product. If changes in the Chinese rate of
capital formation and personal consumption had something in common
with both the Soviet economy and a certain kind of less-developed
economy, what can be said about other changes in the structure of Chinese national product?

A rising share of industry in national product is such a universal feature of the development process that it is included as part of the definition of modern economic growth. In spite of much talk in China in the
1960's of making agriculture and rural development the leading sectors,
the share of Chinese industry in national product is no exception to the
general pattern. The relevant estimates are presented fully in Appendix A, and are summarized and translated into three different sets of
prices in Table 8.

As one would expect of a nation undergoing growth, the share of
industry in China rose steadily between 1952 and 1970 while the share
of agriculture fell. There was a similar movement in these shares between 1933 and 1952, though some of this change may simply reflect
errors in the underlying data. The share of the services sector shows no
discernible trend, and this too is consistent with the past performance
of other industrializing nations. The much-publicized Chinese attacks
on bureaucracy and reductions in the number of university students
may have slowed growth of this sector to a small degree. But the bulk
of this sector's share is accounted for by trade, finance, housing, and the
like, which had to grow along with national product or population if

TABLE 8

Effect of Prices on Gross Domestic Product Shares

Sector	1933[a]	1952	1957	1970
Manufacturing+				
1957 prices	.198	.262	.318	.416–.476
1933 prices	.178	.228	.257	.347–.404
Indian prices	.123	.165	.207	.281–.332
Agriculture				
1957 prices	.592	.479	.459	.361–.324
1933 prices	.640	.532	.527	.429–.392
Indian prices	.618	.510	.504	.421–.391
Services				
1957 prices	.210	.259	.223	.223–.200
1933 prices	.182	.240	.216	.224–.204
Indian prices	.259	.325	.289	.299–.277

Sources:
1957 price estimates. Table 1.
1933 prices estimates. Price ratios for each sector were obtained by dividing the Liu-Yeh 1952 price sector estimate by the Liu-Yeh 1933 price sector estimate and then multiplying by an index to take into account the change in prices between 1952 and 1957. The resulting ratios for 1957 (also used for 1970) were M+, 2.899; A, 2.036; and S, 2.408; the value-added figures for 1957 and 1970 from Table 1 were then divided by these ratios to obtain the figures in the above table. Similar procedures were followed for 1933 and 1952.
Indian prices. The ratios used are those of Subramanian Swamy, "Economic Growth in China and India, 1952-1970, A Comparative Appraisal," in *Economic Development and Cultural Change*, *P* 18-19, 49-51 (July 1973). The Swamy figures for M+ were converted to 1957 prices by dividing by .898, the agricultural sector by dividing by 1.088 (the resulting ratios being 1.091 and 1.838). The services sector ratio was obtained by dividing Swamy's services sector estimate in Indian prices for 1957 by the services sector (including transport) figure in Table A.13 (a ratio of 2.17). The figures in Table 1 were then multiplied by these ratios.
[a]The 1933 depreciation share was distributed between the various sectors in exact proportion to their share in net domestic product.

the economy was to function effectively and minimal living standards were to be maintained.

However, to say that industry's share rose while agriculture's fell and services remained unchanged does not take one very far. Hollis B. Chenery and Lance Taylor have carried the analysis a step further by attempting to establish a more precise relationship between these shares and per capita income. To do so, they have had to break the nations of the world into three groups: small primary producers, small industry-oriented countries, and large countries.[30] We shall be concerned here only with the large-country pattern.

The issue is whether the rate of change in the shares of Chinese national product as per capita income rises is typical of large countries undergoing growth, and, if not, why not. The Chenery-Taylor estimates, together with the Chinese data and estimates for a few selected developing nations, are presented in Figures 1, 2, and 3. There are nu-

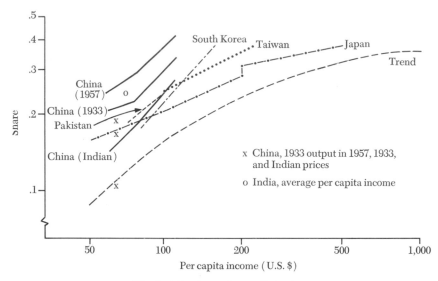

Fig. 1. The share of manufacturing

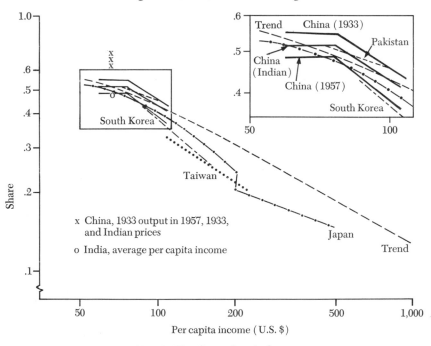

Fig. 2. The share of agriculture

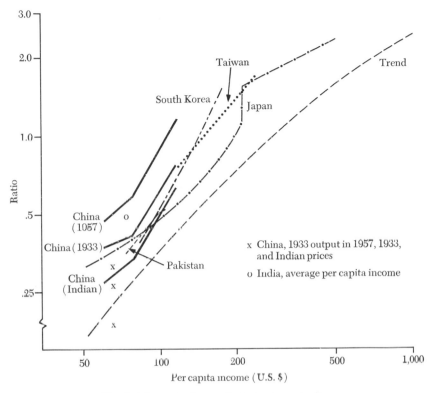

Fig. 3. The ratio of manufacturing to agriculture

SOURCES: The trend lines in Figs. 1 and 2 are those of the "large country" pattern of Hollis B. Chenery and Lance Taylor, "Development Patterns Among Countries and Over Time," *Review of Economics and Statistics*, 50.4:401 (1968). The trend line in Fig. 3 derives from the Chenery-Taylor data in Figs. 1 and 2. The Japanese pattern is Peter Temin's as reported in Chenery-Taylor (except Fig. 3, which derives from the data in Figs. 1 and 2). The Chinese figures are point estimates for the years 1933, 1952, 1957, and 1970 as reported in Table 8, except that the figures in the table have been modified to make them comparable to Chenery-Taylor (i.e., mining has been subtracted from the M+ sector and added to the A sector).

The other estimates in Figs. 1 and 2 (except those of India) are simple regression lines relating per capita income (the independent variable) to the share of M— or A (+ mining) (the dependent variables). Fig. 3 estimates were then derived from the estimates in Figs. 1 and 2. Regressions were run solely for the purpose of converting numerous point estimates to a single line in order to simplify the diagrams. No "theory of growth" is implied by the form of the equation or the independent variables selected, hence no tests of significance were run. There was so little change in Indian per capita income in the 1960's that a simple average, rather than a regression line, was used.

Indian, Pakistani, and Taiwan data for the 1960's: United Nations, *Statistical Yearbook for Asia and the Far East (1970)*, pp. 78, 113, 282. Taiwan data for the 1950's: *China Yearbook, 1960–1961* (Taipei, 1961), p. 311. All South Korean data (1953–70): Bank of Korea, *Economic Statistics Yearbook, 1971*, pp. 14–15.

NOTE: Per capita income figures were converted to U.S. dollar estimates using official exchange rates. The dollar figures are in U.S. prices of 1960.

merous data problems connected with estimates of this sort, not the least of which is the somewhat arbitrary procedures necessarily used when one converts all per capita incomes into U.S. dollars at an official or other exchange rate. We also know very little about the price structure of many of the countries in the sample, and differences in price structures can create a considerable number of differences in product shares, differences that do not necessarily reflect underlying physical dissimilarities. In addition, there are only nine nations in the Chenery-Taylor large-country sample with per capita incomes below U.S. $200, and none of these nine behaved in a "typical" way. That is, none of them had a development pattern conforming to that of the regression line derived from the nine taken together.

From Figures 1–3, it is clear that China was typical of the poorer large developing countries only in the sense that it too performed differently from the "average." The most striking difference is in the share of the Chinese manufacturing sector, which was well above that of the "average" large less-developed economy at comparable levels of per capita income no matter what prices one uses. There is also some indication that the share of manufacturing was increasing more rapidly relative to income as well. But differences in the slopes of the lines in Figure 1 mean less than differences in their levels, mainly because the methods used to estimate the Chinese and "trend" lines were not the same (see the notes to the figures).

China's agricultural (plus mining) share seems to have behaved in a more "typical" manner, but the significance of the difference between China and the trend lines in both Figure 1 and Figure 2 is obscured by the nature of the services sector in less-developed countries. The pertinent data for these countries are not only very poor, but notoriously difficult to interpret. Is, for example, a rapid increase in the bureaucracy really a contribution to national product or only a method of providing welfare payments to otherwise unemployable school graduates? In many less-developed countries, it is clearly the latter. To remove this source of "static," the ratio of the shares of manufacturing to agriculture were estimated in Figure 3, from which it is readily apparent that manufacturing was at a higher level and was also probably increasing its share relative to agriculture more rapidly than in the "average" less-developed country at a comparable level of income. Put differently, agriculture was at a lower level and its growth was probably lagging behind manufacturing to a greater degree than in the "average" less-developed country.

The more rapid rate of increase in industry's share, if in fact it is real and not a product of the method of estimation, could simply reflect some of the problems inherent in using cross-section data to "predict" change in economic structure over time. Investigations of time-series data for selected European nations has led Alexander Gerschenkron to the generalization that the later a country enters into modern economic growth, the more likely it is that the first stage of its development will be characterized by a spurt in the industrial growth rate.[31] Thus what matters is not so much a country's level of per capita income at the time that modern economic growth is initiated, a condition that has a major influence on the Chenery-Taylor regressions, but at what time the process began relative to other industrializers. An accelerated spurt in the rate of industrial growth, of course, does not necessarily imply an equivalent spurt in the rise in the industrial share; agriculture could experience a similar acceleration, but such a performance would be atypical.

Seen in this light, China becomes a not unusual case of a late developer enjoying some of the "advantages" of backwardness. The great backlog of industrial technology built up over two centuries in the advanced nations has finally begun to be systematically tapped by Chinese firms.

Still, such an explanation taken by itself is not completely satisfying because, as pointed out above, the significant point is not so much that the share of Chinese industry has grown rapidly, but rather that it began from a relatively high base compared with most other nations with low per capita incomes, so that by 1970 the ratio of industry to agriculture had reached a level (over .7) normally achieved only by nations with per capita incomes of over $200.

The usual explanation of China's accelerated industrialization and slowed pace of agricultural development is that it resulted from a policy decision by the Chinese government to emulate the Stalinist pattern of development. Agriculture was to be sacrificed on the altar of machine tools and steel, and consumer dissatisfaction was to be suppressed by keeping society closed off from outside influences and under a tight political rein.

Certainly China did make an effort to learn from Soviet experience, particularly during the first Five-Year Plan (1953–57), but Chinese economic planners never enjoyed the leeway available to Stalinist planners. Most significantly, China was never in a position to sacrifice the agricultural sector the way Stalin did in the 1930's and 1940's. When agriculture was damaged inadvertently in the aftermath of the Great Leap Forward in 1959–61, the resulting decline in farm output contributed in a major way to a severe economy-wide depression.

Since 1961, far from ignoring the farm sector, Chinese planners have poured in investment in the form of domestic resources and foreign exchange, in addition to encouraging the rural sector to continue seeking ways to help itself. Precise figures are not available, but what evidence we have suggests that the state funds supplied to agriculture rose from an average of about one billion yuan a year in the 1952–58 period to nearly five billion a year in the 1960's and early 1970's.* In addition, the state drastically reduced prices on fertilizer, insecticides, and farm machinery, in effect raising the real value of investment by rural brigades out of their own funds. And yet the share of agriculture in domestic product declined more rapidly between 1957 and 1970 than between 1952 and 1957.†

One possible explanation for this comparatively rapid decline in the relative importance of the agricultural sector may be that it was more difficult to raise farm output in China than in many other large developing countries. The reason for this situation was presumably that China was a labor-surplus, land-short economy. That is, increases in investment had to be combined with a labor force whose marginal product was very low and a stock of land that was for all practical purposes fixed. Added to this could be the fact that China's climate was not suitable to the raising of valuable tropical crops such as coffee, cocoa, and rubber.

"Land shortage" perhaps means more in this context than "labor surplus" because the latter term has been applied to any society where there is structural unemployment or underemployment whether urban or rural and whatever the nature of the structural causes of unemployment. Thus rural neglect by the government, property laws that inhibit land development, and numerous other institutions and policies can create a situation where the modern sector can draw on a large pool of unemployed workers without raising wages (that is, it faces a horizontal supply curve of labor). "Land shortage" as used here implies a society where the cultivated acreage cannot be extended except at prohibitive cost. It also implies that existing arable land is intensively utilized in the sense that yields per hectare are approaching the maximum levels readily achievable within the limits of existing technology. The second

---

* According to the *Peking Review*, Dec. 15, 1972, p. 17, state funds for agriculture in the 1953–71 period were 23.4 percent greater than the agricultural tax of the same period. Since the agricultural tax was probably maintained in the 1960's at roughly the same absolute level as during the 1950's (or about three billion yuan a year), the total tax for the 1953–71 period would be about 55–60 billion yuan and state funds for agriculture would be roughly 70 billion yuan. Subtracting state funds supplied to agriculture during 1953–58 (of 6.82 billion yuan) one ends up with an average investment between 1959 and 1971 of nearly five billion yuan a year. If one includes loans to agriculture in 1953–57 as part of state funds (a total net increase of 3.1 billion yuan), the estimate of the level of state funds for the 1959–71 period is reduced, but by only 200 million yuan a year.

† The concept of rate of decline as used here is in relation to a given increase in per capita income, not a specific length of time.

part of this definition lacks precision, but it clearly excludes countries where land is allowed to lie fallow and where water supplies depend on rainfall, and includes countries with extensive multiple cropping and irrigation networks. Under this definition, China, Korea, Japan, and Taiwan are all land-short economies. Most of Latin America, much of Southeast Asia, and all of Africa south of the Sahara, in contrast, clearly are not short of land by either of the two criteria, and India falls somewhere in between (meeting the first criterion but not the second).

That China is land-short according to both criteria can be readily documented. First, although China's cultivated acreage did rise slowly through 1956, it declined in the late 1950's and in the early 1970's had still not achieved the 1956 peak. And second, Chinese rice yields are high by world standards. Japan's heavily subsidized rice fields yielded 5,600 kilograms of paddy per sown hectare in 1970 and Taiwan's fields yielded 4,000 kilograms.[32] Though China's average yield in 1957 was only 2,700 kilograms per hectare, the figure had risen to around 4,000 kilograms by 1971.* Rice yields for 1970 in Thailand, India, and the Philippines, by contrast, were only 1,700 to 1,900 kilograms per sown hectare. China's dry-land crops were less advanced relative to world standards, but these crops had to be raised under conditions of severe water shortage in North China.

Thus China in the 1960's and 1970's was not in a position to achieve easy and rapid breakthroughs in farm technology that would in turn make possible an accelerated agricultural rate of growth. Even with the diversion of large funds to the agricultural sector, the rate of growth achieved was only about 2 percent a year between 1957 and the early 1970's. If the estimate of state funds to agriculture of five billion yuan a year is correct and communes themselves supplied at least five billion yuan,† then the rate of return on farm investment must have been very low. In effect some ten billion yuan in investment per year achieved

---

* The Chinese figure for 1971 is an estimate based on the assumption that roughly two-thirds of the increase in grain output between 1957 and 1971 was accounted for by rice, and that the rice-sown acreage did not change in that period. Equally plausible assumptions could lower the rice-yield figure to 3,500 kilograms or raise it to 4,300 kilograms per hectare.

† The "reserve fund" of the Chinese commune was the main source of investment funds, and it generally appears to have amounted to a bit under 10 percent of the gross income of the commune. In one sample of 11 communes the "reserve fund" was 8 percent of gross income (Shahid Burki, *A Study of Chinese Communes, 1965,* Cambridge, Mass., 1969, p. 20; I eliminated two very large "showpiece" communes from the Burki sample). Eight percent of the gross value of agricultural output in 1970 would be 5.8 billion yuan (less in years when gross value output was lower). Gross income and gross value output, of course, are not identical (the former would

an average yearly increase of 1.2 billion yuan in agricultural value-added between 1957 and 1971. And the ten billion figure presumably does not include many investment projects undertaken by communes without drawing on their reserve funds, though it may include some double counting.

If this analysis is a reasonable description of China's current situation, one would expect a similar pattern in the development of other labor-surplus, land- and resource-short economies. There is some evidence that this may be the case. Japan, Taiwan, Pakistan, India, and South Korea, according to Figure 1, had manufacturing shares well above those of other large nations at comparable levels of income. In Korea and Pakistan, the rates of change in the share of the manufacturing sector also appear to have been above the rate represented by the regression line (but not in Taiwan or Japan). Changes in per capita income in India in the 1960's were too small for any trend to be discerned. Most significant, the ratio of manufacturing to agriculture was in each and every country higher than the "average" of all large less-developed countries at comparable levels of per capita income.

There are, of course, numerous problems connected with comparisons of this sort, beginning with the fact that apart from China and India there has been little comparative study of the price structures of these countries. Nor is there reason to believe that the official exchange rates used to convert their national products into U.S. dollars accurately reflect purchasing power parity. Thus there is an element of faith in the view that the price structures of these nations are similar enough to allow comparisons. Another potential source of bias is the fact that the trend line was derived from data for the years 1950–63, whereas the data for China were for 1933–70 and those of some of the other nations were for 1959–69. Perhaps many nations, including those with a surplus of land and natural resources, are industrializing much faster than the "average"; if so, this would be consistent with the Gerschenkron hypothesis (and would also have the effect of raising the trend line as more recent data were included).

In any case, since the list of large, labor-surplus, land- and resource-short economies is not long,* there is little more evidence of the Kuznets-

include commune industrial income, for example), but they are close enough for the purposes of crude estimates of the type made here.

* One could perhaps add Egypt, but I know nothing about the quality and nature of Egyptian national income estimates and hence cannot make use of them. Java (but not all of Indonesia) would be another possibility, but Indonesian data are of very low quality where they exist at all. Figures 1 and 2, of course, also include Taiwan, whose population was only a little over ten million in the 1960's.

Chenery sort that can be mobilized in support of the hypothesis that China's product shares reflect the country's factor endowment at least as much as they do any deliberate Stalinist industrialization policy. Certainly given the smallness of the sample, there is little point in attempting to identify and estimate by regression analysis the specific contribution of the labor-surplus–land-short factor endowment to the share of agriculture and manufacturing in national product. All that can be said is that the available data are consistent with the hypothesis.

4. Conclusion

Beginning in the early 1950's, China entered into a period of sustained and rapid, if uneven, modern economic growth. By 1971 or 1972, Chinese gross domestic product was triple the level of 1952 (or 1933) and per capita product had doubled.

This economic performance, however, did not rise miraculously out of nothing. The process of modernizing the Chinese economy had begun in the late nineteenth century. Although progress was slow and frequently interrupted, so slow that per capita income barely kept ahead of the increase in population, China in the late 1930's had acquired a modern transportation network and a modern consumer goods industry. In the Japanese-occupied territory of Manchuria there was also the beginning of a modern producer goods industrial sector. Rehabilitation and expansion of these existing enterprises accounted for most of the growth during the years 1950–57. Probably more important, these enterprises and their personnel were the training ground for the workers and managers of the hundreds of new modern plants that began operating in the late 1950's and after.

It was not just the pre-1949 growth of the modern sector, however, that influenced developments in the 1950's and 1960's. Conditions in China's traditional sectors also fundamentally shaped changes in the structure of national expenditure and product. The economic planners of the People's Republic were able to influence these trends, but often to a lesser degree than the Soviet planners of the 1930's. Thus the Chinese departed from Stalinist precedents when in the early 1960's they began to divert large amounts of resources to investment in the agricultural sector. And yet, largely as a result of China's land-poor resource endowment, all this increased investment was able to achieve was a 2 percent annual rate of agricultural growth and a rate of decline of agriculture's share in domestic product that was even more rapid than during the period of rural neglect in the 1950's.

Chinese planners did follow Soviet precedents in the early 1950's when they used the great power of the state and the Communist Party to raise taxes and markedly up the rate of investment. But China's rate of investment and taxes (as a percentage of GDP) continued to rise in the 1960's in spite of a considerable shift in emphasis in government policy toward more adequate provision for individual consumption. This attention to consumption was not sufficient to offset the fact that enterprise managers were under little pressure to raise real or money wages. And this lack of pressure in turn resulted in part from the fact that Chinese managers faced a nearly perfectly elastic supply curve of labor. In many ways, therefore, China even in the early 1970's was at least as much like a number of other less-developed economies, particularly labor-surplus–land-short economies, as it was an Asian version of the Soviet model.

What has given the Chinese economy a distinctive character that separates it from both the Soviet and the less-developed-country pattern does not show up clearly in the aggregate data on which this study has largely been based. It was the redistribution of income and improvements in the marketing of commodities that accounted for the improvement in living standards of a large portion of the population in the 1950's; it was not an increase in the average per capita availability of consumer goods as a whole. Aggregate data measure the economic resources available to a society. They are a crude guide at best to the way that society makes use of its limited resources.

China's National Product, an "Official" Estimate for 1957–1971

(In 1957 prices)

The Chinese blackout on the publication of statistics, never complete, began to lift a bit in 1970 and 1971. As a result it has become possible to reconstruct several of the major components of Chinese national product without extensive resort to heroic assumptions to fill gaps (except in the services sector). What follows is a sector-by-sector discussion of these figures and their plausibility vis-à-vis certain alternative estimates.

1. Agriculture

The agricultural sector is the easiest to deal with because data for that sector are more complete than for other sectors. For example, a nearly complete series of official grain output figures is available (see Table A.1), and grain alone constitutes over half of the gross value output of the sector.

Official estimates of gross value output itself, however, are available only for the 1950's and for 1970 (see Table A.5). Furthermore, when Chou En-lai gave the 1970 figure to Edgar Snow, he made no mention of what year's prices were used in the calculation. In fact, there is good reason to believe that the 1970 figure is in 1957 prices, but the argument for this position depends on an acceptance of a number of the key physical output series, and hence they are dealt with first.

Grain. In addition to the "official" grain series presented in Table A.1, which is constructed from data leaked or published by official sources in the People's Republic of China, mention must also be made of the Burki-Swamy series and the various series of estimates by United States government economists. The reasons for preferring the "official" series over the others are simple and straightforward, though only a summary version of the arguments can be presented here.

The Burki-Swamy series is an "official" series too, in that it was given by Chinese officials to Shahid Burki on his visit to China in 1965. One suspects the series after 1958 includes soybeans and other non-grain crops (or perhaps potatoes at a different conversion ratio) or some similar phenomenon. Whatever the case, the series is not really very consistent with what we know about the period. We know, for example, that 1961 was a year of severe food shortages and sharp cuts in the grain ration, and yet the Burki-Swamy series indicates that 1961 grain output was 2.3 percent above 1957 or down only about 5 percent in per capita terms, hardly enough to warrant the drastic measures that were undertaken in this period. Similarly, by 1964 grain output had risen by 28 percent over 1957 for a rise of over 10 percent in per capita terms, and yet China continued grain imports at the same high level. Finally, if the 1964 Burki-Swamy figure is correct, grain output in 1970 and 1972 was essentially the same as in 1964 and hence per capita output declined by perhaps 17 percent by 1972 (from 1964). Such a decline is not plausible, given what we know of conditions in China in the early 1970's.

Estimates by United States government economists vary considerably in quality. As argued at length elsewhere, estimates published in the mid-

TABLE A.1
Grain Output Series
(Million metric tons)

Year	"Official"	Burki-Swamy	Erisman
1957	185	185.5	—
1958	—ᵃ	215.2	200
1959	—ᵃ	192.7	165
1960	150	161.3	160
1961	162	189.2	160
1962	174	203.8	175–80
1963	183	218.9	175–80
1964	200	237.8	180–85
1965	200	258.0	190–95
1966	220	—	195–200
1967	230	—	210–15
1968	—	—	195–200
1969	—	—	200–205
1970	240	—	215–20
1971	246	—	215–20
1972	240	—	—

Sources:
    Subramanian Swamy and Shahid Javed Burki, "Foodgrains Output in the People's Republic of China, 1958-1965," *The China Quarterly,* Jan.-Mar. 1970, p. 62.
    Alva Lewis Erisman, "China: Agricultural Development, 1949-1971," in *People's Republic of China: An Economic Assessment* (Washington, D.C., 1972), p. 121.
    "Official" figures. 1957, State Statistical Bureau, *Ten Great Years* (Peking, 1960), p. 119; 1960-65, Edwin F. Jones, "The Emerging Pattern of China's Economic Revolution," in *An Economic Profile of Mainland China* (Washington, D.C., 1967), p. 93; 1966, Han Suyin, *China in the Year 2000* (New York, 1967), p. 54; also Hsieh Fu-chih's statement that output in 1967 was 18-21 billion catties (9-10.5 million tons) above 1966, translated in *Survey of the China Mainland Press,* no. 4076 (Dec. 8, 1967); 1967, Anna Louise Strong, "Letter from China," Jan. 15, 1968; 1970-72, published in various official sources, including Chung Li-cheng, "China's General Principle for Developing the National Economy," *Peking Review,* Aug. 17, 1973, p. 6.
    ᵃOfficial figures are generally known to have been greatly inflated.

1960's were implausible because they were not consistent with what was known about Chinese grain consumption or the increase in sector inputs in agriculture.* The most recent estimates by A. Lewis Erisman, in contrast, are within the plausible range, given what is known about consumption (the lack of a significant decline), population growth, and factor inputs (a considerable increase). But Erisman's figures are not very different from the official estimates, and it seems more reasonable, given the considerable degree of consistency between the two sets of figures, to use the estimates of trained

    * The figures referred to here are the once widely quoted estimates of the U.S. Consulate General in Hong Kong. My views on the reliability of these figures were developed at greater length in "Economic Growth in China and the Cultural Revolution," *The China Quarterly,* Apr.–June 1967, pp. 36–39.

TABLE A.2

Cotton Output Series

(Million metric tons)

Year	"Official"	Erisman	Year	"Official"	Erisman
1949	0.44	0.44	1964	1.70	1.40
1952	1.30	1.30	1965	2.10	1.50
1957	1.64	1.64	1966	—	1.60
1958	2.10	1.75	1967	—	1.80
1959	1.80	1.60	1968	—	1.70
1960	1.02	1.28	1969	—	1.58
1961	0.88	.90	1970	—	1.66
1962	1.03	.92	1971	2.22	1.60
1963	1.24	1.03	1972	down	—

Sources:
"Official" figures. 1949, 1952, 1957, 1958, State Statistical Bureau, *Ten Great Years* (Peking, 1960), p. 119; 1959-65, reconstructed from percentage increases, statements that one year was above another but below still another, etc., as cited by Kang Chao, *Agricultural Production in Communist China, 1949-1965* (Madison, Wis., 1970), p. 270; 1971, *Peking Review*, Oct. 13, 1972, p. 12 (reporting a fivefold increase in cotton output between 1949 and 1971); 1972, New China News Agency, Dec. 28, 1972, in *Foreign Broadcasts Information Service*, Dec. 29, 1972, p. B3 (reporting output was below that of 1971).
Alva Lewis Erisman, "China: Agricultural Development, 1949-1971," in *People's Republic of China: An Economic Assessment* (Washington, D.C., 1972), p. 124.
Note: The 1958 figure may reflect some of the upward bias so prevalent in data in 1958-1959.

statistical workers in China rather than those reconstructed from incomplete data from a distance of some 10,000 miles away.

One final qualification to the use of the "official" grain series is in order. There are a few indications that China has changed the method of calculating grain output from biological to barn yield[*] and the conversion ratio for potatoes (which China includes in grain output at a percentage of actual weight) from 4 : 1 to 5 : 1.[1] Both changes, if they have in fact occurred, would mean that comparisons between 1970 and 1975 figures would tend to understate the real rate of growth in grain output. But it is unlikely that these changes in definition would change our results much. The availability of the gross value of farm output figures for 1970 is in effect a check on errors introduced in this way.

Cotton. The "official" cotton series is not as complete as that for grain. Such estimates as can be derived are presented in Table A.2. They differ significantly from those of Erisman, who indicates in effect that cotton output in the early 1970's was the same as in the latter half of the 1950's. Given the fact that population grew substantially between 1955–57 and 1971 and that cotton textile exports were negligible in the first period and large (U.S. $480 million) in the second, domestic per capita cotton consumption in 1971

[*] This change was instituted in the aftermath of the Great Leap Forward as part of the effort to reestablish the reliability of the grain estimates. Whether the practice has continued since then is unknown. On the 1959–60 efforts, see Choh-ming Li, *The Statistical System of Communist China* (Berkeley, Calif., 1962), pp. 93–96, 124.

TABLE A.3
Farm Purchase Prices
(Yuan per catty)

Product and year	Price	Product and year	Price
Grain		Hogs	
1950	.0555	1950	.2685
1952	.070	1957[a]	.38
1957[a]	.081	1971	.4850
1971	.1082		
Cotton		Vegetables	
1952	.849	1957[a]	.03
1957[a]	.78	1965–72	.035–.039

Sources:
  Grain prices. *Peking Review,* Oct. 6, 1972, p. 21. 1952, 1957, obtained by dividing the agricultural tax expressed in yuan by the same tax expressed in "grain equivalents"; as a check, this procedure for 1950 (actually the 1950-51 grain year) leads to a figure of .054, virtually identical to that in the table.
  Cotton prices. 1952, T. C. Liu and K. C. Yeh, *The Economy of the Chinese Mainland* (Princeton, N.J., 1965), p. 381; their figure is an average of reported prices in the major cotton-producing provinces; 1957, estimated from the cotton grain price ratios for the years 1952-55, which indicate that cotton prices were reduced by about 8 percent from their 1952 high.
  Hog prices. 1950, 1971, *Peking Review,* Oct. 6, 1972, p. 21; 1957, obtained by assuming that hog prices rose at the same rate as farm purchase prices between 1957 and 1971 (see Table A.4).
  Vegetable prices. 1965-72, British Broadcasting Company monitoring service (hereafter *BBC*), Jan. 10, 1973, p. A4; 1957, obtained by assuming that vegetable prices rose along with the overall farm purchase price index between 1957 and 1971 (see Table A.4).
  Note: 2,000 catties = 1 metric ton
  [a]Indicates prices used here in gross value product calculations

would have been just over half the 1955–57 level. The "official" figures also imply a per capita consumption decline over the same period, but a very modest one.

The "official" series is clearly more consistent with what we know about cotton cloth output, which was reported to be 8.5 billion meters in 1970[2] (as against 5.05 billion meters in 1957 and 5.7 billion meters in 1956), and increases in the capacity of the cotton textile industry (of 1.4 million spindles in 1965, 18 percent of the 1957 total).[3] There is also a report that rural cloth consumption in 1965 was 3.6 billion meters (compared with the 1956 peak of 3.9 billion meters).[4]

Finally we have statements that 1971 cotton output in the middle and lower Yangtze and Hwai River valleys was 5.8 and 5.77 times respectively the 1949 level; and that 1970 output in the Yellow River basin was 2.37 times the 1949 level.[5] These river valleys cover the major cotton areas except Szechwan and much of Hopei. An unweighted average of these figures (we lack the data necessary to weight them properly) would give us an estimate of 4.65, fairly close to the fivefold figure cited in Table A.2 (the Erisman figure is 3.64 for 1971 over 1949).

Hogs and vegetables. Two of the largest items in the gross value of agricultural output are hogs and vegetables. Because a high proportion of the output of these items is accounted for by the private sector (e.g., farmers' production on private plots), data on their output are neither plentiful nor very reliable. Still, there are a few relevant "official" figures.

TABLE A.4

Price Indexes

Year	Agricultural purchase prices	Industrial products in rural areas	Retail prices (8 large cities)
1950	82.2	91.2	106.7
1951	98.3	100.5	101.0
1952	100.0	100.0	100.0
1953	110.1	98.5	104.9
1954	113.8	100.2	106.9
1955	113.2	101.4	107.9
1956	116.6	100.4	107.8
1957	122.4	101.6	109.1
1958	125.1	101.0	108.2
1963	154.7	114.3	118.4
1971	156.2	114.0(?)	115.6

Sources:

1950-58. Indexes taken or derived from data in State Statistical Bureau, *Ten Great Years* (Peking, 1960), pp. 172-74.

1963. Based on the increase between 1951 and 1963, as reported in *Peking Review*, Nov. 20, 1964, p. 7.

1971. Agricultural purchase price, based on a 90 percent increase between 1950 and 1971, as reported in *ibid.*, Oct. 6, 1972, p. 21; industrial products price, based on the report in the same source that the parity rate between industrial and agricultural products in 1971 was 40 percent below 1950 and the assumption that this meant a decline from 100 to 60 (not 140 to 100); retail prices, based on the fact that the Shanghai price level fell by 2.4 percent between 1965 and 1970 and the assumption that this was typical of the other seven large cities (*Liang-chung she-hui, liang-chung kung-tzu*; Two kinds of societies, two kinds of wages, Shanghai, 1973, p. 16).

The hog situation as of the early 1970's is the clearest. Not only do we have a national percentage increase of 330 percent between 1949 and 1971,[6] but we also have figures for five provinces (seven if 1964-65 data are used).* Although these provinces were undoubtedly the star performers, the figures indicate that there were nearly three hogs per family in many southern provinces in 1971 and nearly two per family in many northern provinces. Since there were more than 100 million farm families in 1971, perhaps 120-30 million, a figure of 248 million head, implying about two hogs per family, is not unreasonably high.

The only 1970's information available on vegetables deals with urban areas alone, an imperfect guide to total vegetable production and consumption, since the urban population was only about 20 percent of the total. Still, the substantial rise in urban vegetable consumption that appears to have occurred was probably matched by increases in rural areas as well.

Other products. There are scattered "official" figures for several lesser items

* To wit: Chekiang (1971), three per family (*Peking Review*, Jan. 3, 1972, p. 23); Kwangtung (1969), 2.89 per family (*ibid.*, Jan. 1, 1971, p. 17); Hopei (1971), 1.5 per family (British Broadcasting Company monitoring service, Jan. 5, 1972, p. A13); Shensi (1971), six million head (*ibid.*, Jan. 12, 1972, p. A7); Yunnan (1965), two per family (*Peking Review*, Oct. 29, 1965, p. 28); Szechwan (1965), 25 million head (*ibid.*, Jan. 7, 1966, p. 26); and Kansu (1971), four million bred (BBC, Jan. 26, 1972, p. A7).

TABLE A.5

The Components of Gross Agricultural Product

(Million yuan)

Gross value of:	1957 (1957 prices)	1970 (1957 prices)	1970 (1970 prices)
(1) Farm output	53,700	72,000	72,000
(2) Grain	29,970	38,880	51,936
(3) Residual (1 – 2)	23,730	33,120	20,064
(4) Cotton	2,560	3,350 ⎤	—
(5) Hogs	4,440	6,380 ⎬	21,480
(6) Vegetables	4,390	7,100 ⎦	—
(7) Residual (3 – 4 – 5 – 6)	12,340	16,290	–1,416

Sources:

Farm output values 1957, State Statistical Bureau, *Ten Great Years* (Peking, 1960), p. 118; 1970 (1957 prices), Edgar Snow, "Talks with Chou En-lai," *The New Republic,* Mar. 27, 1971, p. 21 (this figure is in fact somewhat rough since Chou said that agriculture was "about 25 percent of the total combined output value of industry, transportation, and agriculture"); Chou did not specify the prices used in making the estimate.

Grain values. Derived from data in Tables A.1 and A.3.

Cotton values. Derived from data in Tables A.2 and A.3. Cotton output in 1970 was a bit below 1972; an estimate of 2.15 million tons was used.

Hog values. Obtained by assuming that the average weight of hogs was 100 catties and the hog utilization rate was 80 percent (the rate used by T. C. Liu and K. C. Yeh, *Economy of the Chinese Mainland* [Princeton, N.J., 1965]). To obtain the 1970 figure in 1970 prices, I added the 1970 figures in 1957 prices for cotton, hogs, and vegetables and multiplied by the 1957-71 farm purchase price index.

Vegetable values. These figures are not precise estimates but rather are suggestive of an order of magnitude. They were obtained by assuming that national per capita vegetable output grew between 1955-57 and 1957-70 at the same rate as vegetable sales in Peking.

(e.g., silk, the number of sheep, sugar), but most such products make up only a small percentage of the gross value of agricultural output and hence will not be presented here because of space limitations.

Prices. To convert the above physical output figures into gross value output, price data are required. The prices used in this study are presented in Table A.3. The one remaining issue is to make a case for the view that the 1970 gross value of agricultural output figure was probably calculated in constant 1957 prices or at least prices not very different from those of 1957.

An alternative possibility is that the Chinese used mid-1960's or early-1970's prices. Since there was virtually no change in farm purchase prices between 1963 and 1971 (see Table A.4), the use of the prices of either period would imply that roughly 26 percent of the increase in gross value output between 1957 and 1970 reflected price changes, not changes in real output. This in turn would indicate that real farm output had risen only 6 percent and that real per capita farm output had fallen nearly 20 percent. The 6 percent figure is not consistent with what we know about the performance of individual crops (see Table A.5) and the nearly 20 percent decline would imply that China suffered a major food shortage in 1970, something that clearly did not happen.

Gross value of farm output. On the basis of the above analysis, the estimates for 1957 and 1970 (in 1957 prices) are accepted as reasonably reliable estimates of farm output in those two years. Illustrative figures for intervening

TABLE A.6
Gross Value of Farm Output
(Million 1957 yuan)

Year	Output	Grain	Other
1957	53,700	29,970	23,730
1960	37,420	24,300	13,120[a]
1962	42,400	28,190	14,210[a]
1965	58,960	32,400	26,560[a]
1970	72,000	38,880	33,120
1971	73,800	39,850	33,950

Source: For the method used to derive the figures in columns 2 and 3 (grain, other), see text and Tables A.1, A.2, and A.3.

[a] For purposes of calculation I converted knowledge of the general order of magnitude of hog production into precise figures: 75 million head in 1960, 85 million head in 1962, and 150 million head in 1965.

years were estimated by assuming that the gross value output of products other than grain maintained a constant ratio to that of cotton plus hogs. This assumption clearly makes possible a wide margin of potential error, but it serves to illustrate certain major trends that undoubtedly did occur (e.g., the much sharper drop in non-grain crops as compared to grain in the crisis years of 1959–61). These estimates are presented in Table A.6.

2. Industry

The gross value index. One can reconstruct from official sources a nearly complete series for the gross value of industrial output between 1957 and 1971, but not without difficulty or without resort to certain assumptions that introduce a potential for error. Because there are so many different industrial products and no one product dominates the way grain dominates agriculture, one cannot rigorously check the gross value figure for consistency with output series for individual industries without a great many such series. Unfortunately, Chinese policy on releasing data has not liberalized to the degree necessary to provide all the relevant figures. Thus a measure of uncertainty surrounds the gross value of industrial output series. Have we reconstructed it properly and, even if we have, has the ratio of industrial value-added to gross value output been sufficiently stable to allow one series to act as a proxy for the other?

The reconstructed industrial gross value output series is presented in Table A.7. Reconstruction begins with the figure given by Chou En-lai to Edgar Snow and the published reports that output in 1971 was about 10 percent above 1970 and about 20 times that of 1949, which would make 1949 output (in 1957 prices?) about 12 billion yuan. The figures for the 1960's can then be reconstructed from reports of percentage increases over either 1949 or some adjoining year. If these percentage increases have been correctly reported, then reconstruction error is introduced in the 1960's estimates only by inaccuracies in the reconstructed 1949 figure (in 1957 prices) and from rounding of numbers in the official reports (e.g., reporting a tenfold increase

TABLE A.7
Gross Value of Industrial Output—"Official" Estimates
(Million yuan)

Year and price index	Gross value output	Year and price index	Gross value output
1952 prices		1957 prices	
1949	14,020[a]	1961	–
1952	34,330	1962	100,000
1953	44,700	1963	111,000
1954	51,970	1964	127,650
1955	54,870	1965	141,700
1956	70,360	1966	170,000
1957	78,390	1967	–
1957 prices		1968	144,000
1957	70,400	1969	173,000
1958	117,000[a]	1970	216,000
1959	163,000[a]	1971	237,600
1960	–		

Sources:

1949-58. State Statistical Bureau, *Ten Great Years* (Peking, 1960), p. 87.

1959. Li Fu-chun, "Report on the Draft 1960 National Economic Plan," *Second Session of the Second National People's Congress* (Peking, 1960), p. 2.

1962. Based on the report that 1963 output was 11 percent above 1962. There is also a report that 1962 light industry output was above 1957, and there is little question that 1962 heavy industry output was well above 1957.

1963. Based on the report (*Ta kung pao*, Oct. 9, 1964, cited by R. M. Field, "Chinese Communist Industrial Production," in *An Economic Profile of Mainland China*, p. 273) that handicraft output was four times the 1949 level (3,237 million yuan in 1952 prices) and 10 percent of the combined output of industry and handicrafts (3,237 x 4 ÷ .10 x 12/14.02 = 111,000).

1964. Based on the report (Chou En-lai, *Peking Review*, Jan. 1, 1965, p. 8) that 1964 output was 15 percent above 1963.

1965. Based on the numerous reports that the plan for that year, which called for an 11 percent increase over 1964 (*Peking Review*, Jan. 1, 1966, pp. 19-23), was probably overfulfilled.

1966. Based on the report in a number of sources (e.g., *ibid.*, Jan. 6, 1967, p. 15) that 1966 output was 20 percent above 1965. .

1968. Based on the report (New China News Agency, May 11, 1969, cited by R. M. Field, "Industrial Production in Communist China, 1957-1968," *The China Quarterly*, Apr.-June 1970, p. 47) that 1968 output was twelve times the output of 1949.

1969. Derived from a sample of 17 provinces and major cities whose average (weighted) industrial growth between 1969 and 1970 was 24.8 percent.

1970. Edgar Snow, "Talks with Chou En-lai," *The New Republic*, Mar. 27, 1971, p. 21.

1971. Based on the reports that industrial output for 1971 was 10 percent above 1970 (New China News Agency, Dec. 31, 1971, in *Foreign Broadcasts Information Service*, Jan. 3, 1972, p. B10); and was 20 times that of 1949 (*Peking Review*, Sept. 29, 1972, pp. 11-12).

[a]The 1958-59 data are widely believed to be inflated. The 1949 figure, in contrast, is generally believed to be underestimated.

when the actual increase was perhaps 965 percent). There is also the possibility that the 1970 figure was not calculated in 1957 prices, but it is at least plausible to believe that industry and agriculture were treated alike, and the case for the agriculture figure's being based on 1957 prices has already been made.

Checks for consistency. Two major efforts have been made to construct a Chinese industrial output series from various kinds of disaggregated data, one by R. Michael Field and the other by Thomas Rawski. Subramanian Swamy

TABLE A.8
Industrial Output Indexes

Source	1957	1965	1970
"Official"	100	201	307
Rawski (1)	100	199–227	319–64
(2)	100	182–205	281–318
Field	100	148–61	199–230
Swamy (1)	100	163	240
(2)	100	146	212
Liu-Yeh	100	145	177

Sources:
"Official." Table A.7. These figures were probably in 1957 prices and included handicrafts.
Thomas Rawski, "Chinese Industrial Production, 1952-1971," *Review of Economics and Statistics,* 55.2: 169 (1973). Rawski's original figures (1) were calculated in 1952 prices and excluded handicrafts. In row (2) I have recalculated the figures including handicrafts.
R. M. Field, "Chinese Industrial Development, 1949-1970," in *People's Republic of China: An Economic Assessment* (Washington, D.C., 1972), p. 63.
Subramanian Swamy, "Economic Growth in China and India, 1952-1970, A Comparative Appraisal," in *Economic Development and Cultural Change,* 2: 44, 51 (July 1973). (1) represents gross value of output in Indian prices. (2) represents net value-added in Indian prices.
T. C. Liu and K. C. Yeh, "Chinese and Other Asian Economies: A Quantitative Evaluation," *American Economic Review,* May 1973, p. 218. The index here is based on Liu-Yeh's "most probable" estimate.

has also calculated an industrial index, but in Indian prices, though he largely follows Field in other respects. Finally, mention should be made of the index of T. C. Liu and K. C. Yeh (1973), which is calculated as part of their estimate of Chinese gross domestic product. Summary versions of these indexes are presented in Table A.8.

With the exception of the "official" index, all the indexes have been constructed from disaggregated output series for individual products (Rawski for 1965–70 also uses provincial gross value output data). The principal difference between Rawski's index and those of the others is that he has used only "officially" published or leaked data, whereas they rely in large part on output series independently estimated by various United States government economists. Only Rawski's reconstructed series, therefore, can be used as a check on the internal consistency of Chinese gross value output figures and the disaggregated data that went into the overall figure. It is encouraging to note that the two indexes are virtually identical for both 1965 and 1970. Internal consistency, of course, is not the same thing as reliability.

There remains the question of whose individual product output series, those of China (where they are available) or those of Field et al., are most reliable. Unfortunately no definitive answer to this question is possible, but a case can be made that where Field's data appear to err, or at least differ, they are invariably on the low side. A number of the key figures are presented in Table A.9. In three of four cases, Field's figures are lower than official estimates, and in five of seven cases, his figures are also below those estimated by Soviet economists.

There is not sufficient space in this appendix to deal with each commodity

TABLE A.9

Industrial Product Figures

(Million metric tons except where otherwise noted)

Product	"Official"				USSR 1970	Field 1970
	1957	1970	1971	1972		
Steel	5.35	18	21	23	15–16	18
Chemical fertilizer	.86	14	16.8	19.9	12	7.4
Petroleum	1.46	20+	25+	29+	18–19	18
Cotton cloth (billion meters)	5.05	8.5	–	–	8–8.5	7.5
Electric power (billion kwh)	19.34	–	–	–	73–75	60
Coal	130	–	–	–	250–60	300 –
Cement	6.86	–	–	–	14–16	13

Sources:

"Official." 1957, State Statistical Bureau, *Ten Great Years* (Peking, 1960), pp. 95-96; 1970, Edgar Snow, "Talks with Chou En-lai," *The New Republic,* Mar. 27, 1971, p. 20; 1971, New China News Agency, Dec. 31, 1971, in *Foreign Broadcasts Information Service,* Jan. 3, 1972, p. B10; 1972, New China News Agency, Dec. 26, 1972, and Jan. 3, 1973, in *Foreign Broadcasts Information Service,* Jan. 3, 1973, pp. B6 and B7, respectively.

USSR. *Voprosy ekonomiki,* no. 11, 1971, as reported in *Radio Liberty Dispatch,* Dec. 2, 1971.

R. M. Field, "Chinese Industrial Development, 1949-1970," in *People's Republic of China: An Economic Assessment* (Washington, D.C., 1972), p. 83.

individually. Where the differences between "official" and Field estimates are small, it seems reasonable to prefer the "official" figures, given the problems inherent in making estimates from afar. The chemical fertilizer differential, however, is anything but small. It is true that the "official" figure includes the output of many small plants, and the nutrient value of their output may have been below that of large plants, but large- and medium-scale plants in 1970 accounted for 60 percent of total output.[7] Even if the nutrient value of the small plants was half that of the large plants, chemical fertilizer output (in large-plant output equivalent) would still be 11.2 million tons in 1970, not 7.4 million tons.[8]

Field's figure for cement also appears to be well below Chinese output claims. For 1964, China indicated that cement output had risen to 10.6 million tons[9] (Field's figure for 1964 is 8.7 million tons), and after that year cement output in small plants alone rose from low if not negligible levels to 40 percent of total output in 1971.[10] Even if large-plant output did not rise at all, this percentage would imply a total output of 17–18 million tons in 1971 (against Field's figure of 13 million tons).*

The main source of potential bias in the Field index, however, arises from his estimates of machinery output. Various attempts have been made to estimate Chinese machinery output, and the results are presented in Table A.10. Machinery output is extremely difficult to estimate without access to a great

* If small-plant output was negligible in 1964, then my statement is correct (10.6/.6 = 17.67). If small-plant output in 1964 was not negligible, my estimate would have to be reduced accordingly.

TABLE A.10
Machinery Output Indexes

Source	1957	1965	1966	1970	1971
"Official"	100	600–700	—	—	1,300
Rawski	100	282–529	—	—	—
Cheng	100	236	283	—	—
Field	100	177	204	265	—

Sources:
   Based on the report (*Peking Review*, Nov. 2, 1973, p. 22) that machinery output increased 13 times between 1957 and 1971 and the statement that China's machine-building industry "more than doubled" its gross output between 1965 and 1972. 1972 was undoubtedly above 1971, but by an unknown amount, so the 1965 estimate is very rough.
   Thomas Rawski, unpublished supplement to his essay in this volume, p. 178.
   Chu-yuan Cheng, *The Machine-Building Industry in Communist China* (Chicago, 1971), p. 108.
   R. M. Field, "Chinese Industrial Development, 1949-1970," in *People's Republic of China: An Economic Assessment* (Washington, D.C., 1972), pp. 78, 80, 83.

deal of data. Field used a simple formula whose parameters were estimated by regression. This formula related the index of total machinery output to a slow-growing index of machine tools (method of estimation unknown) and the official crude steel index. It is in fact the performance of steel that largely dominates his machinery index. What Field seems to be implying is that machinery accounted for a significantly smaller proportion of steel output in 1970 than in 1957 (he does not state this, but it follows from the formula and individual output series for machine tools he uses), and that there was little or no increase in the quality of machinery output (including the shift to more sophisticated and expensive machinery as well as improvements in specific types of machinery). The declining share is possible, but stagnant or declining quality is not.[*]

Field's index is also well below those estimated from a considerably greater amount of disaggregated data by Chu-yuan Cheng and Rawski. On the other hand, the "official" percentage increase between 1957 and 1971 is extraordinarily high, and the rough 1965 "official" estimate is probably above even Rawski's high estimate for 1965. It may be, for example, that the "official" estimate is distorted by the inclusion in the late 1960's of rapidly expanding rural repair services and the like at too high a valuation. In any case, the figure is not usable until much more is known about it.

Whatever the correct machinery index turns out to be, the switch from Field's to Cheng's index fills nearly 15 percent of the gap between Field's estimate and the "official" 1965 industrial index. The substitution of Rawski's high figure closes most of the gap in 1965.

Provincial data. Because the greatest source of controversy is likely to be over the rate of increase in industrial output between 1965 and 1970, one final consistency check is in order even though it partially duplicates work

[*] The principal emphasis during much of the 1960's and in the early 1970's was on improved quality and greater variety, not greater quantity. If quality did indeed improve, that would imply an even sharper decline in the share of steel used in machinery.

TABLE A.11

A Comparison of Provincial and National Data on Industrial Output

Industrial output	1965	1966	1967	1968	1969	1970	1971
National index	100	120	–	102	–	152	167
Provincial weighted index	100	–	–	96	129	161	182

Sources: The national figures are based on Table A.7. Sources for the individual provincial percentage increases (for 18 provinces and three cities) are available from the author.

done by Rawski. The rather plentiful data in recent years on percentage changes in provincial industrial output can be checked for consistency against the national figures. The provincial percentages are presented in summary form and compared with national figures in Table A.11.

As is apparent from the table, the national and provincial estimates are broadly consistent with each other. The provincial series, which covers about 60 percent of national industrial output, rises somewhat faster than the national index, but this is not surprising. To the degree that data publication was selective, one would expect it to favor the faster-growing provinces in any given period.

Conclusion. On the basis of the above analysis, the industrial index used in this essay will consist of a range bounded on one side by the "official" gross value of industrial output series. Because of uncertainties about the consistency of coverage of the "official" series and a possible decline in the ratio of value-added to gross-value output, the lower end of the series will rely on Field's data.

3. Services

There are few figures available for estimating the output of China's services sector, and there are major conceptual problems involved in interpreting the information that does exist. An important illustration of the conceptual problem can be seen in Swamy's treatment of this sector in his national product estimates. For the latter half of the 1960's and 1970, Swamy takes China's well-publicized attacks on the bureaucracy during the Cultural Revolution as a basis for projecting a decline in services in this period. But such a conclusion is not warranted. Reduction of the central bureaucracy was in many cases temporary, and in others it simply meant that a given set of services was provided by other, lower-level governmental units or by nongovernmental units.

The services sector in Chinese GDP is made up principally of commerce (42 percent in 1957), transport (23 percent), finance (6 percent), and government (18 percent).[11] The first two and a significant portion of the third are bound to be highly correlated with what is happening in certain sectors of the economy. If those sectors are rising, the relevant services must also rise, or there will soon be a breakdown of the system, complete with underutilized capacity (due to shortages), long queues, and the like. Such problems did arise during the height of the Cultural Revolution in 1967–68, but

TABLE A.12
Estimates of the Services Sector
(Billion yuan)

Category	1957	1962	1965	1970	1971
Grew with economy					
Transportation	6.25	6.34	8.89	12.22	13.03
Trade	11.45	11.61	16.29	22.38	23.87
Finance	1.77	1.79	2.52	3.46	3.69
Grew with population					
Government					
administration	5.03	5.55	5.89	6.51	6.64
Personal services	0.51	0.56	0.60	0.66	0.67
Residential rents	2.55	2.82	2.99	3.30	3.36
Total	27.56	28.67	37.18	48.53	51.26

Sources: Population was assumed to have grown at 2 percent per annum throughout the period. The growth rate for transportation et al. was assumed to be the same as that for industrial value-added plus agricultural value-added in Table A.13.

TABLE A.13
Estimates of Gross Domestic Product
(Billion yuan; 1957 prices)

Year	GDP	Industry value-added	Agriculture value added	Services value-added
1957	95.71	24.22	43.93	27.56
1962	97.75	34.40	34.68	28.67
1965	134.15	48.74	48.23	37.18
1970	181.73	74.30	58.90	48.53
1971	193.36	81.73	60.37	51.26

Sources: Services are from Table A.12. For industry and agriculture it was assumed that the ratio of net value-added to gross value output remained the same as in 1957, and these ratios were applied to the gross value figures in Tables A.6 and A.7. The official ratios used are those of Shigeru Ishikawa, *National Income and Capital Formation in Mainland China* (Tokyo, 1965), pp. 56, 64.

all indications are that they had disappeared by 1970 (or at least the situation had returned to a normal level).

Unlike Swamy, Liu and Yeh, using an input-output table, estimate that the services sector remained nearly constant at 27–28 percent of GDP. No one argues that the share of the services sector rose dramatically. To take such a position one must be prepared to agree that trade, transport, housing, and military personnel grew much faster than the economy as a whole.[12] What evidence we have on these and other basic services in China would generally suggest the opposite (except for rural barefoot doctors and the like, whose services are only a tiny fraction of the whole sector). However, trade has grown faster than GNP during the early stages of development of many other countries. Thus an assumption that trade grew only as fast as industry plus agriculture could be considered conservative.

The procedure used to estimate services here is a very simple one. Certain services were assumed to grow at the same rate as value-added in industry plus agriculture, and others to have matched population growth, at least over the long run. The results of these calculations are presented in Table A.12. They are clearly subject to a wide margin of error. They also cannot be considered "official" figures.

4. Gross Domestic Product

All that remains is to convert the gross value figures for industry and agriculture and add the results to the estimates of the services sector. This is done in Table A.13. The use of a constant ratio of value-added to gross value output for industry may introduce some upward bias in the final estimates, but there is insufficient data to correctly estimate the precise ratio for the 1960's and 1970's.

APPENDIX B

An Estimate of China's Rate of Capital Formation in 1970

There is no completely reliable basis for estimating the Chinese rate of investment in 1970. Even for the years for which data are relatively plentiful, there are major conceptual problems, particularly if one is attempting to estimate the rate of investment in 1933 as contrasted to current prices. All that is attempted here is to reach some notion of the effect of the rapid rate of growth of industrial producer goods (plus mining and utilities) on the rate of investment.

The principal assumption underlying the analysis in this appendix is that domestically manufactured producer goods were mainly used for investment purposes and that their growth was reasonably closely correlated with that of other investment goods and hence with the rate of investment as a whole. Actually both of these assumptions are too strong. Many items classified as producer goods were in fact military equipment and hence a part of consumption, and there are many indications that the share of this military equipment in the total rose sharply after the Soviet break in 1960, which cut China off from its principal source of military supplies. There is also hard evidence that the share of imports of producer and related goods in investment declined slightly in the 1960's and early 1970's. For both of these reasons, the rise in the rate of investment can accordingly be assumed to have fallen short of the increase in domestically manufactured producer goods.

The second step in the analysis is to estimate the growth of the industrial producer goods sector between 1957 and 1970. No precise estimate is possible, but there is little doubt that output of this sector rose much more rapidly than GDP.

In the 1952–57 period there was an almost perfect correlation between the growth of producer goods industry and steel output,[*] but it does not automatically follow that there was an equally close correlation in the 1960's. In the 1950's steel itself and machinery (a big steel user) accounted for a high proportion of the industrial development program, but in the 1960's the leading sectors were chemicals, petroleum, nuclear weapons and missiles, and conventional weapons. Nevertheless, steel and machinery growth continued to account for a substantial portion of the development of producer goods industry. Further, there were apparently a number of slow-growing sectors (e.g., coal) that would offset the impact of chemicals and the like on the growth rate. In addition, electricity, which is an input into all industrial processes (and has been increasingly important in rural development as well), may have grown at only a slightly higher rate than steel (11.0 percent per year).[1] Thus it is reasonable to assume that producer goods industry as a whole (including mining) grew at a rate of 9 percent to 10 percent a year, though rates somewhat higher or lower than this are certainly possible.

There are also bits and pieces of evidence that suggest that the share of producer goods in total industrial output rose between 1957 and 1970, and hence that the rate of growth of producer goods must have been higher than

[*] Regressing producer goods industry value-added (y) and crude steel output (x) using 1952–57 data, one arrives at the following parameters: $y = .82 + 1.95x$, with an $R^2 = .99$.

the rate for industry as a whole. The share of producer goods in Shanghai industry, for example, increased from 43 percent in 1957 to 50 percent in 1971.[2] Of all the large projects undertaken by the state during the great burst of activity in 1958–59, "heavy" industry accounted for the great majority. In 1958, for example, "heavy" industry plus transport and communications accounted for 730 of 1,185 "above-norm" projects, and in 1959 the figure was 879 of 1,092 such projects. Light industry meanwhile, accounted for only 92 and 161 projects in 1958 and 1959, respectively.[3] Although the enterprises set up in these years had many difficulties as a result of mismanagement and the Soviet pull-out in 1960, they accounted for most of the industrial growth in the early 1960's.

We also have the statement that the rate of investment in "light" industry in the entire 20-year period through 1970 was only equal to the profit accumulation of light industry in one year—1970.[4] This statement can be used to deduce that investment in "light" industry in the 1960's was perhaps double that of the first Five-Year Plan period (1953–57),* but it also implies that "light" industry profits from 19 of 20 years went elsewhere, i.e., to producer goods and agriculture for the most part.

The amount of investment also rose in agriculture, but not by enough to cut deeply into the share of producer goods industry. State investment in agriculture in each year of the 1960–71 period was several times that of the low levels of the 1950's,[5] but the increase in total state revenue was much greater in absolute (not percentage) terms. Thus, this increased revenue must have been spent on military equipment and construction or investment goods to make more investment goods or, more likely, both. Under such circumstances, it is difficult to see how the rate of investment could have failed to rise.

Finally, we know that personal consumption expenditures have risen only slowly in the 1960's and early 1970's. As indicated elsewhere in this essay, real wages rose by only about 6 percent between 1957 and 1971. Hence urban personal consumption could only have increased substantially if there was a rapid rise in the urban population, and we know this rise has been modest, though no precise figure is available. Rural consumption is made up mainly of personal farm output plus purchases out of income from the sale of agricultural products. Since farm output rose only 34 percent and farm product prices only 28 percent between 1957 and 1970, it follows that rural purchasing power and consumption increased at a rate well below that of GDP. If the two main components of personal consumption accounted for a declining portion of GDP, then the share of other components (investment, the military, etc.) must have risen.

Because of uncertainties surrounding estimates of the level of Chinese military expenditures, any estimate of Chinese investment or capital formation is bound to be subject to a wide margin of error. The figures in Table B.1 are based on plausible assumptions about the rate of growth of producer goods industry, imports of investment goods, and military expenditures. There is

---

* One can estimate the profit rate on "light" industry for the 1950's and apply that rate to an estimate of "light" industry output in 1970. Though crude, the results give one a notion of the order of magnitude of the increase in investment in "light" industry.

TABLE B.1
Estimates of Gross Domestic Capital Formation for 1970

Category	1957	1970(1)	1970(2)
Producer goods industry and mining			
(1) Net value-added (billion 1957 yuan)	14.68	47.77	41.25
(2) As pct. of GDP	15.34%	26.29%	25.29%
Net imports of producer goods			
(3) Billion 1957 yuan	3.90	6.44	—
(4) As pct. of GDP	4.08%	3.54%	3.95%
(5) Military consumption of producer-type goods (as pct. of GDP)	2.00%	6.00%	6.00%
(6) Net available producer goods (2 + 4 − 5) (as pct. of GDP)	17.42%	23.83%	23.24%
Gross domestic capital formation			
(7) As pct. of GDP, 1952 prices	23.5%	32.2%	31.4%
(8) As pct. of GDP, 1957 prices	20.9%	28.6%	27.9%
(9) As pct. of GDP, 1933 prices	17.4%	23.8%	23.2%

Sources:

(1) The 1957 figure was obtained by multiplying the official gross value of producer goods industry figure by .4291, the average of official net to gross value ratio for 1952 and 1955. The 1970 figures were obtained by multiplying the 1957 figure by (1) the rate of growth of 9.5 percent a year (see text); and (2) an index of fuel, industrial materials, and machinery derived from data in R. M. Field, "Chinese Industrial Development, 1949-1970," in *People's Republic of China: An Economic Assessment* (Washington, D.C., 1972), pp. 78, 80. The GDP figures were taken from Table A.13, but were adjusted downward for the 1970 (2) estimates to be consistent with the lower industrial output figure.

(3) Net imports of producer goods (exports-imports) in current U.S. dollar prices were obtained from Alexander Eckstein, *Communist China's Economic Growth and Foreign Trade* (New York, 1966), pp. 106-7, 114-15; and A. H. Usack and R. E. Batsavage, "The International Trade of the People's Republic of China," in *People's Republic of China: An Economic Assessment*, p. 353. The 1970 figure was converted into 1957 prices by dividing by the U.S. wholesale price index (of 117.9). For the year 1955, one has available net trade figures of producer goods in both yuan and current U.S. dollars; dividing one by the other gives an implied exchange rate of 5.792, and that rate was used to convert the 1957 dollar figures into yuan. This exchange rate reflects the high valuation the Chinese price system places on producer goods.

(5) These figures assume a very large increase in military equipment production, from 15 percent of all producer goods in 1957 to 30 percent in 1970, or a nearly sixfold increase in absolute terms.

(7) (9) The 1957 figures are those of K. C. Yeh, "Capital Formation," in Eckstein et al., eds., *Economic Trends in Communist China* (Chicago, 1968), p. 511. The 1970 estimates were derived by assuming that the ratio of net available producer goods (row 6) to gross domestic capital formation (rows 7 and 9) was the same in 1970 as in 1957. Some distortion is caused by the fact that the GDCF figures are in 1952 and 1933 prices while the data in row 6 are in 1957 prices, but this is only one of many sources of potential error in these estimates.

(8) The procedure was the same as described in the preceding paragraph except that the 1957 estimate in 1957 prices is the official figure as given in Nai-ruenn Chen, *Chinese Economic Statistics* (Chicago, 1967), p. 145. The "official" and K. C. Yeh percentages in 1952 prices were virtually identical.

also considerable potential error introduced by assuming a constant ratio between net available producer goods output and the rate of gross domestic capital formation.

What the estimates in Table B.1 do indicate is that a substantial rise in the rate of capital formation was possible even with a very large assumed increase in military expenditure, whether producer goods industry rose at the rate indicated by "official" gross value output figures or a rate consistent with the estimates of R. M. Field.

Kang Chao

The Growth of a Modern Cotton Textile Industry and the Competition with Handicrafts

As IN many countries, the modern consumer goods industry of pre-1949 China grew rapidly in comparison with the producer goods industry. But whereas many of the Chinese producer goods industries involved "new products" in the sense that they had no counterparts in the traditional economy, the modern consumer goods were inevitably in direct competition with handicrafts producing similar items. Such competition has long been a controversial subject to students of China. The majority are inclined to believe that though industrialization benefited the economy over the long run, the transition was painful for certain sectors. The pain seems to have been made more intolerable by the existence in China of foreign capital and colonial power during the transition period.

Given the constraints of space, which do not permit us to embark on a broad-ranging inquiry, and the relatively good data for textile production in both the modern sector and the traditional sector, we here select the cotton textile industry as a case study.

It is imperative at the outset to define what we mean by modern production and by handicrafts. The distinction, not always so easily made in many fields of production, is rather straightforward in our case: by handicraft production I mean production activities with instruments moved by human power,* and by modern or factory production, processes involving the use of mechanical power such as electricity or steam.

Importation of Modern Textile Goods Before Domestic Manufacture

China exported cotton cloth to Europe and America at least as early as 1730,[1] and for some 50 years thereafter remained exclusively an exporter of such goods, selling what was commonly referred to as nankeen in the world market and importing neither yarn nor cloth from any other

* The use of hydraulic power in spinning in the Chinese countryside was extremely rare and can legitimately be ignored.

country. The first attempt to penetrate the Chinese market came in 1786, when the East India Company tried to sell some British cotton cloth to China.[2] Despite heavy losses in this transaction, the company persisted; eight more attempts were made over a period of years, but none was successful. The situation was altered only after 1829, when the East India Company gave up its monopolistic position in the Chinese market and allowed individual British businessmen to apply their more vigorous selling practices.

Statistics of gross exports of Chinese cloth in the years before the Opium War, though admittedly inaccurate, are nevertheless indicative of the general trends. The total export of cotton cloth was drastically reduced from more than one million bolts in 1830 to a trickle of only 31,000 bolts in 1833.[3] There are no statistics on exports of Chinese native cotton cloth from 1834 to 1866, but since the average amount of cotton cloth exported in the 1867–74 period, as reported by the Chinese Maritime Customs, was about the same as in 1833,[4] we may safely assume that exports remained at a low level in the years 1834–67.

The precipitous decline in China's export of cotton cloth coincided with a sharp rise in imports of cotton goods into China. After the Opium War (1840–42), cotton textiles replaced opium as the leading Chinese import. However, imports of cotton cloth soon reached a "saturation point"—and at a level considerably lower than the Lancashire producers had expected. At the same time, the British manufacturers were equally surprised to find machine-spun cotton yarn being absorbed by the Chinese market at a rapidly rising rate. This general trend continued for decades without major interruption, though textile exporters from America, Holland, India, and, somewhat later, Japan came to join the British producers in competing for the Chinese market. The net value of textile imports recorded by the Chinese Maritime Customs increased from 14.6 million Haikwan taels in 1867 to a peak of 246.8 million Haikwan taels in 1920.[5]

Manufacture of Cotton Goods in China, 1890–1936

The beginning of the modern textile industry in China may be dated from 1890, when after long preparation a public-private joint enterprise known as the Shanghai Machine Weaving Bureau was established in order "to prevent benefits from flowing out to foreign countries."* It

---

* The planning for this textile mill was initiated in October 1878; two years later, in 1880, the machinery was ordered, a construction site was selected, and A. D. Danforth, an American textile expert, was hired as chief engineer. But the mill did not begin operating until 1890, and it was completely destroyed by fire three years later, in 1893. See Chuang Chi-fa, "The History of the Shanghai Machine Weaving Bureau in the Ch'ing Dynasty," *The Continental Magazine*, 40.4: 23–27 (Feb. 1970).

started operating with 35,000 spindles and 530 power looms. Two more government-sponsored mills, based on the same *kuan-tu shang-pan* (official supervision, merchant management) principle of organization, were established in the ensuing years in Shanghai and Wuchang.

The Manchu government granted a ten-year monopoly on the manufacture of modern textile goods to the semiofficial Shanghai Bureau. The edict provided that a private citizen could participate in the textile industry only by investing in this mill.[6] Fortunately, the long period of preparation for the Bureau shortened the effective time period of its monopoly, and beginning in 1894 several new mills were built in Shanghai with purely private capital. Unaware of the great demand for yarn, as reflected in the rapid increase in imports, the planners of these mills placed their emphasis on finished cloth. This initial misdirection of effort was tested in the market and quickly found wanting. Consequently, from 1897 to about 1910, new investors in the textile industry concentrated exclusively on spinning.[7]

As is well known, the nominal import duties imposed by the Nanking Treaty (1842) did not provide effective protection for infant Chinese industries. Theoretically, given an equal level of technology, a country with relatively abundant labor would receive a natural protection if it engaged in labor-intensive industries. Textile production is undoubtedly a labor-intensive industry. The crucial question then would be: how fast could the Chinese textile producers attain the technological level of their competitors?

However, there soon came a new complicating factor. The Treaty of Shimonoseki (1895) permitted Japanese businessmen to establish manufacturing concerns inside China, a privilege that became immediately applicable to the nationals of the Western powers by virtue of the "most-favored-nation" clause. Theoretically, one would expect to see two important economic effects resulting from the new treaty. On the one hand, the Chinese producers would completely lose the natural protection just mentioned; whatever advantages they used to enjoy would now be shared by the foreigners who opened up factories in China. On the other hand, the learning process on the part of local producers could be substantially shortened simply because the model for imitation was now right next door.

So far as textile production is concerned, the privilege granted by the Shimonoseki Treaty was first exercised not by Japanese businessmen but by British, Americans, and Germans. Four foreign-owned cotton mills were built in 1896.

The two decades from 1890 to 1910 may be termed a trial period for both the Chinese mills and the foreign adventurers. Altogether 19 Chi-

TABLE 1

Distribution of Cotton Spindles in China, by Ownership, 1913–1936

Ownership	Number of spindles	Percent	Ownership	Number of spindles	Percent
1913			1931		
Chinese	484,192	58.8%	Chinese	2,566,642	54.7%
Japanese	111,936	13.6	Japanese	1,946,840	41.5
Other nationals	227,024	27.6	Other nationals	170,610	3.8
Total	823,152	100.0	*Total*	4,684,092	100.0
1925			1936		
Chinese	1,907,504	55.4	Chinese	2,919,708	51.8
Japanese	1,326,920	38.5	Japanese	2,485,352	44.1
Other nationals	205,320	6.1	Other nationals	230,006	4.1
Total	3,439,744	100.0	*Total*	5,635,066	100.0

Source: Yen Chung-p'ing, *Chung-kuo mien-fang-chih shih-kao* (Draft history of China's cotton textile industry; Peking, 1963), pp. 354-55.

nese mills were erected during this period, but only one (the Ta Sheng Cotton Mill in Nan-t'ung) was able to reinvest for expansion. The other 18 mills all changed hands in one form or another due to business failure.[8] Nevertheless, the industry as a whole managed to go on and even expand, thanks to a reserve army of capitalists who were willing to try their luck in the exciting new field. Or to put it in another way, a high birth rate cancelled out the high death rate.

The second decade of the twentieth century marked the beginning of a new era. A group of vigorous new competitors—the Japanese—now began participating in the domestic production of cotton textiles. At first the Japanese businessmen only bought bankrupt Chinese mills or leased factory facilities from Chinese owners. But after 1911 they began to build their own mills.

The outbreak of the first World War in 1914 gave tremendous impetus to the industry in China. The curtailed production of civilian goods and decreased shipping capacity of the Western powers led to soaring profits for the textile mills in China. Both Chinese and Japanese investors capitalized on this situation, opening new textile plants in the Chinese coastal cities, a spurt that lasted for many years after the war. But as Table 1 shows, though both groups rapidly increased their spindles, the Japanese outpaced their Chinese competitors. The relative position of the Japanese-owned spinning mills rose from 13.6 percent in 1913 to 41.5 percent in 1931; in the same period the Chinese mills barely maintained the same proportion. Since the Japanese mills usually had a lower rate of idle capacity and a higher rate of output per operating spindle than the Chinese mills, the output of the Japanese mills may have equaled or even exceeded that of the Chinese mills after 1925. But the real losers in this race were the nationals of the Western countries: the American and

German mills closed down, leaving two British mills as the only survivors in this group by the 1930's.

Production Indexes and Other Quantitative Indicators

The textile industry was by far the most rapidly growing field in prewar China. On the eve of the Sino-Japanese War (1936), there were 137 modern textile mills with 5.6 million spindles and 58,439 power looms.[9] However, the capacity was not evenly distributed geographically. About 88 percent of the total spindles and 90 percent of the power looms in 1936 were in the seven coastal provinces of Liaoning, Hopei, Shantung, Kiangsu, Chekiang, Fukien, and Kwangtung.[10] Textile production capacity was especially concentrated in three coastal cities, Shanghai, Tsingtao, and Tientsin, which together had 68 percent of China's total cotton spindles and 70 percent of its power looms in 1936.[11]

Unfortunately, there are no accurate output data for the textile industry for the prewar decades. The most extensive set of data was collected, beginning in 1919, by the Chinese Cotton Spinning Mill Owners Association (CCSMA) and published under the title *The Complete List of Cotton Spinning Mills in China*. Though the CCSMA data on capacity are fairly good, the output statistics are seriously defective in a number of ways. For instance, many integrated mills failed to report as part of their cotton yarn output the portion consumed by their weaving departments. Another shortcoming is that since CCSMA was exclusively an organization of spinning mills, it did not collect data on weaving mills that did not engage in spinning.

Many scholars have attempted to adjust the CCSMA output data in order to present a more complete picture of China's modern production of cotton textiles. The best series are those of Richard Kraus for cotton yarn and cloth for 1918–38.[12] Here we adopt Kraus's output estimates and take them back to 1890 by using the indexes of spinning and weaving capacity in place for the years 1890–1918 as "indicators."* The results are presented in Table 2.

In spite of the uneven pace of growth in various periods, the long-run performance of this industry as a whole must be considered quite satisfactory. As a natural result of this rapid development, there was a continuing process of import substitution. Table 3 clearly reveals the decline

---

* Among different series of estimated capacities for that period, Yen's figures are taken as most reliable because he obtained them by tracing the histories of individual mills. However, there might be a slight downward bias in his estimates, since it is possible he missed one or two mills. See Yen Chung-p'ing, *Chung-kuo mien-fang-chih shih-kao* (Draft history of China's cotton textile industry; Peking, 1963), pp. 354–55.

TABLE 2

Factory Production of Cotton Yarn and Cloth, 1890–1936

Period	Cotton yarn		Cotton cloth	
	Average output *(Thousand bales)*	Pct. increase over preceding period	Average output *(Million sq. yds.)*	Pct. increase over preceding period
1890–94	38.7	–	23.9	–
1895–99	188.7	38%	39.1	63%
1900–1904	276.6	47	40.9	4
1905–9	340.9	23	40.9	0
1910–14	439.0	29	63.4	55
1915–19	698.1	59	123.1	94
1920–24	1,293.5	85	249.0	102
1925–29	2,263.2	75	531.8	113
1930–34	2,725.0	20	965.5	81
1935–36	2,786.8	2	1,294.7	34

Sources:
   Cotton yarn. Output data for 1918-36, Richard A. Kraus, "Cotton and Cotton Goods in China, 1918-1936," Ph.D. diss., Harvard University, 1968, Table III.7, p. 72. Outputs for earlier years are interpolated by using the growth rates of spindles in place in China: the number of spindles for 1890-1913, Yen Chung-p'ing, *Chung-kuo mien-fang-chih shih-kao* (Draft history of China's cotton textile industry; Peking, 1963), p. 354; the annual increments of spindles in 1914-18, H. D. Fong, *Chung-kuo chih mien-fang chih-yeh* (China's cotton textile industry; Shanghai, 1934), p. 9.
   Cotton cloth. Output data for 1918-36, Kraus, p. 72. Outputs for earlier years are interpolated by using the growth rates of power looms in place: the number of power looms for 1890-1913, and 1918, Yen Chung-p'ing, pp. 345, 355; for 1914-17, Fong, p. 9.

TABLE 3

Export and Import of Cotton Yarn, 1922–1932
(Thousand bales)

Year	Export	Import	Year	Export	Import
1922	13	406	1928	117	95
1923	30	254	1929	115	78
1924	49	188	1930	110	53
1925	22	216	1931	206	16
1926	64	153	1932	116	32
1927	113	98			

Source: Shanghai Cotton Textile Mills Association, *Chung-kuo mien-fang-chih tung-chi shih-liao* (Statistical records of China's cotton textile industry; Shanghai, 1950), p. 123.

of imported cotton yarn and the accompanying increase in yarn exports. By 1927—that is, even before the readjustment of tariff rates—China exported more than it imported, achieving a self-sufficiency in cotton yarn for the first time in about a century.*

Impact on Handicraft Textiles: The Traditional View Examined

It has been argued for many decades that the importation and domestic production of modern textile goods destroyed the handicraft textile industry in China, or at least pushed it to the brink of collapse. The contention is accepted by virtually all Chinese intellectuals and by most foreign students in China as a self-evident fact. To the Marxists this is an inescapable conclusion since the theory of imperialism insists on just such a pattern of development. Yet, whether imperialists and indigenous capitalists can so easily displace the old is highly questionable. In the case of China, the complexity of the question is compounded by the existence of many conditions peculiar to that country. At any rate, to establish the plausibility of this theory requires some empirical support, something the Chinese Marxists had neither the desire nor the ability to obtain.[13]

What is puzzling is why so many non-Marxian Chinese economists who were trained in scientific survey techniques and conducted, or at least read, careful surveys about Chinese handicraft production in general and handicraft textiles in particular, could present information in their studies ostensibly consistent with the prevailing theory together with data sharply contradictory to it. Presumably, these scholars chose to use the one type of information without making any attempt to interpret the other.

The traditional view was first challenged, so far as I am aware, by Chi-ming Hou in the middle 1960's.[14] Others have since supported his skepticism to one degree or another, notably Ramon Myers, Richard Kraus, and Albert Feuerwerker.[15] But many questions remain unanswered.

There are many empirical studies, of varying degrees of detail, on handicraft textiles in individual localities or provinces. A survey of these reports reveals that no matter what conclusions the investigators reached or intended to convey, all make note of the fact that the area studied had

---

* Two qualifications should be made in this connection. First, the exported yarn was produced mainly by foreign mills in China; the attention of the Chinese mills was still focused on the domestic market. Second, after 1931 an unknown amount of yarn produced by the Japanese mills in China was shipped annually to Japan and then re-exported to Manchuria in order to take advantage of the preferential tariff the Manchurian authorities granted to Japan. This amount should by rights be subtracted from both the import and the export figures.

TABLE 4
Growth of the Handicraft Weaving Industry in Selected Localities

Locality	Boom period(s)	Locality	Boom period(s)
Hopei		Shansi	
Ting hsien	1910–15	All hsien	1923–29
Pao-ti	1910–23		1935–40
Kao-yang	1915–20	P'ing-yao	1916–26
	1926–30	Fukien	
	1934–37	Foochow	1918–23
Shantung		Szechwan	
Wei hsien	1926–33	All hsien	1922–29
Nan-liu	1929–36	Kwangtung	
Ch'i-nan	1929–36	Hsing-ning	1927–33
	1938–42	Kiangsu	
Kwangsi		Changchow	1925–31
Yü-lin	1931–33		1934–35

Sources:
   Ting hsien: Chang Shih-wen, *Ting-hsien nung-ts'un kung-yeh tiao-ch'a* (Survey of rural industry in Ting hsien; Ting hsien, 1936), p. 113.
   Pao-ti: H. D. Fong, *The Growth and Decline of Rural Industrial Enterprise in North China* (Tientsin, 1936), p. 17.
   Kao-yang: Wu Chih, *Hsiang-ts'un chih-pu kung-yeh ti i-ko yen-chiu* (A study of the rural weaving industry; Shanghai, 1936), p. 18; and Wu Chih, "Kao-yang's Weaving Industry Viewed in the Light of the General Development of the Industrial System," *Cheng-chih ching-chi hsüeh-pao*, 3.1: 63.
   Wei hsien: Lung Chiu, "Rural Subsidiary Production in Wei hsien, Shantung," in Ch'ien Chia-chü, *Chung-kuo nung-ts'un ching-chi lun-wen* chi (Collected essays on China's rural economy; Shanghai, 1936), pp. 541-42; and Liu Tsu-kan, *Min-kuo Wei-hsien chih-kao* (Draft local history of Wei hsien), 24: 10.
   Nan-liu: *Mien-yeh yueh-kan*, 1.2: 306 (1937).
   Ch'i-nan: North China General Survey Research Institute, *Ch'i-nan chih-pu-yeh tiao-cha pao-kao-shu* (Report on the survey of China's weaving industry; Peking, 1945), p. 5.
   Yü-lin: Ch'ien Chia-chü et al., eds., *Kuang-hsi-sheng ching-chi kai-k'uang* (Economic conditions in Kwangsi; Kweilin, 1936), pp. 111-12.
   Hsien of Shansi: South Manchurian Railway, *Mantetsu chōsa geppō*, 21.10: 145-46 (Oct. 1941).
   P'ing-yao: *Chung-wai ching-chi chou-k'an*, 185: 27 (Oct. 23, 1926).
   Foochow: *ibid.*, 110: 43-44 (May 2, 1925).
   Hsien of Szechwan: Bank of China, *Chungking Cotton Textile Industry* (Chungking, 1935), p. 7.
   Hsing-ning: *Kuo-chi lao-kung tung-hsun*, 20: 53 (May 1936).
   Changchow: Wu Yung-ming, "The Weaving Industry in Changchow," *Kuo-min ching-chi chien-she*, 2.4: 118 (Apr. 1935).

undergone a period of rapid development in textile production at some point in the recent past. To be more precise, these reports indicate that the handicraft textile industry in each place had actually developed in a cyclical pattern, though the investigators chose to pay attention primarily to the declining phases, not the rising phases.

Table 4 presents a summary of the relevant information collected from various available Chinese studies. It is interesting to note that all the recorded phases of rapid development in handicraft weaving occurred in the period when the importation and domestic production of modern cotton goods were increasing significantly. For some of the studies, annual growth rates may be computed from relevant data (see Table 5). These rates are hardly lower than the growth rate of the modern textile

TABLE 5

Implied Annual Growth Rates of the Handicraft Weaving Industry in Selected Localities

Locality	Boom period(s)	Rate	Indicator
Hopei			
Ting hsien	1903–15	13%	Sales to other areas, 1903–15
	1910–15	15	Sales to other areas, 1910–15
Kao-yang	1915–20	15	Number of ordinary looms, 1915–26
	1926–30	37	Number of Jacquard looms, 1915–29
	1934–37	24	All looms combined, 1912–26
Shantung			
Wei hsien	1926–33	32	Number of looms, 1926–33
	1915–33	31	Number of looms, 1915–33
Nan-liu	1929–36	20	Yarn consumption, 1929–33
Kwangsi			
Yü-lin	1931–33	52	Yarn consumption, 1931–33

Sources: See Table 4.

industry in the same period. The traditional theory cannot maintain its validity unless it can successfully interpret the booms, however temporary, in an alleged process of destruction.

A few studies mention only a declining phase with no reference to past expansion. But judging from the requirements of labor and raw material, one cannot help concluding that there must have been an expansion phase preceding the decline. Take Nan-t'ung in Kiangsu, for example. This relatively old textile center in East China is reported to have suffered a severe setback in the sale and production of native cotton cloth after 1931. Its output fell to 6,109,480 bolts in 1933 with a total yarn consumption of 1,586,053 bundles,[16] or 21,094,500 catties. If produced by traditional methods, this amount of yarn would have required 2,344,000 spinners, a number that greatly exceeds the total population of the area at that time—1,358,461.[17] This suggests that the pre-expansion level of cloth output, i.e., output prior to the use of machine-spun yarn, must have been only a small fraction of the 1933 level and an even smaller fraction of the peak output.

The Theory of Distinct Demand for Handloom Cloth

If the old theory is invalid, we are then confronted with the problem of explaining how and why handicraft weaving in China managed to survive in the late nineteenth century and early twentieth century. One possible explanation has been suggested by Kraus and Feuerwerker. They theorize that Chinese consumers saw handloom cloth and factory cloth as two distinct products that were not interchangeable to any significant extent. Modern factory cloth, they argue, was a brand new item that had little impact on the market for native cloth. In short, they would place the whole weight on the demand factor. Feuerwerker succinctly states: "The performance of the handicraft weaving sector as it was is a remarkable one, and suggests the existence of a strong and partially discrete market, especially in the rural interior of China, for the generally heavier and longer-wearing handicraft products. Domestic mill cloth and imported goods were not perfect substitutes for the handicraft cloth."[18]

Kraus takes an even stronger position on this point.[19] He divides the market for Chinese cloth into eight types of demand or submarkets, five from within and three from the outside, and distinguishes four sources of supply of piece goods used to "meet the demands of these various markets." Finally, he supplies a chart to show what he sees as the channels and commodity flows from which the markets obtained their supplies, and concludes that the "flows in other directions were quite minor."[20]

Actually, the demand theory is not new. Several Western observers in the nineteenth century, puzzling over why the English textile merchants did not find the huge market in China they had dreamed of, reached the same conclusion after interviewing Chinese consumers. As a British customs agent in China put it in 1876: "The native cloth, though coarser, is more durable and warmer than the foreign rival . . . and the demand for the foreign fabric will be restricted to the impecunious, who cannot afford to purchase at the outset more costly but in the long run less expensive native cloth, and to the wealthy who are able and willing to pay highly for a fabric less durable but of more delicate texture."[21]

Ten years later, the British consul in Amoy conveyed the same message to his countrymen: "It is well known already that the many millions of lower-class Chinese toiling and moiling throughout the 18 provinces, and in huge territories beyond them, do not wear foreign-made cloths, but homespun. Ask a Chinaman why this is, and he tells you that the poor wear suits of native cotton, because such clothing lasts three, four, or five times as long as foreign cloth, because it wears less easily, and because it is much warmer in winter. Why is it warmer? Because, he says, the yarn of which the native fabric is made is quite different from the foreign, and warmer by nature."[22] The same argument was still being advanced in 1892.[23]

There is no doubt that the Chinese rural consumers interviewed by these foreign observers expressed their true feeling. However, the reason Chinese native cloth was more durable and warmer is rather simple. It was woven with handspun yarn, which for technical reasons was limited to very low counts. The Chinese native cloth woven with six- to ten-count yarn was "three times heavier per square area" than imported cloth, which was made with yarn of at least 20 count.

By measures other than weight, however, piece goods manufactured by modern mills were much better than the Chinese native products. This is why the textile experts in Lancashire never accepted the demand theory. As early as 1852 British producers collected 40 samples of Chinese native cloth for study, and two years later an even larger variety of material was shipped back to England for the same purpose.[24] The British manufacturers realized that the Chinese cloth was much heavier than theirs, and technically there was no reason why their mills could not have produced low-count yarn and heavy cloth. They simply refused to imitate the Chinese products because they had confidence in the overall superiority of their own products and believed that the Chinese consumers would soon come to appreciate the fact. They thus rejected the demand theory and inclined instead to the view that what had prevented the Chinese market for British textile goods from expanding was not quality at all, but the "price factor." Accordingly, they pushed the British government to pressure the Chinese, politically as well as militarily, into instituting the so-called transit-pass system. This exempted importers from all likin taxes collected by local authorities along inland transportation routes on payment of a fee amounting to half the import duty.

Subsequent events seemed to support the correctness of the British manufacturers' assessment. Total Chinese imports of cotton yarn increased more than fifteenfold in some 20 years, jumping from 70,000 piculs in 1871 to 1,081,000 piculs in 1890.[25] All the imported yarn was used by handweavers, for China had no power looms before 1890. Why should the Chinese handweavers be so eager to buy factory yarn if consumers preferred heavy cloth woven with low-count yarn? Obviously, Chinese consumers realized the superiority of modern textile products, as predicted by the British producers.

But it is equally obvious that the British textile producers were only partly correct in their analysis of the Chinese market. While rejecting a wrong diagnosis they failed to provide an effective prescription; for in spite of the new "transit-pass" system, cotton cloth imports to China made little progress over the same 20-year period, increasing only from 14,439,000 pieces in 1871 to 15,561,000 pieces in 1890.[26] It is important to note in this connection that the import prices of cotton yarn and cotton cloth fell markedly and by almost the same degree in this period—from a base of 100 in 1870–71, to 75.6 and 76.6 respectively, in 1890.[27]

Developments after 1890 further undermine the demand theory. The owners of modern spinning mills built in China after 1890 were no more

TABLE 6

Exports of Chinese Native Cloth, 1867–1930

(Total for period)

Period	Quantity (Piculs)	Value (1,000 haikwan taels)	Period	Quantity (Piculs)	Value (1,000 haikwan taels)
1867–70	5,038	219	1901–5	129,932	6,124
1871–75	3,903	193	1906–10	178,346	8,548
1876–80	9,328	487	1911–15	221,917	11,454
1881–85	12,917	526	1916–20	258,596	15,698
1886–90	28,086	1,037	1921–25	315,516	19,737
1891–95	88,528	3,289	1926–30	201,486	13,494
1896–1900	139,188	5,855			

Source: Yen Chung-p'ing, *Chung-kuo mien-fang-chih shih-kao* (Draft history of China's cotton textile industry; Peking, 1963), p. 83.

interested in manufacturing the six- to ten-count yarn used in the traditional heavy cloth than the British producers when they found that the strongest demand was for 16- to 20-count yarn.* As will be discussed in greater detail later, more and more handweavers turned to imitating factory cloth to compete with the modern mills. In both quality and design their products were almost indistinguishable from factory goods.† By the 1920's and 1930's, little of the native cloth was of the traditional heavy type woven exclusively with handspun yarn, first because the total amount of handspun yarn was drastically reduced, and second because almost all of what was produced was used only as wefts in combination with factory-yarn warps. The greater proportion of the yarn consumed by handlooms in that period came from modern mills.[28] The most striking illustration of this development in handicraft textiles was in Kaoyang, Hopei, where production flourished in the 1920's with the introduction of a new type of cloth that combined rayon and fine cotton yarn of from 32 to 60 count.[29]

In fact, from the time the Chinese handloom weavers first began using machine-spun yarn, their competitive power was significantly increased, not only in domestic markets but also in certain overseas markets. This

* Twenty-count yarn was the most popular product of mills in Shanghai, whereas 16-count was dominant elsewhere. The average count for all mills was 17. See Wang Tzu-chien and Wang Chen-chung, *Ch'i-sheng hua-shang sha-ch'ang tiao-ch'a pao-kao* (Survey of Chinese cotton mills in seven provinces; Shanghai, 1935), pp. 23, 34, 35.

† That is to say, the handwoven cloth of 20-count yarn was nearly comparable to the factory cloth of 20-count yarn in all physical aspects. But of course product differentiation by trade name still existed.

can be seen from the rapid growth of exports of Chinese native cloth, shown in Table 6. Between 1867, the year of least exports (238 piculs), and 1921, the peak year (75,848 piculs), the volume of exports of hand-loom cloth increased 319 times over.[30]

In view of all the above facts, one cannot but feel that the demand theory is not satisfactory either.

A New Interpretation

In the search for a better explanation of the surprising performance of the Chinese handicraft textile industry in the late nineteenth century and the early twentieth, I suggest we shift our attention from demand to supply. The handicraft textile industry survived not because there existed two separate, non-interchangeable demands, but because the handicraft sector and the modern sector were using two non-competing sets of resources. To clarify this statement, we must first make a crucial distinction between enterprises or firms as production units and the family production system.

Whereas production in enterprises depends on the employment of workers under a wage system, family production rests on the labor of family members; all family members share the family earnings regardless of their individual contributions. As is commonly observed, the two systems exist side by side even in a highly industrialized economy like the United States.

Although the results of the two production systems may not differ greatly in a labor-scarce situation, the distinction is critically important in analyzing economic behavior and performance in countries with a large pool of surplus labor. Surplus labor is defined here not as the Marxist would define it, but as a situation where the marginal productivity of labor falls below the cost of subsistence. In such circumstances the wage rate may be depressed to a level as low as, but not below, subsistence cost. Economic analysis tells us that, motivated by profit maximization, the capitalist firm tends to employ workers up to the point where the marginal productivity of workers equals the going wage rate. Under no circumstances would a firm hire a worker who contributes less to production than it costs to keep him alive.

The family production system would operate quite differently under such extreme conditions. Since the family is not based on the wage system and is obliged to accommodate all members, it tends to use all available labor until its marginal productivity drops to zero. In other words, since the family has to support the member even if his contribution to production is below his subsistence cost, it is better to let him work to

earn some small income than to keep him idle with zero income. Therefore, when there is a substantial amount of surplus labor in the economy,
the two systems of production face two quite different labor demand
and supply curves.

Before 1952, practically the entire agricultural sector in China fell into
the category of family production. This was true of tenant households
as well as peasant families. Both farm institutions followed the same principle in using labor; the only distinction between them was that tenant
households did not own, but had to rent, the other production factor—
land. To dispose of their surplus labor during the idle season, most Chinese rural families engaged in various subsidiary industries, sometimes
called sideline production. This was the very foundation of Chinese
handicrafts. Farmers and their family members had to feed themselves
the year around. They were therefore willing to take any small remuner-
ation for work done in the off-season as long as it was the best they could
get. Even one penny was better than none. This is the key to the per-
sistence of Chinese handicrafts. The handicraft industry could meet
head-on competition from the modern sector at almost any price as long
as enterprises in the modern sector had to pay subsistence wages to their
workers.

If an individual subsidiary industry is singled out for examination,
however, we must consider its opportunity cost. A rural household could
choose from any number of sideline productions. One sideline activity
in effect becomes the opportunity cost for engaging in any other. Rural
households thus tended to select the most profitable sideline or sidelines,
and to earn as much as they could. It is for this reason that we have com-
plexities in the responses of the Chinese handicrafts to the rising pressure from modern industries. The introduction of factory production
with modern machines put all lines of handicrafts in "disadvantageous"
positions. But various handicraft lines did not suffer to a uniform degree, and so rural households made adjustments based on new assess-
ments of the relative advantages of various subsidiary industries, moving
into those that had become the least "disadvantageous." As a result of
this adjustment process, some handicrafts declined sharply while others
prospered.

The Fate of Handicraft Spinning

Even before China's contact with the Western powers, handicraft
spinning and weaving were carried on in every part of the country except the northwestern and northeastern frontier provinces. Though
people produced primarily for their own consumption, certain quan-

tities of cotton cloth were transferred annually from surplus to deficit areas. This basic situation was not altered by the presence of modern textile goods. As late as 1935, farm household spinning and weaving activities were engaged in to varying extents in 19 of 22 provinces of China (excluding Jehol and Manchuria).[31] Only Suiyuan, Ningsia, and Tsinghai among those surveyed reported no such production.

Also unchanged was the fact that handicraft textile production served as a major outlet for disposing of surplus labor in the rural sector. This was true even in the centers of handweaving, where production was the most commercialized. A detailed survey of three villages in Ting hsien, Hopei, one such center, disclosed that the less farm land a household possessed the more hours it tended to devote to sideline production.[32] One can say of this correlation, either that a smaller land holding could absorb less labor in farming, hence more labor was left for sideline production, or that a smaller land holding meant a lower income to the family, hence it was forced to seek more nonagricultural earnings. But in fact, these two interpretations are two sides of the same coin.

The finding from Ting hsien is hardly conclusive evidence, however, since the data do not tell us the average number of persons per family in each class of land holding, let alone the average number of persons of working age per family. Fortunately, we have a set of more revealing data from a similar investigation for Nan-t'ung, Kiangsu, another important production center of native cloth.[33] These data, based on interviews with 94 rural households in 1940, give us the total area of farmland (owned and rented land combined), the number of persons of working age, and the amount of native cloth produced in the year. Discarding, for obvious reasons, those households in the sample that did not have any farmland or produce any cotton goods, we can easily compute the amount of available farmland per person of working age in the rest. The interesting result is that very few of the households with more than two mou of land per person of working age engaged in weaving activities; only families below that critical point produced significant amounts of cloth. Furthermore, within this group of families we find a clear inverse relationship between the amount of available land per person of working age and the textile output per person.

Various reports provide other evidence of the surplus nature of the labor used for handicraft textiles. For instance, in both Kao-yang and Nan-t'ung the surveys show strong patterns of seasonal fluctuation in the output of native cloth, with heavy production during the farming off-season.[34] And in Nan-t'ung we find further that weavers devoted only 60 to 180 days in the year to handloom cloth production.[35] Evidently, this was not a full-time occupation for any of the weavers interviewed.

As postulated earlier, under the family production system surplus labor will be employed even after the marginal earnings have fallen below the level of subsistence cost. Spinners earned on the average about two cents a day in Ting hsien, and even less in Shen-tse, another county in Hopei—under one cent for a full working day.[36] Their daily earnings were thus barely above zero. Though weavers made more than spinners, their earnings were also below the subsistence cost in many places. A weaver of Pao-ti, Hopei, for instance, could earn only enough in a day in 1929 to buy one-third of his daily food requirements.[37] By 1930 his earning rate had fallen to about one-fifth of the cost of food.[38]

The importation of factory-made cotton goods in large quantities from abroad and, later on, the manufacture of those goods in the Chinese treaty ports significantly altered the structure of comparative advantage among various fields of handicraft production. For cotton textile production, the availability of machine-spun yarn gave rise to attractive new handicraft industries like knitting and lace-making. Knitting was in fact a totally new industry in China. More important, modern textile goods stimulated the production of handloom cloth. The two principal aids to this development were (1) the availability of machine-spun yarn, which removed bottlenecks created by the low productivity of traditional spinning, and (2) the example of the mill products, which provided important clues for improving handloom production techniques.

Traditional spinning wheels in China were very simple. Most had only one spindle. The spinner held a bundle of cotton in his left hand, feeding out the lint with his fingers as he turned the wheel with the other hand. In some parts of the country three- or four-spindle units were used. Here the spinner had to manipulate multiple lines of cotton lint simultaneously, an operation that obviously required a much higher level of skill than in the one-spindle technique. But either way, handspinning was a slow and laborious process. On the average it took three hours to make enough yarn for one hour's weaving.[39] The spinning stage thus constituted a formidable bottleneck for all handicraft textile production. Rural households rarely had surplus yarn for sale, consuming virtually all the yarn they produced in their own weaving activities.* However, the end product of this integrated process, cotton cloth, was sometimes in surplus and sold on the market.

Qualitatively, handspun yarn had serious defects. At best, spinners

---

* Though cotton yarn was occasionally sold on the market, the market was neither extensive nor well organized compared with the cloth market, and the amount of yarn sold was usually very small.

could produce only 16-count yarn, and the count was usually far lower,[40] so that cloth of handspun yarn was inevitably coarse. Moreover, the yarn was comparatively weak and could seldom be used in warps of any real length.[41] Consequently, bolts of native cloth were short, and the weaver had to prepare warps for weaving each small bolt—a very time-consuming process. This defect became fatal after the iron-gear handloom came into wide use in China because it required warps that could stand greater strain.

Machine-spun yarn was not only cheaper but also free from all these shortcomings. The only attractive feature of the handspun yarn was its weight, which made warmer and more durable cloth than the high-count yarns. But as noted earlier, if the Chinese consumers had insisted on coarse cloth, the modern mills could well have manufactured low-count yarns.

In terms of productivity, the primitive spinning tools in the Chinese countryside and the modern spinning equipment are beyond comparison. Where the single-spindle wheel could at best produce about a half pound of yarn per day (11 working hours),[42] the same amount of labor at a power spindle of the 1930's yielded an average of 22 pounds of 16-count yarn. Hence the labor productivity ratio between the two types of production was at least 44 to one, not counting the time saved in the modern mills in the various preliminary stages.

All these advances combined to create revolutionary changes in the handicraft textile industry in China. First and foremost, with the availability of machine-spun yarn weaving work was no longer tied to spinning. What used to be an integrated process of handicraft production appeared now as two independent subsidiary industries. Consequently, rural households could weigh the benefits and advantages of one over the other in deciding on a sideline activity. It is hardly surprising that many found handloom weaving more appealing than when the choice was between spinning and weaving combined and some other handicraft. The sharp drop in the price of cotton yarn also made weaving an attractive option. In the circumstances, it is not at all puzzling to find that handloom weaving, far from being destroyed as modern textiles made inroads in China, in fact boomed in many places. The above analysis also helps explain why, quite contrary to the previous pattern, many communities that had no significant production of cotton nearby suddenly emerged as centers of handicraft textiles.

The other side of the story, of course, is the precipitous decline in handicraft spinning. To produce one's own yarn now became not only unnecessary but also unprofitable. This is not to suggest, however, that handicraft spinning disappeared altogether in prewar China. If it is true that handspinning became the most inferior way of disposing of rural surplus labor, it is also true that as late as the 1930's, it was still carried on in many parts of the country. Surveys show that yarn was being handspun in more than half the hsien of Hopei in 1929 and in about a fifth of the hsien surveyed in Kwangsi a few years later.[43]

The reason why some spinning activities survived is not difficult to find. For one thing, a single-spindle wheel cost only 60 cents,[44] and almost every peasant could afford one. But more important, those who engaged in handspinning were either very young girls (of around ten years or younger) or very old women—family members whose labor had practically no opportunity cost in the sense that it could hardly ever be employed in any other production activities. Relevant earnings data can prove this point. It was reported as early as 1887 that the average daily earnings of handspinners were already comparatively low: 20 copper coins, or about five cents in the new currency. This was said to be a much lower rate than could be earned in making straw hats or other handicraft industries.[45] With the continuing fall in the price of factory yarn and the continuing rise in the price of raw cotton, the earning margin for handspinners must have been even lower thereafter. According to the Ting hsien study, handspun yarn was worth about 57 cents per catty in 1930 and the cost of a catty of cotton lint about 45 cents,[46] so that the net income to be derived from the spinning of a catty of yarn was only 12 cents. Since it typically took five days to spin a catty of yarn, the worker might thus earn as little as two cents a day. The Ting hsien spinners usually worked at night, when there was nothing else they could profitably do, and had to confine their activities to nights of good moonlight, since they were hardly in a position to pay for lighting oil.[47] Under such conditions, however efficient the modern spinning equipment, as long as factories had to pay some positive wages or capital cost a certain amount of handspinning was bound to continue.

These developments also explain why, when factory yarn came into wide use, the multispindled spinning wheels all but disappeared, leaving the primitive one-spindle wheels in operation. The single-spindle wheel was so simple that a little girl of seven or eight could be taught to operate it, that is, long before she was old enough to learn any other handicraft technique, whereas the multispindled wheel required considerably more skill, so that only older girls could manage them. But the older girls could easily earn more from other handicrafts than from spinning. In short, the least efficient spinning tool was preferable because it was appropriate for the marginal labor that had no opportunity cost.

By the 1920's and 1930's most hand yarn (as we have noted) was interwoven with factory yarn. Cloth of pure hand yarn was rare except deep inland. According to one study, hand yarn accounted for about 40 percent of the yarn consumed by hand weaving in Hopei province in 1929.[48] This certainly represents a sharp decline from the time when all handicraft weaving depended on native yarn. But the general decline may have been even more severe than this, since Hopei was a cotton-growing province, and so may well not be representative of the country as a whole. Yen Chung-p'ing, for example, estimates that some 104,400 tons of cotton were consumed in China's handicraft spinning in 1934–35, i.e., 17 percent of the estimated total consumption of cotton yarn in that period.[49] Using a similar approach, Kraus concludes that the average annual cotton consumption for handicraft spinning dropped from 4.4 million piculs (about 220,000 tons) in 1925–27 to 3.2 million piculs (about 160,000 tons) in 1934–36, and suggests that the average consumption in 1925–27 was at most only half and perhaps only a third of the average consumption in the late nineteenth century.[50] The accuracy of either estimate cannot be determined without a thorough, quantitative reexamination of the whole cotton textile industry in China.

Innovations in the Handicraft Weaving Industry

The handlooms of China varied widely in construction, productivity, and name, but they may be classified into four general categories: the traditional wooden loom, the improved wooden loom, the iron-gear loom, and the Jacquard loom.

1. *Traditional wooden loom.* This was the most primitive type of handloom, a simple affair that cost no more than ten yuan in the 1920's.[51] The weaver threw the shuttle back and forth from one hand to the other, drawing the weft through the warp strands, and raised and lowered the harness by stepping on a foot pedal. The traditional wooden loom had two bad shortcomings. First, its productivity was low, for the weaver had to stop weaving from time to time to pull warps from the frame and to roll the finished cloth. A good average speed was about 30 rounds of the shuttle per minute, but many weavers could not maintain this pace once their hands began to tire. Second, for physical reasons the weaver was constrained to make the cloth only ten to 15 inches wide. Tailoring with cloth so narrow was obviously wasteful—not only of material but of labor as well.

2. *The improved wooden loom.* The first lesson the Chinese learned from the piece goods produced in factories was that the construction of the shuttle had to be improved so the width of cloth could be increased. The result was a new loom, with a lay suspended from the

ceiling so it could be swung easily; a harness hung from the ceiling by cord and springs, which was connected by cords to foot pedals; and pickers along the sides manipulated by cords that ran through a hook above and extended down over the loom in front of the weaver. Sitting on a bench before the loom, the weaver moved the harness up and down with his feet, pulled the lay back and forth with his right hand, and drew the shuttle back and forth by jerking the cord with the other hand. This loom, with its flying shuttle, was able to turn out cloth more than two feet wide. In addition, the number of shuttle rounds per minute was nearly doubled. However, as with the traditional loom, the weaver still had to interrupt his work to pull the warps and roll the cloth. Being made of wood, these looms cost only about ten to 15 yuan and were thus not substantially more expensive than the old ones.[52] We have no way of tracing when this innovation was introduced, but by 1919–20 this type of loom was in wide use.

3. *The iron-gear loom.* This loom represented a considerable advance, incorporating virtually all the basic mechanical principles in the early factory equipment except that it was still moved by human power. The foot pedals controlled all movements, including the pulling of warps and the rolling of cloth (the so-called take-up roller). Consequently, the speed of weaving was further improved—about 120 rounds per minute or four times as fast as the traditional wooden loom. The new loom had a wooden frame, but its many moving parts and gears were made of iron. The first iron-gear loom is said to have been imported from Japan in 1906,[53] but it did not come into wide use until the Chinese modified the foot pedals to accommodate the bound feet of the Chinese women. By the 1920's thousands of iron-gear looms were being both imported and locally built. In Wei hsien, Shantung, alone some 7,000 iron-gear looms were produced annually in the early 1930's.[54] The price of the looms varied considerably from place to place, costing about 40–50 yuan in Nan-t'ung and other parts of Kiangsu, and 60–78 yuan in Shantung and Hopei in the early 1930's.[55]

4. *The Jacquard loom.* The Jacquard was a special loom for weaving patterned cloth. The Chinese had long had various types of handlooms for weaving patterned silk products, but such looms had never been adapted to cotton textiles. Instead, the Chinese cotton weavers copied the French looms when they turned to making patterned cloth. The contribution of Jacquard looms lay not in increased speed but in the greater variety of native cloth that could be made. According to the economist H. D. Fong, this technique was introduced into China in 1906 by a Japanese textile expert, who taught it to the students of a

government-sponsored textile school in Tientsin.[56] The skill was gradually diffused to other parts of the country. The Jacquard looms varied in size, depending on the pattern, and accordingly the price could range anywhere from 40 yuan to more than 100 yuan.[57] As we shall see, the wide use of these looms tremendously enriched the variety and quality of native cloth produced in Kao-yang and was responsible for the "second boom" of handicraft textiles in that area.

The handspinner could not hope to match or even come close to the productivity of the modern mills, with their multispindled equipment. But in weaving, once the iron-gear loom came into wide use and before the modern mills installed fully automatic looms, the speed differential between the traditional and modern sectors was quickly narrowed. When translated into labor productivity, the differential was about four to one.[58] This did not give modern weavers all that much margin of cost advantage over handweavers, when the capital cost, administration cost, and many indirect costs incurred in modern mills are figured in.

Furthermore, the most important consideration is not the absolute advantage but the relative advantage. As the reader will recall, the productivity differential between hand- and machine-spinning was far greater than in weaving—44 to one. To the extent that there existed a sizable amount of surplus labor in rural communities to be disposed of and given the fact that handweaving and handspinning could be separated as fields of production, peasant households would naturally shift from spinning to weaving. In a very real sense the Chinese rural population was simply applying the famous Ricardian theory of comparative cost; when a poor country finds that all its industries are in a disadvantageous position vis-à-vis those in an advanced country, it should concentrate its resources on the items that are the least disadvantageous. Comparative advantages or disadvantages were unmistakably reflected in the annual average earning rates of handspinners and handweavers in Ting hsien: 3.26 yuan against 22.15 yuan.[59]

In addition to closing the productivity gap handicraft weavers improved their position by imitating the factory-produced piece goods, a possibility that was open to them once they could choose their raw materials from a wide range of factory yarn. Centers of handicraft textiles in the 1920's and 1930's turned out shirtings, sheetings, drills, calicos, pongees, muslins, crepes, cotton poplins, cotton imitations of woolen cloth (serges, gabardines, satin drills), and patterned cloth, plus many local inventions that had no standard terms on the market. The most remarkable case is Kao-yang, whose craftsmen produced at least 97 types of cloth in the 1930's, not counting different patterns and designs.[60] Weavers there were interested in only fine yarn, ranging from 32 to 60 count. Their most popular products were the so-called patriotic cloth woven with 42-count yarn and various types of mixtures of sized rayon and fine cotton yarn.

As noted earlier, unlike the old centers of handicraft textiles, the new production points were not in cotton-growing areas. Kao-yang, for example, was so situated that it was frequently flooded in the late summer, and no crop could be sown after the waters subsided.[61] With an unusually short growing season compared with the rest of Hopei, its rural households thus had an extraordinary amount of surplus labor and were constantly compelled to seek a viable line of subsidiary production. The communities of Pao-ti in Hopei and Ping-yao in Shansi were in a similar plight.[62] More curious is the case of Wei hsien in Shantung, which had a popular cash crop in tobacco but still developed as a handicraft weaving center.[63]

Since in the absence of a cotton crop these areas had no intrinsic advantage over other areas, the success of their handloom cloth industries depended on the skill of the local weavers and the quality of their products. For this reason the regional competition among the new centers was acute, accounting for the sharp fluctuation of their output.

There were two relatively old centers of handicraft weaving in North China: Ting hsien in Hopei and Te-p'ing in Shantung. Ting hsien's sales of cloth to other places increased continuously in the early twentieth century, rising from 600,000 bolts in 1892 to an all-time high of four million bolts in 1915.[64] The prime market for its cloth was Chahar, which normally accounted for about 70 percent of the total sales. Te-p'ing had likewise emerged as an important textile center in the latter part of the nineteenth century; it imitated Sung-chiang cloth, which was marketed chiefly in Jehol.[65] After 1917, both Ting hsien and Te-p'ing lost their positions to the new textile center of Pao-ti, in Hopei. The secret of Pao-ti's success was the quick adoption of new handlooms that led to a substantially improved product.[66] But after a number of highly successful years, Pao-ti in turn gave way to Kao-yang. During the years of high demand, Pao-ti weavers had begun to lower the quality of their products,[67] whereas in 1926 households in Kao-yang began vigorously importing new techniques in order to upgrade theirs.

According to Wu Chih, Kao-yang's textile production in fact underwent two boom periods before 1930.[68] The first, in 1915–20, was triggered by the availability of factory yarn and the adoption of iron-gear looms. After a tapering off in 1921–25, there followed a renewed upsurge with the introduction of Jacquard looms and new varieties of cloth. In 1926 producers in Tientsin devised a way to size rayon yarn so that it could be interwoven with cotton wefts on the Jacquard loom. The sheen of the new type of cloth had the appeal of real silk. Within a few months this new technique had been mastered in Kao-yang, and there was a rush to buy Jacquard looms. Indeed, the number of Jacquard looms in Kao-yang almost doubled annually for several years. Finally, the weaving of cotton yarn below 20 count became completely obsolete, and the whole industry in that area turned exclusively to producing quality piece goods.[69] The second boom ended in 1930, when Wei hsien emerged as the leading center of handicraft textiles in North China.

The Effect of Transportation Cost

Many students of the Chinese economy ascribe the survival of handicraft textiles to high transportation costs, arguing that, because of the expense involved, the modern textile goods of the coastal cities could not be profitably distributed in the vast reaches of the Chinese interior. The high transportation cost is expected to play the role of tariff rates in protecting handicraft textiles in the inland provinces. Though there is some truth to this argument, the effect of transportation cost was only secondary.

Transportation cost is undoubtedly a component in the formation of selling price, and the selling price of a commodity manufactured in the modern sector helped determine the earning rate of handicraft workers who produced comparable goods. In handspinning, for instance, the spinner's earnings represented the difference between the local price of cotton lint and the local price of factory yarn of the same quality as his product. Obviously, transportation cost figured in the local price of comparable factory yarn. But as pointed out earlier, the lowering of earning rates in a sideline industry did not necessarily affect production in that field unless there was an accompanying change in the advantages of this industry relative to other handicraft activities.

Contrary to the anticipation of the adherents of the transportation-cost theory, high transportation cost in China did not serve as an effective means of protection for inland handspinners. Factory yarn was available in almost every corner of the country by the 1930's. As we have seen, cotton spinning activities persisted only in those areas that grew cotton—where its comparative advantage as a sideline presumably justified its survival.

As for handweaving, virtually all the centers of this craft in the 1920's and 1930's were close to treaty ports like Shanghai and Tsingtao. Furthermore, two successive surveys in 1934 and 1935 found that 862

persons in a total of 4,094 from 994 households just outside the city
limits of Shanghai engaged in handweaving as a subsidiary activity.[70]
Clearly, in this case the keen competition of modern cotton cloth and the
lack of "protection" by a transportation cost factor failed to wipe out
these activities. Handweavers in the outskirts of Shanghai probably
earned less than those in the interior, as postulated by the transportation-cost theory, but handweaving there was still the least disadvantageous way of disposing of surplus labor. Hence it survived.

The Putting-Out System and Marketing

Our study of the development of handweaving in China during the
early twentieth century would be incomplete if we were to ignore the
paramount role of the cloth merchants—or what is sometimes referred
to as the putting-out system—in that period. Most of the prewar studies
of the handicraft textile industry discuss, or at least touch on, these
merchants and their relations with rural weavers,[71] but only to conclude
that on the whole they did nothing except to exploit the poor weavers
of the countryside. This may be true, but they did much more than that.

Cloth merchants always appeared on the scene as soon as an area
began demonstrating some potential of emerging as a textile center or
producing cloth in excess of local consumption. Their operations varied
from place to place and from period to period, but in general their
activities tended to develop along the following lines. At first, the merchants acted purely as intermediaries who bought surplus stock from
weavers for cash and shipped the goods to outside markets. Then, as
time passed, many entered into contractual relations with weavers, supplying yarn to a worker who undertook to deliver a specific amount of
cloth in a certain amount of time; the weaver was paid, in cash or in
kind, on a piece-rate basis. This was sometimes called the merchant-
employer system. In many places both systems existed side by side, in
part because the merchant selected as his subcontractors only those
weavers who were trustworthy and skilled, in part because many weavers remained free agents by choice.

The most important contribution of the cloth merchants was their
marketing function. Merchandising was plainly the most serious shortcoming of the family production system. As a part-time operator, the
peasant-weaver could afford to give little time to selling his surplus stock
beyond the local market. Some weavers tried to carry their goods to
neighboring towns or cities every so often, but at best these time-consuming trips extended their marketing area by no more than 20 miles.
The cloth merchants, who in general showed remarkable organizing

ability and high mobility, easily solved this problem for rural weavers. For personal or business reasons, or both, the cloth merchant tended to concentrate his selling activities in one or two regions. In spite of, or perhaps because of, this specialization, the cotton products of Hopei and Kiangsu enjoyed a nationwide market, reaching even the remote provinces of the Northwest and Manchuria. It is fair to say that without the cloth merchants none of the handicraft textile centers could have developed on the scale they did.

Apart from his marketing function but closely connected to it, the cloth merchant served also as a quality control agent and a supplier of information about consumer preferences. In the absence of any effective means of standardization, the quality of handicraft cloth could vary enormously. It was the cloth merchant who imposed on peasant-weavers the rules and standards for their work and saw that substandard pieces were rejected before they had a chance to spoil the reputation of the product on the market. In so doing, the merchants automatically conveyed important market information to producers who had no other way of getting it. This function was essential in a dynamic period when handicraft weaving industries were confronted with both regional competition and competition from the modern sector. For instance, cloth merchants in Kao-yang kept their weavers informed about new products just appearing on the market and the changing tastes of consumers, and determined what patterns and designs might attract the greatest demand.

The merchants were also important in the other aspect of the marketing problem, the supply of raw materials. Supply arose as a problem as soon as rural weavers gave up handspun yarn and depended on factory yarn. It was not so much that factory yarn was unavailable but rather that the mills in China, following Western practice, only sold their yarn in large bales. The cloth merchant thus came to play a double role for weavers—serving as both buyer and supplier. He bought cotton yarn in large bales in the big cities and distributed it in small quantities to the rural weavers.

If a weaver had signed a contract with a cloth merchant, he could get yarn without making a cash payment—in effect obtaining working capital in advance. Since factory yarn was much longer than hand yarn, the weaver in such case could take a roll of warps long enough for perhaps ten bolts, thereby sharply reducing the tedious work of preparing warps. Some cloth merchants went even further in their credit arrangements, occasionally providing the money for a potential weaver to install a loom.

In short, cloth merchants in the early twentieth century must be considered important promoters of the handicraft weaving industry. The handsome profits they gained are not necessarily a sign of exploitation, except in the Marxian sense.* Once the market was enlarged through the efforts of cloth merchants, weavers were likely to receive more earnings both per unit of output and in the aggregate. Still, like any good institution, this intermediary system could not avoid having some bad side effects. The merchants were responsible in some degree for the recessions as well as the booms in handicraft textile centers. In part because they were assuming the bulk of the risk in the whole production-distribution process and in part because there were many alternatives open to them, cloth merchants were highly sensitive to business conditions and profit prospects in various localities. Most cloth merchants were also money-changers or grain dealers, or both;[72] they were thus in a position to close up shop without much hardship anytime they felt the profits were too low or the risks too high in the textile market. Furthermore, their high mobility permitted them to shift operations from one site to another with comparative ease. As records have shown, the migration of cloth merchants aggravated the fluctuations in various handicraft textile centers to a considerable extent.

A Close Examination of the Handweaving Industry in the 1930's

Virtually all the empirical studies of China's handicraft textile industry were conducted and published in the late 1920's and early 1930's. Most take note of the signs of decline in that industry and impute it to the impact of the modern sector. But in fact the decline of various handicraft textile centers can be ascribed to many factors.

One important factor was the regional competition mentioned earlier. Although every textile center underwent a period of recession, this did not occur simultaneously everywhere but was simply a matter of one place rising at the expense of another. Ting hsien was undersold by Pao-ti, which was in turn displaced a few years later by Kao-yang as the leading textile center in North China. Kao-yang began to show signs of decline in 1930 when Wei hsien was in a rising phase (1926–33).[73] Such displacements took place in part because weavers in the old centers tended to lower the quality of their products in order to meet the strong demand[74] and in part because new types of looms or varieties of cloth were introduced elsewhere at a faster pace. In the case of Wei hsien, however, two additional factors contributed to the growth of the weav-

---

* That is, anyone who receives income without engaging in physical labor is regarded as exploiting workers.

ing industry. First, in the late 1920's the Japanese mills in Tsingtao set up offices in Wei hsien and began distributing cotton yarn to weaving households directly;[75] hence the weavers there got their materials at a reduced price. Second, weavers in Kao-yang and other places were often hard put for yarn when Japanese goods began to be boycotted after the Mukden Incident (1931), while the Wei hsien weavers continued to receive Japanese yarn at a below-market price.[76]

The synchronization of the declining phase in one textile center and the rising phase in another is not the only evidence of regional competition. Most studies make a point of how rapidly the number of looms in a textile center fell off during a recession period. The writers uniformly focus on changes in the absolute number of looms as a symptom of boom and slack, but entirely ignore another important implication of such changes. Handlooms, even wooden ones, were fairly durable, lasting 20 to 30 years. It is inconceivable that Chinese peasants would destroy their looms when they found it impossible to weave and sell cloth for one reason or another. Therefore, one would expect to see a rising number of idle looms rather than an absolute reduction in the number of looms in place during a general recession of handicraft weaving. How, then, are we to explain the statistics for, say, Pao-ti, where the total number of looms fell from 10,158 in 1928 to 4,825 in 1933, and most striking of all, from about 8,000 to 375 among weavers working under contract to cloth merchants?[77] Natural depreciation alone cannot account for such a drastic attrition rate in a short five years. The inescapable conclusion is that the peasants of Pao-ti must have sold their looms to other people who were not too far away. In other words, we should look for a place or places where handicraft weaving was expanding during this period and taking over the looms that would otherwise have been left idle.

One may wonder why the regional competition among handicraft textile centers should have had a greater impact than the competition coming from the modern sector. The significant fact here is that the rural handweavers, having no marketing ability, depended too heavily on cloth merchants. As noted earlier, the merchants were so mobile and flexible that their exodus could destroy a textile center in a matter of a year or two. Without them, the peasant-weavers had no choice but to cut their output to whatever the local market would bear. This is clearly what happened to Kao-yang after 1929, when the cloth merchants deserted it for the more profitable products of Wei hsien.[78]

The mechanism of regional competition among handicraft weaving centers was so complicated that an initial change might be followed by a reverse trend later. People in a declining textile center would strive to make innovations or to introduce new products in the hope of regaining markets from their rivals. Again, Kao-yang is a good example. It had experienced two booms (1915–20 and 1926–30) when Wu Chih embarked on his study. He visited Kao-yang at its nadir. But before he could publish his report, the handweaving industry there revived, and Kao-yang was into its third boom (1934–37).[79]

Similar to the regional competition in impact but quite different in basic cause were the increasing weaving activities in many inland provinces, notably Shansi, Kansu, Kweichow, and Yunnan. These areas, which had little or no cotton production, were traditionally cloth-deficient and formed a good market for products from the cloth-surplus areas. This general situation began to change in the late 1920's and early 1930's, which brought improved communications with the coast, and above all, the Lunghai Railway. With the constraint on handweaving set by local supplies of cotton and hand spun yarn thus removed, the peasants of the interior began to purchase factory yarn and to produce more and more of the cloth they used. Many producing centers in Hopei and Kiangsu complained about the shrinking inland market as this development toward self-sufficiency proceeded.[80] The National Agricultural Research Bureau made an extensive survey in December 1935 to ascertain the state of the handicraft textile industry in rural China. Of the 952 localities in 19 provinces that supplied the required information, 26 percent reported that their handicraft textile industry was expanding; virtually all of these were in the inland provinces.[81]

As we have postulated, whether a rural household or community chose handweaving as a subsidiary production depended in good part on the potential earning rate of that industry relative to the potential earnings from alternative handicraft activities. Thus, a community tended to shift its labor resources from textile production to other fields when these became more profitable for one reason or another. Instances of such shifts are not difficult to find. To cite two examples, farmers in Pu-yang, a minor center of handicraft weaving in south Hopei, turned from weaving to producing peanut oil in the early 1930's; and more and more women in Wusih and the outskirts of Shanghai shifted from weaving to knitting and lace-making.[82] With an increased demand in both the domestic and foreign markets, knitting, lace-making, and vegetable oil extraction became the star handicraft attractions in that period.

In any case, the early part of the 1930's was undeniably a period of general depression for the handicraft textile industry as a whole. This is evident from the substantial drop in sales of cloth in several centers. The flourishing phase of some areas ended, and the downswing of others accelerated. All decreases can be ascribed in part to the reduced purchasing power of Chinese consumers following the twin disasters of drought in the Northwest in 1930 and flood in the Yangtze river valleys in 1931.[83] But by far the most important factor was the loss of the prime market in Manchuria and Jehol after the Japanese invasion in 1931–32.

Prior to the Mukden Incident, Manchuria and Jehol absorbed about 26 percent of the surplus cloth produced in China proper.[84] Now the Chinese producers suddenly lost about a quarter of their market. The blow was especially severe for some areas. Nan-t'ung, for instance, saw a drastic decline in cloth sales immediately after the Incident. It sold three million bolts to Manchuria in 1930, or about 60 percent of its total cloth sales; the amount dropped to one million bolts in 1932.[85] Similarly, where Pao-ti had sold 3,982,693 bolts in a total of 4,588,693 in Manchuria and Jehol during its peak year, it shipped only 727,010 bolts there in 1933.[86] Faced with this problem, cloth merchants and weavers made every effort to open up new markets elsewhere in the country. Pao-ti successfully promoted its sales to the Northwest by about half a million bolts, while Kao-yang made significant inroads in the cloth market in the Southwest, and eventually generated its third boom, in 1934–37.[87]

To sum up, when we look long and hard at the gloomiest period of the handicraft weaving industry in the 1930's, we find that the competition of modern mills was by no means the sole cause of the distress. Indeed, it may not even have been a critical factor. As our theoretical model postulates, the pressure from modern mills and the importation of piece goods are likely to have more impact on the earning rate of handweavers than on the total output of handloom cloth. Only when a substantial portion of the national market was cut off by the military force of a foreign power were the Chinese rural weavers compelled to curtail their output regardless of how much surplus labor they still possessed.

Estimates of the Total Output of Handloom Cloth

An American expert observed of the textile industry in China in the early 1910's: "The use of handlooms is far more extensive in China than in any other country in the world."[88] The same observation could probably have been made even in the 1930's. However, what the total handloom cloth output was and what proportion of cotton cloth consisted of handloomed cloth are problematical. Following are some of the better known estimates.

1. Ralph Odell puts the output of cotton yarn in 1913 at 200 million pounds and the amount of imported yarn at 358 million pounds. Out of this total supply of 558 million pounds, he estimates that 15 million pounds were consumed by power looms and 543 million pounds by handlooms—or 3 percent and 97 percent, respectively.[89]

2. Freda Utley estimates that per capita annual consumption of cotton cloth in 1925 was 13.5 yards; that imports accounted for 1.5 yards, and domestic production for 12 yards; and that about 70 percent of the domestic production came from handlooms.[90]

3. H. D. Fong calculates that in 1930 handlooms consumed 78.6 percent of the total yarn used in the cotton weaving industry.[91]

4. Ou Pao-san, in his national income study, puts the value-added of handweaving in 1933 at 154 million yuan, or 83.6 percent of the total for the cotton weaving industry.[92]

5. After a more elaborate computation, Yen Chung-p'ing reaches these figures for the 1934–35 period:[93]

	National total	Handlooms only	Handlooms as a percentage
Consumption of cotton yarn (1,000 tons)	579	318	55%
Cotton cloth output			
(millions of running yards)	5,506	3,993	73%
(millions of square yards)	3,800	2,329	61%

The percentage of yarn consumption by handlooms is smaller than the other two percentages because Yen assumes a figure of 13 percent for yarn consumed in knitting.

6. More recently Richard Kraus, using a different method of computation, suggests somewhat higher percentages for handicraft output:[94]

	National total (million sq. yds.)	Handlooms only (million sq. yds.)	Handlooms as a percentage
1933	3,633	2,525	69.7%
1934	4,200	3,023	72.0%
1935	4,658	3,378	72.5%
1936	3,549	2,240	63.1%

7. The statistical Bureau of the Communist government has made its own independent estimates for 1963. It puts the output of cotton cloth from power looms at 1.66 billion meters, the output from handlooms at 1.80 billion meters, and the total output at 3.46 billion meters.[95]

As the reader will appreciate, in this area even the most knowledgeable experts differ. Still, for all practical purposes, the first six sets may be regarded as consistent so far as the proportion of handloom cloth output is concerned. The Communists' estimates stand conspicuously alone: their figure for power loom output in 1936 is about 20 percent higher than Yen's estimate for 1934–35; and their figure for handloom output is less than half of Yen's.* It should be noted that the proportion of handloom output as estimated by Yen is already the lowest of the six non-Communist estimates.

The question of which authority is closest to the mark cannot be answered without a thorough quantitative investigation of the whole textile sector. For now, all we can say is that handicraft production of cotton cloth still played a dominant role as late as 1936.

Handicraft Textiles During the Communist Era

What happened to the handicraft weaving industry in China during wartime can only be speculated. The destruction, partial or complete, of modern spinning mills in the coastal cities and the shortage of raw cotton in that period seriously cut the output of factory yarn. The situation was exacerbated by the disruption of transportation, which had to have curtailed the rural weavers' supply of factory yarn and hence the output of handloom cloth. In the meantime, peasants probably had to resume handspinning in order to fill their own needs so far as they were able. In other words, wartime conditions tended to force the rural sector back toward a subsistence economy. This should be especially true of the unoccupied areas where people were cut off from the supplies of modern goods manufactured in the coastal cities.

The interesting thing is that the new government established in Peking in 1949 made no attempt to restore the production level of handloom cloth. This can be clearly seen from the official statistics compiled in Table 7, which are either stated figures or figures derived from related official data. I have chosen to present them in published form (except for rounding) instead of converting meters into yards or running meters into square meters. As the table indicates, the total output of handloom cloth remained approximately constant throughout the period 1949–56. The average amount for that period was much below the estimated output for 1936, a figure that is itself suspected of being a serious understatement.

The Peking government adopted two policies that had an important

---

* 1 meter = 1.0936 yards. Therefore, 1.66 billion meters = 1.81 billion yards; Yen's estimate for the output by power loom is 1.51 billion yards. The Communists' 1.80 billion meters of handloom cloth output converts to 1.97 billion yards, which is only 49 percent of Yen's estimate of 3.99 billion yards.

TABLE 7

Cotton Cloth Production, 1936–1956

(Million meters)

Year	Wide cloth (1) By power looms	Wide cloth (2) By handlooms (3) – (1)	(3) Total	(4) Narrow cloth	(5) Total handicraft cloth (2) + (4)	(6) Total cotton cloth (3) + (4)
1936	1,656	1,131	2,787	671	1,801	3,458
1949	1,103	786	1,889	262	1,048	2,151
1950	1,692	831	2,522	274	1,104	2,796
1951	2,171	887	3,058	285	1,172	3,343
1952	3,060	769	3,829	329	1,098	4,158
1953	3,693	993	4,685	317	1,309	5,002
1954	4,083	1,147	5,230	311	1,458	5,541
1955	3,477	884	4,361	150	1,034	4,511
1956	4,644	1,160	5,803	75	1,235	5,878

Sources:

Col. (1). With 1949 = 100, output index numbers for power loom production are given in People's Republic of China, Statistical Bureau, Wo-kuo kang-t'ieh tien-li mei-t'an chi-hsieh fang-chih tsao-chih kung-yeh ti chin-hsi (The present and past of our iron and steel, power, coal, machinery, textile, and paper manufacturing industries, Peking, 1958), p. 193. On p. 194, it is said that 79 percent of the 5,878 million meters of cotton cloth produced in 1956 was by power looms; consequently, output of power looms in 1956 is known. This figure is then applied to the index numbers provided on p. 193. For 1936, p. 151 reports that 53 percent of the cotton cloth produced in that year was by handlooms, including the 670.5 million meters of narrow cloth.

Cols. (3) and (4). 1936-52 figures, ibid., p. 155; 1953-56 figures, ibid., p. 166.

effect on the handicraft textile industry. First, it announced at the outset its complete control over all fiber materials including cotton. Henceforward, those materials were distributed to selected users according to predetermined quotas. This policy quickly eliminated the remaining handspinning in China.[96] Second, the government allocated cotton yarn only to weavers who worked in handicraft factories. This policy succeeded, as it was intended to do, in ending handweaving business under the family system. It was only a matter of time before the government, committed to socializing the private sector, took the second step of reorganizing the handicraft factories into cooperatives.[97] This development is apparent in these official data:[98]

Year	Total no. of workers engaged in handicraft textile production	No. of those who were members of cooperatives
1952	917,692	79,486
1953	931,325	98,650
1954	909,692	206,899
1955	862,488	314,192
1956	747,134	691,199

Dividing the handloom cloth output in 1952 as given in Table 7 by the total number of workers in the handweaving industry (917,692), we arrive at a per-worker annual output figure of 1,190 meters. This is higher than the wooden-loom rate but lower than the iron-gear loom rate (2,100 meters),[99] suggesting that wooden looms were still in wide use in 1952. Per-worker output increased to 1,700 meters in 1956, probably because of better equipment.

Some Concluding Remarks

In this essay I have tried to demonstrate that the question of the impact of modern piece goods on the Chinese handicraft textile industry is a complex one. Up to the eve of the Sino-Japanese War (1937–45) there is no unequivocal evidence that a long-run downtrend had set in the handloom weaving industry. If my analysis is close to the reality, some important welfare implications may be deduced. The bulk of power loom cloth probably represented a net increase in total production of cotton textiles. So far as the rural people are concerned, earnings from handicraft production may have been depressed in money terms but not in real terms (e.g., the yardage of cotton cloth consumed per capita), provided the total amount of their surplus labor had not decreased substantially. This would be so because, though the price of the goods produced under the family system could be depressed under

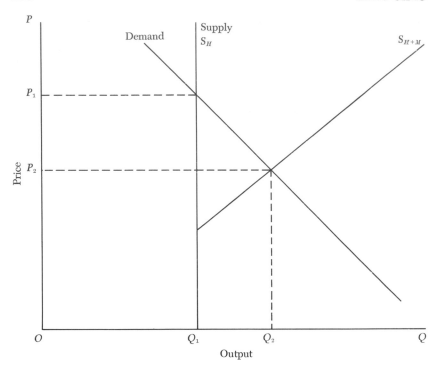

the competition of the modern sector, the total output in the handicraft sector was a function of the total amount of surplus labor.

This process is depicted in the above figure. If we take the handicraft production done by rural households as a whole, supply may be represented by S_H. That is to say, given the amount of surplus labor, supply is independent of the price.* P_1 is the price level prior to industrialization. The shape of S_{H+M} is that of the supply curve in the modern sector in the sense that it is price-elastic and has as its lower limit the supply price. Once the supply of the modern sector is superimposed on S_H, the combined supply curve will be S_{H+M}. The new price level then becomes P_2. Quantitatively, total handicraft production remains at OQ_1 with the output from the modern sector, Q_1Q_2, as a net addition.

In fact, the developments I have described in this essay are not unique to China. Studies of textile production in other countries invariably indicate that handweaving was more persistent than handspinning. For instance, handloom weaving in Japan, India, and Russia continued for several decades after the widespread use of power looms.[100] China is an

---

* Here we follow conventional practice by not including the cost of material in the price. Furthermore, the figure depicts the short-run situation; the line S_H may shift over time.

extreme case only because in the period under study it had extremely large amounts of surplus labor to dispose of.*

However, no matter how long China's handicraft weaving industry survived in the face of a modern textile sector, it was bound to be displaced eventually. Handicraft production as a whole will disappear when any one of the following conditions is met. (1) Surplus labor in the rural sector is eliminated by vigorous industrialization. (2) The income of the rural household rises so high as to make the marginal earning from using its idle labor unattractive. (3) Modern energy sources such as electricity are extended to the rural areas, permitting families to use power tools and machines. When any given handicraft industry, such as weaving, is singled out for consideration, we must add another condition: (4) This handicraft industry tends to disappear if industrialization has altered the comparative advantage of various subsidiary production lines and has made it the most disadvantageous line to pursue.

In the absence of any of these conditions, the strong natural force underlying the family production system would push the handweaving industry to carry on unless a powerful government were to arise that was bent on strangling it by cutting off its supply of raw materials. Such a powerful government did take command in China in 1949. Consequently, the Chinese handweaving industry under the family production system died an unnatural death.

The premature elimination of handweaving in rural households in China is unfortunate. True, the family production system is not an efficient institution. But it is very useful when the economy is confronted with an extreme imbalance in production factors. Modern economics can easily prove that where there is a large amount of surplus labor, the family production system can help maximize employment and output. Under no circumstances will an enterprise hire a worker whose contribution to output falls short of the subsistence cost. But the family production units are not subject to such a limitation; they can apply labor beyond that critical point until its marginal productivity becomes zero. Only then is the output in the labor-surplus country maximized.

---

* The handweaving industry in India could have survived longer if people there did not attach so much disutility to the use of their surplus labor.

Thomas G. Rawski

The Growth of Producer Industries, 1900-1971

THE SUBJECT of this essay is the development in China of manufacturing, mining, and utilities whose output is destined primarily for productive use elsewhere in the economy. These industries produce both intermediate and capital goods, including fuels, power, metals and metal products, machinery, chemicals, and building materials. The producer sector occupies a central position in the process of economic growth, providing the materials and equipment needed to transform the economy from dependence on human and animal power to the use of fossil and mineral fuels, and from hand to machine production. As one Chinese author observes, the producer sector constitutes the core of industrialization, "using modern technology to equip agriculture, industry, the military, and science for achieving the modernization of all these sectors."[1]

The creation of a producer sector capable of responding to changing economic and military needs by appropriately restructuring the stock of physical capital, and ultimately the flow of intermediate and final products, has claimed the attention of Chinese governments since the early 1930's. For this reason, the selection of producer industries as the focus of this essay, though dictated by the structure of available post-1949 output data, is not inappropriate from the viewpoint of present and past Chinese economic policy.

Political changes divide the history of China's producer industries into two periods: the years to 1945, which witnessed development under China's Republican government as well as Japanese-dominated administrations in Manchuria; and the post-1949 period of Communist leadership.

The author gratefully acknowledges comments by the Conference participants, especially John C. H. Fei and K. C. Yeh, and by Scott M. Eddie, Victor C. Falkenheim, and Evelyn S. Rawski, as well as financial support from the Canada Council and the SSRC Committee on the Economy of China.

Since the outbreak of war between China and Japan prevented the implementation of economic plans prepared by Kuomintang economic authorities during the mid-1930's, the prewar development of producer industries in China proper occurred largely within the framework of a market economy. In some manufacturing sectors, the volume and quality of output expanded through a gradual process of backward linkage and import substitution. Progress also occurred in mining and utilities, though here the important role of foreign investment and demand makes it difficult to study developments from the viewpoint of domestic economic transformation adopted in this essay. In other sectors, expansion was limited by technical and financial indivisibilities. We shall examine the engineering and iron-steel industries as examples of these two groups.

In contrast to the market economy of China proper, Manchuria's producer industries operated in an environment of state influence. After decades of concentration on resource-based export industries, Japan sponsored an attempt to create an integrated producer sector during the late 1930's. Initially, Manchuria's producer sector was to be tied to Japan's economy, but by 1938 wartime conditions altered the objective of Manchukuo's Five-Year Plan (1937–41) toward regional economic and military self-sufficiency. Despite increases in productive capacity and output, the Manchukuo Five-Year Plan failed, with production falling short of both targets and capacity, and even beginning to decline before serious war damage was sustained.

The accession of a Communist government in 1949 led to a renewed effort to install an integrated producer sector. China's First Five-Year Plan (FFYP; 1953–57) involved far larger outlays than Manchukuo's and was national in scope, but resembled the earlier program in its emphasis on producer industries and in the central role of imported technology and state finance and control. This investment program showed both the strengths and the weaknesses of the Manchukuo experience, characteristics probably shared by any balanced growth attempt.

The analogy between the industrial economies of Manchukuo and post-1949 China does not end here. As in Manchukuo, industrialization in Communist China soon encountered a period of crisis that left the nascent producer sector isolated from important sources of capital funds and imported machinery. Unlike the Manchukuo producer sector, however, China's postwar industry successfully endured a period of consolidation in which state policies simulated many features of a market economy, providing an artificially created producer sector with some of the strengths typical of industries arising in a market context. Having previously surmounted the shortcomings of the earlier market environment, China's producer sector now seems able to fulfill its intended function of providing flexibility and new technology, as well as capital widening, to all sectors of China's economy.

Producer Industries in China Before 1945

The origins of China's large-scale producer industries lie in the efforts of nineteenth-century regional officials to bolster military capabilities by introducing the manufacture of modern weapons. An early interest in arsenals, shipyards, and training schools broadened to include the promotion of a wider range of industries with potential military importance, such as mining and metallurgy. The tradition of officially sponsored regional industrialization was extended by twentieth-century warlords, notably Yen Hsi-shan, and by the Japanese rulers of Manchuria.

Early official enterprises had checkered careers, often passing under foreign control. Foreign-owned producer industries, including those in Manchuria, typically directed their attention to external markets, and by the 1930's substantial shares of domestic producer output went abroad.[2] Despite growing output and capacity, raw and semifinished products dominated the prewar producer sector. On the eve of World War II, China depended heavily on overseas suppliers of steel, machinery, and other processed goods. The continuing inability of domestic industry to supply the basic intermediate and capital goods needed to expand modern investments has led Chinese and foreign observers to conclude that China failed to industrialize prior to 1949.

Beginning in the late nineteenth century, however, a second group of producer enterprises appeared, largely without government assistance. Modern transport and manufacturing created demands for maintenance, repairs, spare parts, and other ancillary services. Some tasks, such as the repair of railway equipment, were undertaken mainly by large state or foreign organizations. Others, however, became the province of Chinese enterprises that often began as tiny craft shops but gradually evolved into substantial factories capable of manufacture as well as repair.

During the first three decades of the twentieth century these enterprises multiplied and expanded, and began to take on the character of an embryonic engineering sector, particularly in the Shanghai area. The development of this private and indigenous segment of producer industry resulted in a slow but marked process of import substitution. By 1937 Shanghai's engineering industry turned out complete sets of equipment for cotton-spinning and match factories, as well as a variety of engines, pumps, simple machine tools, and other products.[3]

We begin our discussion of China's pre-1949 producer industries by examining this evolutionary growth in engineering. The extent of development and its limitations are contrasted with China's iron and steel industry, in which different circumstances seem to be responsible for the slow pace of advance. Finally, we consider Manchuria's producer industries, and the relative strengths and weaknesses of the market economy of Republican China and Manchurian state-supported industrialization for developing producer industries to support national economic growth and transformation.

Backward linkage and import substitution in engineering to 1945. The development of China's engineering industry arose from a cycle of backward linkage and import substitution associated with new modes of production introduced from abroad. The appearance of steamships, railroads, and telegraphs during the second half of the nineteenth century created immediate demands for parts and repair services. Initially, imported parts and mechanics were employed, but Chinese inevitably became involved as helpers and apprentices. As they became familiar with new machines, the simpler tasks were assigned to them, and later to the Chinese enterprises that grew up to service modern transport and communications. As Chinese experience and capital grew, Chinese mechanics increasingly replaced foreigners. Later, the domestic manufacture of spare parts expanded until, by the 1930's, Chinese enterprises produced railway equipment and even small ships.

The growth of manufacturing, principally of textiles and foodstuffs, and of modern mining after 1895, led to a similar sequence. Imported spinning, milling, mining, and other equipment required repairs and parts that eventually came to be supplied by Chinese firms. By the 1930's domestic producers could supply complete sets of equipment for several consumer industries, and the process of import substitution was gradually extending to include new capital equipment as well as parts.

The unique significance of import substitution in engineering is the transferability of techniques, skills, and equipment used to service one sector of the economy to equip other trades. Whereas the machinery and methods imported to produce cotton yarn, for example, offer little or no benefit to coal mining or grain milling, the industrial history of many countries shows that the equipment and skills needed to service and manufacture spinning machinery readily lend themselves to the repair and manufacture of a broad range of engineering goods. The accumulation of experience in one type of engineering may be expected to accelerate the pace at which new products and techniques are mastered and costs reduced in other branches of this industry.[4]

These considerations lead to the hypothesis that gradual mastery of casting, forging, machining, design, and other engineering operations will push individual firms toward a technological threshold beyond which they can apply their resources of machinery and skill to produce a variety of equipment. A similar threshold may be supposed to exist for the entire sector: following a period in which skills and experience are accumulated, the engineering sector will suddenly develop competence in producing many types of machinery and equipment.[5]

We shall argue that such thresholds were attained by individual firms beginning in the mid-1930's, and by the entire engineering sector after 1949.

The most detailed case study of this pattern of development comes from a history of the Ta-lung Machinery Works established at Shanghai in 1902. The founder, Yen Yü-t'ang, an associate of foreign merchants, recognized the potential profit from ship repairing and used his foreign contacts to solicit business. A partner managed the actual work, which consisted mainly of general steamship repairs. The small capital of 7,500 *liang* came from three partners, and the initial labor force of 11 men was recruited from foreign-owned factories and the Shanghai dockyard.[6]

Ta-lung's origins are typical of many engineering enterprises. Small machine shops were often established by men with experience in foreign firms, and later, with overseas technical training. The Hua-feng Machine Works was founded in 1920 by a former apprentice trained to repair German warships at the Ch'ing-tao Marine Engineering Office.[7] Yi Chih-chung, an entrepreneur in needle- and nail-making, studied at a factory in Japan.[8] Engineering entrepreneurs frequently had studied abroad.[9]

The formation of new enterprises without recourse to organized financial markets is another feature shared by other firms. The absence of technical indivisibilities and scale economies in the repair tasks initially undertaken by engineering firms enabled groups of friends, relatives, or classmates to begin business with their pooled personal savings. A limited survey of company histories shows no instance in which a private engineering firm obtained bank loans in its early years.[10]

Men with factory experience provided a growing pool of skilled labor to private engineering firms. The machine shops attached to railways and mines, which were far larger than small plants like Ta-lung, must have trained large numbers of entrepreneurs and workers for the private sector.* Apprentices trained at Ta-lung, totalling an estimated 10,000 prior to 1949, became workers, managers, and owners of machine shops throughout China.[11] Former employees of steel and textile plants also founded small machinery works.[12]

Ta-lung's growth provides a classic example of Schumpeterian entrepreneurship. Yen Yü-t'ang bought out his partners around 1906, when Ta-lung's work force had risen to about 50 men. When easy entry created competition among shipyards, Yen, facing a probable decline in profits, promptly shifted his attention to repairing machinery for Shanghai's burgeoning textile industry.† The pulley-driven spindles of this period needed frequent repairs, and since breakdowns idled large numbers of workers, mill owners paid well for swift and competent repair work.[13]

Though Yen's foreign contacts again proved useful, it was the skill and experience of Ta-lung's workers, readily transferred from ship to factory repair work, that brought continued success. When an English firm failed to replace a broken steam pipe satisfactorily, Ta-lung completed the job, thereby winning as a customer Naigaiwata (with over a quarter of a million spindles) and other Japanese textile mills as well.[14]

Bolstered by continued high profits, Ta-lung added new buildings, machinery, and workers.‡ After 1911 its business began to include the manufacture as well as the repair of textile machinery.§ Once again, the absence of technical indivisibility and the easy transfer of skills within engineering facilitated the firm's development. But though World War I partially isolated Chinese textile mills from foreign competitors and

* In 1919, 35 railway factories under the transport ministry employed 11,428 workers and staff (Nung-shang pu, *Ti-pa-tz'u nung-shang t'ung-chi piao;* Statistical tables of agriculture and commerce, no. 8; Peking, 1923, pp. 280–83). In 1930 government railways employed 99,754 workers, of whom 73,944 were classified as "mechanical" or "engineering" personnel. On most lines, 20–30 percent of the workers were classified as skilled. ("Statistical Study of Working Conditions of Railway Employees," *Chinese Economic Journal,* 14: 202–8 [1934].)

† Chung-kuo k'o-hsüeh yuan Shang-hai ching-chi yen-chiu so and Shang-hai she-hui k'o-hsüeh yuan ching-chi yen-chiu so, comps., *Ta-lung chi-ch'i-ch'ang ti fa-sheng fa-chan yü kai-tsao* (Birth, development, and reform of the Ta-lung Machinery Works; Shanghai, 1959), pp. 3–6. Shanghai factories housed 98,580 cotton spindles in 1894, 525,488 in 1904, and 625,876 in 1914 (Onoe Etsuzō, *Chūgoku no sangyō ritchi ni kansuru kenkyū;* Studies in the location of Chinese industry; Tokyo, 1971, p. 301).

‡ *Ta-lung,* pp. 8–9, 17. The work force exceeded 100 in 1913 and 300 in 1920.

§ *Ibid.,* p. 7, lists the parts produced. At that time, cotton spinning machinery consisted of over 50 components that could be produced and sold separately. No special materials or production techniques were needed; aside from the spindle itself, operation of the equipment involved neither high speeds nor great pressure. Precision was relatively unimportant, and no special steels were used. (*Ibid.,* pp. 20–21.)

machinery suppliers and inflated the domestic prices of both textile products and machinery,[15] neither Ta-lung nor any other Chinese enterprise attempted to capitalize on the situation by undertaking full-scale manufacture of textile machinery. At this time, the obstacles to domestic manufacture of textile machinery were linked with supply rather than demand.

Growing technical strength enabled Ta-lung to produce textile equipment on an increasing scale during the 1920's. The first breakthrough occurred with the successful trial manufacture of a series of components, including looms, cotton gins, and packing machines.[16] More changes followed on the move to a new plant in 1926. A new management team, headed by Yen Ch'ung-ling, a son who had studied engineering in Germany, divided the work force into shops and work groups, and formed a design department with a staff of 11 engineers and technicians. Improved British loom designs were adapted to Chinese requirements, and a newly hired Japanese engineer introduced advanced casting techniques. As a result, spinning machinery was successfully produced for the first time.[17]

The problem of marketing textile machinery now came to the fore. British products still dominated the trade, thanks to the formidable array of services offered by British suppliers.[18] To avoid a head-on clash, Yen Yü-t'ang created his own sheltered market by purchasing a bankrupt textile plant and re-equipping it with Ta-lung machinery; eventually he formed a group of seven textile plants, all equipped with Ta-lung machinery and managed by sons, former apprentices, or close friends of the Yen family. The large profits of these plants provided excellent advertising for Ta-lung's machinery within Shanghai industrial circles.[19]

The outbreak of war with Japan cut short Ta-lung's campaign to penetrate the domestic textile machinery market. Ta-lung's Communist historians argue that imperialist restrictions on China's trade policy and the irrational preference of both Chinese and foreign managers for imported machinery condemned the Ta-lung plant to a secondary role as supplier exclusively to captive textile firms controlled by the Yen family.[20] Such pessimism seems unwarranted. It was certainly not shared by Yen Ch'ung-ling, who believed that the low cost and high quality of his product would open markets not only in China, but elsewhere in Asia, and accordingly ordered sales brochures printed in English as well as in Chinese.[21]

The status of Ta-lung's factory appears to vindicate Yen's optimism. On the eve of the Sino-Japanese War, Ta-lung occupied a modern plant equipped with over 500 machine tools and operated by an experienced force of about 1,300 men. Trained engineers directed manufacturing operations, and continually introduced innovations in heat treatment, design, and measurement that lowered costs and raised quality.[22] Business decisions rested in the hands of men with a knack for decisive entry into profitable fields and quick recognition of mistakes.* With its strong financial base and technically trained management, Ta-lung compared favorably with some of its leading foreign competitors in the textile machinery industry.†

Whether or not Ta-lung could have carved out a place for itself in the textile machinery market of a peaceful China after 1937, its history testifies to a very real development of private engineering in the preceding decades. What began with a few men tinkering in a small shop had grown into a modern manufacturing enterprise based on the systematic application of technological knowledge to problems of machinery production.

Ta-lung's subsequent history demonstrates the quality of its equipment, and especially of its labor force.[23] When Shanghai fell to Japan in 1937, the best machinery was moved inland and the plant occupied. The remaining staff moved equipment to Shanghai's foreign concession and built a new plant, which turned out 65,000 spindles prior to Japanese occupation in December 1941. The two Ta-lung plants produced munitions for Japan during the Pacific War. After 1949 they successively produced spindles, machine tools, mining machinery, and other items before receiving a long-term assignment to supply the petroleum industry in 1955.

Though Ta-lung specialized in machinery repair and later in textile machine manufacture, it accumulated a stock of expertise that could be transferred to a broad range of engineering operations. This is shown not only by the shifting output mix of the 1950's, but by the wide variety

* Successful ventures included the invasion of the North China market for furnaces previously dominated by German imports; Ta-lung provided comparable furnaces at one-third the German price and sold about 10,000 before withdrawing in the face of political instability (*Ta-lung*, p. 50). Unsuccessful initiatives included several efforts at mass production of agricultural machinery and a short-lived apprenticeship program for women (*ibid.*, pp. 20, 27, 32–33).

† Between 1913 and 1926 the largest textile machinery producer in the United States employed between 2,800 and 6,000 workers in at least four plants. As late as 1912 central managerial control was notably absent in at least one plant, with foremen responsible for hiring and training workers. Only in the 1920's did research and "scientific management" become important managerial concerns (George S. Gibb, *The Saco-Lowell Shops*, Cambridge, Mass., 1950, chaps. 12, 13).

of machines produced before 1937.* By the late 1930's this enterprise had achieved a threshold of technical competence at which it could produce textile machinery meeting international standards of cost and quality and, furthermore, could shift to the production of many other types of machinery with a minimum of dislocation and adjustment.

Though Ta-lung was the leading firm in Shanghai's engineering industry, it no longer stood in virtual isolation as it had 15 years before.[24] Industrial surveys show that hundreds of entrepreneurs had taken advantage of the lack of scale economies to establish machinery plants in Shanghai (Table 1) and elsewhere, characterized by low levels of capitalization and labor productivity.[25] The number of these plants and their average size and output jumped sharply between 1930 and 1933, at least in Shanghai.† Though most of these were unsophisticated repair plants, there were, by 1930, several dozen machine shops in Shanghai that specialized in the manufacture of various types of machine parts.[26]

Further research may reveal gradual import substitution in branches of engineering other than textile machinery. Match-making is one industry that may have shifted toward domestic equipment suppliers during the 1930's. Though productive capacity rose significantly and output apparently reached unprecedented levels, imports of matches plunged from 8.5 million gross to .073 million gross between 1930 and 1933, due to higher tariffs, and imports of match-making machinery declined in 1934–36.[27] The domestic producers responsible for the implied import replacement must have experienced technological transformation similar to that recorded for Ta-lung and suggested for the small number of private firms that competed with it in selling textile machinery.[28]

A few firms do not make an industry, of course, and it is clear that the Ta-lung Machinery Works stood at the forefront of China's machinery producers prior to World War II. Its history, however, shows that many entrepreneurs eagerly followed a course charted by the initial success of leading firms. Just as Yen Yü-t'ang's firm initially occupied a nexus between foreign enterprise and the domestic economy and gained technical strength through association with foreign firms, new companies

* The list includes textile machinery, engines, pumps, rice milling equipment, stoves, machine tools, and agricultural tools.

† Liu Ta-chün, *Shang-hai kung-yeh-hua yen-chiu* (The industrialization of Shanghai; Changsha, 1940), pp. 55ff, reports that the number of standard enterprises (using mechanical power and employing over 30 persons) in metal processing and machinery rose from 82 to 173 betwen 1931 and 1933, with capital, output, and labor for all enterprises in this sector rising by approximately 100, 300, and 60 percent, respectively.

TABLE 1

Interindustry Comparison of Shanghai Industrial Firms, 1928 and 1933

Sector and period	Number of firms	Gross output value (Million yuan)	Capital per firm (Yuan)	Capital per worker (Yuan)	Gross Output value per worker (Yuan)	Workers per firm (Average)
1928						
Machinery[a]						
Largest plants	6		50,000+	677		
Smaller plants	49		5,000–50,000	322		
Electrical machinery[b]						
Largest plants	2		50,000+	923		
Smaller plants	8		5,000–50,000	356		
1933						
Metal industries[c]	972	52.0	15,900	700	2,354	23
Cement	1	2.3	1,638,600	7,300	11,420	220
Cotton yarn and cloth	248	162.3	233,000	790	2,214	296
Flour milling	15	74.2	406,000	2,440	29,669	167
Sugar milling	8	6.5	47,000	1,825	31,410	26
Rice milling	49	10.3	19,444	1,557	17,197	12
Power and water supply	2	3.6	3,625,000	28,769	14,394	126
All firms	3,485	—	54,769	776	—	70

Sources:

1928. Machinery plants, Shang-hai she-hui-chü, *Shang-hai chih kung-yeh* (Shanghai's industry; Shanghai, 1930), pp. 126-31. Electrical machinery plants, *ibid.*, pp. 137-38.

1933. Ōtsuka Reizō, *Shina kōgyō sōkan* (Comprehensive survey of Chinese industry; Tokyo, 1942), 1: 300-310. (Vol. 1 is a translation of Liu Ta-chün, *Chung-kuo kung-yeh tiao-ch'a pao-kao shu* (Report on a survey of Chinese industry; 3 vols, Shanghai, 1937). All plants using mechanical power were included in this compilation.

Note: The average capital per worker for the 55 machinery plants in 1928 was 459 yuan; and the average for the 10 electrical machinery plants was 688 yuan.

[a]Excludes nine plants with incomplete data or values in liang rather than yuan.

[b]Excludes one plant with incomplete data.

[c]Includes forging, smelting, machinery manufacture and repair, electrical machinery and parts, shipbuilding and repair, railway shops, and transportation equipment.

later benefited from the links of their founders with Ta-lung and began their careers as Ta-lung subcontractors.[29] Through this mechanism, the domestic economy created successive generations of engineering concerns.

There seems little reason to doubt that this evolutionary growth, similar in nature to the growth of engineering in nineteenth- and early-twentieth-century Europe and America, could have continued to gather momentum in a China free of foreign and civil war and political revolution. Indeed, the spurt in machinery output from existing enterprises unexpectedly achieved during 1952–57 may largely reflect expansion potential left over from the prewar years when industry was pent up by political instability and economic depression.

Capital shortage and development in ferrous metallurgy to 1949. If China's engineering sector had achieved a foundation for future expansion and technical transformation prior to 1949, no such favorable conclusion can be suggested for ferrous metallurgy. With the partial exception of Japanese installations at Anshan and Pen-ch'i, the history of China's iron and steel industry between 1900 and 1945, summarized in Table 2, is a record of declining output, foreign takeover, and idle capacity.

Why this dismal contrast with progress in engineering? Table 2 suggests no failure of foreign or domestic demand. Promoters of China's iron and steel industry committed egregious blunders, but the Japanese hardly did better at Anshan, installing blast furnaces only to find that nearby lean ores could not be used until a new enrichment process was developed.[30] Instances in which Chinese firms survived only at the cost of growing indebtedness to foreigners cannot be blamed solely on the unequal treaty system, which merely created the possibility of foreign takeover. A scarcity of capital from domestic sources opened the door to foreign control of China's nascent metallurgy sector and acted as the chief constraint to the growth of iron and steel before 1949.

Ferrous metallurgy requires large capital facilities and a high rate of output from the start.[31] The gradual buildup of capacity through the accumulation of experience and profits cannot generate modern enterprises from small workshops. Prior to World War II, there was no alternative to dependence on imported technology and equipment to build China's iron and steel industry. Accordingly, investment in ferrous metallurgy called for heavy initial outlays not only on the main smelting apparatus but also on mines, ore and fuel preparation plants, and various ancillary services.

Moreover, once the physical plant is installed, start-up costs are likely

TABLE 2

Annual Output and Demand for Iron and Steel, Five-Year Averages, 1900–1944

(Thousand tons)

Period	Pig iron output			Ingot steel output		Iron and steel market		
	China proper	Anshan	Total	Anshan	Total	Imports	Exports	Apparent consumption
1900–4	198	0	198	0	–	–	–	–
1905–9	223	0	223	0	23[a]	–	–	–
1910–14	258	0	258	0	38	209[b]	54[b]	451[b]
1915–19	319	54[c]	373	0	46	174	156	437
1920–24	278	102[c]	380	0	47	362	212	577
1925–29	185	225[c]	410	0	28	497	201	734
1930–34	251	305	556	–	26	533	235[d]	880
1935–39	–	647	–	441	406[e]	–	–	–
1940–44	62[f]	1,137	–	628	–	–	–	–

Sources:

Pig iron output. China proper, 1915-34, derived from data in cols. 2 and 3; 1940-44, Ch'en Chen, ed., *Chung-kuo chin-tai kung-yeh shih tzu-liao* (Collected material on modern Chinese industrial history; reprint ed., Tokyo, 1966), collection 4, vol. 2, p. 765. Anshan (and Pen-ch'i), 1915-29, *ibid.*, p. 746; Anshan only, 1930-44, M. Gardner Clark, *Development of China's Steel Industry and Soviet Technical Aid* (Ithaca, N.Y., 1973), p. 12. Total figures, 1900-29, Ch'en Chen, p. 746; 1930-34, Yen Chung-p'ing et al., *Chung-kuo chin-tai ching-chi shih t'ung-chi tzu-liao hsüan-chi* (Selected statistical material on modern Chinese economic history; Peking, 1955), p. 142.

Ingot steel output. Anshan, 1935-44, Clark, p. 12. Total figures, 1905-29, 1935-38, Ch'en Chen, pp. 748, 786; 1930-34, Yen Chung-p'ing, p. 142.

Imports, exports, and consumption. 1910-29, Ch'en Chen, p. 754; 1930-34, imports, Yen Chung-p'ing, p. 142, exports, Ch'en Chen, p. 754; consumption, derived from other data in the table.

[a] Average for 1907-9 only

[b] Average for 1912-14 only

[c] Pen-ch'i and Anshan combined

[d] Average for 1930-31 only

[e] Average for 1935-38 only; this may account for the inconsistency with the Anshan output for 1935-39.

[f] Free China only

to be high. Product quality may be decisively altered by small impurities: rails produced by the Han-yeh-p'ing ironworks developed cracks because they contained excessive phosphorus.[32] Cost and quality also depend on the appropriate selection and blending of raw materials. The selection process "cannot be carried out . . . on the basis of *a priori* chemical analysis," but "requires patient and careful full-scale experimentation, which means years of painstaking effort to determine the best combinations." [33]

Since initial production costs are often high and quality low, new plants will find survival difficult without large capital reserves, subsidies, or some form of protection. In China these difficulties were compounded by the scarcity of raw materials rich enough to bypass expensive preliminary treatment without endangering product quality and by the long depression of iron prices following World War I, an unfortunate coincidence that hastened the downfall of several ironworks.[34]

The history of the Japanese-owned ironworks at Anshan illustrates the magnitude of the capital and start-up cost requirements in iron and steel. Construction began in 1917, and included two blast furnaces intended to produce 150,000 tons of pig iron annually, coal washing and coking plants, a power plant, and waterworks.[35] Production began in 1919, when year-end capital, presumably reflecting the cost of construction and equipment, was 38 million yen.[36] Output rose only slowly, and by the time the first 150,000 tons had been produced, total outlay had surpassed 100 million yen.[37] Because of low iron prices and unexpected beneficiation problems, no profits were recorded until 1928. Between 1919 and 1933 annual returns were negative in 12 of 15 years, with cumulative net losses of 28.5 million yen, or three-fourths of the initial investment.[38] Anshan continued to operate only because of an ongoing subsidy from the parent South Manchurian Railway Company.

Chinese businessmen could not amass the resources needed to build plants even half the size of the original Anshan project and to carry new enterprises through initial technical and marketing difficulties. Profit flows from existing enterprises were too small: though annual losses of two–three million yen were not uncommon in Anshan's history, Chinese industries rarely generated profits of this magnitude, not to mention the initial investments needed in metallurgy. After writing off 15 million yen for continued losses, Anshan's capital was still valued at 29 million yen in 1932, a figure matched by only a few Chinese firms.[39]

Organized financial markets offered little aid to prewar producer industries. Despite the rapid growth of modern banking after World War I, financial intermediaries did not begin to influence the growth of modern industry until the 1930's.[40] Even then, exceptional yields on government securities drew funds away from industrial finance.[41] Further, those loans that were advanced to industry went almost exclusively to textiles and flour milling.[42] Finally, plans for state participation in iron and steel were nullified by World War II.[43]

Under these conditions, Chinese iron and steel producers found it difficult to survive. Some, including the Hanyang and Tayeh ironworks, borrowed heavily from foreigners and subsequently failed to meet their debt obligations.[44] Others, such as the Ho-hsing plant in Shanghai, were driven out of business by foreign competitors; and the blast furnace at Shih-ching-shan, hailed by contemporaries as the finest in Asia outside India, consumed its promoters' entire capital in construction and produced nothing until captured by the invading Japanese.[45] By 1929 Anshan and Pen-ch'i were the only large modern ironworks still in operation.[46]

Indivisibilities, business fluctuations, and scarce capital combined to thwart the development of an iron and steel industry in Republican China's market economy. Although the present existence of active metallurgy enterprises on nearly all the sites developed in prewar China shows the basic soundness of early ventures, prewar entrepreneurs failed because technological and financial indivisibilities prevented them from going through the same kind of evolutionary growth that permitted the engineering sector to achieve substantial progress in the decades preceding World War II.

Development under government auspices in Manchuria. Japan exercised semicolonial control over key sectors of the Manchurian economy following the creation of the South Manchurian Railway Company in 1906. Japan valued Manchuria as a market for its own producer industries, and limited its sponsorship of producer enterprises to a network whose ultimate task was to deliver raw and semifinished materials to the home economy. These units, including the Anshan and Pen-ch'i ironworks and the Fushun colliery, were large, modern, vertically integrated enterprises, which had their own power supply and repair shops and even built their own machinery.[47] Links with local suppliers were minimal: Japanese policy did not encourage the type of engineering development that occurred in Shanghai.[48]

Despite the Japanese monopoly of positions of skill and responsibility in large modern enterprises, the mechanized Fushun coal fields, the modern ironworks, the engineering plants attached to these enterprises, and the South Manchurian Railway itself undoubtedly created a pool of trained Chinese mechanics, machinists, and metalworkers that sup-

TABLE 3
Engineering and Metallurgy in Manchuria, 1931

	Number of plants		Gross value of output *(Thousand yen)*	
Category	Japanese	Non-Japanese	Per plant	Total
Metallurgy and metal products—*106 plants*			95	10,030
Large metallurgy plants: Anshan, Pen-ch'i, Ta-lien	3		2,970	8,910
Others	40	63	11	1,120
Machinery and tools, incl. repair—*184 plants*			232	42,680
Large plants:			4,795	38,360
Feng-t'ien arsenal		2	11,730	23,460
Shao-ho-k'ou railway works	1		6,870	6,870
Ta-lien railway works	3		1,966	5,898
Fushun colliery machine works	2		630	1,260
Anshan ironworks machine shops	1		512	512
Ta-lien shipyard	1		360	360
Others	69	105	25	4,320
Japanese			16	1,130
Non-Japanese			30	3,190

Sources:
 Gross value of output, Shao-ho-k'ou railway works, Fushun colliery machine works, and Ta-lien shipyard. Manshū kaihatsu yonjūnenshi kankō kai, comp., *Manshū kaihatsu yonjūnenshi* (Forty years of development in Manchuria; Tokyo, 1964-65), 2: 494.
 All other data. South Manchurian Railway, keizai chōsa kai, comp., *Manshū sangyō tōkei, 1931* (Manchurian industrial statistics; Dairen, 1933) as follows: number and total value of output of all plants, pp. 60-61; total value of output, Anshan, Pen-ch'i, Ta-lien metallurgy plants, p. 62; total value of output, Feng-t'ien arsenal, Ta-lien railway works, Anshan ironworks machine shops, pp. 74, 76, 72, respectively.
 Note: To compare the state of Shanghai's metallurgy industry, see the metal industries entry in Table 1. The Manchurian data for 1931 are in Japanese yen, which were equivalent to approximately 2.2 Chinese yuan or dollars in 1931 (Arthur N. Young, *China's Nation-Building Effort, 1927-1937*, Stanford, Calif., 1971, p. 474; *The China Yearbook*, 14 [1928]: 406), but had achieved rough parity with both the Chinese yuan and the Manchukuo yen by 1933 *(Manchoukuo Yearbook, 1942*, Hsinking, 1941, pp. 254-55).

plied entrepreneurs and skilled workers to the private engineering sector, as Ta-lung's apprenticeship program had done at Shanghai.[49]

Even without Japanese encouragement, one survey noted 69 Chinese-owned machinery plants in Manchuria by 1928, most serving the needs of oil pressing and other native food-processing industries.[50] The largest of these, the Northeast University Ironworks at Feng-t'ien, employed more than 700 workers, who engaged in a wide variety of manufacture and repair work.[51]

Table 3, however, shows that Japanese policies did succeed in limiting the growth of private engineering to a level considerably behind that achieved in Shanghai. Apart from several large South Manchurian Railway–sponsored enterprises and the two Feng-t'ien arsenals established by Chang Tso-lin, the engineering plants in Manchuria were smaller in average size and in contribution to overall industrial output than Shanghai's.[*]

With the creation of Manchukuo in 1932, Japan's policy toward the local economy began to shift. Earlier exploitative aims were supplemented and eventually superseded by a policy of encouraging local industrial and military self-sufficiency. New attention to engineering development reflected this change.

The construction boom that followed the establishment of Manchukuo included growing investment in the machinery sector.[†] However, as far as can be determined from the confusing array of output data in Table 4, machinery production responded only sluggishly to sharply rising demand; additional capital equipment came primarily from abroad.[52]

Following the first economic construction program, promulgated in 1933, which focused on transport development, Manchukuo enacted several versions of a five-year industrial development plan (1937–41) that increasingly emphasized the growth of engineering industries. The initial plan allotted 108 million yen to the machinery industry—including 28 million yen for expansion of railway-equipment production, or 8.3 percent of the 1.3 billion yen to be invested in mining and industry.[53] The revised plan of 1938 called for expending 823 million yen on machine-building, including provision for capacity to produce 5,000 (later 50,000) machine tools, an item omitted from the initial plan.[54]

The response of the engineering sector to the ensuing investment push is problematic.[55] The output data in Table 4 and retrospective claims

---

[*] Since other large Japanese plants may be hidden in the remainder, this comparison possibly exaggerates the size of Manchuria's private engineering sector. Coverage of the two surveys—all plants employing five or more in Manchuria and all plants employing mechanical power in Shanghai—is quite similar (South Manchurian Railway, keizai chōsa kai, comp., *Manshū sangyō tōkei, 1931*; Manchurian industrial statistics for 1931; Darien, 1933, p. 59; T. C. Liu and K. C. Yeh, *The Economy of the Chinese Mainland*, Princeton, N.J., 1965, p. 430).

[†] Construction outlays rose from 15 million yen in 1930 and 10 million in 1931 to 29 million yen and 104 million yen in the following two years (Manshū kaihatsu yonjūnenshi kankō kai, comp., *Manshū kaihatsu yonjūnenshi*; Forty years of development in Manchuria; Tokyo, 1964–65, 2: 351); capital of newly incorporated enterprises in machinery and tool manufacture, which amounted to less than one million yen during 1905–31, reached 59 million yen during 1932–36 (Ch'en Chen, Yao Lo, and Feng Hsien-chih, eds., *Chung-kuo chin-tai kung-yeh shih tzu-liao*, Collected material on modern Chinese industrial history; reprint ed., Tokyo, 1966), collection 2, p. 472).

TABLE 4

Manchurian Output of Machinery and Tools, Including Repairs, 1931–1940

(Million current yen)

Year	Yeh	Manshū kaihatsu	Other sources	Machinery price index for Japan	Manchurian imports of machinery and tools, vehicles and vessels
1931	29.0		42.68	72.5	
1932	29.0		28.2	87.1	
1933	27.1		25.0	100.0	31.243
1934	37.2		19.6; 44.6	102.0	59.002
1935	34.6		42.9	99.9	74.457
1936	40.4	24.2	50.4	101.9	78.468
1937		31.0		143.0	112.307
1938		37.2 (35.17[a])		150.2	211.158
1939		178.78 (88.93[a])	71.5	150.8	395.205
1940		(152.86[a])		156.1	

Sources:

Kung-chia Yeh, "Capital Formation in Mainland China, 1931-36 and 1952-57," Ph.D. diss., Columbia University, 1964, p. 225. This series covers only machinery and parts and has been converted to constant 1935-37 prices.

Manshū kaihatsu yonjūnenshi kankō kai, comp., Manshū kaihatsu yonjūnenshi (Forty years of development in Manchuria; Tokyo, 1964-65), 2: 372, except for the 1938 figure in parentheses, both 1939 figures, and the 1940 figure, which are from p. 509 and exclude repairs.

Other. 1931, South Manchurian Railway, keizai chōsa kai, comp., Manshū sangyō tōkei, 1931 (Manchurian industrial statistics, Dairen, 1933), p. 71. 1932, Manshū sangyō tōkei, 1932 (Dairen, 1934), pp. 80-81; and Manshū ni okeru kikai kigu kōgyō no geniō (Current state of Manchuria's machinery and tool industry; n.p., 1937), p. 40. 1933, Manshū ni okeru kikai kigu kōgyō, p. 40. 1934, Manchoukuo Yearbook, 1942 (Hsinking, 1941), p. 515; and Manshū ni okeru kikai kigu kōgyō, p. 40. 1935, derived from Manchoukuo Yearbook, 1942, p. 515, by assuming that the 1934-35 output increase in the Kwantung (Kantō) area was half the increase reported for 1934-36, the 1934-35 output growth for the other areas is shown on p. 515. 1936, ibid. 1939, Kantōkyoku, comp., Kantōkyoku dai-34 tōkei-sho (34th Kwantung statistical volume, 1939; Dairen, 1940), p. 96.

Machinery price index for Japan. Calculated from Kazushi Ohkawa et al., eds., Estimates of Long-Term Economic Statistics of Japan Since 1868, vol. 8: Prices (Tokyo, 1967), p. 159.

Manchurian imports. Manchoukuo Yearbook, 1942, p. 550. The figure given for 1933 is 321.243 million yen, an obvious misprint.

[a]Indicates data that specifically exclude the province of Kantō (Kwantung)

of large increases by Japanese historians may not accurately reflect changes in real output.[56] Inflation accounts for a substantial share of recorded output growth. Since Manchurian wholesale prices outpaced Japanese prices after 1936, it is likely that the Japanese machinery price index in Table 4 understates the impact of inflation in Manchuria.[57] Evidence that sales prices of Anshan pig iron, ingot, and steel plate rose by 38, 101, and 133 percent, respectively, in 1939–40 while Japanese machinery prices fell supports this view.[58] In addition, certain individual output claims appear dubious.[59]

Regardless of the rate of output growth after 1936, it is clear that though production of mining machinery, metallurgical equipment, loco-

motives, and rolling stock previously manufactured by large South Manchurian Railway Company factories increased, plans to produce machine tools, automobiles, aircraft, and other new items were never
realized. Deprived by war of imported equipment, foreign financing,
and certain raw materials, the Manchurian producer sector was inca-
pable of developing new lines of manufacture. The appearance of gaps
between output, targets, and capacity revealed growing imbalance even
in the well-established coal and metallurgy sectors.

War-imposed isolation exposed the weakness of Manchuria's producer sector. Though Japanese investment brought impressive output
gains, particularly in sectors that developed only slowly in China's private sector, Manchurian producer industries never acquired the flexibility essential to permit industrial diversification without continuing
outside aid.

This essay only begins to tap the rich materials describing China's industries before 1949. Our findings emphasize the distinctiveness of the
economic forces influencing various sectors. Though China's lack of organized financial markets decisively influenced ferrous metallurgy, financial constraints operated less severely in engineering. Some machinery
producers certainly perished because of undercapitalization, but others
managed to accumulate sufficient funds to prosper and expand.

The effect of economic forces on various producer sectors also shifted
with the passage of time. World War I, which simulated the effects of
tariff and quota restrictions on textile machinery imports, apparently
curtailed textile investment without stimulating domestic production
of spindles or looms. But two decades later, when the Sino-Japanese
conflict again isolated Shanghai's textile mills from foreign suppliers,
domestic spindle production rose sharply.

These circumstances suggest that broad analyses based on such general factors as imperialism or entrepreneurial failure, though perhaps
valid for certain sectors at particular times, cannot explain the totality of
China's complex pre-1949 industrial experience.

China's prewar history also reveals some strengths and shortcomings
of various institutions as vehicles for industrialization. The free market
environment of China proper nurtured enterprises strongly linked with
suppliers and customers. To survive the harsh discipline of an unstable
and cycle-ridden environment, firms must respond promptly to shifting
patterns of price and demand; otherwise, they die. Successful businesses
must quickly abandon unprofitable activities and produce only market-

able items of satisfactory cost and quality. These are all virtues of the classical competitive model.

Free market development also creates problems. Whole sectors may be stifled by technical or financial indivisibilities, as was China's iron and steel industry. Even in growing sectors, promising firms are often wiped out by the accident of business fluctuations. Others fail to negotiate the obstacles of start-up costs. Finally, even a successful free market evolution of producer industries seems painfully slow.

Manchuria's experience shows that public participation can overcome many delays and obstacles encountered in a market system. Official investments and formal or informal trade barriers eliminate capital scarcity, shield infant industries from the threat (and goad) of external competition, and circumvent the demand problem by the simultaneous creation of supplier and customer firms, with government standing ready to absorb the initial losses of both.

Though state action may hasten the rise of new industries, the balanced investment method attempted in Manchukuo's five-year plan entails disadvantages best studied in the post-1949 period, on which more information is available. Planning is never perfect, and the frequently revised Manchukuo plans were no exception. What begins as an integrated cluster of investment inevitably emerges as a group of enterprises whose supply and demand relations include grave imbalances. Unless these difficulties can be overcome by forging the type of firm input-output links that characterize free market relations between buyers and sellers, planned industrialization may result in the cycle of falling output and idle plant that marked Manchukuo's final years.

Producer Industries in China Since 1949

Quantitative trends: output, input, and productivity. Our estimates of output, input, and total factor productivity for the producer sector during 1952–71 appear in Tables 5–8.* The derivation of these series is sketched in the Appendix (p. 234, below) and is fully described in a supplement available from the author. Though each series, as well as the scope of the producer sector, is subject to significant ambiguity and qualification that cannot be elaborated here, the problems are not large enough to obscure the basic trends discussed below.

The Chinese define producer industries as mining, metallurgy, fuels and power, metal processing (including machinery), basic chemicals,

---

* The recovery years 1949–52, for which data are poor, are omitted.

TABLE 5
Gross Output Value in Industry and Major Components, 1949–1971
(Billion 1952 yuan)

Year	Industry	Producer goods		Consumer goods	
		Output	Share	Output	Share
1949	10.781	3.100	27.9%	7.681	72.1%
1952	27.014	10.730	39.7	16.284	60.3
1953	35.577	14.670	41.2	20.907	58.8
1954	41.513	17.578	42.3	23.935	57.7
1955	44.748	20.578	46.0	24.170	54.0
1956	58.660	29.241	49.8	29.419	50.2
1957	65.020	34.330	52.8	30.690	47.2
1963	104.1–126.7				
1964	119.7–145.7				
1965	132.9–161.7	87.7–116.6	66.0–72.1	45.1	34.0–27.9
1966	159.5–194.0				
1970	260.9–271.3	207.8	79.6–76.6	53.1–63.5[a]	20.4–23.4
1971	297.0–311.8	246.5	83.0–79.0	50.5–65.3[a]	17.0–21.0

Sources:
1949-57. Nai-ruenn Chen, ed., *Chinese Economic Statistics* (Chicago, 1967), p. 210; the 1957 share of producer goods is taken from SSB, "Communique on Fulfillment and Overfulfillment of China's First Five-Year Plan," translated in *Current Background,* 559: 4 (1959).
1963-71. See Table S-1 of the supplement to this essay (see Appendix).
Note: Consumer output totals include the household share of fuel and power, amounting to 60 percent of 1952 output but only 16 percent of incremental output during 1952-71 (Thomas G. Rawski, "The Role of China in the World Energy Situation," unpub. paper, June 1973, p. 31); bicycles, radios, sewing machines, and other consumer items amounting to 7 percent of 1956 and 3 percent of 1971 machinery output (see Table S-3 of the supplement to this essay available from the author); and miscellaneous metal products for daily use, such as washbasins. The first two items account for 2-3 percent of estimated 1971 producer output. Producer items buried in the consumer sector include portions of textile and paper output.
[a]Figures derived from other estimates

TABLE 6
Average Annual Growth Rates, 1952–1971

Year	Industry	Producer goods	Consumer goods
1952–57	19.2%	26.2%	13.5%
1952–65	13.0–14.8	17.5–20.1	8.1
1952–71	13.5–13.7	17.9	6.1–7.6
1957–65	9.4–12.1	12.4–16.5	4.9
1957–71	11.5–11.8	15.1	3.6–5.5
1965–71	14.2–11.6[a]	18.8–13.3[a]	1.9–6.4[a]

Source: See Table 5.
[a]Calculated by pairing the high and low estimates for 1965 and 1971

TABLE 7

Estimated Total Input into the Producer Sector, 1952–1965

(Billion 1952 yuan)

Year	Employment (Millions)	Wage bill (1952 yuan)	Average capital		Total input		
			Fixed	Working	$r = .05$[a]	$r = .20$[a]	Arbitrary weights[b]
1952 level	2.76	1.656	8.426	1.350	2.570	4.036	—
Index: 1952 = 100							
1953	116.3	121.8	99.8	126.8	110.8	108.2	111.4
1954	123.2	135.0	102.3	157.9	118.7	115.5	116.9
1955	129.0	147.5	108.1	190.6	127.8	124.8	122.7
1956	140.9	181.9	118.6	238.5	152.7	146.3	134.2
1957	159.0	214.3	135.4	290.7	176.9	169.6	151.9
1965 – High output[c]							
Low C, L	158.7	203.7	562.7	987.3	317.9	428.2	279.9
Low C, high L	231.5	361.4	562.7	987.3	403.8	482.8	365.9
High C, low L	158.7	203.7	945.9	987.3	431.2	620.3	394.9
High C, L	231.5	361.4	945.9	987.3	517.1	675.0	480.8
1965 – Low output[c]							
Low C, L	158.7	203.7	562.7	743.1	311.5	411.8	279.9
Low C, high L	231.5	361.4	562.7	743.1	397.4	466.5	365.9
High C, low L	158.7	203.7	945.9	743.1	424.8	604.0	394.9
High C, L	231.5	361.4	945.9	743.1	510.7	658.7	480.8

Source: Tables S-7, S-9, and S-10 of the supplement to this essay available on request from the author (see Appendix).

Note: High and low C and L refer to high and low 1965 estimates of fixed capital and employment.

[a] Calculated using the formula described in the Appendix.

[b] Weighted average of indices of employment (weight of 0.7) and fixed capital (weight of 0.3).

[c] Total input depends on 1965 output level because of the assumed dependence of 1957–65 increase in working capital on the growth of output

TABLE 8

Estimated Total Factor Productivity in the Producer Sector, 1953–1965

(1952 = 100)

Year	Input with r = .05		Input with r = .20		Input with arbitrary weights	
1953	123.4		126.3		122.7	
1954	138.0		141.8		140.1	
1955	150.1		153.7		156.3	
1956	178.4		186.3		203.0	
1957	180.8		188.6		210.6	
1965	Output estimate		Output estimate		Output estimate	
	High	Low	High	Low	High	Low
Low C, L	341.8	257.1	253.8	190.9	388.2	292.0
Low C, high L	269.1	202.4	225.1	169.3	297.0	223.4
High C, low L	252.0	189.5	175.2	131.8	275.2	207.0
High C, L	210.2	158.0	161.0	121.1	226.0	170.0

Source: Tables 6 and 7. Productivity index is the quotient of output and input indices.
   Note: High and low C and L refer to high and low 1965 estimates of fixed capital and employment.

and building materials, a classification that is nearly identical with their concept of "heavy industry."[60] Though the output data in Table 5 include some final consumer products and exclude certain items that should appear in the producer category, the quantities involved are small and of decreasing importance. Chinese treatment of military products is uncertain: weapons were apparently classified as machinery in the official output data for 1952–57 shown in Table 5, but their subsequent classification is unknown.[61]

The output series consists of official gross value data for 1952–57 and estimates based on published physical output data for various products in subsequent years. I have argued the validity of this procedure elsewhere, and note only that the use of 1952 prices results in a higher growth rate and output share for producer goods than would emerge from a series valued in prices of a later year, were such prices available.[62]

Employment figures come from Chinese sources and our own crude estimate for 1965. Wage data are from Chinese sources.

The large size and substantial average gestation period of industrial investment necessitate the use of time lags to obtain estimates of fixed capital available for productive use. The lag structure underlying our capital series is based on construction and trial periods for large and small investment projects. The accuracy of the resulting estimates is limited by reliance on 1952 capital stock figures generated by China's then poorly organized statistical agencies, and by our own crude post-1957 investment estimates.

Factor productivity is calculated as a quotient of output and input indices. The latter are derived both by summing wages and imputed capital costs and by applying arbitrary 7:3 weights to separate indices of employment and fixed capital.[63]

Tables 5–8 suggest a division of the past two decades into two periods: (1) the years 1952–57, characterized by rapid growth of output; slow growth of inputs, especially fixed capital; and the consequent rapid expansion of productivity; and (2) the years after 1957 in which output continued to increase, though less rapidly; inputs, notably fixed capital, grew much faster than before; and productivity growth slowed markedly. The discussion below focuses on factors responsible for the performance of China's producer industries in these two periods.

The output spurt of 1952–57. Output of producer goods grew rapidly during 1952–57. The new Communist government prepared ambitious industrial production targets under the FFYP (1953–57), which were generally exceeded. Within the producer sector, machinery grew fastest, with 1957 output surpassing the planned level by more than 80 percent.[64] As is evident from Tables 5–8, producer output grew much more rapidly than inputs, and productivity growth in the machinery industry was substantially above that recorded for the entire producer sector.[65]

Why this output spurt? There are several obvious explanations. Restoration of political and monetary stability benefited every sector of the economy. The government's concern with industry, its conferral of new prestige and material rewards on industrial workers, the influx of Soviet engineers and technicians into Chinese factories, and the results of new on-the-job training programs all stimulated industry, particularly the favored producer sector. Though trends in the size of China's industrial capital stock during 1933–52 require detailed study, the large rise in producer output between 1933 and 1952 suggests massive idle capacity in 1933 or major post-1933 additions to fixed assets that survived war and civil strife, or both.*

* With 1933 = 100, T. C. Liu and K. C. Yeh, *The Economy of the Chinese Mainland* (Princeton, N.J., 1965), p. 66, estimate 1952 value added by mining, utilities, and producer goods factories at 280 or 333, depending on the price base used. Heavy wartime and postwar damage to Japanese industrial assets in Manchuria described in the Pauley Report (cited in Onoe Etsuzō, *Chūgoku no sangyō ritchi ni kansuru kenkyū*; Studies in the location of Chinese industry; Tokyo, 1971, pp. 228–29) and declining industrial output and power consumption in Shanghai after 1940 (*ibid.*, p. 314; Yu-kwei Cheng, *Foreign Trade and Industrial Development of China*; Washington, D.C., 1956, p. 116) suggest the absence of major post-1937 fixed investments (or in the Manchurian case, surviving fixed investments) in China's leading centers of producer industry. Since Liu and Yeh find that output per worker in all factories, mines, and utilities rose by over 13 percent between 1933 and 1952

Socialist economic organization also stimulated industrial output by sweeping away restraints formerly imposed by the market. The iron-works of North China, for example, idled during the 1930's by scarce working capital and low prices, were quickly returned to production.[66] Officials urged producers to maximize output, often as it turned out with little regard for demand. Industrial enterprises commonly disregarded assortment plans, for even substandard products could be sold to state commercial organs.[67] Ready availability of bank loans and assured sales at cost-plus prices enabled output per unit of labor or fixed capital to exceed levels achieved during the 1930's.[68]

These factors, which affected all producer sectors, cannot explain the startling performance of machinery plants. China's FFYP, approved and published in mid-1955, set a 1957 target for machinery output that was exceeded by 67 percent in the following year. Although the 1956 output total included quantities of useless items, such as the notorious double-bladed plows, the still larger 1957 output, now 80 percent above the target, was produced with much greater attention to demand factors. Since enterprises under the First Ministry of Machine-Building (which controlled the largest, most modern plants) operated at 80 percent of capacity in 1957, 1957 productive capacity in machinery clearly exceeded the 1955 forecast by more than 100 percent.[69]

Chinese planners, surprised by this unanticipated output growth, announced reductions in future investment in machine-building and began to study the relationship between the growth of machinery and that of other sectors of the economy.[70] Unexpected output growth could not have stemmed from military industries, from new facilities, or from the impact of Soviet advice, for Chinese economic planners and their Soviet associates could have foreseen the result of these factors.[71] Gross underestimation of the number and size of inherited machinery plans is possible but unlikely, in view of the extensive destruction of Japanese plants in the northeast.[72]

In the machinery sector, and apparently only in that sector, the relation between inherited capacity and output was very different during the 1950's from what might have been anticipated on the basis of earlier performance.[73] This finding supports our hypothesis that the Ta-lung Machinery Works was not unique. It now appears that before or during

---

despite an 82 percent increase in employment (pp. 66, 69), further research is needed to determine whether this outcome resulted from the survival of prewar capacity that had been idled in 1933, from post-1933 investments that survived the war, or from a production function that permitted higher employment without lowering average productivity.

World War II, many engineering plants reached the type of technological threshold described above, and that as a result the removal of
previous constraints imposed by raw materials, working capital, and
sales led to a unique and unexpected breakthrough to higher levels of
machinery output during the 1950's.

Once again, the Ta-lung Machinery Works, where both gross output
value and output per worker nearly doubled between the prewar years
and 1952, and doubled again between 1952 and 1956, provides some firm
evidence.* As before, the paucity of direct evidence makes it difficult
to confirm the threshold hypothesis, but the behavior of machinery output during 1952–57 is otherwise difficult to explain.

Whatever its causes, by 1957 the output spurt in producer goods had
revealed the need for an interlude of adjustment and consolidation.
With investments in the pipeline amounting to 148 percent of fixed
assets available for production as of December 31, 1957, there was evident need to prepare for the smooth integration of major FFYP investment projects into the expanded industrial sector.[74] In addition, the re-
laxation of economic discipline, though conducive to rapid growth, had
created undesirable effects that required correction.

Some plants had produced goods that could not be used anywhere in
the economy. This problem was especially serious in machinery and
led the government to suspend agricultural machinery production in
the first half of 1957.[75] With customers assigned to suppliers by official
fiat, many enterprises shipped defective or incomplete merchandise, especially near the end of the planning year.† Together with lax financial
controls, the unreliability of suppliers encouraged a trend toward vertical integration that led to high costs and widespread excess capacity;
utilization rates for forging equipment in 11 major machinery plants, for
example, averaged only 52 percent of capacity in 1957, and integrated
plants were attacked for producing hardware at many times the cost
levels attained by specialist firms.[76]

Adjustments were needed also to cope with changes in the structure

---

* Pre-1949 peak output was equivalent to about three million post-1949 yuan
(*Ta-lung*, p. 119); this is assumed to have occurred in the years prior to 1937, described as the peak of Ta-lung's preliberation history (p. 29) when employment
reached 1,300 (p. 46). Average output of six million yuan for 1949–53 (p. 121) is
assumed to apply to 1952, when employment was above 1,400 (p. 99). In 1956 output was 26.28 million yuan (p. 121), and the work force numbered 2,950 (p. 119).

† A typical report concerns the T'ai-yüan Machinery Plant, which fulfilled 42
percent of its output quota for the first quarter of 1953 during the last 15 days of
March. With office staff pressed into service in the shop, workers remained at their
posts up to 19 hours a day during the final three days, during which inspection
standards were suspended. (*Jen-min jih-pao*; People's daily; May 26, 1953.)

of inherited industries. Unplanned expansion of machinery output, for instance, contributed to shortages of iron ore, steel, coal, and electricity, and threatened to disrupt the supply of raw materials to newly completed plants.

Finally, the completion of major investment projects led to many problems. Although the FFYP was designed in the aggregate as a balanced program of investments, planning errors, construction delays, and changes in output and demand patterns elsewhere in the economy inevitably created a host of imbalances at the microeconomic level. New units often had difficulty obtaining materials, equipment, labor, transport services, and markets for their products: among projects built with Soviet aid, the Harbin Electric Meter Plant was idle for want of customers, the Loyang Bearing Works reported that plants designated to supply special steel were unaware of its existence, and the Wuhan Steel Works could find no supplier for needed equipment.[77]

By 1957 Chinese planners recognized the inappropriateness of the past policy of output maximization. Their prescription, implemented in 1957, brought on an interlude of retrenchment that saw a new emphasis on product quality, cost reduction, customer service, and interenterprise cooperation; a reduced rate of accumulation; and sectoral investment shifts from machinery to basic raw materials.[78]

Consolidation, 1961–66. These timely changes were swept away by the Great Leap Forward of 1958–60, a campaign that obliged industry to focus almost exclusively on raising the volume of physical output to the detriment of cost, balance, and customer service. The Leap accentuated weaknesses already inherent in China's industrial economy. Efforts of some executives to divert Great Leap energies into more productive channels at best only delayed the harmful impact of successive years of uncoordinated output maximization.[79]

By 1960 the partial breakdown of normal planning and reporting procedures greatly increased the need for a policy of industrial consolidation. The situation was exacerbated by the Soviet withdrawal of technical aid, which left major investment projects unfinished and threatened China's petroleum supplies, and by consecutive poor harvests, which signaled the need to raise industry's support for agriculture. Consequent shifts in the composition of demand for producer goods turned an unavoidable process of adjustment and integration into a crisis in which economic collapse became a real possibility.

The restructuring of producer output to bolster agricultural production and support the petroleum and defense sectors demanded the utmost exercise of the technical skills and fixed capital acquired both before and after 1949. This was particularly true in the machinery industry, where the composition of output shifted most markedly from the anticipated pattern. To facilitate a quick and flexible response to new demand conditions, Chinese leaders did not flinch from introducing policies that simulated free market selection processes unknown in Chinese industry since 1949.

Unproductive resources were abruptly dismissed from the industrial sector. Cultural Revolution sources have focused attention on the role of Liu Shao-ch'i and other "revisionists" in eliminating small enterprises, especially ironworks, that diverted labor and funds from agriculture and produced expensive, low-quality products. The cutbacks, however, were not confined to small units. Shih-ching-shan Iron and Steel Company sent 40 percent of its workers into agriculture in 1960–63; the Shanghai Steel Plant's number one blast furnace shop cut labor requirements by 56 percent between 1959 and 1961; and the Shansi Machine Tool Works fired more than 2,000 workers in July 1961.[80] This trend continued for several years. After eliminating 27 percent of its labor force in 1961–63, the Chi-hsi Mining Bureau reported in 1964 that "after major studies of the Chairman's works, of the People's Liberation Army, and of Ta-ch'ing, we raised our ideological awareness, strengthened political work, and again recorded new achievements, reducing personnel by 8 percent."[81] Chinese journals of the early 1960's listed dozens of enterprises that had reduced their work forces.[82]

The government now strongly opposed the earlier policy of raising output at all costs. Pressure for quality improvements obliged some units to suspend production until reforms could be made.[83] Producers found themselves forced to consider the customer's viewpoint: employees of one mining machinery plant were dispatched to the mines to learn the importance of product quality, and a work team including "participants from fraternal units" made an inspection visit to verify quality claims of the Chi-nan Number One Machine Tool Plant.[84] Suppression of output value data was probably enforced as much to convince industrial managers of the reduced importance of output quantity as to conceal China's economic woes.

As monetary controls tightened, firms that had once ignored financial criteria began struggling to reduce costs and raise profits.[85] Large reductions in labor norms—Peking Sewing Machine Plant cut assembly time by 54 percent, and Shenyang Number Two Machine Tool Plant enforced successive cuts of 34 and 62 percent—revealed the extent of earlier laxity.[86] Reductions in working capital, in input coefficients for raw materials, and in transport costs were reported as part of the crackdown on waste.[87] As a result, journals were filled with descriptions of falling costs and prices and rising profits.[88]

The government also renewed previously unsuccessful efforts to foster specialization and division of labor within the producer sector, especially in machine-building. A barrage of articles extolled the cost advantages of specialized hardware production and subcontracting arrangements for machine parts; news media carried testimonials from once-skeptical executives who now supported interenterprise cooperation.[89]

Despite periodic reports indicating the survival of the output-first mentality, a resistance to innovation, excessive stockpiling, and other institutionally based inefficiencies, strong central leadership undoubtedly succeeded during the early 1960's in simulating certain beneficial features of free market economic organization within industry. This reform facilitated the concentration of material and human resources on the task of redirecting producer industries from their previous focus on expanding the circular flow of products among themselves toward the new objective of supporting all sectors of the economy, notably agriculture, transport, and the military. The ability of economic planners to force enterprises to abandon output maximization and turn to providing new products (such as equipment for the fertilizer and petroleum industries, items needed to finish construction and begin production at new plants initiated with Soviet aid, and the tools, materials, and spare parts required to maintain steady operations throughout the economy) was an essential ingredient in reversing the economic decline that threatened China in the wake of the Great Leap Forward.

I have argued elsewhere that the success of the producer sector in meeting unexpected shifts in the composition of demand shows that China's industry has acquired one significant characteristic of industrial maturity.[90] Two aspects of this achievement deserve closer examination.

First, the cost of abandoning the planned output mix in the producer sector was very high. The productivity estimates in Table 8, though subject to several qualifications, show that the pace of productivity growth declined sharply after 1957 despite the acquisition of large amounts of sophisticated capital equipment, growth in the quality and quantity of engineers and technicians, and a strong campaign to eliminate waste. Although this measure might be suspected of downward bias because it fails to account for the need to traverse new learning curves when new products are introduced or to deflate the value of fixed assets shifted to unintended tasks, the earlier productivity estimates incorporate the same faults. The consistency of results based on a variety of assumptions and weights indicates that the downturn in productivity growth shown in Table 8 is a real phenomenon.

The slow growth of productivity reflects the problems that many plants experienced in their efforts to master new processes and manufacture unfamiliar products. Unfortunately, we get only occasional glimpses of these difficulties from Chinese sources or visitors to the mainland, as when Barry M. Richman reported a plant newly converted to diesel-engine production to be among the worst-organized factories he visited in 1966, or when an agricultural machine plant complained of the veteran workers' inability to master new techniques.[91] We may surmise, however, that frequent references by Chinese industrial commentators to the strenuous effort required to overcome technical problems of the past decade have a solid factual basis.[92]

Second, it is important to note the surprisingly large role that small enterprises inherited from pre-1949 days played in overcoming the difficulties of the 1960's. This role emerges from the recognition of Shanghai as the source of urgently required new products and techniques and from the ability of small firms to outperform newer and larger competitors.

In machine tools, it was the Shanghai Machine Tool Plant, an expanded version of an old agricultural machine shop, that led the nation, and not the three Shenyang plants built with Soviet and Czech aid. Frequent coupling of exhortations to "learn from the advanced" with advice to "learn from Shanghai," embodied most clearly in the nationwide "emulate Shanghai" movement of 1964, shows that despite a decade of low investment and substantial emigration of skilled workers, Shanghai maintained its technological lead over the rest of China.[93] Producers of machine tools, pumps, pneumatic tools, sewing machines, and many other goods judged their technological prowess by comparing their products with Shanghai's.[94]

Petroleum machinery provides one example of this trend. The Lanchow Petroleum and Chemical Machinery Plant, China's only large firm specializing in these products, was still under construction in 1963. Furthermore, its management was described as "chaotic" up to the end of 1962, and the plant completed only 23 percent of its annual construction tasks in the first five months of 1963.[95] The implication that large increases in output of petroleum machinery during 1962–64 came from small enterprises is borne out by a description of "The Developing Petroleum Equipment Manufacturing Industry" published in 1964, which mentions only the Shanghai Petroleum Machinery Parts Plant, a one-time textile machinery repair shop that had been merged with some 40 small plants, and a medium-scale plant in Lanchow that was descended from Tso Tsung-t'ang's nineteenth-century arsenal.[96] Elsewhere, the Ta-lung Machinery Works is identified as an important supplier of machinery for the petroleum industry.[97]

There are other indications that small enterprises, which account for major output shares in chemical fertilizer, cement, and some types of machinery, retain an important role as sources of innovation within engineering.[98] Shanghai is a city of small factories, accounting in 1955, for example, for 50 percent of China's machine-building enterprises but only 25 percent of output value and 24 percent of employment in that industry.[99] Its prominence therefore suggests the importance of smaller producers. In 1963 and 1964 small Shanghai firms triumphed in cost reduction contests among producers of machine tools and pneumatic tools.[100]

This evidence may unfairly favor older and smaller plants. Many Soviet-equipped plants, such as the Shenyang Number One Machine Tool Plant, were designed for mass production of specific general-purpose machines and were not intended as centers of research and development. Victories by small units in interfirm competitions may be a device for compelling advanced enterprises to improve their performance. Even so, there remains the strong possibility that as late as 1965, small industrial enterprises inherited from the past, neglected by analysts both within and outside China, still formed a key link in China's expanded producer sector.

In the 1950's and 1960's China built a large and progressive producer sector on an inherited foundation that now appears considerably stronger than previous studies by Chinese and Western economists would suggest. Following an extremely rapid process of import substitution, which reduced the share of imports in aggregate machinery supply from about 50 percent to under 5 percent between 1952 and 1965, Chinese enterprises have become active in every major branch of producer industry and at a level of technological sophistication that has often surprised competent foreign visitors.[101]

This does not mean, of course, that China has become an advanced industrial nation. As its own leaders have been quick to admit, as late as the mid-1970's most sectors of industry still lagged far behind international developments. In chemicals, for instance, one survey of the 1960's indicated that 60 of 100 major products failed to achieve advanced world quality standards, 226 of 272 new products fell short of world standards, and only 35 of 89 major new techniques were introduced at relatively high levels of technique.[102] Chinese eagerness to increase imports of steel, fertilizers, trucks, ocean freighters, aircraft, and equipment for the metallurgy, petroleum, chemical, and communications sectors indicates the range of industries in which China's isolated producers cannot keep abreast of world technological advances.

Such comparisons, however, are not a suitable gauge of progress for the semi-industrialized Chinese economy, and should not divert attention from the important gains China's producer sector achieved after 1949. Output rose rapidly, though erratically; a skilled work force was developed; whole new industries appeared; productivity increased, and should rise further as growing imports alleviate bottlenecks and reduce the need to assign existing capital equipment to ill-suited tasks. The most significant achievement, however, is the ironic legacy of the sudden Soviet withdrawal of technical assistance in 1960. It was this hostile gesture, coupled with poor harvests, that stripped industry of its comfortable reliance on external support and forced the producer sector to develop the innovative capacity which is an important characteristic of industrialized, as opposed to backward, economies.

China's past success in autarkic producer development, superficially reminiscent of Rosenstein-Rodan's theory of the big push, does not imply that recent Chinese experience is a suitable model for emulation. China's current leaders feel that expanded imports of capital goods and technology will promote their present objective of developing "basic industries, particularly petrochemicals, machinery and metallurgy."[103] And in light of our finding that inherited enterprises have made important contributions to resolving the economic difficulties of the 1960's, China's experience cannot be held to support the view that massive investment and hard work alone can quickly create a viable producer sector within a framework of economic backwardness.

APPENDIX

This Appendix briefly summarizes the methodology underlying the estimates of capital stock and productivity appearing in Tables 7 and 8. Full details are presented in a supplement that is available from the author.

For 1952–57 Chinese data on basic construction investment are used as estimates of gross fixed capital formation for the producer sector. Fixed investment is divided into expenditures destined for major and minor projects. Major projects typically require three to five years for completion, whereas minor projects are completed within a year. For years after 1957 a lower boundary to annual fixed investment outlay in the producer sector is obtained by assuming that investment in industry grew in proportion to an index of aggregate investment estimated by T. C. Liu and K. C. Yeh, and that three-fourths of annual industrial investment went to the producer sector. An upper boundary to annual fixed investment outlay is derived by assuming that annual investment in the producer sector increased in proportion to a maximal index of machinery output. It is assumed that three-fourths of producer sector investment after 1957 went to major projects, and that the post-1957 structure of investment lags is identical with the system derived for the FFYP period. With an initial value derived from Chinese capital stock data for 1952, fixed capital stock estimates for 1951–71 (single values for 1951–58; upper and lower boundaries for 1958–71) are derived from the following equation:

$$K^f_t = K^f_{t-1} + \tfrac{1}{3} \left(I^M_{t-3} + I^M_{t-4} + I^M_{t-5} \right) + I^m_{t-1} - .05\, K^f_{t-1}$$

where K^f_t indicates year-end fixed capital stock in year t; I_t indicates gross fixed capital formation (1952 prices) in year t; superscripts M and m designate outlay on major and minor projects, respectively; and the final term on the right is an estimate of retirement of fixed assets, assumed to occur at an annual rate of 5 percent.

Industrial working capital for 1952–57 is estimated from Chinese data and separated into producer and consumer components in proportion to the annual shares of these branches in overall industrial output value. It is assumed that after 1957 working capital in the producer sector increased in proportion to gross output value.

Total factor productivity is estimated by Jacob Schmookler's method of calculating the quotient of separate output and input indices. Input series are derived from the following formula:

$$\text{Total input in year } t = WB_t + D_t + rK_t$$

where WB, D, and K are the annual wage bill (in 1952 yuan), depreciation (assumed to equal 5 percent of previous year-end fixed capital), and average annual fixed plus working capital; t is a time subscript; and r is an arbitrarily chosen rate of return, which is set at .05 or .20.

Since the identity of Chinese factor prices with marginal factor productivities implicitly assumed by this method is doubtful, we compute a third input series derived by applying arbitrary 7:3 weights to indices of employment and fixed capital in the producer sector.

John C. H. Fei

The "Standard Market" of Traditional China

WE ARE indebted to G. William Skinner for the important idea of a "standard market" as a self-sufficient unit in the economic and cultural sense in traditional China.[*] It is the purpose of this essay to analyze a set of issues suggested by his paper in respect to the forces that determine certain quantitative aspects of the standard market: size, shape, population density, regional variations, process of formation, and so on. The theory presented here is essentially an economic theory.

Although the theory can be formulated rigorously, we shall concentrate in the text on the major economic ideas—relegating the mathematical details to the appendix. We first present Skinner's conclusions in the larger spatial perspective of traditional China (Section 2). The quantitative aspects of the standard market are issues of the economics of space. One major determinant of the shape of the standard market is transportation cost; minimizing this cost constitutes a rationale for the marketing system (Section 3). The standard market is next examined as an institution of agrarian dualism (i.e., the coexistence of agricultural and nonagricultural production and exchange) in which agriculture is exalted (Section 4). The efficiency of large-scale nonagricultural production is shown to be a basic advantage for larger standard markets over smaller ones, and this finding is integrated with the transportation cost argument to form a positive theory of market area (Section 5). The regional variation in size of standard market areas, as traced to differentiated population density and agricultural production conditions, can then easily be explained as a theoretical consequence (Section 6). The dynamic process by which standard markets are formed is explored in Section 7, and finally (Section 8) intermediate market towns are considered.

[*] G. William Skinner, "Marketing and Social Structure in Rural China, Part 1," *Journal of Asian Studies*, 24.1:3–43 (1964).

2. *Spatial Perspective of Traditional China*

The spatial perspective of traditional China is presented at three levels of aggregation in Figure 1. At the most general level (Fig. 1a) is a transportation network (river and roads) linking urban centers forming a hierarchy that represents a coincidence* of economic centers (from larger manufacture and wholesale trading centers to small-scale local manufacture and retail centers) and political centers (capital, provincial capital, etc.). This diagram portrays the urban aspect of traditional China, emphasizing a pattern of connectivity as well as the distance that is one major attribute of space.

In Figure 1b the rectangle *ABCD* of Figure 1a is enlarged. Here we have a more local view of the spatial structure of standard markets: the cells of the beehives. Skinner pointed out the hexagonic nature of the cells, the standardization of their size in a homogeneous plane, and a tendency for this size to shrink from thinly populated to more densely populated regions. Although the standard markets are linked up with the national network (Fig. 1a), there is a second dimension of space which is brought out in Figure 1b, namely, the area of the space. The area included in a standard market is primarily the area of cultivable land—a most important primary factor of production in any agrarian economy. Thus the standard market structure is basically a rural market structure in which agricultural production is a central phenomenon.

Figure 1c is a microscopic view of one cell of Figure 1b, containing the marketing center (c) and nucleated villages $a_1 a_2, \ldots, a_{18}$. An essential characteristic of the standard market, Skinner observes, is that although peasants must live close to the land at a_1, they have numerous reasons for making frequent trips to c. There are sometimes cultural purposes for such trips, but the very notion of a standard *market* implies that their basic purpose is economic.

Three attributes of space must be sharply distinguished in the formulation of a positive theory of the standard market, namely, distance, area, and non-homogeneity. In Figure 1a, which portrays the urban part of traditional China, the distance of space and transportation cost considerations are analytically crucial. In 1b, which portrays the rural part of traditional China, the area of space and agricultural production considerations are as important as distance. The non-homogeneity of land space will be interpreted mainly in terms of the differential fertility of China's various agricultural regions as described by Buck. We shall

---

* In the long run, the political or administrative hierarchy of cities is probably determined by the economic hierarchy, hence by economic forces.

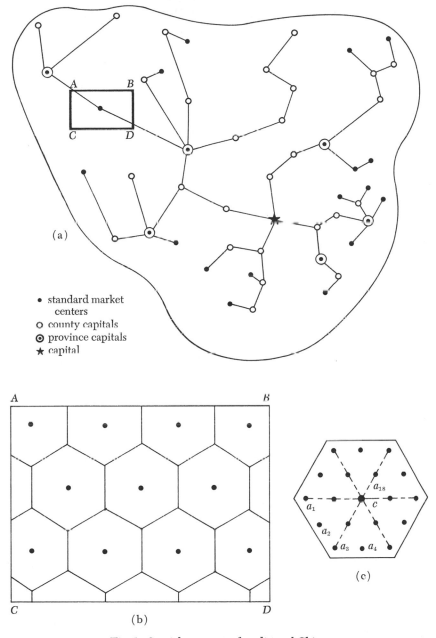

Fig. 1. Spatial structure of traditional China

first assume a homogeneous plane, deferring region-related issues to Section 7.

From Figure 1c we see that the marketing centers (c) of standard market areas are the "nerve ends" of the aggregate urban structure (Figure 1a), and thus the focal points of contact between the urban sector and the rural sector. The economic significance of standard markets will be explored from this point of view in Section 4. Intuitively, it is obvious that a formal theory of the standard market must take into account both agricultural and nonagricultural production—the key phenomenon of any agrarian dualism.

3. *Minimization of Transportation Cost*

A part of our theory of the size and shape of the standard market area is based on the notion of the minimization of transportation cost in a "densely populated" agrarian society. In such a society the homogeneous plane must by definition be completely covered by standard market areas, with no wasteland in between. (By contrast, in the tenth-century "three-field system" in Western Europe, although there were local self-sufficient units comparable to the standard market, there was wasteland between the units so that the land space was not entirely covered.) It can be assumed that China reached the "densely populated" state in the Southern Sung dynasty at the latest.* It is intuitively obvious that without the dense population assumption it is impossible to establish the hexagonic shape of the standard market; under the three-field system, for example, the spatial unit is a three-leaf clover.

In the standard market an important economic cost is the local transportation cost associated with frequent trips from nucleated villages to the marketing center. In the typical standard market observed by Skinner, the least advantageously located village has a round trip of 5.4 miles to the market center. Assuming he carries no extra load besides his own weight (150 pounds), each trip costs him "work" (as the physicists would say) of 810 pound-miles. Multiplying this figure by the number of trips he makes each year (as determined by the frequency of marketing schedules) and the number of people in a typical standard market area (about 1,350) suggests the magnitude of this cost, even if allowance is made for the shorter distances traveled by other villagers (see below). The cost could conceivably be of the same order of magnitude as the

---

* In the period from T'ang to Sung, land abundance gave way to labor abundance. This transition was manifested in many ways (e.g., in changing ideas on land versus labor as wealth, on population pressure, and on the nature of government rural overhead investment; and in new kinds of population migration). Issues of this type have not been fully explored from the point of view of economic theory.

other "work" (cultivating the land, manufacturing activities, etc.) performed in the standard market area.

In traditional rural China, where local transportation was supplied by human or animal power, small increases in distance meant large increases in cost; as an old Chinese proverb had it, "The distance of 90 miles is half the distance of 100 miles." A fair assumption is that the cost is proportional to the square of the distance traveled. Thus, when the distances traveled are 1, 2, 3, 4, . . . miles, the total transportation costs are 1, 4, 9, 16, . . . ton-miles instead of 1, 2, 3, 4, . . . ton-miles. In such circumstances, there is clearly economic pressure to keep marketing areas small.

The implications of this assertion are explored in Figure 2. Let us assume that a market area A and an urban center c located in A are postulated arbitrarily as in Figure 2a. Suppose one ton of goods is to be delivered directly from c to each of the nucleated villages $a_1, a_2, \ldots, a_6$, which are respectively 2, 2, 1, 3, 3, and 3 miles from c. Then the transport cost (T.C.) coefficient is 36 ton-miles with increasing cost. Since the T.C. coefficient clearly depends only on the shape and size of A and the precise location of the urban center, we may denote it by $T(A, c)$.*

A fundamental hypothesis in this paper is the principle of rationality in minimizing local transportation cost—i.e., minimizing $T(A, c)$. On the strength of this principle, we hope to establish both a theory of market boundary (i.e., the optimum size and shape of A) and a theory of location (i.e., the optimum location of the marketing center c once A is given; see Section 7). Once A is given, the principle implies that the optimum urban center c should be located in such a way as to minimize $T(A, c)$. If, furthermore, A is assumed to be a regular polygon, then the optimum location of c is the geographic center of gravity.† For regular triangles, squares, and hexagons, the optimum location of c is indicated in Figure 2b. As Skinner has shown, marketing centers do indeed tend to be located near the geographic center of gravity of the hexagonal marketing area.

Let us next try to determine the optimum shape and size of A. For the time being, let us assume that the A's are in fact regular polygons of the same size; we defer the proof of this assumption to Section 7. It is

* When the nucleated villages are spread evenly in A, the value $T(A, c)$ is what physicists refer to as the second moment of A with respect to c. (See Appendix.)

† If A is of arbitrary shape (i.e., not necessarily regular), the optimum location of c may not be the geographic center of gravity when transportation costs are directly proportional to distance. However, when this direct proportion does not hold, as in the present case, the optimum location of c is *always* the geographic center of gravity.

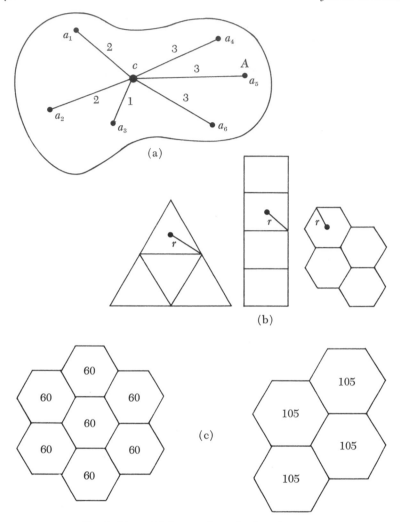

Fig. 2. Potential shapes of standard market areas

easy to prove that only three kinds of polygon can fully cover a homogeneous plane, namely, triangle, square, and hexagon (Fig. 2b). Next imagine that the total area in the three cases is the same and occupied by the same number of polygons (e.g., four, as shown). Thus the areas of the individual triangles, squares, and hexagons are the same. It can be readily proved (see Appendix, equations A2–A4) that $T(A, c)$ is the smallest for the hexagon pattern. The fact that the standard market area indeed tends to be a hexagon, as observed by Skinner, thus lends support to the principle of minimizing local transportation cost.

Next, with respect to the size of the market area, Figure 2c shows that equal total area can be covered by a large number of small hexagons or a small number of large ones. Intuitively, it is obvious that the total transportation cost for the whole region is smaller in the former case. From the formula in the Appendix we see that $T(A, c)$ is proportional to the third power of the radius, i.e., as the radius increases by 1, 2, 3, 4, ..., $T(A, c)$ increases by 1, 8, 27, 64, ..., testifying to the disadvantage of a large standard market area.

In summary, the principle of minimizing transportation cost tells us (1) that the optimum location of market centers tends to be at the geographic center of gravity, (2) that the optimum shape of marketing area tends to be hexagonic, and (3) that the optimum shape of marketing area tends to be the smallest commensurate with considerations other than transportation cost. Clearly we must search for those economic forces that prevent the standard market from becoming too small. The optimum size is then determined by a balancing of forces making for larger market areas against the principle of minimizing transportation cost (see Section 5).

4. Agrarian Dualism and Standard Market

In the land space of traditional China, different regions have different population density. On a map, equal population density contour lines would run from the southwest to the northeast—indicating diminishing population density as one moves away from the Lower Yangtze Valley. Skinner has shown that as population density increases, the area of the standard market shrinks. It takes two steps to explain this phenomenon. In the first step, we may raise the question of what forces determine the size of the standard market in a homogeneous plane when population density is *given and uniform* (see Section 5). The explanation of the regional variation of size as population density varies then follows as an easy consequence (see Section 6).

Referring to Figure 2c once again, imagine that for the two cases portrayed (with the same total area) the population density is also the same, i.e. 420,000. Thus the individual market areas number 105,000 people in one case and 60,000 in the other. Why is the larger area not smaller? For one thing, because all important cultural considerations point to the advantage of a larger population—but this need not detain us. From the economic standpoint, the basic advantage of a larger population is that it enables the community to enjoy the efficiency of large-scale production.

The role of the standard market in traditional China may be explained with the aid of the Economic Tableau of the French Physiocrats (Fig.

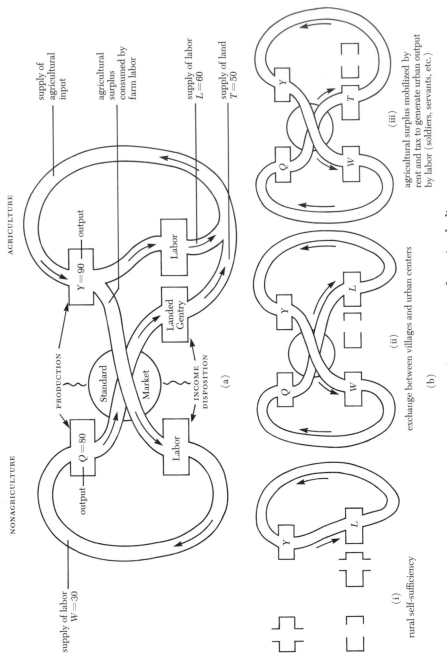

AGRICULTURE

NONAGRICULTURE

supply of
agricultural
input

agricultural
surplus
consumed by
farm labor

supply of labor
L=60

supply of land
T=50

output — Y=90

PRODUCTION

Standard

Market

INCOME
DISPOSITION

Labor

Landed
Gentry

Labor

Q=80 — output

supply of labor
W=30

(a)

(i)

rural self-sufficiency

(ii)

exchange between villages and urban centers

(iii)

agricultural surplus mobilized by
rent and tax to generate urban output
by labor (soldiers, servants, etc.)

(b)

Fig. 3. Circulation patterns of agrarian dualism

3a), which depicts the regularity of major economic events in the European agrarian economy before the Industrial Revolution. The Physiocrats envisioned an agrarian dualism typified by the coexistence of agricultural production (output $Y = 90$) and nonagricultural production (output $Q = 80$), using as inputs land ($T = 50$) and labor ($L = 60$) in the agricultural sector and labor force ($W = 30$) in the nonagricultural sector. The economic tableau can be decomposed into three types of "circulation" (Fig. 3b):

(i) *Agricultural self-sufficiency*: Part of agricultural input is used to produce goods (Y) that flow back to feed the agricultural labor force (L).

(ii) *Dualistic exchange*: Part of agricultural input is used to produce agricultural goods (Y) that flow through the market to feed the industrial labor force (W), which in turn produces nonagricultural goods (Q) that flow back to agricultural labor (L) through the market. This amounts to an exchange of agricultural goods for nonagricultural goods by the two types of labor in the market.

(iii) *Utilization of agricultural surplus*: The input of land (T) leads to agricultural output (Y) that is supplied to nonagricultural labor (W) which produces nonagricultural goods (Q) that flow back to the landlord class.

It does not stretch the imagination too far to see that the same pattern of life prevailed in traditional China—and that the role of the standard market can be explained in terms of this dualism. To a large extent, there is self-sufficiency in the nucleated villages (Figure 1c), which renders frequent trips to the market center unnecessary from an economic standpoint. When such trips are made, it is for the purpose of exchanging agricultural goods for products produced not only by the laborers living in the marketing center, but also, indirectly through trade, by laborers living in urban centers higher in the hierarchy.* Thus the standard market is an institution of exchange and production specialization in a dualistic agrarian economy.

The standard market is also a part of the institutional arrangement for channeling agricultural surplus to the urban labor force (soldiers,

---

* The aggregate view of the urban sector in Figure 1a describes only the spatial structure (i.e., location patterns) of nonagricultural production. The pyramid (or hierarchy) of urban centers has its own rules of formation—an aspect of industrial location theory that will not be explored in this paper. Since our emphasis is on the "dualistic exchange" between the agricultural and nonagricultural sectors, the reader may from now on ignore the existence of urban centers higher in the hierarchy than standard marketing centers.

domestics, civil servants, producers of luxury consumer goods, etc.) that produce goods and services for the landowning gentry class and the government they control. The agricultural surplus in this sense corresponds to the agricultural tax and rental payments, which in traditional China may account for as high as 60 percent of the production of the nucleated villages. The standard marketing centers are the last link in this arrangement; the instruments of their smooth functioning are the landlords, the tax collector, the civil servants, and others residing in the town or nearby.

The Physiocrats not only help us to understand the economic-institutional significance of the standard market, but also teach us that a prosperous agricultural sector is a prerequisite for flourishing nonagricultural activities.* A modern version of the principle of agricultural primacy may be stated in terms of agricultural labor productivity, $p = Y/L$; nonagricultural labor productivity, $q = Q/W$; the proportion of nonagricultural labor to the total labor force, $\theta = W/(L + W)$; and the per capita consumption of agricultural goods, $c = Y/(L + W)$, and nonagricultural goods, $n = Q/(L + W)$. Since the total supply of food is Lp and the total demand is $c(L + W)$, the equality of supply and demand immediately leads to

$$(1) \qquad\qquad\qquad c/p = 1 - \theta$$

For example, if as in China per capita consumption of food (c) is 80 percent of agricultural labor productivity (p), then 80 percent of the total population must be farmers to grow enough food for the remaining 20 percent. Similarly $\theta = n/q$, when substituted in (1), leads to

$$(2) \qquad\qquad\qquad n = q(1 - c/p)$$

which states that the per capita availability of nonagricultural goods (n) can be increased not only by productivity gains in nonagricultural labor force (q), but also by productivity gains in the agricultural labor force (p). The latter effect comes about because more labor can be released from agricultural to nonagricultural production after the per capita food demand (c) is met.

To make the argument clearer, in Figure 4 the nonagricultural labor force (W) is measured on the horizontal axis and the total output of nonagricultural goods (Q) is represented by the total output curve OAB.

---

* To be sure, they refer somewhat misleadingly to land as the source of all wealth and regard the nonagricultural labor force as nonproductive. We must add that the French Physiocrats allegedly imported the idea of the primacy of agriculture from the Chinese during the early Ch'ing dynasty.

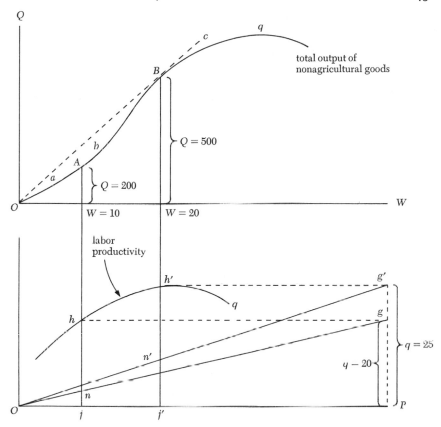

Fig. 4. Effects of increases in productivity. OP is total labor force. Increasing agricultural productivity leads to an increase of the nonagricultural labor force from j to j' with the following effect on per capita consumption of nonagricultural goods: at j we have $\theta = Oj/OP = jn/Pg$, hence $\theta q = jn$; at j' we have $\theta q = j'n'$. Since both θ and q become higher at j', it follows that $j'n' > jn$.

When $W = 10$, total output is 200, leading to a labor productivity of $q = 20$ (plotted in the lower deck). When W increases to 20, total output increases more than proportionally to $Q - 500$, leading to labor productivity of $q = 25$. Between point A and point B there is efficiency of large-scale production—i.e., the total output curve AbB is concave. The efficiency of large-scale production is exhausted after point B, when the total output curve becomes a straight line (or even becomes convex after point c).

Thus as agricultural productivity (p) expands, the nonagricultural labor force (W) expands accordingly—e.g. through a, A, b, B, c, C . . . .

More output will be available on a per capita basis (n). Not only will there be a larger nonagricultural labor force (higher θ), but its productivity will increase because of the efficiency of large-scale production —at least to the point where such efficiency is exhausted. The primacy of agriculture must basically be argued in these economic welfare terms; the standard market is merely an institution to implement such an agrarian system.

5. *Theory of the Size of Marketing Area*

The various threads of thought above may now be integrated to explain the economic forces that determine the size of the standard market. Referring back to Figure 2c, let us once again assume a fixed population density (ε) and a total population of 420,000 in each case. Let us also assume that agricultural productivity (p) is fixed, so that the nonagricultural labor force represents a fixed proportion (θ) of the total population (P). Suppose $\theta = .1$ so that in each standard market the nonagricultural labor force (W) accounts for 10 percent of the total. All this is summarized in Figure 5, which is a reproduction of Figure 2c with labor allocation figures added.

When there is no efficiency of large-scale production, the smaller labor force ($W = 6$) and the larger ($W = 10.5$) will have the same labor productivity (q). The economic welfare of the two cases (in terms of per capita supply of agricultural and nonagricultural goods) will be the same (see equation 2). The principle of minimizing transportation cost immediately implies that under "constant returns to scale in non-

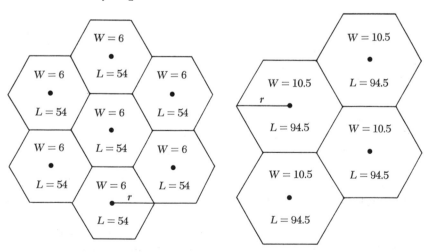

Fig. 5. Hypothetical allocation of agricultural and nonagricultural labor in two regions of equal area and population

agricultural production," the smaller market area is to be preferred. However, when there is efficiency of large-scale production, the larger labor force will have higher labor productivity, implying higher economic welfare. The larger market area will be chosen in any rational society in the absence of transportation cost considerations. Realistically, the optimum market area is the one that maximizes consumer welfare by balancing the low transportation cost of the small area against the efficiency of large-scale production in the large area.

The outline of this deterministic theory is sketched in Figure 6. The two axes in the third quadrant (linked by a 45-degree line) are used to measure r, the radius of the hexagon (i.e., the distance traveled by the least advantageous villagers). The dotted curve in the fourth quadrant measures the total population in the standard market area ($P = kr^2\varepsilon$), i.e., population density (ε) multiplied by the area of hexagon (kr^2).* The solid curve in the same quadrant is the size of the nonagricultural labor force ($W = \theta P$), i.e., a fraction (θ) of the total population. The total output curve of Figure 4 is reproduced in the first quadrant and is translated to the second quadrant (i.e. the total output curve) with the aid of the rectangles. This curve shows for each radius r the total output of nonagricultural goods produced by W in the market area with that radius.

In the same quadrant, the total transportation cost associated with each r is shown by the transportation cost curve (see Appendix, equation A4). With proper adjustment of the unit of measurement,† the shaded gap between the two curves then represents the net gain (i.e., industrial output less transportation cost). In any rational society, the optimum market area (or the optimum value of r) is determined at that level (in our case r_m) where the net gain is a maximum (the distance uv).

According to Skinner, a typical standard market in traditional China is located in a region with population density of 109 persons per square kilometer. The hexagonal market region has a radius of 4.34 kilometers, hence an area of 64.56 km², hence a population of 7,037 (109 × 64.56). Since the average family size in traditional China is 5.21 persons, there are 1,350 families. Assuming $\theta = .2$, there are 270 urban families living in the urban centers and 1,080 families living in the nucleated villages.‡

---

* For any polygon, the area is proportional to the square of the radius.

† Though the unit of measurement of Q is output and that of transportation cost is labor, the two may be converted into the same unit of measurement (e.g., labor) by considering the relative price of labor and output, e.g., according to the labor theory of value.

‡ The 64.56 km² of market area amounts to 15,953 acres. With a degree of land utilization of .34 (John Lossing Buck, *Land Utilization in China*, Nanking, 1937,

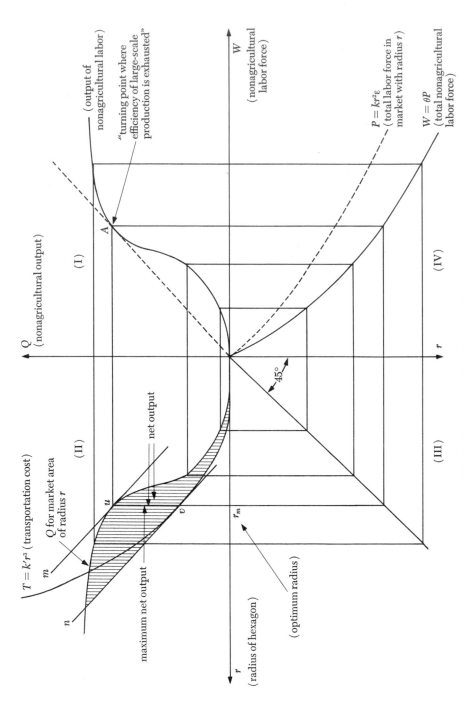

Fig. 6. Optimum radius of standard market area

The theory we have constructed helps to explain these observed magnitudes.

With the aid of the theoretical framework, we can now see why the market area cannot be too large. Basically, two factors restrict market area: a rapid increase in transportation cost proportional to the third power of the radius r, and a much slower expansion of output—proportional at most to the second power of r—as the efficiency of large-scale production is exhausted. The optimum market radius (r_m) is established at the level whereby the marginal transportation cost is equated with the marginal output as the radius varies (indicated by the parallel lines m and n).

The reasonableness of our theory may be examined both deductively and inductively. Deductively, the theory envisions the standard market as a rational economic institution for a dualistic agrarian economy in which technological factors (production and transportation) delimit its operation. The theory envisions an expansion of the market area associated with every improvement in transportation facilities (i.e., lowering of the transportation cost curve) and with any significant gain in the efficiency of large-scale nonagricultural production. These theoretical predictions will now be examined in the light of inductive (i.e., statistical) evidence.

6. Regional Variation of Market Area

Skinner introduces statistical evidence to show that the size of the standard market shrinks from the thinly populated to the densely populated regions in China (except in the case of very densely populated large urban centers, which do not concern us here). To analyze this phenomenon, we have to take into consideration yet a third property of land space, namely regional non-homogeneity of fertility and natural resources. We shall confine ourselves here to fertility as a first approximation.

It is reasonable to assume that more fertile regions have both a higher population density (ε) and a higher agricultural labor productivity (p) than nonfertile regions,[*] and thus a higher proportion (θ) of nonagricultural labor (see equation 1). Returning to the fourth quadrant of Figure 6, we see that as (θ, ε) increases the two curves shift upward, which

---

p. 162), the cultivated acreage is 5,424 ($15,953 \times .34$), implying 5.0 acres ($5,424/1,080$) per family.

[*] Ricardo's theory of rent first formally recognized the differential fertility of land as a basic factor determining population allocation and differences in rent between regions. The "conclusion" cited here without proof can be proved rigorously by Ricardo's theory.

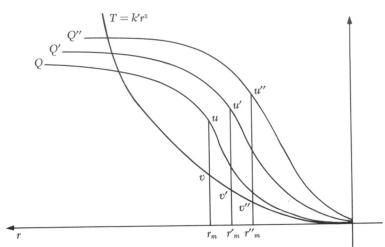

Fig. 7. Shrinkage of optimum radius with increasing population density

means that for a given r the total population as well as the nonagricultural labor force is higher in regions with higher agricultural productivity. This in turn raises the total output curve in the second quadrant. The situation is reproduced in Figure 7, where with a fixed transportation cost curve the upward shift of the total output curves $(Q, Q', Q'', \ldots)$ corresponds to higher agricultural productivity in the more densely populated regions. The equilibrium optimum value of the radius is seen to shrink accordingly $(r_m > r'_m > r''_m)$. This establishes the rationale for the shrinkage of market area observed by Skinner.

Intuitively, the basic reason for smaller market areas in more densely populated regions is the decreasing efficiency of large-scale production as the industrial labor force expands. In an agrarian economy, the traditional technology of nonagricultural production places a limit on the advantage to be gained from increasing the labor force. When the population density rises, a given market area will have a larger total population as well as a larger nonagricultural labor force than before. Since there is no further advantage to be gained from the efficiency of large-scale production, the market area shrinks in order to economize transportation cost.*

* Skinner's exception for large urban centers can be explained by the same principle. Such centers are typically located where the efficiency of large-scale production is relatively conspicuous and at river and road junctions, where the local transportation cost is lower. Both factors make for an expansion of the standard market area.

7. The Formation and Shape of the Standard Market

It takes a different kind of theory to explain how the standard market in traditional China was formed. Since the development of such a theory is as yet incomplete, we shall only provide an outline. To begin with, the process of formation took a long time: probably at least 500–600 years after the cultivable wasteland disappeared during the Southern Sung dynasty. Furthermore, as population increased in a given homogeneous land space, standard markets increased in number and decreased in area. In this process, the shape of the standard market became gradually regularized: i.e., the shape asymptotically became hexagonal. Finally, the process was "experimental" in that deviations from rationality tended to be corrected by a trial-and-error process. In particular, whenever an irrational (or inefficient) market structure* was destroyed by war, famine, or other calamities causing large-scale population dislocation, it tended to be rebuilt in the direction of rationality.

Suppose that at some point in the long process the population density (ε) warranted the coverage of the land space by n standard markets $A_1, A_2, \ldots, A_n$ with n marketing centers $c_1, c_2, \ldots, c_n$. Since the transportation coefficients are defined for each market, the total transportation cost is:

$$(3) \qquad T = T(A_1, c_1) + T(A_2, c_2) + \ldots + T(A_n, c_n)$$

By rational coverage (or efficient coverage) we shall mean that the shape and size of the A's as well as the location of the c's must be such that T is minimized.

We can immediately identify two necessary conditions of the efficiency of the coverage:

(i) When $(A_1, A_2, \ldots, A_n)$ are given, the urban centers $c_1, c_2, \ldots, c_n$ must be located at the geographic centers of gravity (see Figure 8a).

(ii) When $(c_1, c_2, \ldots, c_n)$ are given, the market areas $A_1, A_2, \ldots, A_n$ must be determined by the perpendicular bisectors to the lines connecting the adjacent urban centers, i.e., the c's (see Figure 8b).

These conditions ensure that the transportation cost is minimized within each marketing area individually, a necessary condition for minimizing total transportation cost. The two conditions, however, are

---

* For example, a marketing center might be wrongly located because it was there historically; or a nucleated village might choose to affiliate with a distant marketing center for reasons of historical loyalty.

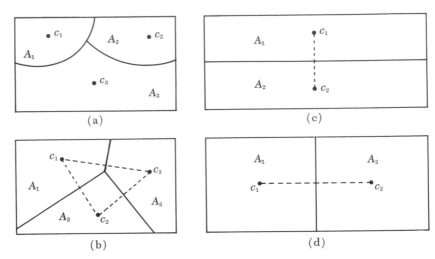

(a) (c)

(b) (d)

Fig. 8. Necessary conditions for optimum market structure

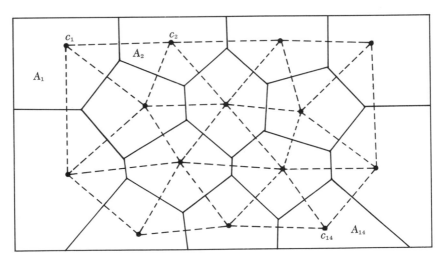

Fig. 9. Long-run process of forming standard markets

not sufficient, as can be seen from Figure 8c; here the two urban centers are too close and the coverage is not as efficient as the one portrayed in Figure 8d.

Now suppose that an increased population density in a given land space warrants an increased number of standard markets in that space ($m > n$). The situation is now depicted in Figure 9, a magnified version of Figure 8 in which both conditions are fulfilled. Here we begin to sense that the marketing regions all *tend to be* hexagonal in shape. This phenomenon suggests the following theorem:

> *Under the principle of minimizing total transportation cost, the coverage of a given land space by a marketing structure will be equal-area asymptotically regular hexagonal as the number of market areas increases to infinity.*

This theorem, purely mathematical in nature, is as yet unproved, but the analysis that has led to it represents an advance on the mere assumption of hexagonality that we made in Section 2. Note that the effect of the theorem is to emphasize the increasing rationality of the spatial structure of standard markets in the context of continuous long-run population pressure.

8. Conclusion

In this paper, we are concerned with the analysis of the spatial economics of a traditional agrarian economy. In such an economy the land space has four properties relevant to economic analysis: area, distance, fertility, and resource endowment (i.e., natural resources other than land fertility). It is essential to know which of these properties are relevant to our argument at a particular level of abstraction.

Let us assume there is no transportation cost (i.e., no real cost, even in time, required for transportation). Then the distance property is irrelevant. Let us further assume a land space homogeneous in land fertility and resource endowment. Then only the area property is relevant to economic analysis, as represented in Figure 10a by the region S. Since the marginal productivity of labor is by definition the same throughout the region, the agricultural population (represented by the dots) will be distributed evenly in the land space. The efficiency of large-scale production, if unlimited, leads to the emergence of one urban center (represented by point a), whose location is quite arbitrary because of the absence of transportation cost.* This "distanceless economy"

---

* This corresponds to the classical analysis of Ricardo. If the efficiency of large-scale production is limited, there may be several urban centers, whose locations are again arbitrary.

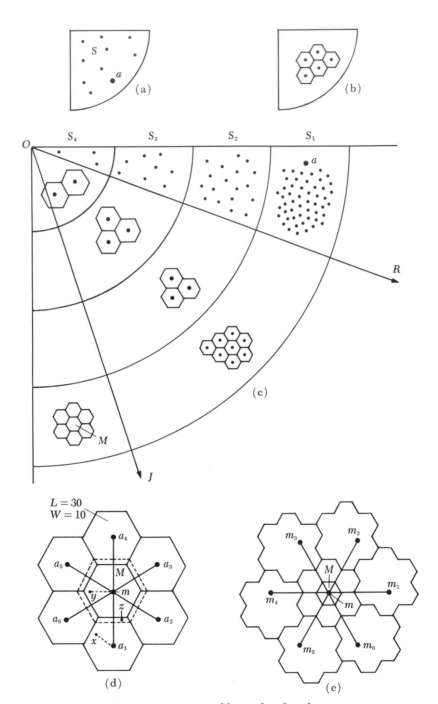

Fig. 10. Location, size, and hierarchy of market towns

leads to the picture of agrarian dualism shown in the Economic Tableau of the French Physiocrats (Fig. 3a).

Figure 10b portrays an economy that has significant transportation costs; i.e., both area and distance are relevant to economic analysis. Now agrarian dualism has one additional property, namely the appearance of a localized market structure of uniform size covering the land space—i.e., Skinner's standard market structure. It is distance and transportation costs that give rise to the localized market structure pattern.*

In Figure 10c the land space is divided into strips S_1, S_2, S_3, S_4 in decreasing order of fertility. The total population of S is distributed such that population density increases with increasing fertility and each homogeneous strip has uniform distribution of population. Such a pattern of settlement is implied by Ricardo's theory.

In this figure the line OR marks off two subregions. In the subregion above OR, we assume there is no transportation cost; hence, as in Figure 10a, there is only one urban center, a, with an arbitrary location. In the region below OR, where we assume transportation cost, each strip is covered by standard markets of uniform size (as in Figure 10b) and the size decreases as we move from less fertile to more fertile strips. This is the situation envisioned by Skinner and dealt with in Section 6.† Thus, differences in size of market area are caused by differences in land fertility in a land space with transportation cost.

In the subregion below the dotted line OJ, we observe in the most fertile region (S_1) a standard market M surrounded by six other standard markets and forming what may be called a market complex; in Skinner's terminology, the market town m of M is an "intermediate market town." This complex is shown in detail in Figure 10d. Usually the intermediate market area m has a higher population density than the surrounding area, and the market area of m (represented by the dotted line) is larger than that of the satellite market towns. Thus, although as we move from S_4 to S_1 the size of the standard market shrinks as the population density increases, there are some large urban centers

---

* The determination of the size of these markets is the main focus of Section 5. In classical economic analysis, transportation cost is usually neglected. On the other hand, some good analyses of the economics of transportation costs are only tenuously related to the main concerns of classical economics; see, for example, August Losch, "Die raumliche Ordnung der Wirtschafts," translated in *Economics of Location* (New Haven, Conn., 1954), cited by Skinner.

† My argument in the earlier section is formally concerned with this case. The rest of this section is heuristic and suggestive of future research.

that have both more area and greater population density than the average for their strip.

To account for this phenomenon, consider m in Figure 10d, an intermediate market town surrounded by six satellite market towns such that there is now a two-tier hierarchy of marketing centers. Heretofore we have assumed that every standard market is completely self-sufficient, but the existence of the intermediate market town m implies a different order of economic relations, namely, an exchange of goods between m and its satellite towns $a_1, a_2, \ldots, a_6$ (shown by the lines linking m and a_i). A standard market is no longer either self-sufficient internally or symmetrical externally.

The existence of a market complex can be explained by recognizing that different industrial goods are produced with optimum efficiency at different levels of large-scale production. Suppose needle-making has a higher efficiency of scale than rice-milling. Then it is likely that needle-making will be located at m and rice-milling at the satellite cities (and m as well). Throughout the complex, the consumers will buy needles manufactured in m, but rice will be produced and consumed locally within each standard market.

Let us investigate the emergence of the market complex in these terms. In Figure 10d, suppose that in each standard market there were originally 30 agricultural workers and ten industrial workers, of which nine are rice-millers and one is a needle-maker. Let us assume that needle-makers migrate to m because of the scale efficiency of needle-making (so there are now seven needle-makers and nine rice-millers at m). Now assume that two farmers, x and y, are equidistant to their respective market centers. Since for purchasing needles x pays more transportation cost than y, his real income is lower than y's. Some farmers from the satellite areas will accordingly migrate to M, and since this population shift will simultaneously decrease the demand for rice in the satellite areas and increase it in M, some rice-millers will necessarily move to m. In due course the population density of all three types (i.e., needle-makers, rice-millers, and farmers) will be higher in and around m than in any of the satellite areas.

Once this situation exists, the market area of m is likely to expand if there is external economy of production, e.g., if rice-milling can be done more efficiently in m than in the satellite towns because it is done side by side with needle-making. When this occurs, a person like z who previously bought rice at a_1 may now choose to buy rice at m because the price is lower there. Thus, the emergence of a market complex with a larger population density and market area at the center can be explained by (1) the existence of some industries with conspicuous economies of scale (e.g., needle-making) and (2) the existence of external economies for other industries (e.g., rice-milling).

The concentration of the manufacturing industries of the Philippines in Manila (or those of Thailand in Bangkok) is due mainly to the fact that the external economies of an industrial complex in these large cities far outweigh the transportation cost incurred in shipping commodities to the provinces.

In Figure 10e the marketing complex of Figure 10d is shown surrounded by six other marketing complexes (only the intermediate market towns are shown) to form a marketing complex of a higher order. As before, those commodities with a higher scale of efficiency are produced at m but not at m_1, m_2, ... , m_6. External economies will greatly increase the size of the standard market M with center at m (in Skinner's terminology, a "central market town"). Proceeding in this way from the economic standpoint, we can see the logic of the formation of a hierarchy of urban centers.

From the above analysis, we might expect to see a uniform and symmetrical pattern of industrial location. But this is to reckon without the fourth property of land, namely the irregular distribution of natural resources (e.g., minerals, salt) and natural features (e.g., mountains, rivers). When such features are introduced, the regularity of the pattern becomes distorted by long-distance trade, which is based not on efficiency of scale but on differential resource endowment: thus herbs from Szechwan are shipped east down the Yangtze, salt from the coast is shipped west to the interior. The existence of such trade further contributes to the expansion of large cities, which may further increase the efficiency of large-scale production in those cities and thus further expand their marketing area. These ideas, of course, are no more than intuitively obvious; rigorous models remain to be formulated.

APPENDIX

Let A be a simply connected region in two-dimensional space, and let c be a point in A. Let dA be a differential area, and let x be the distance between (any point in) dA and c. Suppose the tonnage of shipment is s per unit area; then the shipment from dA to c is $xsdA$ ton-miles (without increasing transportation cost) and is x^2sdA (with increasing cost). The total special transportation costs are then

$$T = s \int_A x dA = sM^{(1)}(A, c) \qquad \text{(without increasing cost)}$$

$$T = s \int_A x^2 dA = sM^{(2)}(A, c) \qquad \text{(with increasing cost)}$$

where $M^{(1)}$ and $M^{(2)}$ are respectively the first and second moments of A with respect to c. If, in particular, A is a regular polygon of n sides with radius r and c is located at the "center," we easily have (without increasing cost)

(A1) $\quad T(A, c) = (n/3) \cos^3(\pi/n) [\tan(\pi/n) \sec(\pi/n) +$
$\qquad\qquad \ln \tan(\pi/n) + \sec(\pi/n)] r^3$

which shows that the spatial transportation cost is proportional to the third power of the radius. For the special cases $n = 3, 4, 6$ (triangles, squares, hexagons), we have

(A2) $\quad T(A, c) = \dfrac{1}{4}\left[\sqrt{3} + \dfrac{1}{2} \ln(2 + \sqrt{3})\right] r^3 \qquad$ (triangle)

(A3) $\quad T(A, c) = \dfrac{8}{3}\dfrac{1}{\sqrt{2^3}}\left[\dfrac{1}{\sqrt{2}} + \dfrac{1}{2}\ln(1 + \sqrt{2})\right] r^3 \qquad$ (square)

(A4) $\quad T(A, c) = \dfrac{3\sqrt{3}}{2}\left(\dfrac{1}{3} + \dfrac{1}{2}\ln\sqrt{3}\right) r^3 \qquad$ (hexagon)

On the other hand, the area of the hexagon, $R = kr^2$, is proportional to the second power of the radius.

In the theory of Section 5 the following equations are postulated:

$Q = f(W)$ $\qquad$ (production function for nonagricultural output)
$R = kr^2$ $\qquad$ (area of hexagon)
$P = \varepsilon R$ $\qquad$ (ε is population density)
$W = \theta P$ $\qquad$ (θ is percentage of population in nonagricultural labor force)
$T = k'r^3$ $\qquad$ (equation A1)
$u = (Q - T)/P$ $\qquad$ (per capita net consumption of nonagricultural goods)*

* In Figure 6, we have defined u as $Q - T$ to simplify exposition.

To determine the optimum market area, we must determine that r which maximizes u; i.e., we must maximize

$$u = [f(\theta \varepsilon k r^2) - k' r^3]/k r^2 \varepsilon = [f(\theta \varepsilon k r^2)/k r^2 \varepsilon] - (k'/k)\,(r/\varepsilon)$$

Differentiating u with respect to r, we obtain the first-order condition

(A5) $du/dr = \phi(r; \theta, \varepsilon) = 0$

The first-order condition implies that the optimum value of r (i.e., r_m) is a function of θ, ε, which are being held fixed in the differentiation of equation A5. Thus conceptually $r_m = F(\theta, \varepsilon)$. In order for r_m to be a true maximum, the sufficient condition is

(A6) $d^2u/dr^2 = d\phi/dr < 0$

The problem of the regional variation of the market area is a comparative static analysis based on the above static equilibrium problem. The basic argument is that as we move from a less fertile to a more fertile region, both θ and ε increase. Thus we may postulate $\theta = g(\varepsilon)$ with $g' > 0$. We can then differentiate r_m with respect to ε, obtaining

(A7) $$dr_m/d\varepsilon = \frac{\delta F}{\delta \varepsilon} + \frac{\delta F}{\delta \theta} g'$$

The heart of the theory of regional variation of the market area is to prove that equation A7 is negative—i.e., that r_m decreases as ε increases. In the text, we have not given a rigorous proof; we only demonstrate the likelihood that r_m decreases as the efficiency of large-scale production becomes exhausted (Figure 7). A rigorous proof would involve the second-order condition (equation A6), which in turn would necessitate a careful specification of properties of the production function $Q = f(W)$ in respect to the efficiency of large-scale production.

We may add here that whereas the optimum size of a standard market (Sections 5 and 6) is a typical comparative-state economic problem in the Samuelson sense, the optimum shape of a standard market is an entirely different (and more difficult) analytical problem of space. The theorem formulated in Section 7, which is a purely mathematical theorem of two-dimensional space, is merely a conjecture. The validity of the elementary discussion of the shape of the standard market in Section 3 depends on the proof of our assumption in that section that when the number of standard markets is large, they all tend to be regular *polygons* of the same shape and size. If this can be proved, it is easy to show that the hexagon is the optimum polygon.

Ramon H. Myers

Cooperation in Traditional Agriculture and Its Implications for Team Farming in the People's Republic of China

THE BASIC socioeconomic unit in Chinese society has always been the household, a group composed of persons of the same blood residing under the same roof. Although households were many times interconnected by kinship ties to constitute a lineage or clan, the household, irrespective of its size, served as the unit on which other cooperative forms were created. To preserve the peace, safeguard the empire, and ensure prosperity, China's rulers inevitably administered their far-flung territories by mobilizing and organizing households. And though the tasks demanded of them varied in the burden and time involved, and the organizations centered on them differed in function and size, certain similarities of household organization persisted throughout.

After the collapse of the Nationalist government, the Communist Party rapidly replaced family farming with a system of team farming. The traditions, customs, and experiences that characterized village cooperation in the past made it possible for the Party to achieve this transformation without vigorous opposition. The purpose of this essay is to show how the cooperative aspects of family farming before 1949 contributed to the establishment of a new farming system based on closer cooperation between households.

The State and the Rural Community

During imperial times the county magistrate represented the furthest extent of state power over Chinese society. Beyond the magistrate lay a world of villages governed by their own leaders and local custom. The magistrate exercised some authority over this world via various village

I wish to thank the Social Science Research Council for supporting the preparation of this essay. I am especially grateful to Dwight H. Perkins for critical comments on an earlier draft of this paper. I naturally assume entire responsibility for remaining errors and omissions.

organizations that made the peasantry fairly responsive to his demands. In the Ch'ing period local gentry or literati also provided a bridge linking the magistrate to village leaders and their organizations. During the Republican period this relationship between state and rural communities changed markedly. The state became weaker and failed to provide relief when villages suffered natural disasters. Groups that claimed to represent state power merely tried to extract additional taxes from villages. As a result, village leaders used their household organizations to protect themselves as best they could under the new circumstances. After the 1949 Revolution the Communist Party eliminated the old village ruling elite, replaced it with leaders of its own choosing, and made the township instead of the county seat the lowest unit of local administration.

The minimal number of households making up the basic village organizational units has remained remarkably constant since the 1870's or so. In the Ch'ing period, groups of ten households made up *li* of 110 households, *pao* of 100 households, and *she* of 20 to 50 households. The *li-chia* formerly collected taxes, the *pao-chia* provided police service and registered people, and the *li-she* supplied "mutual assistance in farm work in the event of death or sickness in any of [the households] during the farming season."[1] Between 10 and 110 households constituted the range between the smallest and largest groups of households in any village.

In the Republican period a modified pao-chia system continued to operate with the same group range of households. For example, the 89 households of Teng k'ou *hsiang* village outside of Paotow were organized into four *lu*, forming the *lin-lu* system.[2] The peasants in Chang yao t'un village in Chiao county near Tsingtao used the *lin-pao* system, with five families making up a *lin* unit and the entire village organized into five lin.[3] In Nan-ching village outside of Canton the households were organized into 20 pao and two chia, both forming part of a hsiang of five villages with headquarters in another village two miles away. The pao each contained about 50 persons or roughly 10 households, the chia slightly over 500 persons, and the hsiang about 6,000.[4]

After the Revolution the Communist Party established mutual aid farming teams of six or fewer households. Later, it ordered these teams enlarged, to form first lower and then higher agricultural producer cooperatives that ultimately accounted for all households in a village. In 1960 the current three-tier system based on the commune, the production brigade, and the production team was installed. The production team usually incorporates between 20 and 40 households, though some teams have been reported to have as many as 80 to 100.[5] Thus, despite the considerable variation in the relationship between state and village under the Ch'ing, Republican, and Communist regimes, the number of households making up any basic village organizational unit has typically ranged between 10 and 100.

Moreover, in all three periods the smallest cluster of households has consisted of families living close to one another. Within this basic group, whether it is today's production brigade or the chia, the lin, the li, or the pao of the past, a member from one household was selected to represent all the other households. This leader in turn met with the village head and council. This organizational hierarchy carried out different tasks over time as demands by the state changed. During the early Ch'ing period the li unit collected tax revenue, but by the late nineteenth century and perhaps even earlier, this function fell under the pao-chia system.[6] In the Republican period the pao-chia or lin-lu system continued to be used for this purpose, as well as to mobilize labor for corvée duty.[7] By the 1960's groups of neighboring households organized as production teams farmed the land.[8]

Before the Communist Revolution the village leadership usually consisted of a headman, an assistant, and a village council of a half dozen farmers. The council members were invariably the same household heads who were in charge of a lin, a lu, a chia, or a pao.[9] These village leaders were responsible during the Ch'ing period to the county magistrate and his underlings, the *ti-pao*, and later, after 1911, to the county official (appointed by a warlord or the Nationalist government) and the local police. From about 1900 onward, the village leaders' principal responsibility was ensuring that the villagers paid their land taxes and any surcharges or special tax levies. They also were expected to manage the financing of the village school, the temple, the crop-watching association, the village granary, and the peace preservation corps.[10] Village leaders naturally used the pao-chia or lin-lu system to collect the extra revenue to support these organizations.

After 1949 a new village leadership ascended to power. During the next two decades Party cadres frequently replaced these leaders when policies changed or when they failed to carry out Party directives. In 1958 the hsiang, or township, formerly a market town surrounded by a cluster of villages, was made the lowest administrative unit in each county and renamed the commune. Each commune formed a council to manage the affairs of all villages under its jurisdiction. Many villages were amalgamated to form a unit called the brigade, and large villages simply dropped their names and became brigades. Within each of these brigades the new village leaders organized production teams. Each brigade also had a council made up in part of leaders from the production teams. Since each brigade maintained close contact with the commune council, rural communities were now brought more tightly under government administration and made more responsive to the demands of the state than at any time in Chinese political history.

Finally, there is one other important similarity in village organization in these three periods. The households in the lowest unit have always met and thoroughly discussed the basic issues and problems in order to reach a consensus. Just as household heads in the chia or lu groups always gathered to decide how the new tax or levy burden was going to be equitably distributed among families,[11] production team members now participate in group sessions to discuss how farming will be undertaken.

But for all these similarities, there is an important difference between the production team and pre-Revolution organizations like the pao-chia or lin-lu, namely, that families now farm the land together in small teams rather than as families. In 1960 a Party directive granted production teams the right to manage their farm capital and a portion of brigade land.[12] Although the Party tried to transfer these rights to the commune in 1967–68,* Party leaders later rejected this move in favor of the former three-tier system, confirming the production team's right to make farming decisions. As this system has operated in the 1970's, team leaders first meet with brigade leaders to agree on general brigade farming goals, and the teams then select their crops accordingly. The teams also work out the procedures for irrigation, fertilizing, weeding, and pest control. After the harvest, team leaders meet to decide which village projects should be undertaken to improve future farm production.[13] The brigade permits team households to farm small plots around the family residence, and these private plots vary with village size and available land.[14] The household thus has much less freedom to use its family labor compared with family farming before the Revolution.

* The left-wing character of Communist Party rural policy during the Cultural Revolution has been missed by Western commentators and students. The very vigorous efforts of the Party to gradually make the production brigade instead of the production team the unit of account and chief dispenser of resources in some provinces came to my attention in an essay by Lin Pang, "Tui Kung-fei chiu-cheng kuo-tso nung-ts'un ching-chi cheng-ts'e chieh-shih chih fen-hsi" (Analysis of the Communist "bandit" policies toward the village economy: The policy of "correcting errors" and the policy of "extreme leftism"), *Fei-ch'ing yüeh-pao*, 14.4: 43–44 (Mar. 1971).

Cooperation in Agriculture Before the Communist Revolution

In a country so vast as China, with great differences of climate and landscape, farming conditions vary greatly. The central and southern provinces contain areas of higher fertility, a longer growing season, and greater rainfall than the northern provinces. In traditional China, then, the farther south one traveled, the higher the crop yields and the more numerous the people supported by the land.* But even under the most favorable farming conditions, villagers had to solve two problems. The first was to correct for the unequal distribution of land and labor among households. The second was to satisfy the irregular, high demand for labor during certain farming periods. In any village the households could be divided into two groups: the wealthy households with more land than their family labor could handle and the poor households with more labor than their land would support.[15] Certain crops also needed more labor than others, requiring soil preparation in the early spring, followed by weeding in the late spring and early summer and then by harvesting in the late summer and early fall.[16]

Both problems could be solved by households entering into informal and formal agreements with each other to rent or lease land, loan or borrow carts and work animals, hire or sell labor, and lend or borrow money. These agreements really were exchange transactions based on the subjective evaluations of each party of the costs and benefits. Sometimes, however, households found a different solution: cooperation. Households of long standing friendship or of the same lineage cooperated and shared their resources to overcome a certain resource scarcity.

On first glance at the standard village studies it appears that households preferred commercial transactions to cooperation. For example, C. K. Yang makes no mention of widespread household cooperation by Nan-ching villagers, but speaks only of the peasants renting land, hiring or contracting out their labor, and leasing and renting work animals.[17] Japanese researchers investigated many villages in Kwangtung province in 1940–41; they described the numerous labor markets and how lineages used their land, but they do not mention households cooperating in farming.[18] Daniel Kulp does not report any households engaged in cooperative farming in Phenix village up the Han river from Swatow in Fukien.[19] Fei Hsiao-t'ung remarks that the farmers in K'ai-hsien-k'ung of Kiangsu avoided any "ritual ceremony at the beginning of the agri-

---

* This was true not only of the southeast provinces but also of the east-central provinces. In both regions crop yields were much greater than in the northern provinces, and population density was also higher.

cultural work and every household [was] free to determine its own time for starting."[20] Martin Yang makes no reference to cooperation between households in Taitou village southwest of Kiaochow Bay during the farming season.[21] In short, although these works comment on household cooperation for village irrigation, they fail to mention such cooperation in the direct working of the land.

There are studies, however, that do cite instances of household cooperation, notably those of the Japanese who surveyed villages in North China between 1939 and 1942. Their research turned up cases in which several households shared labor, land, or capital with one another. In Sha-ching village, situated several miles from the county seat of Hsun-i in Hopei, the peasants described how such farming cooperation took place.

QUESTION: "What do you call examples of cooperative activity?"

ANSWER: "They are called *ta-t'ao*. In this village and even in nearby villages, ta-t'ao is widespread. Ta-t'ao means tying ropes together in the form of a chain. This custom takes place throughout the year. When a household has a cart but no horse, ta-t'ao allows that household to borrow a horse from another household. There are even cases where more than two households will cooperate with two other households. There is no reason for households practicing ta-t'ao to be the same households every year. In fact, long-term cooperation of this sort is rare. At most the same households will use ta-t'ao for only two or three years. If there is disagreement between them, they will break off cooperation."

QUESTION: "What are some examples of this custom?"

ANSWER: "An example would be if a household has a cart but no draft animals to pull it, then that household would borrow a strong horse from another household."

QUESTION: "Is this practice used between households to borrow goods?"

ANSWER: "It merely permits the exchange of labor and for households to help one another."[22]

The peasants did not use ta-t'ao to accumulate farm capital or to exchange money. They simply exchanged labor and farm capital to sow, harvest, and build or repair their homes.[23] Their cooperative efforts depended on the goodwill and trust established between households of the same lineage or of friends and neighbors.[24]

The Japanese found similar cases of such farming cooperation in other Hopei villages as well as in Shantung.[25] Nor was this kind of household cooperation peculiar to North China. In Imahori Seiji's account of agrarian conditions in Kwangtung during the Ch'ing period, we are informed that a dozen poor families would obtain water buffalo, take turns providing it with the necessary grass and fodder, and then cooperate to plough their fields for rice planting.[26] The peasants referred to fields prepared in this manner a *niu-t'ien* (water buffalo fields) as opposed to *jen-t'ien*, those ploughed by human hand. Very likely cooperation of the sort was quite prevalent among poor families throughout rural China.

Household cooperation in agriculture was also common in the sugar-cane regions of southern Taiwan during the Ch'ing period.[27] The processing of sugarcane, an expensive operation that few individual farmers could afford, was frequently undertaken by a group of 15 to 40 farmers. Each man contributed a water buffalo, or a large stone for rolling, or some of the building materials for a small mill. The value of these contributions was measured according to a unit equivalent to three bullocks drawing a large stone to crush the cane stalks. This unit also had its money equivalent, so that farmers could supply either cash or kind. If the mill had to be expanded to process more sugarcane, the farmers supplied additional resources or money. Each farmer brought his harvested cane to be processed, awaiting his turn to supervise the crushing and to tend the fires that boiled the extracted juice. The amount of cane he was allowed to process was governed by his original contribution toward establishing the mill, and his share of the processed sugar was determined in the same way.

Water control was also frequently a cooperative endeavor among landowning peasants, and indeed often required the cooperation of several or even many villages. There is considerable controversy over the relationship of water-control cooperation and village administration, some arguing that the one determined the other, some saying it did not. In fact, we have examples that show water-control cooperation functioning independently of village administration and others that show the selfsame men handling both responsibilities.[28] In any event, this issue has no real bearing on our concern, which is with how household cooperation was organized. Several examples will suffice to show that all such cooperation had certain common features.

In eastern Hsing-t'ai county, Hopei, the villages were organized into pao-chia or lin-lu systems with the headman of each pao or lin assisting the village headman on the village council.[29] These groups of households raised funds to finance village organizations and pay the levies imposed by the county tax office and the police. Numerous rivers flowed through this section of the county across the North China Plain. During the early Ming period, a system of canals and embankments had been built along these rivers to channel irrigation water to the villages. Each year the water gates (*cha*) that connected the canals and controlled the flow of water had to be repaired, and the canals dredged to prevent silting and blockage of flow. Repairs were also required periodically on the embankments, which were frequently eroded or swept aside by floods.

For the system to function smoothly the water flow to each village had to be carefully coordinated so that all the farmers in the region had sufficient water for their fields. One or more villages might be serviced by a water gate and several canals. Management of the system was handled by a hierarchy of well-to-do peasants experienced in irrigation matters, who were selected annually by their predecessors. At the top of the hierarchy were supervisors called *lao-jen* or *hao-lao*. Next came their assistants, the *ho-cheng* or *ho-fu*, and at the lowest level were a group of agents known as *hsiao-chia, kung-chih,* or *pang-pan*. Each of these agents was in turn responsible for several households, usually about 20, seeing that the water-using village families, called *lien-hu* or *po-lien*, supplied labor to maintain the system and paid their annual fees. The water managers' principal duties were to inspect the system thoroughly before each spring planting and to see that the water gates were opened at whatever time and for whatever period custom prescribed. At the end of the year they were rewarded for these services with small payments of grain from their clients. This organization for water control existed quite independent of the village administration.[30]

This form of cooperation had four principal features. First, the managers of the water-control system were always well-to-do, experienced farmers who had the respect of other villagers. Second, all the water-using households were landowning; tenants did not participate in the system. Third, the participating households paid fees and supplied labor on the basis of the amount of land they wanted watered, so that those households deriving the most benefit shouldered the major costs. Finally, the water-control managers were rewarded in a small way for their supervisory efforts, and leadership perpetually rotated among the more able, landowning peasants of these farming communities.

Another cooperative form of water control was practiced in Nan-hai county in Kwangtung province, a low-lying region in which the peasants were able to grow mulberry trees between their rice paddies, thanks to the embankments constructed in the Ch'ing period against the monsoon floods. This area, which the inhabitants called Sang-yüan-wei, contained more than 190 villages. Local officials had established special offices to inspect and supervise the maintenance of the embankments, naming two men to see to the repair of each section.[31] The landowners (*yeh-chu*) of the area held the subsurface (*t'ien-ti*) rights to the land, their tenants the surface (*t'ien-shang*) rights. The landowners, whether working or absentee owners, had to make annual payments toward the support of the flood-control offices. They also had to supply rice, bamboo, straw, and the like, and transport these to the repair sites. Each landowner provided at least four workers, and in cases of heavy repairs, they were notified to supply additional materials and workers. In the event of enormous damage to the system the county magistrate helped pay for the repairs. Unlike the Hopei system just discussed, this water-control system was paid for by the landowning farmers but was not run by them. Households no doubt agreed to cooperate in maintaining these embankments because of the economic advantages of combining sericulture with rice cultivation.

During the Ch'ing period, water was channeled from Lake Lien, located near Chinkiang in Kiangsu, into a narrow passage-way, allowing grain tribute boats from Kiangsu and Chekiang to enter the Grand Canal to the north.[32] The lake water was also used for irrigation by villages at both ends of the lake. The villagers at the upper end had been mobilized by the local elite to build a dam with sluices and water gates, thereby ensuring themselves of a regular flow of water for their fields. Each village had managers, often the village leaders, who fixed the amount of labor and materials the water-using households were to contribute for the annual repair of the system in proportion to their land holdings.[33] Similarly, farmers at the lower end of the lake jointly built and maintained a network of canals capable of diverting enough water to irrigate 40,000 *mou* of land. This area, containing about 180 villages, was divided into sections, each of which looked after its part of the irrigation system. Managers selected from the villages cooperated to coordinate the flow and rationing of water and to assess the water-using households for the upkeep of the system. The county magistrate and his assistants made certain that villages carried out their cooperative responsibilities.[34]

Water-control systems involving intervillage and intravillage household cooperation were not unique to any particular area of China. Fei Hsiao-t'ung reported that in K'ai-hsien-k'ung the villagers were organized into teams to pump water to different sections of the village. "The amount of labor contributed by each member of a certain land area, taking the household as a unit, is proportional to the size of his holding."[35] The members of these land-area groups were divided into teams, each headed by a manager and assigned to specific pumps and specific sections of the village. At the beginning of the year, the chief of all the managers called them to a meeting to name a chief manager for the coming year, and a feast was given for the formal inauguration of his successor.[36]

In Tung-ho village, near Paotow, Inner Mongolia, some 100 landowning Chinese households, working through an association called the *nung-p'u-she* (society of farmers with vegetable gardens), supported an irrigation system fed by three canals.[37] All the landowners receiving water benefits belonged to this association and paid annual fees according to the amount of land they owned. The head of the association had several assistants, including a record keeper, plus a number of lower-level agents to supervise groups of households. The association leaders managed the flow of water into the village at prescribed periods and collected funds to keep the system repaired and in working order. The same men also managed village affairs. In this case, water rights were tied to property rights, passing to a new owner along with the land deed.

As these examples make clear, cooperation was part of rural life in much of China. Both villages and teams of households within villages frequently cooperated to manage complex water-control systems, some number of which were built in the first place through the joint efforts of villagers and the state. Households worked together in order to process cash crops. Poor families often shared their labor and farm capital. The tradition of household and village cooperation was strong in the countryside, and when households saw that participation in a team or organization brought benefits they could not otherwise afford, they chose cooperation.

Family-Farm Economic Decision Making and Social Mobility

Villagers used cooperative arrangements because they perceived that it was in the family interest to do so. Yet the same villagers also often engaged in commercial transactions with each other, shuffling their resources of land and labor. How was such a combination of systems possible? An examination of how the typical farm family made its economic decisions and used its resources reveals certain patterns of household economic behavior that will partially explain why family cooperation and private exchange coexisted.

To begin with, we may describe the Chinese farm family itself as a cooperative unit—in the words of Fei Hsiao-t'ung, a group whose members "possess a common property, keep a common budget, and cooperate together to pursue a common living through division of labor."[38]

The number of persons in such households, or *chia*, varied both according to farming region and according to whether the residents comprised a nuclear, stem, or joint family. The nuclear or elementary family was made up of parents and their children; the stem family of parents and one or more married sons; and the joint family of parents, two or more married sons, and the sons' children. As Irene Taeuber's large sample shows, in the 1930's the rural household typically took the form of the nuclear family. In about three-fifths of the farm families in her survey, no more than two generations resided in the household; only 10.2 percent of the families had four generations of males living in a single household.[39]

Rural custom dictated that the family head, or *chia-chang*, should be a male, usually the eldest; upon his death the position was occupied by his eldest son, or if he had no sons, by an adopted son (*kuo-chi*).[40] The chia-chang represented the household in all contractual matters with other families and outsiders. He also made the key decisions on family work schedules, sources of income, and expenditures.[41] Family members, however, played a certain role in these decisions, which were taken only after group discussion, so that the household's sharing of income and expenditures very much resembled that of a cooperative unit. The household tried to allocate its resources to activities where income gain might be highest; the earnings of family members were then redistributed according to family goals and concerns. Apart from its day-to-day needs, the household spent its income to fulfill ceremonial obligations and improve its income sources.

Every chia was linked to chia before it in an endless chain made possible by ancestor worship and ceremonial display.[42] Veneration of the chia's common ancestors established a connecting thread with previous chia, which in turn had venerated the ancestors on the paternal male side. At the same time the chia-chang also looked toward the future when he would be venerated by his descendants. Each chia head realized the necessity of managing the family's resources so as to provide security and an adequate standard of living, but he was also strongly motivated to try to do better than his ancestors. In the same way, his sons in their turn would identify with his goals and strive "for more wealth, for larger family honor, for more advantageous graveyards, for bigger clan temples, for costlier ceremonials, and for a host of other measures which were calculated to increase the welfare and prestige of the living and of the dead."[43] The internal tensions created from this pull toward the past and concern for the future encouraged hard work, accumulation of wealth, and relentless struggle to improve family social status and economic welfare. Each member of the household was expected to cooperate in this struggle, and to carry out his or her assigned role over the life-span of the chia.

For this cooperating unit to achieve its goals, family members had to work at various tasks. Though agriculture was a full- or part-time occupation for 75 to 90 percent of the men in China,[44] farming was only one of the possibilities for advancing the family's fortunes. Household members were sent into many other occupations depending on the location and available opportunities. At one end of the occupational continuum were laboring jobs of low status, inconvenient and usually performed away from home. Next came commercial jobs, such as peddling, clerking in shops, and brokering, tasks that required certain skills, carried higher status, and were convenient to perform. The wages and profits from these activities varied enormously, but some were more desirable than others in terms of prestige, and this could figure in the chia-chang's decision of which jobs were appropriate for which sons. Toward the middle range of the continuum came farming, an occupation of greater security, status, and convenience because it could be performed in one's own village.[45] For these reasons the majority of households strove to accumulate some land in the community. Toward the upper end of the continuum were entrepreneurial jobs—managing land, lending money, operating shops, and the like—and finally, at the top were the positions of officialdom, the posts in the bureaucracy and the military.

Peasants did not record their preferences for particular occupations, nor did they have the opportunity to make their desires known to outsiders. But rural survey information about household income sources, labor allocation, and social mobility makes it possible to cite certain wealth and occupation patterns. For example, very poor households with few members and a limited pool of labor tended to own little or no land. Such families had to obtain most of their income from wages or farm several plots of land as tenants. Households with some land and more labor could devote their resources primarily to farming. Households with relatively extensive landholdings usually leased part of it, and sometimes participated in entrepreneurial pursuits as well. During the slack farming periods, almost all households tried to earn income from other sources, and some families with special skills regularly supplemented their farm income with sideline activities like sericulture, fishing, peddling, or handicrafts. We observe that in Kwangtung and Fukien the farmers engaged in various trades, whereas farther north, in Honan and Hopei, they went to the market towns to seek work.

Households entered into all kinds of formal and informal contractual arrangements, both written and oral, to exchange, borrow, or rent equipment and land, to hire, supply, or exchange labor, even to borrow or lend money. These arrangements reduced the element of risk and guaranteed recovery of land or other assets. Households that managed successfully and escaped calamities or personal tragedies such as sickness and the early death of a family member usually accumulated some wealth. The accumulation of wealth gradually permited the household to revise its work schedules and put its resources to different use. What perhaps more than anything else prevented households from accumulating wealth sufficient to achieve and hold upper-class standing for a long period of time was the inheritance system. The rules of rural inheritance varied slightly according to local custom, but the basic principle was that all land and wealth were to be divided equally among the sons residing in a household. A son who received a slightly larger share was expected to support his aged parents or provide for their funeral. This practice continually redistributed land and wealth in the countryside.

We have barely begun to understand the complex process of change in rural China over the past centuries. Clearly, village social and economic change must have been more dynamic than we hitherto believed. For what were communities, after all, but aggregations of households that were strongly motivated to achieve certain social and economic goals and that constantly tried to improve their standard of living and social status? At the same time, the periodic redistribution of wealth by the few large extended families created some downward social and economic mobility. This same trend might involve all villagers if certain disasters caused a widespread loss of property and reduced the number of workers and managers in households.

Rural survey evidence collected in 1934 sheds light on certain mobility patterns that might have been fairly common. I have arranged the information for Ho-san-ma-chia village in Hai-lun county, north Manchuria, according to land tenure categories of landlord, cultivator, tenant, and farm laborer.[46] When one compares the status of these households in that year with their status on arrival in Ho-san-ma-chia, an interesting pattern can be observed. In 1934 only 11 of the village's 52 households were in the rural laborer category, and five of these families had been resident there under five years. At one time 27 households or nearly half the households then in the village had been farm-laborer families, newly resident and trying to become farmers. Half of the households in the cultivator and landlord classes (14 of 28) had once been rural laboring families. Nine of these families had lived longer than ten years in the village, suggesting that they had gradually acquired land and elevated their tenure status after a long period. Of the 11 farm-laboring households in 1934, only four had formerly farmed any land, indicating that at some point their status and ranking had declined.

In this single village, more than half of the chia had improved their status, a few fell in ranking, and an even smaller number maintained their status over a long period. Manchuria, of course, was an expanding frontier region, but in other areas of substantial migration and commercial growth, it is likely that a similar development took place. The mobility pattern might have been different in densely populated, long-settled areas. Although the precise degree of change and mobility may never be learned for mainland China, our limited information about cooperation before the Communist Revolution must be placed in the context of family-farm behavior and mobility described above.

The Basis for Cooperation in Chinese Agriculture

Although numerous examples of family-farm cooperation can be cited, we have insufficient evidence to argue that peasants preferred cooperation over private transactions in solving resource scarcities and correcting imbalances between land and labor. Indeed, the evidence seems to suggest that private transactions were the acceptable solution, and that peasants participated in group cooperation only under unusual circumstances. Why did certain villages engage in cooperation and others reject it? This is an extraordinarily difficult question, because we have very little firm evidence about the conditions within which households decided to cooperate. Yet this question must be examined if we are to understand how the shift to cooperative farming could have occurred so rapidly in the 1950's.

There is no particular reason to believe that village cooperation was the result of strong, single lineage influence in a community. On the contrary, Burton Pasternak's recent study of two villages in southern Taiwan shows that more tension and rivalry existed in a single lineage village where geographic and farming conditions had not promoted the development of irrigation through cooperation than in a multilineage village where the cooperatively run irrigation system had contributed greatly to increasing farm income and expanding village employment.[47]

Second, there is no reason why cooperation should have automatically occurred in areas where climatic fluctuations routinely caused great loss of the annual harvest. Even though the peasants stood to gain by cooperating to stabilize the harvest through water control or other measures, the costs of undertaking such large-scale projects might have appeared too high. Usually, only when village or clan leaders perceived substantial benefits from large-scale projects, or continued high costs to the community in the absence of these projects, did they initiate cooperative action. Such was the case described by C. K. Yang for Nan-ching village in 1935–36.[48] The decline of prices and incomes in the early 1930's intensified economic difficulties for the Nan-ching villagers, and they began to recognize the need to farm more land to maintain their standard of living. Many owned sections of a mud flat along the southern edge of the village near a river, but only one crop a year could be grown on this flat because of flooding in May and June. The peasants had long recognized that two crops could be grown in the area if dikes were built, but the cost had always appeared prohibitive until economic conditions worsened in the early 1930's. At that point the Wong clan decided to use its funds and manpower for this purpose. Once the dikes were built, each clan family was allowed to rent the reclaimed land for a period of 15 years in an amount determined by the number of males in the family, after which the land was to revert to the owners. Previously, some agricultural experts who had visited Nan-ching had proposed that two reservoirs be constructed on the nearby hills to capture water and supply it to the dry land below. But the high construction costs of this project discouraged the clan leaders from considering it. Apparently the alleged benefits and worsening economic conditions still failed to change the minds of the clan leaders in this case.

On the positive side, several things can be said. First, any cooperative effort involving more than just a couple of families sharing their labor and farm capital required the participation of landowning families that could afford to contribute some resource or income to the common goal. Second, these families had to perceive that substantial direct benefits would accrue quickly from cooperation; therefore, favorable geographical circumstances had to exist so that income from farming could be increased after households cooperated. Third, an outsider like an official or a member of the gentry or an insider like a clan leader could provide financial assistance to eliminate a large share of the high initial cost of constructing a large-scale project involving peasant cooperation. Finally, households were encouraged to cooperate in face of a real or potential decline of village living standards through the action of the state or some other outside agency; confronted with increased taxes, the expropriation of grain or savings, and the like, village leaders and peasants were forced to cooperate simply to protect themselves. One or more of these circumstances can be found in the examples of household cooperation found in the historical records.

In the early fifteenth century officials of Hsing-t'ai county helped the local peasants construct a series of canals and water gates to supply their villages with water.[49] The peasants themselves maintained the system for some 500 years thereafter, into the twentieth century. Officials also played a key role in constructing and maintaining the dikes in Nan-hai county, Kwangtung, and constructing dams and canals around Lake Lien in Kiangsu during the Ch'ing period.

The state promoted cooperative activity on an even larger scale in the early 1930's, when the Nanking government organized members of rural cooperatives in the countryside, particularly in the seven provinces of Kiangsu, Shantung, Kiangsi, Chekiang, Hopei, Hunan, and Hupeh. A few such cooperatives had been organized in Hopei before then, in the early 1920's, to supply credit in areas stricken by famine, but the movement did not go much beyond that until 1932, when the government published new rules and procedures for launching rural cooperatives.[50] Each village was supposed to form a cooperative with a manager, an assistant, and several clerks for the purpose of either supplying credit, purchasing farm capital, engaging in marketing, or producing specific crops. Between 1932 and 1936 the number of rural cooperatives increased from 3,976 to 37,319, and the membership climbed from around 151,000 peasants to over 1.6 million. By 1936 only 55 percent of these organizations dispensed credit and accepted peasant savings; the rest were concerned wholly with marketing, production, and other services. The speed with which the Nationalist government organized this movement and obtained peasant support for it indicates how quickly new cooperative forms could be developed in the Chinese countryside if the state decided to use its authority.

The rapid spread of crop-watching associations (*ch'ing-miao-hui*) in North China after the 1880's apparently came about because of new taxes and levies imposed on the peasants.[51] Such actions by outsiders encouraged peasants to pilfer from the fields of others to obtain extra grain. At first households merely tried to protect their own fields with privately hired watchmen, but when this proved too costly, they joined with other villagers to make crop watching a common effort. In these associations all landowning families paid a fee, assessed according to the land they owned, to the lin or chia headmen, and the village council or headmen used these monies to hire some poor peasant to patrol the fields several weeks before the harvest. By taxing themselves on an ability-to-pay basis, households established an organization to provide crop-watching services for all. The benefits derived from reducing crop loss through theft far outweighed the small cost each household shouldered for these services.

Village cooperation on a large scale invariably involved families that owned and rented land. Since these households made up the majority of villagers, their participation was essential for cooperation to be successful and lasting. The cost of household cooperation was typically calculated by labor and money contributions determined by the amount of land the household owned. This was true also of the southern Taiwan sugarcane farmers, whose assessed resources were pegged to the amount of cane to be processed and whose rewards were commensurate with the resources contributed.

The strong family-farm cooperative tradition and the historical precedent of household organizations within villages to raise revenue and mobilize labor suggest that cooperation could be increased or extended in different directions (or both) rather easily if the state could tighten its control over rural communities and influence village leadership decisions. Of course, if the state could also provide assistance to villages to undertake projects that increased village income, there is every reason to expect that peasants would participate willingly as long as they observed that direct benefits would accrue to them. On the other hand, given the strong tradition of interhousehold contractual relationships by which families hoped to increase their wealth and improve their status, excessive state intervention in community affairs might provoke passive resistance by the peasantry. Over the centuries state power had often succeeded in influencing peasants in their use of land and labor, and state encouragement of team farming after the Revolution was precisely in that tradition.

Peter Schran

On the Yenan Origins of Current Economic Policies

THE SWEDISH journalist Jan Myrdal recounts the following conversation with Mao Tse-tung on the occasion of the National Day celebrations in Peking in 1962:

MYRDAL: I have just come back from a trip to the Yenan area.

MAO: That is a very poor, backward, underdeveloped and mountainous part of the country.

MYRDAL: I lived in a village, Liu Ling. I wanted to study the change in the countryside of China. (I meant historical change; Mao seemed to understand it as just economic.)

MAO: Then I think it was a very bad idea that you went to Yenan. You should have gone to the big agricultural plains. Yenan is only poor and backward. It was not a good idea that you went to a village there.

MYRDAL: But it has a great tradition—the revolution and the war—I mean, after all, Yenan is the beginning—

MAO: (interrupting me): Traditions—(laughing). Traditions—(laughing).[1]

This brief exchange struck Myrdal as "surrealistic and inconsequential." Yet it poses the intriguing question of why Mao laughed. Was the old revolutionary amused by the interest in tradition? Or did he find it funny that one should look for it in Yenan? Or was he merely thinking of what had become of his "Yenan model" by 1962, under the influence of those old comrades who were treating their chairman like a "deceased ancestor"? Unfortunately, Mao did not add to this disconcerting response, which was doubtless wholly unexpected.

In spite of Mao's reaction, Jan Myrdal's interest in the traditions of the Chinese Communist movement was not all that surprising. Certainly, it was shared by many students of China. Most eyewitness accounts of the Chinese Communists' struggle for power during the 1940's had stressed several aspects of their behavior that seemed to set them apart from their Russian comrades, and some reports had attributed strategic significance to this divergence from the Soviet prototype. The comprehensive adoption of Soviet institutions and policies by the Chinese Communists after their rise to power in 1949 tended to belie such interpretations—besides giving rise to charges of naïveté, superficiality, or worse against those who apparently had mistaken tactical expediency for strategic principle. After a few years of seeming conformity, of course, the Chinese began to deviate again from the Soviet line. And the institution of such new methods and organizations as the Great Leap Forward and the Rural People's Communes had to be explained. In search of experiences which could account for them as well as for other strategic innovations, many studies have looked to the formative period of Chinese Communist thinking about the transition to socialism, and specifically to the thought of Mao Tse-tung, who by all indications provided the inspiration for both the earlier and the more recent departures from the Soviet path to socialism.

Needless to say, this deviation in theory as well as in practice aroused violent opposition not only from the Soviet Union but also within the Chinese Communist movement. In the continuing dispute between the proponents and opponents of Maoist thinking, the principal difference of opinion concerned the malleability of man. Mao's insistence on collective forms of incentive and entrepreneurship, for instance, did not follow simply from his Marxist interpretation of fundamental human needs, to which the advocates of the Soviet view could agree. It depended further on a conception of the relations between man's ideological and technological progress with which they had to disagree. To them, Mao's assessment of the Chinese people's ability and willingness to live and act collectively appeared to be "anti-scientific" and "voluntaristic" because it was premature, i.e., because China's state of backwardness could not be conducive to such behavior according to their reading of Marx.[2]

The indications are that Mao's optimistic assessment was based on wartime experiences in the Chinese Communist base areas during the 1930's and 1940's. In order to be "rational" in the sense called for, the trust in the feasibility of reenacting those experiences required one of two things: either that the circumstances of the 1950's and 1960's had to be comparable in all essential respects to those of the preceding two decades; or that they were irrelevant to the transfer of the experience. In other words, if the "Yenan way" was to be pursued, China's situation had to be fundamentally similar to Yenan's, or else the "spirit of Yenan" had to be communicable to the Chinese even though China's situation was different. In the latter case in particular, tradition had its role to play. A 1972 article in the *Peking Review* says as much in its opening lines: "YENAN, cradle of the Chinese revolution, is the symbol of the glorious tradition of the Chinese revolution. Known as the Yenan spirit, hard struggle and self-reliance make up an important part of this tradition."[3]

Of course, the cultivation of tradition easily gives rise to myths. To sort out so far as possible what is fact and what fiction, I propose to explore the elements of continuity and change in Chinese Communist economic policy over four decades by focusing on four critical topics. The lack of summary descriptions of Chinese Communist base area economies makes it advisable, first, to identify their principal economic problems and to examine possible solutions to these problems. Such an account provides a contrast, second, to a review of the actual emergence of solutions, most of which are attributed to Mao Tse-tung. It also facilitates, third, an exposition of the differences in circumstances between pre-Liberation and post-Liberation times, which called for different solutions in view of the experiences of the Soviet Union. These considerations in turn serve, fourth, to suggest to what extent tradition has been manifested in post-Revolutionary attitudes and policy.

Problems of Guerrilla Economy

In 1927, after the urban revolutionary strategy of the Chinese Communist Party had failed and its urban positions had become untenable, Mao Tse-tung and other Chinese Communists relocated their struggle from the cities to the countryside. There they established themselves in highly backward areas, remote from existing centers of power, first in the hills of south-central China. At the end of seven years of war with the armies of the Nationalist government, they were forced on their famous Long March, which brought them in one year to the loess plateau of northern Shensi in the bend of the Yellow River. Throughout this "soviet" period (1927–37), their primary concern was agrarian revolution, especially the redistribution of land. After the Japanese invasion of China proper in 1937, the Chinese Communists sent out units to set up additional base areas behind Japanese lines. Moreover, in order to promote national resistance against Japan, they adopted a "united front" policy and limited their activities in all bases to social reform rather than revolution for the duration of the war (1937–45), which may be called the Yenan period. At the end of the war against Japan, the Chinese Communists moved once more to extend the territory under their control. After the complete collapse of the wartime alliance with the Nationalists, they also reverted to redistributing land in their areas, a policy that was pursued throughout the final phase of their rise to power (1946–49).

By redistributing land and other assets from the rich to the poor, the Communists sought to achieve two effects: to deprive the dominant classes—landlords, well-to-do merchants, moneylenders, and even rich peasants—of their sources of power, and to secure the support of the dominated masses—tenants, farm laborers, and poor peasants in general—in whose behalf they claimed to rule. During the Yenan period, these objectives were scaled down temporarily. For instance, the three-thirds system of political representation limited the Communists to one-third of the membership of any representative assembly, and their enforcement of Kuomintang land laws tended to diminish payments of land rent by 25 percent. Their shift from revolutionary to reform practices thus served to redistribute power and income to relatively limited degrees. The Communists attributed this conscious self-restraint to their desire to bring about anti-Japanese unity among the Chinese people. Their moderation consequently extended to all patriotic base area residents. It clearly did not apply to collaborators, who continued to be subjected to the extreme retributions of the soviet period.

In reaction to such challenges from within, the respective "host" states attempted to eradicate the pockets of insurrection or resistance inside their territory. During the soviet period, the Chinese Nationalists with the help of some of their warlord allies waged "encirclement and suppression campaigns" against the Communists. These military expeditions into the soviet areas had a twofold aim—not only to "search and destroy" the activists but also to do away with all visible means of support for the entire population in the base areas. Economic blockades at the same time aimed at keeping both the Communists and the local people from replenishing their resources by means of external trade or aid. During the Yenan period, the Japanese army and its puppet regimes resorted to the same practices, especially after the Japanese adopted their "three-all" (burn all, kill all, destroy all) policy and began to build strategically located strong points throughout the countryside. In support of these counterinsurgency measures, both the Chinese Nationalists and the Japanese sought and found cooperation among those who had been hurt by the Chinese Communists' revolution or reforms, in particular members of the propertied classes and public officials.

The Chinese Communists had to cope with this predictable retaliation in order to ensure their survival. To rehabilitate and defend the base areas required additional resources that could be obtained in either or both of two ways. On the one hand, they could occupy additional territory and confiscate wealth as well as recruit people there. But such a tactic conflicted with the interests of merchants, local officials, and other segments of the outside population who had to collaborate in order to break the blockade. On the other hand, the Communists could rely on the wealth and contributions of the people within their areas. Yet the support of local people did not flow automatically from the enemy's atrocities or even from the Communists' redistribution of land or income. It depended also on a variety of concrete improvements in the living conditions of the local population. Such improvements necessitated at the least better government and perhaps even the diversion of resources that were needed for purposes of defense.

In order to rid themselves of this dilemma, the Chinese Communists had to render their base areas self-sufficient. A state of autarky could be approached from two directions. The supply of goods could be increased by developing production within the base areas, especially of import-substituting goods and goods for public uses. Given the backwardness of the area and its isolation, this had to be accomplished through technically primitive methods with locally produced machinery and equipment. As a consequence, it was to be expected that the gains in production would be correspondingly limited, again notably in the cases of import-substituting goods and goods for public uses. Yet since the blockade fully "protected" all production activities, almost any gain had to be worthwhile.

On the other side, it was possible to limit the demand for various goods and services within the base areas. The Chinese Communists could attempt to convince the indigenous population of the need for austerity. However, where it took improvements in living conditions to gain adequate popular support, these improvements had to be provided as well as possible. Increases, say, in the personal consumption of food and clothing or in the collective consumption of health, education, and welfare services by the poorer strata had to diminish the amount of redistributed surplus that could be appropriated for the support of the Communist movement. As a consequence, the restrictions on demand had to be imposed primarily in the public sector, where the Communists had to bring their outlays into line with the base areas' surplus-producing capacities as well as with their redistribution policies. Their change from soviet-type revolution to united-front reforms added difficulties in this connection (which were solved temporarily by Nationalist transfer payments).

The Chinese Communists adjusted to these constraints generally by

devising and implementing methods of administration and forms of warfare that matched the modes of production and the ways of living in
their base areas. Above the level of village administration, the public
sector consisted almost exclusively of persons serving in army units,
central administrative organs, public factories, and (boarding) schools,
most of whom lived collectively in households organized by their service
units. To keep personnel costs in these "institutional households" as
low as possible, the Communists adopted two measures: they sharply
diminished earnings differentials among functionaries, troops, workers,
teachers, and students; and they put all of these groups on rations of
food, clothing, and housing that were similar to those of the base area
populations. In addition, they called on all members of their movement
to provide part of their own rations as well as other goods and services
as best they could by their own production. Toward the end of the
Yenan period and especially during the years 1943–45, such subsidiary
subsistence production by army units and government offices, factories,
and schools became an important activity that supplied a large part of
the total public revenue—in kind.

By coming "close to the masses" and "serving the people" in these
and other ways, the Communist movement could provide various public
services increasingly as net benefits to their base areas. Such contributions, which contrasted sharply with the balance of governmental costs
and benefits elsewhere, doubtless accounted in large measure for the
evident popularity of the Chinese Communists. But they also required
a considerable number of personal sacrifices from the members of the
Communist movement, something that plainly depended on total commitment to the cause. Such profound partisanship was not easy to
achieve in the best of circumstances, that is, when the movement consisted primarily of youths who were idealistic and quite prepared to
act like Boy Scouts. It was even more difficult to bring about in the case
of public functionaries and industrial workers in the base areas, who had
to forgo many of the traditional privileges and rewards of official status
and technical skill that continued to be accorded on the outside. In
practically all instances, there thus was a need for the inculcation of "correct" thinking and for the "rectification" of behavior in all lines of work.

In addition to extremely positive attitudes on the part of the members
of the Communists' institutional households, the development of subsidiary production rested on appropriate opportunities for gain. The
technical production conditions had to be such that the returns to specialization in any activity were small in comparison with the returns
to overall activism, so that the combination rather than the division of

many activities appeared as the preferred solution. The rewards for relatively unskilled work could materialize in many lines of production, and most importantly of all, for the survival of the Communist movement, in agriculture if the primary occupation—soldiering or administering or manufacturing or studying—could be adapted to agriculture's seasonal pattern. Adaptations of this kind could be made most easily in the relatively secure headquarters regions of the base areas, especially in Free China's "little rear," the Shensi-Kansu-Ninghsia Border Region. As a consequence, institutional households were most heavily engaged in subsidiary production in these locations.

Similar opportunities for the development of many kinds of subsidiary production existed in most private households. Farm households in particular, that is to say, the vast majority of private households, could supplement their regular seasonal work in agriculture with many sideline activities, e.g. home handicrafts such as spinning and weaving, the mining of various minerals, various construction activities, and transportation, especially if they reduced their traditional engagement in trading, which tended to be a form of hidden unemployment. The search for economies of scale in most of these subsidiary ventures led to the introduction of rudimentary forms of cooperation as alternatives to capitalistic organization.

Of course, all such subsidiary work had to be in the household's interest in order to be undertaken effectively. The Chinese Communists could not expect that the peasants of the base areas would respond en masse to the ideological incentives that—hopefully—motivated the members of the institutional households. But at the same time they knew that the blockade itself provided material incentives—through changes in the terms of external trade that raised the prices of imported goods and made efforts at import substitution highly rewarding. Such positive inducements could be made known to everybody. And they could be magnified by appropriate fiscal and financial policies (for example, tax exemption and credit rationing) as well as by efforts to diminish various kinds of business risks.

In order to assure the development of production within their base areas in this "retrogressive" form, the Chinese Communists further had to equip the institutional and private households alike with adequate technical knowledge, primitive as that seems to have been in the majority of cases. The dissemination of such knowledge was necessary because the increasing division of labor between city and countryside or coast and interior in the previous quarter century or more had led to the abandonment of several subsistence and market-oriented crafts and trades, with the result that many traditional skills had disappeared long since. Spinning and weaving are cases in point. In addition, the pursuit of autarky naturally involved the introduction of many activities and techniques that had never been practiced in these areas, most notably in the field of modern arms. Whether old or new, and however rare, all such knowledge had to be spread so that each person would be able to take advantage of every opportunity in his (ideological or material) interest.

The Communists promoted this acquisition and dissemination of relevant information principally in two ways: first, they encouraged all producers to be inventive, to learn from others, and to teach others, so that the best practices in every field would come to be adopted everywhere; and second, they induced teachers as well as students in the newly developing school system to relate their studies to the requirements of production, in both their own institutions and the base areas at large. To facilitate this integration of work and study, the Chinese Communists published and distributed 4-H–type "how to do it" pamphlets on various improvements as well as the success stories of various "labor heroes." Further, in an effort to instill such behavior, they made the unity of theory and practice one of the principal issues of rectification. Of course, the social distinction bestowed on exemplary producers constituted an additional incentive to perform.

In summary, all of the preceding changes could be expected to increase the self-sufficiency of the base areas, perhaps eventually to a great degree. But substantial results could also be expected to take a considerable period of time. In the meantime, the Chinese Communists had to make do as best they could. This meant in particular that they had to remain dependent to some extent on external resources and on smuggling in both directions, since imports typically had to be paid for with exports for lack of adequate reserves of external currencies or specie. Moreover, distortions in the price and commodity terms of trade due to the blockade could complicate the external payments problems, so that it would become necessary to develop the production of exportable commodities in addition to the production of import substitutes.

To be sure, even such a development did not have to solve all payments problems. Deficits in the external accounts tended to be related to deficits in the budgets of the base area governments, and both gaps could be stopped basically in two ways. In the absence of opportunities for the funding of both debts by the sale of government bonds in exchange for external currencies or specie, there remained the possibility of depreciating and inflating the base area currencies. But stop-gap measures of this sort were used only as a last resort, for they were bound to lead to additional burdens either on the Communist movement or on the masses of the base area populations—and as a result, to the potential loss of allegiance and support. The Chinese Communists therefore acted in their own interest when they made minimum use of such temporary financial expedients and tried to do away with them at the earliest possible moment.

In carrying out this strategy of base area development, finally, the Chinese Communists had to keep in mind that their ultimate aim was not merely survival but the conquest of China. They therefore could not be satisfied simply with maintaining themselves but had to strive to produce a surplus that could be used to carry their revolution or resistance into enemy territory. Needless to say, their circumstances limited the forms in which this transfer of resources could be accomplished. Under conditions of backwardness and isolation, the transfer could most easily be made if the surplus were to be embodied in persons rather than things. It consequently took the form of food, clothing, housing, and training for an excess of political and technical cadres whose services would be used later to establish or strengthen base areas elsewhere. The development of appropriate cadre training programs was thus seen as crucial to the final success of the strategy.[4]

The Historical Significance of Yenan

From the collapse of the first united front to the eve of the conquest of the entire mainland, the Chinese Communists faced more or less the same principal economic problem. But their attempts at solving this problem changed during the course of these 20-odd years—on a pattern of strategic evolution that gave prominence to the area and era of Yenan, that is, to the Shensi-Kansu-Ninghsia Border Region during the years 1937–45.

The indications are that during the initial phase of their struggle in the countryside, the Chinese Communists were preoccupied with problems of soviet statehood and questions of agrarian revolution. Those who operated in the base areas, however, could not help being concerned about the extreme economic difficulties they encountered. Mao himself expressed this concern as early as 1928 in his essay "Why is it that red political power can exist in China?" Referring specifically to the Communists' logistics problems, he wrote:

The shortage of necessities and cash has become a very big problem for the army and the people inside the White encirclement. Because of the tight enemy blockade, necessities such as salt, cloth and medicines have been very scarce and dear all through the past year in the independent border area, which has upset, sometimes to an acute degree, the lives of the masses of the workers, peasants and petty bourgeoisie, as well as of the soldiers of the Red Army. The Red Army has to fight the enemy and to provision itself at one and the same time. It even lacks funds to pay the daily food allowance of five cents per person, which is provided in addition to grain; the soldiers are undernourished, many are ill, and the wounded in the hospitals are worse off. Such difficulties are of course unavoidable before the nation-wide seizure of political power; yet there is a pressing need to overcome them to some extent, to make life somewhat easier, and especially to secure more adequate supplies for the Red Army.[5]

A more profound understanding of the situation as well as references to the elements of an appropriate strategy began to appear at about that time, apparently with the help of the Comintern. The Sixth Congress of the Chinese Communist Party (Moscow, June 1928) adopted a "Resolution on the Agrarian Question," that "proceeded to instruct the Chinese Communists in the basic economic and social policies of the agrarian program to be followed inside each soviet" and outlined some of the ways in which agricultural production could be made to grow by internal means.[6] At issue was the pace at which such policies could be implemented. It is clear that requisitioning in outside territory remained an important source of soviet finance for some time thereafter. But it is also clear that the growth and stabilization of the soviet territory in the next few years made it possible as well as necessary to solve economic problems more and more with current internal resources.

The process of institutional regularization reached its peak at the First Congress of Workers', Peasants', and Red Army Deputies of China (Juichin, Kiangsi province, December 1931). The laws and regulations passed by this congress reiterated the relevant resolutions of 1928 with few changes. The Constitution of the Chinese Soviet Republic enunciated the basic economic and social policies toward the working classes and their enemies in articles 5, 6, and 7. These were amplified by a labor law, a land law, "regulations concerning the privileges extended to the Chinese workers' and peasants' red army," and a resolution on economic policy. This last document specified most of the essential freedoms and controls that had to be instituted in the interest of economic development within soviet territory; called for the formation of appropriate organizations (for example, the Workers' and Peasants' Bank with the exclusive right of note issue); and encouraged cooperation in all lines of production, trade, and finance—not only in aid of development but also in aid of the struggle against capitalism. More specific regulations appeared subsequently in the form of decrees issued by the newly established soviet government.[7]

The laws and regulations passed by the First Congress carried the signature of Chairman Mao. But the indications are that Mao did not agree fully with their provisions. The CCP "Resolution on Certain Questions in the History of Our Party" of April 20, 1945, which presented Mao's appraisal of these events long after the fact, contained the following criticism of the then-dominant "exponents of the third 'Left' line":

> They were mistakenly afraid to acknowledge that the Red Army movement was a peasant movement led by the proletariat, and they mistakenly opposed what they called the "peculiar revolutionariness of the peasants," "peasant capitalism" and "the rich peasant line." Instead, they carried out a number of so-called "class line" policies going beyond the democratic revolution, for instance, a policy of eliminating the rich peasant economy and other ultra-Left economic and labor policies.[8]

The resolution did not specify these "other ultra-Left" economic policies. But the context suggests a general objection to a dogmatism and bureaucratism that were conducive to irrelevant solutions and therefore to organizational ineffectiveness or even counterproductivity.

Of course, many regulations focused on problems of a more technical and less political economic nature, such as military logistics. Measures of this kind may well have evolved in a pragmatic manner, with little reference to conflicting policy lines. But they could also be fashioned to fit in with these alternatives, and they soon appeared as an integral part of Mao Tse-tung's strategic outlook, apparently under the impact of two events. In an effort to erode Mao's power, the Russian Returned Students, who espoused the "class line" policies, diverted him from military and organizational to civilian and economic responsibilities. Yet the tightening of the Nationalist blockade at the same time made solutions to economic problems increasingly important.[9] At a construction conference in the fall of 1933 and again in his report to the Second Congress of the Chinese Soviet Republic (Juichin, January 1934), Mao presented his answer. He stressed as a fundamental requisite of his "mass line" the need to serve the "immediate interests of the masses":

> Our central task at present is to mobilize the broad masses to take part in the revolutionary war, overthrow imperialism and the Kuomintang by means of such war, spread the revolution throughout the country, and drive imperialism out of China. Anyone who does not attach enough importance to this central task is not a good revolutionary cadre. If our comrades really comprehend this task and understand that the revolution must at all costs be spread throughout the country, then they should in no way neglect or underestimate the question of the immediate interests, the well-being, of the broad masses. For the revolutionary war is a war of the masses; it can be waged only by mobilizing the masses and relying on them.

If we only mobilize the people to carry on the war and do nothing else, can we succeed in defeating the enemy? Of course not. If we want to win, we must do a great deal more. We must lead the peasants' struggle for land and distribute land to them, heighten their labor enthusiasm and increase agricultural production, safeguard the interests of the workers, establish co-operatives, develop trade with outside areas, and solve the problems facing the masses—food, shelter and clothing, fuel, rice, cooking oil and salt, sickness and hygiene, and marriage. In short, all the practical problems in the masses' everyday life should claim our attention. If we attend to these problems, solve them and satisfy the needs of the masses, we shall really become organizers of the well-being of the masses, and they will truly rally round us and give us their warm support. Comrades, will we then be able to arouse them to take part in the revolutionary war? Yes, indeed we will.[10]

The Second Congress responded with a "Resolution on Soviet Economic Construction," that presented previous declarations of intent in a new perspective. It specified in 11 points numerous measures that could be taken to "improve the well-being of the masses"; the first eight of these constituted a fairly comprehensive development program:[11]

Point one listed methods of developing agricultural production that reappeared time and again in agricultural policy statements, and pointed to cooperation as a pivotal policy instrument.

Point two discussed the need for the development of small handicraft production of armaments, exports, and necessities. It too endorsed cooperatives but advocated state enterprises in special cases and even promised support for capitalist ventures in many instances.

Point three called for development of socialist labor attitudes among workers and peasants, the increased labor participation of women, the increased labor productivity of all, and the need for "distribution according to labor" generally.

Point four explained why it was necessary to break the blockade and develop external trade, outlined the desirable pattern of exchange, and indicated the roles and opportunities of both state trade organizations and individual merchants in this connection.

Point five dealt with internal trade, emphasized the importance of consumer cooperatives for its development, and advocated the formation of a hierarchy of cooperative organizations throughout the soviet.

Point six identified grain marketing as the critical development problem and listed several ways in which it could be improved. Again, cooperatives figured prominently among the suggested solutions.

Point seven specified the shortage of capital as another critical bottleneck and suggested ways in which its formation could be increased and its use improved. Two of the suggested solutions were the establishment of credit cooperatives and the sale of government bonds.

Point eight considered problems of deficit financing and warned against it. Positively, it proposed that changes in the money supply be tied to the development of trade, and that public finance be regularized in the form of a discriminatory taxation of exploiters.

The final three points reviewed problems of security, leadership, and ideology in economic work, and no doubt to Mao's great alarm, tended to orient the development program toward the Comintern-inspired "class line" of the Russian Returned Students rather than his "mass line," thereby probably jeopardizing its success from his point of view.

In summary, by 1934 at the latest the Chinese Communists had found a promising strategic response to their economic problems. But within the year, and thus well before most of these latest provisions could be carried out, the Communists were forced to abandon their base areas in south-central China. Mao and his followers, who returned to the fore of the movement because of the defeat, saw their objections to the "class line" vindicated by this failure. And now, with several years of trials and errors behind them, they knew what to attempt on the next occasion.

Yenan afforded them this opportunity. By the time the survivors of the Long March (1934–35) had enlarged the existing base area in the northwest,[12] established the Northwest Soviet, carried out land reform, restructured public burdens, and raided the warlord Yen Hsi-shan's territory for machinery and equipment with which to develop their new base area, a new set of circumstances had arisen to put the problem of survival in a wholly different perspective. The second united front, which was formed in the wake of the Sian Incident (December 1936), obliged the Communists to refrain from revolutionary activities such as land redistribution. But it also offered them two windfalls: "peace" in the sense of a state of truce between Nationalists and Communists, and Nationalist support in various forms for the Red Army, now renamed the Eighth Route Army (under the Nationalist government). Both changes affected in particular the Shensi-Kansu-Ninghsia Border Region (SKN), the successor state to the Northwest Soviet.

Objectively, these two changes created favorable conditions for the development of the border region. Military inactivity and territorial stability made it both easier and more rewarding to engage in economic construction. In addition, the state of truce enabled the border region garrison, which did not have to fight and which was not to confiscate wealth anymore, to participate in production. At the same time, Nationalist aid made it unnecessary to reimpose the previous public burdens on the border region population. Moreover, Nationalist financial support could be used not only to sustain the production activities of the army but also to import the necessary means of production from Nationalist territory. The Chinese Communists evidently were quick to take advantage of both opportunities; according to Edgar Snow, this is precisely how they spent their very first grants of aid.[13] Finally, the first border region congress (January 1939) adopted an economic development program that added to previous resolutions on economic construction the call for a production movement and an economizing movement in all government organs, schools, and rear army units.[14]

Yet the very changes that seemed so promising gave rise to responses that conflicted with the Communists' economic program. The availability of imports stifled efforts to develop the production of import substitutes. Similarly, the flow of Nationalist aid lessened concern about developing exports. In addition, it discouraged endeavors on the part of the institutional households to support themselves through subsidiary subsistence production. These and other conflicting reactions may have figured at first mainly in the continuing struggle over strategies.[15] But they soon became more and more problematic in real terms, because of the deterioration of the anti-Japanese united front. Wartime inflation eroded the value of the Nationalist support payment extremely rapidly, and increasing restrictions on trade limited the uses to which it could be put. Both events added to the negative changes in the border region's terms of external trade owing to the increasing isolation of "Free China." Moreover, by 1941, the Chinese Communists in Yenan experienced not only a renewed (partial) blockade but also a sporadic recurrence of military conflict with the Nationalists. Under this threat, they were compelled to reinforce the border region garrison, thereby increasing public demand and thus aggravating their economic problems in the area.

The mounting difficulties necessitated drastic action. To make ends meet immediately, substantially higher taxes had to be imposed on a much larger fraction of the total population. To alleviate this burden eventually in relative terms, the output of the private sector had to be enlarged. And to reduce the imposition in absolute terms, the product of the public sector had to be increased and its expenditure decreased, if possible. The success of these measures depended on the appropriate behavior of those functionaries who had to impose taxes, educate the people about possible improvements in production, and in general provide a model of austerity and hard work. Such behavior could not be expected to emerge spontaneously, since it differed too sharply from the traditional norms of official conduct as well as from the bureaucratism and "commandism" of the "third left line."

Efforts to inculcate "correct" attitudes and approaches to these and other problems culminated in the "rectification" (*cheng-feng*) campaigns of 1942–44.[16] But the principle was far from new. Indeed, Mao's concern with cadre policy dated back to the founding of the first revolutionary base area in the Chingkang mountains, and the problem assumed paramount importance in his struggle with the legacy of the Russian Returned Students during the early years in the northwest. At the national conference of the CCP on May 7, 1937, Mao described the ideal cadre in these terms:

> They must be cadres and leaders versed in Marxism-Leninism, politically far-sighted, competent in work, full of the spirit of self-sacrifice, capable of tackling problems on their own, steadfast in the midst of difficulties and loyal and devoted in serving the nation, the class and the Party. It is on these cadres and leaders that the Party relies for its links with the membership and the masses, and it is by relying on their firm leadership of the masses that the Party can succeed in defeating the enemy. Such cadres and leaders must be free from selfishness, from individualistic heroism, ostentation, sloth, passivity and sectarian arrogance, and they must be selfless national and class heroes; such are the qualities and the style of work demanded of the members, cadres and leaders of our Party.[17]

A year and a half later, in his report to the CCP central committee of October 1938, Mao repeated these norms of cadre conduct. And this time, to help the cadres achieve these lofty standards, he outlined a specific program of guidance, upgrading, supervision, persuasion, and assistance.[18] But the cooperation of those who were to be formed by this program was not so easily obtained. In fact, these fairly conventional methods of inducing improved cadre conduct yielded only passing success while the deteriorating circumstances made lasting and increasingly positive reactions ever more necessary. The result was a more drastic reform effort—and one that soon immersed the entire Chinese Communist movement.

The initial phase of this rectification campaign focused on two critical issues—the movement's mode of learning and its style of work. But the concern soon broadened: improvements in ideology and organization were to lead at once to the more effective implementation of the Party's development program—not only in the SKN border region but in all base areas. To this end, additional campaigns were initiated, notably the campaign for "better troops and simpler administration" promoting production and economies in the public sector plus the transfer of superfluous administrative personnel to the villages (*hsia hsiang*); the campaign to "reduce rent, increase production" offering material incentives to peasants who had not yet benefited from land reform; and the campaign to "support the government and cherish the people" encouraging more cooperation and goodwill between private and institutional households.

The specific effects of these campaigns are hard to determine, though statements claiming full success are by no means lacking. Our data, which are largely limited to the results in the SKN border region, are best analyzed by distinguishing between two segments: the private households in the area, which accounted for close to 95 percent of the border region population; and the institutional households, which included the rear army units, some government organs, the advanced schools, and most of the factories. The following developments are indicated:

1. Cooperation in production occurred more or less automatically in most institutional households, where it was tied to collective material incentives. Among the private households, cooperation appeared early and grew strong in import-substituting activities like spinning and weaving, where it was promoted by state-directed putting-out systems that emphasized individual material incentives. It developed later and much less certainly in the form of mutual labor aid in agricultural production. More advanced forms of collective production in all branches accounted for minute shares of the total labor force.[19]

2. The attempt to mobilize more people and added effort for production was evidently successful in several respects. The indications are that practically all soldiers, probably most students, and a good many functionaries became deeply involved in subsidiary work. Altogether, close to 5 percent of the border region population and perhaps 10 percent of its entire labor force were thus shifted from full-time public service to a combination of public service and production, notably in agriculture. The reallocation policy was plainly least effective in the administrative organs, for the number of administrative employees grew in spite of repeated attempts to economize and to transfer superfluous personnel to the villages.

Private employment grew substantially as a result of immigration (which between 1937 and 1944 added close to 12 percent to the stagnating SKN population) and the absorption of vagrants (who were said to have constituted 5 percent of this population at the beginning of the period). It grew less strongly as a result of internal migration, and to an uncertain degree because of increases in the average number of annual workdays, in the participation of women in production, and so forth. Increases in the number of persons employed in priority branches have been reported.[20] Increased efforts in agriculture may be inferred from the dramatic expansion of the cultivated area,[21] a development that was attributable in part to the rear army units.[22] Interestingly, much of the private expansion occurred prior to 1943, that is, before the campaign to cooperate in production began to be waged on a large scale.

3. According to Chinese Communist reports, output in most sectors and branches of production increased strongly as a result of these increases in the number of employed persons and in their work efforts. Many of these claims, however, are open to question. In the case of the SKN's grain production in particular, the implicit yields are unusually low. Moreover, the changes in grain output do not reflect evident variations in natural conditions or the comparatively low fertility of the large areas of added (hill) land, where efforts to develop irrigation had no success.[23] Finally, the reported output totals could not possibly have supplied the rations purportedly issued to the population in both sectors. For all of these reasons, it appears that the official claims understated the level and overstated the rate of growth of grain production.[24]

In the case of cotton production, which was a critical part of the import substitution program, declines in yields due to the expansion into marginal lands and inclement weather were anticipated. But the differences between expected and reported yields were such that either the severity of these effects was greatly underestimated or much of the output was unreported. In any event total cotton output as reported did not develop as projected. Nevertheless, it increased greatly and in 1943–45 approximated the region's austere autarky requirements.[25] How much was consumed by internal spinning and weaving is once again uncertain, however. The reported increases in both activities, which were great indeed, did not exhaust the internal supplies of textile fibers. The residuals were incredibly large, and probably simply reflected the government's inadequate accounting for spinning and weaving by private households for their own consumption.[26]

Official data on the production of salt, the most important export commodity of the border region, also appear to be subject to question.[27] The reports on most other products are not sufficiently complete to permit consistency checks. But it may be noted that the output of many producer goods—from simple wooden looms to old-fashioned "backyard" furnaces—had to grow strongly in order to permit the indicated increases in the production of various consumer goods. Such an accelerator effect is clearly evident.

4. The successful development of production was apparently reflected in improvements in living conditions, but here again the official reports

are hard to verify. The claim is obviously well founded in the case of the institutional households of the army, government organs, schools, and factories. The initial rations of food, clothing, and incidental expenses were highly egalitarian but apparently much larger than those issued to common soldiers elsewhere. Though they were reduced for a time after 1938 because of the renewed conflict with the Nationalists, the earlier levels were regained by 1942–43 and were surpassed thereafter,[28] largely as a result of the institutional households' growing self–sufficiency through subsidiary production. The indications are that by 1944 these activities accounted for close to 40 percent of all public revenues in the SKN border region.[29]

In contrast, changes in the living conditions of the private population have not been made explicit, and the implications of the production data are inconclusive. The available figures suggest a pattern of change similar to that in the public sector, with reductions in the standard of living due to the tax increases of 1941, followed by recovery and further gains with the continuing expansion of cultivated land and some minor tax decreases. This pattern seems plausible. But the standard of living that is implicit in the data is so low and the data themselves so shaky in several respects, one cannot safely draw many conclusions about the actual developments. Certainly, income in the private sector was much more evenly distributed as a result of the land reform measures carried out in parts of the territory prior to 1937 and the income tax increases of 1941.[30] There was also a rent reduction in 1943, but this apparently added merely marginally to these effects.

5. Besides raising the level and reducing the differences in the standard of living, the Chinese Communists greatly increased the rate of accumulation. Most of the capital in import-substituting and export-supplementing branches seems to have been formed in the years prior to the mass campaigns. Additions to the capital stock consisted not only of producer goods imports procured with external aid prior to the breakdown of the united front, but also of internally produced means of production, and notably of construction works. Both types of investment in fact facilitated the subsequent production mass movement, which in turn yielded excess supplies of basic staples that were earmarked for the future conduct of the struggle. In addition, the border region accumulated a surplus of human capital: during the years 1937–45, its educational institutions trained more than 40,000 political and military cadres, plus thousands of cultural and technical cadres for the liberated areas behind Japanese lines.[31]

The exportation of the "Yenan model" in this form was the crowning achievement, the true mark of the historical significance of Yenan. For there, Mao and his followers not only had managed to adapt their earlier strategy to the circumstances of armed truce and to carry it out effectively in the face of worsening external relations; they had been so successful in this endeavor that they could contribute to the struggle elsewhere thousands of experienced cadres who had absorbed the lessons of Kiangsi, the Long March, and Yenan.

The Contemporary Relevance of the Guerrilla Period

The strategy and tactics that had helped the Chinese Communists in their rise to power were not abandoned in one stroke on October 1, 1949. On the contrary, the Communists' inability to conclude the civil war with the conquest of Taiwan coupled with the involvement in the Korean War preserved an atmosphere of militancy akin to that of Yenan. Moreover, the economic and social problems of rural China did not change greatly as a result of the termination of military actions on the Chinese mainland. Similarly, the cadre force remained largely unchanged and continued to rely on its accumulated experiences and training. In fact, the molding of vast numbers of new cadres in the recently liberated areas was to be the principal organizational problem of the new regime for a considerable period of time. These and many other factors made for strategic continuity and limited tactical adaptation during the period of rehabilitation.

By the same token, most of the specific policies of the guerrilla period appeared increasingly as partial and even temporary solutions to China's problems of social transformation and economic development. The reforms within the private agricultural sector had not gone beyond land redistribution, voluntary elementary cooperation, and minor technical change—limitations that had made the Chinese Communists look like agrarian reformers. Moreover, the development programs of the guerrilla period, fashioned in the remote reaches of the base areas, had not had to deal with the problems of large urban areas, of modern industry and commerce, of urban-rural, modern-traditional, coastal-interior relations, of large-scale government, and the like, which now loomed large in the New China. Indeed, in October 1949 the Chinese Communists had yet to learn how to cope with these new tasks, though Mao for one had stressed the necessity of such learning repeatedly during the final years of war.[32]

Here the Chinese Communists could—and once again did—draw on the pioneering experiences of the Soviet Union. At first in the northeast (Manchuria) and then in all of China, they introduced Soviet forms of organization in many spheres of life. In particular, they adopted Soviet institutions and methods of economic planning, administration, and control as instruments for the formulation and implementation of the First Five-Year Plan (1953–57), which in addition depended heavily on Soviet loans and direct technical assistance. This decision gave rise to elaborate bureaucratic structures and procedures, increasing technical and administrative specialization and professionalization, intersectoral differentiation, status and income hierarchies, and so on,[33] all of which ran counter to the norms that had been propagated and practiced previously. The end of the Yenan era appeared definitely in sight when the state administrative organs in 1955 substituted a straight wages system for the supply system that had provided them for so long with rations of food, clothing, housing, and allowances.

One may guess that this development was profoundly disturbing to those veterans of Kiangsi, the Long March, and Yenan who had been formed so strongly by their guerrilla experience that they had come to think, work, and live in a different style, in the "Yenan way."[34] Many could well have seen ominous parallels between past and present developments in internal organization, in international relations, and so on that argued strongly against the wholesale dismissal of past strategy and tactics as outmoded and for the formulation of new variants to match the new circumstances. This reconsideration of the "Yenan model" did not have to have been made explicitly. But it could be implicit in several policy initiatives after the mid-1950's that attempted to modify the emerging Soviet-type system in critical respects.

In a sense the most consequential reversion occurred on the day after the formal adoption of the First Five-Year Plan, when Mao modified the prevailing conceptions about the relations between socialist transformation and technical modernization in agriculture. The mechanization of farm production appeared as the ultimate goal. But collectivization had to precede rather than follow it. In the meantime, the collectives were to introduce more limited technical changes by making improvements in traditional farming methods as specified in the model regulations for advanced agricultural producers' cooperatives of 1956 and the agricultural development program for 1956–67.[35] There are indications that Mao's trust in the effectiveness of such improvements was based on his experiences in the SKN border region, where the same set of measures had been tried.[36]

Efforts during the 1950's to promote the development of irrigation and other forms of water conservancy were tied to the formation of Rural People's Communes, which may well have been patterned after the institutional households of the Chinese Communist movement during the Yenan period. The most striking similarity between the earlier units and the communes as originally constituted was the collective organization of consumption as well as production. In the case of the communes, collective living was designed to transfer womanpower from household services to advance the agricultural development program, especially with respect to irrigation. A related similarity between the communes and the Eighth Route Army garrisons in particular was the combining of military training and production work. In both instances, this policy seems to have been based on the expectation that substantially greater efforts could be made by almost anyone, and that the gains from such increased efforts would outweigh any possible loss from decreased specialization.[37]

The simultaneous and not so coordinated expansion of the traditional and modern sectors of production by intrasectoral means ("walking on two legs") also had its precedent in the guerrilla period. But the relationship is tenuous, for the Yenan concern was with the incentives and organization of production, not the techniques of production. By necessity, almost all enterprises in the base areas had to make use of traditional technology, and modern industry had existed only as a rare exception to the rule. In technical perspective, a base area therefore was comparable to a Rural People's Commune rather than to the Chinese economy at large. Accordingly, the problems of rural development under communal auspices were similar to the problems of guerrilla economy under conditions of armed truce, whereas communal organization resembled that of an institutional household rather than that of a base area as a whole.

The strategic reorientation of the late 1950's called for an administrative reorganization, which the reforms of 1957–58 were meant to provide. This departure from the Soviet organizational model[38] also had its parallels and possible antecedents in the Yenan period. In both periods there seems to have been a reaction against bureaucratic inadequacies that made centralized administration relatively ineffective, rather costly, and—most important—detrimental to the initiative of the people. Indeed, the fundamental premise of both the production mass campaigns in the base areas and the Great Leap Forward was that the masses could be counted on to help themselves (and thereby the Chinese Communists) if properly aroused.

Dissatisfaction with the results of bureaucratic administration in general and with its inhibiting effects in particular also led to efforts at debureaucratization in both periods. These were similar in at least two important respects, namely, in the expectation that simplifying administrative processes would permit the reassignment of superfluous office personnel to production, and in the belief that the performance of all leaders would be improved if they were to involve themselves with the masses. For both reasons, and to benefit the masses in the end, movements were launched during both periods to transfer people on a temporary or permanent basis. During the early 1940's, cadres, students, and artists were sent *hsia-hsiang* (to the villages) because that was where the masses lived, and the transformation of their lives as well as the development of agriculture were the important things.[39] During the late 1950's, people were sent *hsia-fang* (to the grass roots) anywhere, essentially for the same reasons.[40]

The preceding examples obviously do not exhaust the list of correspondences between the policies of the early 1940's and the late 1950's.[41] But they suffice to reveal their fundamental relationship. To the extent that the Great Leap Forward, the administrative reforms, and most other innovations of the late 1950's drew on the lessons of Yenan, they tended to refer to the experiences of the institutional households. Accordingly, it may be said that *these new policies tended to place the entire population of China and especially all members of the traditional sector into the position of Eighth Route Army men, revolutionary students, refugee workers, and other members of the Chinese Communist movement in the base areas.* It had not been easy for Mao then and there to get even such highly select groups to commit themselves to his norms of cadre conduct: activism, frugality, integrity, self-sacrifice, and adherence to the mass line. Indeed, it had taken mounting educational efforts and finally the rectification campaign of 1942–44 to induce the desired response. To gain the commitment of the masses, the entire population, to the same principles had to be a much more formidable task, requiring profound and prolonged exertions despite the intervening social changes.

There is no need to recount the history of the late 1950's and early 1960's—the surprising ease with which the masses seemed to have been transformed during the Great Leap Forward and the similar rapidity with which they appeared to revert to earlier behavior patterns during the subsequent Three Hard Years. Here, especially, who can say where fact ends and fiction begins? But of one consequence there is no doubt: the widespread demoralization of cadres and masses alike, and their "separation" from each other, as in the aftermath of a lost war.* This experience may have led many old Yenanites to recall still another lesson from their past: how, in similar circumstances, material incentives had

---

* Indeed, the Great Leap Forward was waged as a war—a war on "nature," which was to be "conquered" so that its "laws" could be overcome.

induced the vast majority of the base area peasants to increase their output substantially, and largely on their own! Of course, the same impression could be derived from a study of the developments in, say, Yugoslavia or Poland or of previous Chinese attempts to cope with the impact of collectivization. Consequent moves to decentralize economic organization, to individualize decision making, and to rely more heavily on material incentives in turn raised the specter of "revisionism"—at least in the form of a reversion to the Soviet model and perhaps even to the more extreme pattern of market socialism.[42]

Mao's "Yenan way" thus appeared doomed once again after a brief respite, and with more finality if the crisis could be attributed to its inadequacy as an approach to problems of economic development. However, Mao and a seemingly much-reduced number of old comrades refused to admit the possibility of such an error and looked for other causes of failure,[43] settling finally on the combination of unprecedented natural disasters, inappropriate cadre conduct, and mass inertia. Little if anything could be done about the weather. But the shortcomings of human beings and especially of Party cadres could be attacked by a nationwide reenactment of the policy that had culminated in the rectification movement of 1942–44. The recommitment of the People's Liberation Army to these norms, the "learn from the People's Liberation Army" campaign, the "socialist education" campaign, and the movement for a "great proletarian cultural revolution" thus appeared as phases of an ever-widening struggle to remold everyone and at the least every cadre.

Like the 1942–44 movement, this development had to result in improved practice in all fields and especially in production. Of all the parallels that could be mentioned,[44] I shall note only the campaigns to emulate Ta-chai and Ta-ch'ing in production, both of which were endorsed by Mao in early 1964. The successful efforts of the peasants of the Ta-chai Agricultural Production Brigade to improve their living conditions in the worst possible circumstances and without outside help had their precedent in the accomplishments of the 359th Brigade at Nanniwan.[45] The entire design of the Ta-ch'ing oil field operation likewise had its antecedents there as well as in the experiences of state-operated enterprises in the SKN border region.[46] The Yenan origins of these two models have been asserted officially as recently as October 1972:

The Yenan spirit has been carried forward and yielded fruitful results in the ensuing period of the War of Liberation (1946–49) and, after the nationwide victory in 1949, in the struggle for rehabilitating the national economy and carrying out socialist revolution and construction. The mass movements "In industry, learn from Taching" and "In agriculture, learn from Tachai" now in full swing throughout China are a continuation and development of the Yenan spirit.[47]

In addition, the Cultural Revolution gave new vigor to efforts at administrative rationalization, seemingly on the pattern of the earlier campaign for "better troops and simpler administration."[48]

Conclusion

Our review of the Chinese Communists' problems of guerrilla economy during their 20-year struggle for power, of the significance of Yenan for the development of solutions to these problems, and of the contemporary relevance of these solutions may not really tell us why Mao laughed at Myrdal's mention of tradition. But it does reduce the number of possible interpretations. In particular, it leaves little doubt about strong lines of continuity from the 1930's and 1940's to the present.

In tracing this "tradition," one could go to the extreme of transposing the model of guerrilla economy to the current world economic scene, so that China appears in the position of a revolutionary base area, so that the conflicting development strategies of the late 1950's represent the conflicting lines of the late 1930's, and so on. Such a single-minded approach might yield plausible interpretations of current events. But it would clearly ignore many other interesting relationships—for example, those to Marxist classics and to Soviet practice—that might provide similarly persuasive explanations of many occurrences.

If one therefore looks rather for specific correspondences between the past and the present in support of the assertion of continuity, one comes to focus in the end on visions of particular possibilities of improving man in technological and in ideological dimension—and specifically to the belief in the possibility of combining minor changes in the traditional methods of production with major changes in the traditional relations of production to the great benefit of all.

This conviction seems to be rooted in the wartime experiences of members of the Chinese Communist movement, many of whom became "good revolutionary cadres" and, as such, prototypes of Mao's "new man." But it extends conceptually to the masses as well. And it shapes the policies toward both during the transition to socialism, when all Chinese are to be made into "new men." Since neither the cadres nor the masses seem to pass through this metamorphosis easily, "rectification" will presumably continue to be a critical element of the "Yenan way."

Reference Material

Notes

Introduction: The Persistence of the Past

1. For urban population data around 1900, see Dwight H. Perkins, *Agricultural Development in China, 1368–1968* (Chicago, 1969), Appendix E.

2. See Thomas C. Smith, *The Agrarian Origins of Modern Japan* (Stanford, Calif., 1959); and R. P. Dore, *Education in Tokugawa Japan* (Berkeley, Calif., 1965). The specifically Confucian aspects of this tradition have been developed at length in a forthcoming book by Dr. Kee Il Choi.

3. Albert O. Hirschman, *The Strategy of Economic Development* (New Haven, Conn., 1958), pp. 17–19.

4. David C. McClelland, *The Achieving Society* (Princeton, N.J., 1961).

5. This conclusion is a major theme of such recent works as Yen-p'ing Hao, *The Comprador in Nineteenth-Century China* (Cambridge, Mass., 1970), and Edward LeFevour, *Western Enterprise in Late Ch'ing China* (Cambridge, Mass., 1970).

6. This statement is based on rather impressionistic evidence (quantitative and otherwise). Systematic studies of income distribution in Malaysia are currently under way but not sufficiently far along to use here.

7. The subject could be properly treated only in a book length manuscript. These remarks are based on my own research and observation during periods of work and residence in Hong Kong, Kuala Lumpur, and Seoul, and on my findings on trips elsewhere in the region.

8. See Everett E. Hagen, *On the Theory of Social Change* (Homewood, Ill., 1962).

9. This theme is dealt with in a number of fairly recent works, including Ping-ti Ho, *The Ladder of Success in Imperial China* (New York, 1962), and Evelyn S. Rawski, *Agricultural Change and the Peasant Economy of South China* (Cambridge, Mass., 1972).

10. This argument is generally associated with the name of M. J. Levy.

11. This point is made in village studies such as that of O. Lang, *Chinese Family and Society* (New Haven, Conn., 1946).

The Role of the Foreigner

1. Jack M. Potter, *Capitalism and the Chinese Peasant* (Berkeley, Calif., 1968), p. 177.

2. Chi-ming Hou, *Foreign Investment and Economic Development in China, 1840–1937* (Cambridge, Mass., 1965), p. 1.

3. See especially Marion J. Levy, Jr., "Contrasting Factors in the Modernization of China and Japan," *Economic Development and Cultural Change*, 2: 161–97 (Oct. 1953).

4. Albert Feuerwerker, *China's Early Industrialization* (Cambridge, Mass., 1958), p. 245.

5. For an excellent summary and critical review of village studies especially focused on the arguments concerning the disruptive and negative impact of the foreigner, see Potter, pp. 174–203.

6. Two noteworthy examples are Jack M. Potter and Chi-ming Hou.

7. Though the discussion that follows differs in several important respects and refers to a somewhat later period in Chinese economic history, it is based on the essential argument presented in Mark Elvin's "The High-Level Equilibrium Trap: The Causes of the Decline of Invention in the Traditional Chinese Textile Industries," in W. E. Willmott, ed., *Economic Organization in Chinese Society* (Stanford, Calif., 1972), pp. 137–72.

8. Dwight H. Perkins, *Agricultural Development in China, 1368–1968* (Chicago, 1969).

9. Simon Kuznets, "Quantitative Aspects of the Economic Growth of Nations: IX, Level and Structure of Foreign Trade: Comparisons for Recent Years," *Economic Development and Cultural Change*, 13.1, pt. 2 (1964); and "X, Level and Structure of Foreign Trade: Long-Term Trends," *ibid.*, 15.2, pt. 2 (1967).

10. Chi-ming Hou, *Foreign Investment and Economic Development*, p. 97.

11. Simon Kuznets, *Modern Economic Growth: Rate, Structure, and Spread* (New Haven, Conn., 1966), p. 332.

12. Chi-ming Hou, p. 101.

13. Simon Kuznets, *Modern Economic Growth*, p. 324.

14. John K. Chang, *Industrial Development in Pre-Communist China* (Chicago, 1969), p. 71.

15. For a detailed analysis of the changes in China's export trade, see C. F. Remer, *The Foreign Trade of China* (Taipei, 1967); and Yu-kwei Cheng, *Foreign Trade and Industrial Development of China* (Washington, D.C., 1956).

16. Hollis B. Chenery and Paul G. Clark, *Interindustry Economics* (New York, 1965), pp. 205–11. The average ratio of purchased inputs to the value of total production in the agricultural and mining sectors in Italy, Japan, and the U.S. was 0.31 and 0.23, respectively, compared with an average of 0.42 for all industries (*ibid.*, pp. 206–7).

17. Yu-kwei Cheng, pp. 19, 32.

18. The average ratio of intermediate to total demand for the products of these two sectors in Italy, Japan, and the U.S. was 0.15 and 0.12, respectively, compared with an average of 0.45 for all industries (Chenery and Clark, pp. 205–7).

19. Yu-kwei Cheng, pp. 19, 32.

20. As late as 1933, the handicraft sector accounted for 29 percent of the total nonagricultural labor force—eight times the level of employment in

modern factories and mining and utility enterprises (T. C. Liu and K. C. Yeh, *The Economy of the Chinese Mainland*, Princeton, N.J., 1965, Table II, p. 69). For an extensive discussion of developments in the cotton textile handicrafts sector before 1949, see Kang Chao's contribution in this volume.

21. Remer, *Foreign Investments*, p. 97. The statistics I use here and in the next few paragraphs are from this source and from Yu-kwei Cheng.

22. Remer, *Foreign Investments*, p. 95. The foreigner's contribution to China's mining industry, however, is much larger than these data indicate. Since coal is a major input in industry, especially in industries like iron and steel that in turn produce other major industrial inputs, coal-mining has a very significant forward linkage effect. In addition, though comparatively small, this category of foreign investment dominated the *relevant* domestic industry much more than other categories did theirs. If coal mined by native methods is excluded, foreign-owned mines produced 81.7 percent of the coal extracted with modern equipment in China (Yu-kwei Cheng, *Foreign Trade*, p. 40).

23. We define the linkages effect as follows:

$$L = \frac{\sum_{1}^{j}\{X_j - [(\bar{u} - u_j)X_j] + [(\bar{w} - w_j)X_j]\} + \sum_{1}^{j}\{M_j - (\bar{w} - w_j)M_j\} + \sum\{I_j - (\bar{u} - u_j)I_j - (\bar{w} - w_j)I_j\}}{\sum_{1}^{j}X_j + \sum_{1}^{j}M_j + \sum_{1}^{j}I_j}$$

where:

X = exports
M = imports
I = direct foreign investment
j = sector
$\bar{u}$ = average ratio of purchased inputs to total output, all sectors
u_j = average ratio of purchased inputs to total output, sector j
$\bar{w}$ = average ratio of intermediate to final demand for output, all sectors
w_j = average ratio of intermediate to final demand, sector j.

The figures for this estimate are drawn from the foreign trade statistics for 1928, China's peak level of prewar foreign trade; from the sectoral allocation of cumulative foreign direct investment, estimated for the four major countries that accounted for 91 percent of the total foreign private investment in China in 1931; and from the structure of foreign production within the industrial sector in 1933. Values of u and w: Chenery and Clark, *Interindustry Economics*, pp. 205–11.

24. Feuerwerker, *China's Early Industrialization*, p. 5.

25. Yu-kwei Cheng, pp. 39–40.

26. Feuerwerker, pp. 4–6.

27. Yu-kwei Cheng, pp. 39–40; H. D. Fong, *Industrial Capital in China* (Tientsin, 1936), p. 66; Liu and Yeh, *Economy of the Chinese Mainland*, Table F-1, p. 428.

28. Feuerwerker, p. 5.

29. Data provided by Bruce Reynolds from his research for a Ph.D. thesis on the Chinese textile industry in the 1920's, now in progress at the University of Michigan.

30. For detailed illustrations of the contributions of the modern foreign sector to the Chinese adoption of Western technology referred to in this section of the paper, see especially G. C. Allen and Audrey G. Donnithorne, *Western Enterprise in Far Eastern Economic Development* (New York, 1954), p. 54; Yen-p'ing Hao, *The Comprador in Nineteenth-Century China* (Cambridge, Mass., 1970), pp. 53, 104, 117, 140–45, 217; and Feuerwerker, p. 226.

31. Remer, *Foreign Investments*, pp. 294, 400, 551; Chi-ming Hou, *Foreign Investment and Economic Development*, pp. 114–15.

32. A rate of profit for Chinese firms can be estimated by applying the weighted average profit per unit value of output in the Chinese textile industry, 1914–22 (0.115), times the unit value of output (factor price) per unit value of capital in 2,000 Chinese factories in 1930 (0.948), which implies a rate of profit on investment of 10.9 percent. A biased sample of Chinese textile firms is available, a sample of 17 firms for nine years in the period 1905–37, which shows an average rate of profit of 14.4 percent. The weighted average annual rate of profit on investment for Chinese coal-mining enterprises in 1922–34 was 8.5 percent. (Yen Chung-p'ing et al., *Selected Statistical Material on Modern Chinese Economic History*, Shanghai, 1955, pp. 155, 165, 168.) Finally, according to Feuerwerker's study of the Chee Hsin Cement Company, the weighted average annual profit on investment for that firm in 1908–39 was 8.45 percent (Albert Feuerwerker, "Industrial Enterprise in Twentieth-Century China: The Chee Hsin Cement Co.," in Feuerwerker et al., eds., *Approaches to Modern Chinese History*, Berkeley, Calif., 1967, pp. 315–16).

Surplus and Stagnation in Modern China

1. Paul A. Baran, *The Political Economy of Growth* (New York, 1957), pp. 23–24. In an earlier version of the concept, Baran excluded the fourth category. See "Economic Progress and Economic Surplus" (1953) in Paul A. Baran, *The Longer View: Essays Toward a Critique of Political Economy* (New York, 1969), p. 300. On pp. 32–38 of *The Political Economy of Growth*, Baran explains and gives examples of what he means by the second and third categories.

2. Baran, *Political Economy*, p. 23. The term "potential" thus refers not only to the fact that some of the surplus is not produced at all, but also to the definitional characteristic that none of it currently takes the form of saving (i.e. *actual* surplus).

3. This diagram evolved from one suggested to me by John Gurley.

4. See Amartya K. Sen, "Peasants and Dualism With or Without Surplus Labor," *Journal of Political Economy*, 74.5: 425–50 (Oct. 1966).

5. For a discussion of the relation of income distribution to work incentives in China, see my essay "Maoism and Motivation: A Discussion of Work Incentives in China," in Victor Nee and James Peck, eds., *Uninterrupted Revolution* (New York, 1975).

6. Marion J. Levy, Jr., "Contrasting Factors in the Modernization of China and Japan," *Economic Development and Cultural Change*, 2: 161 (Oct. 1953). Levy also rules out "climate, population size, the forces introduced from out-

side, etc." as factors that can alone account for the different modernization experiences (pp. 195–96).

7. John K. Fairbank, Alexander Eckstein, and L. S. Yang, "Economic Change in Early Modern China: An Analytic Framework," *Economic Development and Cultural Change*, 9.1: 3–4 (Oct. 1960). See, for example, their discussions of trade and luxury consumption among "the Chinese upper classes" (p. 7); of the uses of accumulated savings and hoarded capital (p. 9); of the "inefficient proliferation of services" associated with the distributive process (p. 11); of the "dead weight of official and quasi-official forms of taxation" and the expropriation of income by a profligate and inefficient state apparatus (pp. 11–13); of the ability of "many large households and favored families" to escape taxation altogether at periods of dynastic decline (p. 13); and of the enormous drain of savings in the servicing of foreign loans and the payment of indemnities (pp. 22–26). All of these, needless to say, represent what Baran would regard as nondevelopment-oriented uses of the potential surplus.

8. Ramon H. Myers, *The Chinese Peasant Economy: Agricultural Development in Hopei and Shantung, 1890–1949* (Cambridge, Mass., 1970), pp. 14–24. Fei's affiliation with the distributional school is evidently only partial.

9. For an excellent discussion of the issues surrounding the existence of surplus labor in the countryside, see Sen, "Peasants and Dualism." See also Gerald M. Meier, *Leading Issues in Economic Development*, 2d ed. (Oxford, 1970), pp. 187–88.

10. Mark Elvin, "Last Thousand Years of Chinese History," *Modern Asian Studies*, 4.2: 106 (1960).

11. Fei Hsiao-t'ung, *China's Gentry* (Chicago, 1953), pp. 124, 98–99. For a good description of the contrast in consumption habits of landlords and various classes of peasants in one South China village, see C. K. Yang, *A Chinese Village in Early Communist Transition* (Cambridge, Mass., 1959), pp. 36 62. For a brief but clear discussion of the economic significance of luxury consumption, see Albert Feuerwerker, *The Chinese Economy, 1912–1949* (Ann Arbor, Mich., 1968), p. 28.

12. C. K. Yang, pp. 57, 78.

13. See Arthur N. Young, *China's Wartime Finance and Inflation, 1937–1945* (Cambridge, Mass., 1965), p. 190, for a description of private gold imports for hoarding purposes during World War II.

14. Buck, *Land Utilization*, p. 328.

15. Report of Kwangtung Pacification Commission, April 1933, cited in Victor Lippit, "Land Reform in China: The Contribution of Institutional Change to Financing Economic Development" (unpub. ms., 1972).

16. Feuerwerker, p. 58.

17. See Ping-ti Ho, *Studies on the Population of China* (Cambridge, Mass., 1959), p. 222. See pp. 204–5 for a description of the values motivating elite use of the surplus.

18. *Agrarian China: Selected Source Materials from Chinese Authors*, compiled and translated by the research staff of the Secretariat, Institute of Pacific Relations (London, 1939), pp. xii–xiii. A good example of their view of the link between technological and socioeconomic factors is provided by

John K. Fairbank, *The United States and China* (Cambridge, Mass., 1972), pp. 237–39. See also Fei Hsiao-tung, *China's Gentry*, pp. 125–26.

19. Elvin, "Last Thousand Years," p. 108.

20. Jack M. Potter, *Capitalism and the Chinese Peasant* (Berkeley, Calif., 1968), p. 188, citing George B. Cressey, *Land of the 500 Million* (New York, 1955).

21. Muramatsu Yuji, *Chūgoku keizai no shakai taisei* (The social structure of the Chinese economy; Tokyo, 1949). But compare Muramatsu's "A Documentary Study of Chinese Landlordism in Late Ch'ing and Early Republican Kiangnan," *Bulletin of the School of Oriental and African Studies*, 29: 566–99 (1966), in which he holds that "landlordism in China remained overwhelmingly powerful at least until the early 1920's."

22. Buck, *Land Utilization*, pp. 194, 196. Buck presents two alternative sets of figures as well. These are rejected by Perkins, *Agricultural Development*, p. 91, as "much too low." Potter, p. 188, cites one of these alternative sets as being what Buck's "figures show" without mentioning the others, presumably because Buck himself in *Land Utilization*, p. 194, cited only this one in his text. For summaries of other findings regarding land concentration and tenancy in the first third of this century, see Potter, p. 168; Perkins, p. 91; and Feuerwerker, p. 34.

23. Feuerwerker, p. 33; Elvin, "Last Thousand Years," p. 97.

24. Perkins, pp. 102–6, 93; Myers, *Chinese Peasant Economy*, pp. 241–43.

25. Theodore Schultz, *Transforming Traditional Agriculture* (New Haven, Conn., 1964).

26. Mark Elvin, *The Pattern of the Chinese Past* (Stanford, Calif., 1973), p. 306.

27. *Ibid.*, p. 309.

28. *Ibid.*, p. 312.

29. *Ibid.*, pp. 286–98.

30. Potter, *Capitalism*, p. 180.

31. Lippit, "Land Reform," pp. 85, 80.

32. Buck, *Land Utilization*, pp. 289–301, especially pp. 294–96. It is thus evident that Buck used the term idleness to mean just that, and not to encompass rural subsidiary production. Otherwise, the employment of such labor in any new pursuit would entail an opportunity cost in output forgone of subsidiary products.

33. The total figure cited is that of T. C. Liu and K. C. Yeh, *The Economy of the Chinese Mainland* (Princeton, N.J., 1965), pp. 128–29. Buck found that "removal of graves from farm land," "elimination of land in boundaries," "consolidation of fragmented holdings," "profitable cultivation of arable lands not now cultivated," and "an economic unit size of farm which would lessen the proportion of area in farmsteads . . . might make available nearly another twenty-five million acres of China" (p. 10). I have taken "nearly twenty-five million acres" to mean 23 million acres. This estimate pertains only to the eight regions of China proper that Buck studied, and omits potential surplus inherent in underutilized land in the regions of the Northeast, Mongolia, Sikang, Sinkiang, and Tibet. In addition, it is unclear to what degree Buck intended to express as equivalent to the productivity of additional land the

output lost because of inefficiencies in land utilization owing to gravesites and boundaries in the middle of fields, to fragmentation, and to the uneconomic size of farms.

34. See Anthony M. Tang, "Policy and Performance in Agriculture," in Alexander Eckstein, Walter Galenson, and Ta-chung Liu, eds., *Economic Trends in Communist China* (Chicago, 1968), p. 484, on this subject.

35. Liu and Yeh, p. 101.

36. The second procedure results from a suggestion by Victor Lippit.

37. A much higher estimate of S_e would result from the lower figure for average peasant consumption given by Research Office, State Statistical Bureau, "Wo kuo kuo-min shou-ju sheng-ch'an ho fen-p'ei ti ch'u-pu yen-chiu" (Preliminary research on the production and distribution of China's national income), *T'ung-chi yen-chiu*, no. 1 (1958). Unlike the data used in Table 6, however, this figure is based not on samples of actual peasant budgets but on analysis of the consumption component of national income. Because of the relatively narrow definition of national income used in China (Nai-ruenn Chen, *Chinese Economic Statistics*, Chicago, 1967, p. 10), this method captures only part of peasant expenditures on means of livelihood and is not appropriate for our purposes.

38. Liu and Yeh, p. 68.

39. K. C. Yeh, "Capital Formation," in Eckstein et al., *Economic Trends*, p. 510, gives gross investment rates for these years. Subtracting a reasonable percentage for depreciation leads to this conclusion.

40. Liu and Yeh, p. 89.

41. This is the average annual growth rate of John Chang's index of modern industrial production from 1920 to 1929. See John K. Chang, *Industrial Development in Pre-Communist China* (Chicago, 1969), p. 67.

42. *Ibid.*, p. 60.

43. Perkins, *Agricultural Development*, p. 29.

44. John Lossing Buck, *Chinese Farm Economy* (Chicago, 1930), pp. 57, 86.

45. *Ibid.*, p. 64.

46. *Ibid.*, p. 61.

47. P'eng Tse-i, *Chung-kuo chin-tai shou-kung-yeh shih tzu-liao, 1840–1949* (Materials on the history of the handicraft industry in modern China, 1840–1949), vol. 3 (Peking, 1957), appendix 3, cited in Chi-ming Hou, *Foreign Investment and Economic Development in China, 1840–1937* (Cambridge, Mass., 1965), pp. 169–70.

48. Liu and Yeh, *Economy of the Chinese Mainland*, p. 66.

49. Feuerwerker, *Chinese Economy*, p. 48.

50. Mary Clabaugh Wright, "Introduction: The Rising Tide of Change," in Wright, ed., *China in Revolution: The First Phase, 1900–1913* (New Haven, Conn., 1968), p. 61.

51. Alexander Eckstein, "The Economic Heritage," in Eckstein et al., *Economic Trends*, p. 44.

52. James I. Nakamura, "Meiji Land Reform, Redistribution of Income, and Saving From Agriculture," *Economic Development and Cultural Change*, 14.4: 428 (July 1966).

53. Susan Mann Jones, "Finance in Ningpo: The 'Ch'ien Chuang,' 1750–1880," in Willmott, ed., *Economic Organization*, p. 52.

54. Chung-li Chang, *The Income of the Chinese Gentry* (Seattle, 1962), pp. 372–78.

55. Ping-ti Ho, *Studies on the Population of China* (Cambridge, Mass., 1959), p. 226.

56. Rhoads Murphey, *The Treaty Ports and China's Modernization: What Went Wrong?* (Ann Arbor, Mich., 1970), p. 59.

57. Feuerwerker, pp. 66, 75.

58. Thomas C. Smith, *The Agrarian Origins of Modern Japan* (Stanford, Calif., 1959), pp. 157–58.

Skills and Resources in Late Traditional China

1. Walter Endrei, "Le Moulin à organsiner, source des techniques de notre temps," *L'Industrie textile*, 958 (1967); Walter Endrei, *L'Evolution des techniques du filage et du tissage du moyen âge à la révolution industrielle* (Paris, 1968), pp. 56–58. See also A. Schwarz, "Silk Reels and Silk Mills," *Ciba Review*, 59 (1947); and F. Edler de Roover, "Lucchese Silks," *ibid.*, 80 (1950).

2. Wang Chen, *Nung shu* (Treatise on agriculture; pub. 1313), 22: 4. See also Mark Elvin, "The High-Level Equilibrium Trap: The Causes of the Decline of Invention in the Traditional Chinese Textile Industries," in W. E. Willmott, ed., *Economic Organization in Chinese Society* (Stanford, Calif., 1972), pp. 137–38, 142–45.

3. The earliest use of wooden rails on inclined ways at collieries occurred some time between 1597 and 1606. See John U. Nef, *The Cultural Foundations of Industrial Civilization* (Cambridge, Eng., 1958), p. 58. Steam power —of a sort—was of course known to the Alexandrians. Some investigations into its potentialities began again in the fifteenth century and were pursued with more effect in the early seventeenth. Savery's patent for the first really useful steam-driven engine was in 1698. See Joseph Needham, "The Pre-Natal History of the Steam-Engine," *Transactions of the Newcomen Society*, 35: 3–58 (1962–63).

4. Meaning, essentially, those related to a blockage on the expansion of per-capita demand and supply because of the sharply diminishing returns in a highly developed agriculture and water transport to any further technological improvements that did not depend for their existence on modern science and/or industry. See Mark Elvin, *The Pattern of the Chinese Past* (Stanford, Calif., 1973), pp. 298–315.

5. The definition of a science-based input is of course by no means straightforward. Thus the pulsed irrigation invented in Israel by Dr. Benjamin Zur was inspired by theoretical calculations, but it is simple to conceive and apply, and could perfectly well have been stumbled on empirically by the premodern Chinese. Peter Bunyard, "Squeezing the Best Out of Water," *Ecologist*, 3.8: 284–85.

6. Richard G. Wilkinson, *Poverty and Progress* (London, 1972).

7. Ku Yen-wu, ed., *T'ien-hsia chün-kuo li-ping shu* (Documents on the ad-

vantages and disadvantages of the commanderies and principates of the empire; *Ssu-k'u shan-pen ts'ung-shu* ed., 1936 [orig. comp. 1639–62]), 8: 100ab; *Sung-chiang fu-chih* (Gazetteer of Sung-chiang prefecture; pub. 1817), 5: 6; and Ch'en Yü-ch'i, *Nung-chü chi* (Farm tools; pub. Ch'ing period), pp. 5ab.

8. *Chung-kuo nung-ts'un tiao-ch'a tzu-liao wu-chung* (Five collections of materials on investigations of Chinese villages), comp. Hsing-cheng-yüan nung-ts'un fu-hsing wei-yüan-hui (Taipei, 1971), vol. 1, photographs and accompanying legends.

9. Wu Ch'i-chün, *Tien-nan kuang-ch'ang t'u-lüeh* (An illustrated summary of the mines of Yunnan; pub. 1845), 1: 1b, 4ab. On Wu and the Yunnan mines, see two articles by E-tu Zen Sun, "Wu Ch'i-chün: Profile of a Chinese Scholar-Technologist," *Technology and Culture*, 6.3: 394–406 (1965); and "The Copper of Yunnan: An Historical Sketch," *Mining Engineering*, July 1964, pp. 118–24.

10. Pao Shih-ch'en, *Ch'i-min ssu-shu* (Four arts for the governance of the common people), in Pao Ch'eng et al., eds., *An-wu ssu-chung* (Four works by Pao Shih-ch'en; pub. 1846; rev. ed. 1851; reprint ed., Taipei, 1966), pp. 1758–59.

11. Ch'en Yüan-lung, *Ko-chih ching-yüan* (Reflected sources on the sciences; pub. 1735; reprint ed., Taipei, 1971), p. 3628.

12. Ch'ü Ta-chün, *Kuang-tung hsin-yü* (New discourses on Kwangtung; pub. 1700; reprint ed., Taipei, 1968), p. 1121.

13. Franklin H. King, *Farmers of Forty Centuries*, 2d ed. (London, 1927), p. 158.

14. *Nung-sang chi-yao* (Essentials of farming and sericulture; pub. 1273) in *Ts'ung-shu chi-ch'eng* ed. (Shanghai, 1936), 4: 71; Wang Chen, pp. 49, 46, 462–63. See also E-tu Zen Sun, "Sericulture and Silk Textile Production in Ch'ing China," in Willmott, *Economic Organization*, pp. 84–85.

15. Pao Shih-ch'en, pp. 1731–32; Wei Chieh, *Ts'an-sang ts'ui-pien* (Collected notes on sericulture; pub. [?] 1898; reprint ed., Shanghai, 1958), pp. 133–34.

16. Wei Chieh, p. 133.

17. Hsieh Ch'ao-che, *Wu tsa-tsu* (Fivefold miscellany; pub. 1608; reprint ed., Taipei, 1971), p. 857.

As this essay goes to press, a passage has come to hand from Chou Mi's *Ch'i tung yeh yü* (Untutored discourses from Ch'i tung) describing the forcing of out-of-season flowers during the Southern Sung, and the techniques of hothouse construction, manuring, fanning, and steaming. See the *Ts'ung-shu chi-ch'eng* ed. (Shanghai, 1939), ch. 16, p. 213. Chou's family came from near present-day Tsinan, and he is probably speaking of a northern practice. For other descriptions of greenhouses in and around Peking at later dates, see Yeh Lin-feng, *Hsiang-kang fang wu chih* (Monograph on the local products of Hong Kong; Hong Kong, 1970), pp. 247-6. I am grateful to Mr. Stephen Wong for this latter reference.

18. *Mémoires concernant les Chinois* (Paris, 1776–1814), 3: 432–37.

19. Hsü Kuang-ch'i, *Nung-cheng ch'üan-shu* (Encyclopedia of agricultural policy; pub. 1639; reprint ed., Peking, 1956), 2: 708.

20. Joseph Needham, *Science and Civilisation in China*, 4.2: *Mechanical*

Engineering (Cambridge, Eng., 1965), p. 123; Rudolf P. Hommel, *China at Work* (New York, 1937), p. 162. See also the poem by Huang An-t'ao in Chang Ying-ch'ang, ed., *Ch'ing shih-to* (The Ch'ing bell of poesy; original title *Kuo-ch'ao shih-to*, i.e., The bell of poesy of the present dynasty; Peking, 1960), p. 205.

21. Wang Chen, *Nung shu*, 22: 4a.

22. Wei Chieh, pp. 144–50, 258–59.

23. A tentative reconstruction is given in Mark Elvin, "Mandarini e macchine," a paper presented at the 1973 Venice conference on "Sviluppi scientifici, prospettivi religiose, movimenti rivoluzionari della China classica." See also Li Ch'ung-chou, "Shih-chieh-shang tsui tsao-ti shui-li fang-chi-ch'e—shui-chuan ta fang-ch'e" (The world's earliest water-powered spinning machine), *Wen-wu ts'an-k'ao-liao*, 12: 30, n2 (1959).

24. Joseph Needham, *Science and Civilisation in China*, 5.2: *Chemistry and Chemical Technology* (Cambridge, Eng., 1974), pp. 210–19; Sung Ying-hsing, *T'ien-kung k'ai-wu: Chinese Technology in the Seventeenth Century*, tr. E-tu Zen Sun and Shiou-chuan Sun (University Park, Pa., 1966), p. 258, n12.

25. Miyazaki Ichisada, "Sōdai ni okeru sekitan to tetsu" (Coal and iron in the Sung dynasty), *Tōhōhogaku*, 13: 18 (1957), after pointing to the widespread use of coal for smelting iron ore, mistakenly argues that this would have been possible only with coke. In "A Cycle of Economic Change in Imperial China: Coal and Iron in Northeast China, 750–1350," *Journal of the Economic and Social History of the Orient*, 10: 119 (1967), and "Markets, Technology, and the Structure of Enterprise in the Development of the Eleventh-Century Chinese Iron and Steel Industry," *Journal of Economic History*, 26: 51–57 (1966), Robert Hartwell presents a strongly reasoned case based mainly on inference, but the limited direct evidence he cites seems open to possible alternative interpretation. Thus in *Ou-yang Wen-chung kung wen-chi* (Ssu-pu ts'ung-k'an ed.), 118: 10b, "refining" may refer to iron ore rather than to coal.

26. Sakuma Kideo, "Mindai no tekkōgyō to kokka kanri—chuki kan'ei kigyō o chūshin ni" (The iron-mining industry and state management—with emphasis on the state enterprises of the early period), *Shūkan Tōyōgaku*, 20: 826, n114 (1968).

27. *North-China Herald*, June 29, 1867, p. 131; Wu Ch'i-chün, 1: 12b.

28. J. Needham, *The Development of Iron and Steel Technology in China* (London, 1958), p. 14.

29. Ping-ti Ho, *Studies on the Population of China, 1368–1953* (Cambridge, Mass., 1959), pp. 184ff.

30. Pao Shih-ch'en, *Ch'i-min ssu-shu*, pp. 1770–71; Hosea B. Morse, *The International Relations of the Chinese Empire* (London, 1910–18), 1: 172; Kuo T'ing-i, *Chin-tai Chung-kuo shih-shih jih-chih* (A historical chronology of modern China; Taipei, 1963), 1: 39, 41–43, 59, 70. (Decrees aimed at preventing the domestic cultivation of opium.)

31. Yeh Meng-chu, *Yüeh-shih pien* (A survey of the age; written late 17th century) in Shang-hai t'ung-she, ed., *Shang-hai chang-ku ts'ung-shu* (Collected historical materials relating to Shanghai; Shanghai, 1936), 7: 13ab.

32. Amano Motonosuke, "Mindai no nōgyō to nōmin" (Agriculture and

peasants in Ming times), in Yabuuchi Kiyoshi and Yoshida Mitsukuni, eds., *Min-Shin jidai no kagaku gijutsushi* (Science and technology in Ming and Ch'ing times; Kyoto, 1970), pp. 481–83; *Ch'ing shih-to*, p. 657; King, *Farmers of Forty Centuries*, pp. 23, 163–67.

33. Pao Shih-ch'en, p. 1670.

34. Evelyn S. Rawski, *Agricultural Development and the Peasant Economy of South China* (Cambridge, Mass., 1972), pp. 41–43.

35. Pao Shih-ch'en, pp. 1655–79 *passim*.

36. Ku Yen-wu, *T'ien-hsia chün-kuo li-ping shu*, 6: 35; 29: 103; *Mémoires concernant les Chinois*, 2: 610; Nishijima Sadao, *Chūgoku keizai shi kenkyū* (Studies in the economic history of China; Tokyo, 1966), p. 825.

37. King, p. 153.

38. Pao Shih-ch'en, p. 1691.

39. *Ibid.*, pp. 1655–56.

40. Amano Motonosuke, *Chūgoku nōgyō shi kenkyū* (Researches in the history of Chinese agriculture; Tokyo, 1962), pp. 387–88.

41. Pao Shih-ch'en, *Ch'i-min ssu-shu*, pp. 1661, 1702, 1704.

42. *Ibid.*, pp. 1675-77.

43. *Ch'ing shih-to*, p. 137.

44. Ku Yen-wu, 1: 49.

45. *Ibid.*

46. *Ibid.*, pp. 50b–51.

47. Hsü Kuang-ch'i, *Nung-cheng ch'üan-shu*, 1: 159–60.

48. *Ibid.*, pp. 145–46.

49. Fu I-ling, *Ming-tai Chiang-nan shih-min ching-chi shih-t'an* (A preliminary inquiry into the economy of the urban population of Kiangnan in Ming times; Shanghai, 1957), p. 63; King, *Farmers of Forty Centuries*, p. 92.

50. Pao Shih-ch'en, p. 1760.

51. Katō Shigeshi, "Shina no gaichū kujo-hō ni tsuite" (Methods of exterminating insect pests in China), in Katō, *Shina keizai-shi kōshū* (Studies in the economic history of China; Tokyo, 1953–54), 2: 714–29.

52. Yang Na, "Yüan-tai nung-ts'un she-chih yen-chiu" (A study of the *she* system in farm villages in the Yüan period), *Li-shih yen-chiu*, 4: 123 (1965).

53. *Ch'ing shih-to*, p. 519.

54. *Ibid.*, pp. 521, 523.

55. *Ibid.*, p. 518.

56. Ch'ü Ta-chün, *Kuang-tung hsin-yü*, p. 1113; *Nan-hui hsien hsü-chih* (Continuation of the gazetteer of Nan-hui hsien; pub. 1878; reprint ed., Taipei, 1971), 18: 3b.

57. Shiba Yoshinobu, *Sōdai shōgyō shi konkyū* (Commerce during the Sung dynasty; Tokyo, 1968), p. 57.

58. A. Hoshi, *The Ming Tribute Grain System*, tr. Mark Elvin (Ann Arbor, Mich., 1969), pp. 7–8.

59. Ku Yen-wu, *T'ien-hsia chün-kuo li-ping shu*, 8: 112; 23: 84.

60. Yamaguchi Michiko, "Shindai no sōun to senshō" (The government rice transport and the shipping merchants during the Ch'ing), *Tōyōshi kenkyū*, 17.2: 57–58 (Sept. 1958); *Ch'ing shih-to*, pp. 864–65.

61. Li Chien-nung, *Sung-Yüan-Ming ching-chi shih-kao* (Draft economic history of the Sung, Yüan, and Ming dynasties; Peking, 1957), p. 117.

62. *Ch'ing shih-to*, pp. 71–73.

63. L. Audemard, *Les Jonques chinoises*, 2: *Construction de la jonque* (Rotterdam, 1959), pp. 15–16.

64. Ku Yen-wu, 8: 115ab.

65. D. W. Waters, "Chinese Junks: The Pechili Trader," *Mariner's Mirror*, 25: 62–63 (1939); G. R. Worcester, *Sail and Sweep in China* (London, 1966), pp. 35–38; Joseph Needham, *Science and Civilisation in China*, 4.3: *Civil Engineering and Nautics* (Cambridge, Eng., 1971), pp. 400, 428–29.

66. Shiba, *Sōdai shōgyō-shi kenkyū*, p. 62; Needham, *Civil Engineering*, pp. 618-19, 686.

67. Ku Yen-wu, 23: 75b.

68. O. Ōba, "Hirado Matsuura shiryō hakubutsukan-zō 'Tōsen no zu' ni tsuite" (The *Scroll of Chinese Ships* in the Matsuura Museum at Hirado), *Tōzai gakujutsu kenkyū-jo kiyō*, 5: 23 (Mar. 1972).

69. Hoshi Ayao, *Shinshi-kō sōun-shi yakuchū* (An annotated translation of the monograph on the government grain transport in the *Draft History of the Ch'ing*; Yamagata, 1962), p. 184. On modifications to warship design, see Ku Yen-wu, 8: 119.

70. Yeh Meng-chu, *Yüeh-shih pien*, 7: 9b–10.

71. John Larner, *Culture and Society in Italy, 1290–1420* (London, 1971), pp. 161–62.

72. J. Schreck and Wang Cheng, *Yüan-Hsi ch'i-ch'i t'u-shuo* (Illustrated account of remarkable machines from the distant West; pub. 1627; reprint ed., Shanghai, 1936), pp. 323–24.

73. Chu Hua, *Hu-ch'eng pei-k'ao* (Reference materials on the city of Shanghai; pub. after 1784;) in *Shang-hai chang-ku ts'ung-shu*, 2: 15ab. The poem is in *Ch'ing shih-to*, p. 512; compare the one by Yüan Mei on the same theme, p. 510.

74. G. Agricola, *De Re Metallica* (Basel, 1556), tr. Herbert Clark Hoover and Lou Henry Hoover (London, 1912; reprinted 1950), p. 177.

75. Okumura Shōji, *Hinawajū kara kurofune made* (From the matchlock to the black ships; Tokyo, 1970), pp. 129, 138, 144–45.

76. Wu Ch'i-chün, *Tien-nan kuang-ch'ang t'u-lüeh*, 1: 4b. They were normally used in series. See *ibid.*, pp. 3b–4, 14ab, 27b.

77. Needham, *Civil Engineering*, p. 666.

78. Ku Yen-wu, *T'ien-hsia chün-kuo li-ping shu*, 40: 66b–67.

79. *Mémoires concernant les Chinois*, 5: 475–76.

80. *Ch'ing shih-to*, pp. 174–75.

81. Ku Yen-wu, 24: 71b, 37: 2ab.

82. *Ch'ing shih-to*, pp. 146, 148.

83. *Fan Sheng-chih shu* (The book of Fan Sheng-chih), reconstituted and translated by Shih Sheng-han as *On "Fan Sheng-chih shu": An Agriculturistic Book of China* . . . (Peking, 1959), pp. 29ff; Ku Yen-wu, 3: 42a, 12: 4ab.

84. Amano, *Nōgyō shi*, pp. 364–70.

85. Needham, *Civil Engineering*, p. 328.

86. *Ch'ing shih-to*, p. 115.

87. Wei Chieh, *Ts'an-sang ts'ui-pien*, p. 258.

88. Wu Ch'i-chün, *Tien-nan kuang-ch'ang t'u-lüeh*, 1: 21b.

89. Chang Ch'un-hua, *Hu-ch'eng sui-shih ch'ü-ko* (Street songs on the year's activities in Shanghai; pub. 1839), in *Shang-hai chang-ku ts'ung-shu*,

p. 15; Hommel, *China at Work*, p. 171. The evidence for the existence of multispindle wheels for cotton in other areas is tenuous in the extreme. See, for example, Hatano Yoshihiro, *Chūgoku kindai kōgyō shi no kenkyū* (Studies on early modern industry in China; Kyoto, 1961), pp. 76–77, n62.

90. Hommel, p. 27; Ch'u Ta-chün, *Kuang-tung hsin-yü*, p. 867; *Fo-shan Chung-i hsiang-chih* (Gazetteer of Chung-i district in Fo-shan; pub. 1923), 6: 15b.

91. Hsü Kuang-ch'i, *Nung-cheng ch'üan-shu*, 1: 373–84; Arthur Hummel, ed., *Eminent Chinese of the Ch'ing Period* (Washington, D.C., 1943), pp. 316–17. See also O-erh-tai et al., eds., *Shou-shi t'ung-k'ao* (Comprehensive examination of seasonal practices; pub. 1742), 38: 1–13; and Tai Chen, "Lo-tsu-ch'e chi" (On the Archimedean screw; pub. late 18th century), in *Tai Tung-yüan chi* (Collected works of Tai Chen), in *Kuo Hsüeh chi-pen ts'ung-shu ch'ien pien* (Basic collections of works of national scholarship, 1st series; n.p., n.d.).

92. *Ch'ing shih-to*, p. 149.

93. Hsü Kuang-ch'i, 1: 385; O-erh-tai et al., 38: 13b–14a.

94. Nan-k'ai ta-hsüeh li-shih-hsi, comp., *Ch'ing shih-lu ching-chi tzu-liao chi-yao* (Materials on economics excerpted from the *Veritable Records* of the Ch'ing; Peking, 1959), pp. 204, 206.

95. *Ch'ing shih-to*, p. 930.

96. *Ibid.*, p. 927.

97. *North-China Herald*, June 29, 1867, pp. 129, 131.

98. *Ch'ing shih-to*, p. 926.

99. *Ibid.*, p. 929.

100. Okumura, *Hinawajū kara kurofune made*, p. 146.

101. Needham, *Mechanical Engineering*, p. 351.

102. Agricola, pp. 188–96.

103. Chu Hua, *Mu mien p'u* (Cotton manual; pub. mid-18th century), in *Shang-hai chang-ku ts'ung-shu*, pp. 11b–12.

104. *Ch'ing shih-to*, p. 149.

105. *Ibid.*, p. 145.

106. *Nan-hai hsien hsü-chih*, 18: 3.

107. *Mémoires concernant les Chinois*, 4: 318.

108. *Ibid.*, p. 313.

109. Shih Min-hsiung, *Ch'ing tai ssu chih kung yeh ti fa chan* (The development of the silk textile industry in the Ch'ing period; Taipei, 1968), pp. 35–38, 65.

110. *North-China Herald*, July 22, 1867, p. 165.

111. *Tung-fang tsu-chih*, 1904, 1: 0, 0: 104.

112. Huang Chia-mo, *Chia-wu chan ch'ien chih T'ai-wan mei-wu* (Coal in Taiwan before the Sino-Japanese War of 1894; Taipei, 1961), pp. 2–4.

113. Hoshi Ayao, *Mindai sōun no kenkyū* (The Ming government rice transport system; Tokyo, 1963), pp. 73–74.

114. *Ch'ing shih-lu ching-chi tzu-liao*, p. 146.

115. Ku Yen-wu, *T'ien-hsia chün-kuo li-ping shu*, 30: 36; 31: 33; Hummel, *Eminent Chinese*, p. 109.

116. Ku Ying-t'ai, *Ming-shih chi-shih pen mo* (A chronicle of the Ming; pub. 1658; reprint ed., Taipei, 1956), 31: 82–83; Huang Chia-mo, pp. 2–4.

117. Ku Yen-wu, 26: 36ab, translated in Elvin, *Pattern*, pp. 299–300.

118. Pao Shih-ch'en, *Ch'i-min ssu-shu*, pp. 1653–54.

119. *Ch'ing shih-to*, p. 404.

120. *Ibid.*, pp. 412–13.

121. J. Besson, *Theatrum Instrumentarum et Machinarum* (Paris, 1573), plate 56; Agostino Ramelli, *Le diverse et artificiose machine del capitano Agostino Ramelli* (Paris, 1588), fig. 95 and many others; G. A. Böckler, *Theatrum machinarum novum* (Nuremberg, 1662), plates 135, 138, 150, 151, and others.

122. B. F. de Bélidor, *Architecture hydraulique: ou l'Art de conduire, d'élever et de ménager les eaux, pour les différens besoins de la vie* (Paris, 1737–53), 1: 362.

123. Ku Yen-wu, 8: 100a.

124. Dwight H. Perkins, *Agricultural Development in China 1368–1968* (Chicago, 1969), p. 240.

125. *Ibid.*, pp. 16–17.

126. Lu Wang-ta et al., comp., *Chia-ch'ing Shang-hai hsïen-chih* (Gazetteer for Shang-hai hsien in the Chia-ch'ing reign; Shanghai, 1814), 1: 43.

127. *Ch'ing shih-to*, p. 155. See also p. 166.

Growth and Changing Structure of
China's Twentieth-Century Economy

1. Dwight H. Perkins, *Agricultural Development in China, 1368–1968* (Chicago, 1969), p. 30; T. C. Liu and K. C. Yeh, *The Economy of the Chinese Mainland* (Princeton, N. J., 1965), p. 66.

2. Perkins, pp. 266–71.

3. See Kang Chao's essay in this volume.

4. See Robert Dernberger's essay in this volume for a discussion of the nature and size of China's foreign investment.

5. These figures are from Albert Feuerwerker, *The Chinese Economy, ca. 1870–1911* (Ann Arbor, Mich., 1969), pp. 34–39, which in turn are based on compilations by Wang Ching-yü, ed., *Chung-kuo chin-tai kung-yeh shih tzu-liao ti-erh-chi, 1895–1914 nien* (Materials on modern Chinese industrial history, 1895–1914; Peking, 1957).

6. These figures are from a forthcoming paper by Alexander Eckstein, Kang Chao, and John K. Chang, "The Economic Development of Manchuria: The Rise of a Frontier Economy."

7. See China Maritime Customs, *Decennial Reports, 1922–1931* (Shanghai, 1933), p. 155.

8. For a fuller discussion of these issues, see Perkins, *Agricultural Development*.

9. Eckstein et al.

10. For a breakdown of the components of farm output, see Perkins, p. 30.

11. Chinese trade data are available in the reports of the China Maritime Customs service.

12. *Ibid., 1922–1931*, p. 389.

13. Liu and Yeh, *Economy of the Chinese Mainland*, pp. 426–28.

14. Close estimates of the degree of death and destruction were not made, but attempts to establish general orders of magnitude can be found in Chang

Yu-i, comp., *Chung-kuo chin-tai nung-yeh shih tz'u-liao, 1927–1937* (Materials on the history of modern China's agriculture; Peking, 1957), p. 613; and Walter H. Mallory, *China: Land of Famine* (New York, 1926).

15. These issues are discussed at greater length in Perkins, *Agricultural Development*, chap. 7.

16. See the discussions on this point in Ramon H. Myers, *The Chinese Peasant Economy* (Cambridge, Mass., 1970), pp. 234–40, and Perkins, chap. 5.

17. The gross domestic capital formation figures are those of K. C. Yeh, "Capital Formation," in Alexander Eckstein, Walter Galenson, and Ta-chung Liu, eds., *Economic Trends in Communist China* (Chicago, 1968), p. 510.

18. See the discussion in Gunnar Myrdal, *Asian Drama* (New York, 1968), 3: 2104. I am indebted to Thomas Rawski for this citation.

19. Simon Kuznets, *Modern Economic Growth* (New Haven, Conn., 1966), pp. 347–48, 508.

20. *Asian Drama.*

21. The Soviet figure of 0.7 tons of grain per capita is from Harry Schwartz, *Russia's Soviet Economy* (New York, 1954), p. 358; and the Chinese figure of 0.28 tons is from State Statistical Bureau, *Ten Great Years* (Peking, 1960), pp. 8, 119.

22. Chou En-lai is the most frequent source of such information. See, for example, the *New York Times*, Jan. 28, 1973; and the *Boston Globe*, Apr. 24, 1973.

23. Calculated on the basis of the 1937 ruble factor cost in Abram Bergson, *The Real National Income of the Soviet Union Since 1928* (Cambridge, Mass., 1961), pp. 225, 230, 237.

24. *Ibid.*, pp. 225, 237.

25. For a discussion of the relationship between wages, prices, and the excess demand for labor in the USSR, see Franklyn D. Holzman, *Soviet Taxation* (Cambridge, Mass., 1955).

26. See the discussion in Dwight H. Perkins, *Market Control and Planning in Communist China* (Cambridge, Mass., 1966), chap. 7.

27. Gur Ofer, "Industrial Structure, Urbanization and Growth Strategy of Socialist Countries" (unpub. paper).

28. Bank of Korea, *Economic Statistics Yearbook, 1971* (Seoul, 1971), p. 6.

29. William W. Lockwood, *The Economic Development of Japan* (Princeton, N.J., 1954), p. 484.

30. Hollis B. Chenery and Lance Taylor, "Development Patterns Among Countries and Over Time," *Review of Economics and Statistics*, 50.4:391–416 (1968).

31. Alexander Gerschenkron, *Economic Backwardness in Historical Perspective* (Cambridge, Mass., 1962).

32. United Nations Food and Agricultural Organization, *Production Yearbook, 1970* (Rome, 1971), pp. 73–78.

APPENDIX A

1. Reported at one commune visited by Professor Audrey Donnithorne.

2. Edgar Snow, "Talks with Chou En-lai," *The New Republic*, Mar. 27, 1971, p. 20. There are of course problems in relating cotton output and cotton

cloth production, but Chinese raw cotton imports were small (5 percent of output), and the percentage of cotton used for something other than cloth probably did not change much.

3. *Jen-min jih-pao*, Dec. 25, 1965, as reported by Kang Chao, *Agricultural Production in Communist China, 1949–1965* (Madison, Wis., 1970), p. 291. The number of workers in the textile industry had also increased from 940,000 to 1,500,000.

4. The 1965 figure is from the Hong Kong *Ching-chi tao-pao*, Aug. 8, 1962, translated in Joint Publications Research Service, 38.234:6 (Oct. 19, 1966). The 1956 figure is from *Wo-kuo kang-t'ieh, tien-li, mei-tan, chi-chieh, fang-chih, tsao-chih kung-yeh-te chin-hsi,* (Japanese translation, p. 136).

5. *Peking Review*, Dec. 15, 1972, pp. 15–16.

6. *Hung-ch'i*, Apr. 1, 1973, in *Survey of China Mainland Magazines*, p. 57.

7. *BBC*, Jan. 6, 1971, p. A22.

8. Erisman, in his essay in *People's Republic of China: An Economic Assessment* (Washington, D.C., 1972), p. 140, gives figures in terms of nutrient equivalent that imply that the average nutrient content of all Chinese fertilizers in both large and small firms in 1970 was 7 percent (compared with the usual nutrient-to-gross-weight ratio of over 20 percent).

9. *Peking Review*, May 28, 1965, p. 29, reporting that cement output increased 16 times over in 15 years.

10. *Foreign Broadcasts Information Service*, Jan. 3, 1972, p. B12.

11. T. C. Liu and K. C. Yeh, *The Economy of the Chinese Mainland* (Princeton, N.J., 1965), p. 66.

12. Liu and Yeh do follow the procedure used here of assuming that growth in the services sector was in large part a function of growth in the other sectors. The input-output table they use to estimate this relationship leads to implausible results. Whether this is because it is based on 1952–57 data or for some other reason must await further analysis.

APPENDIX B

1. The electricity figure referred to here is an estimate by Russian specialists. See Table A.9.

2. New China News Agency, Feb. 22, 1972.

3. These figures are from the 1958 plan (*Hsin-hua pan-yueh-k'an*, no. 5, 1958, pp. 16–17) and the 1959 plan (*Chung-hua jen-min kung-ho-kuo fa-kuei hui-pien*, no. 9, 1959, pp. 48–49).

4. *Peking Review*, Oct. 13, 1972, p. 11.

5. See p. 144 of the text and the accompanying footnote.

The Growth of a Modern Cotton Textile Industry
and the Competition with Handicrafts

All Chinese-language articles are cited by English title only. The collection *Chung-kuo chin-tai shou-kung-yeh shih tsu-liao* (Materials on the modern history of China's handicraft industries; Peking, 1957), comp. P'eng Tse-i, is abbreviated as *SKYS* in the Notes.

1. H. B. Morse, *The Chronicles of the East India Company Trading to China, 1635–1834* (Cambridge, Mass., 1926), 1: 224.

2. *Ibid.*, 2: 120.

3. *Ibid.*, 3: 367.

4. According to the data quoted in H. D. Fong, *Chung-kuo chih mien-fang chih-yen* (China's cotton textile industry; Shanghai, 1934), p. 327, the average annual export for 1867–74 was 962 piculs. From the data on p. 322, we know that for the types of nankeen exported in those days one picul contained on the average 36 bolts. Therefore, the average annual export in that period was about 34,600 bolts.

5. *Ibid.*, p. 295.

6. Chuang Chi-fa, "The History of the Shanghai Machine Weaving Bureau in the Ch'ing Dynasty," *The Continental Magazine*, 40.4: 25 (Feb. 1970).

7. This is substantiated by the constant number of power looms over the period. See Yen Chung-p'ing, *Chung-kuo mien-fang-chih shih-kao* (Draft history of China's cotton textile industry; Peking, 1963), p. 354.

8. *Ibid.*, p. 127.

9. *Ibid.*, p. 355.

10. See People's Republic of China, Statistical Bureau, *Wo-kuo kang-t'ieh tien-li mei-t'an chi-hsieh fang-chih tsao-chih kung-yeh ti chin-hsi* (The present and past of our iron and steel, power, coal, machinery, textile, and paper manufacturing industries; Peking, 1958), p. 148.

11. *Ibid.*

12. Richard A. Kraus, "Cotton and Cotton Goods in China, 1918–1936," Ph.D. diss., Harvard University, 1968. See particularly chaps. 3–5.

13. In making field studies in agriculture, the Chinese Marxists were concerned primarily with the tenancy system. This excessively narrow scope in their studies of agricultural production was criticized by Wang I-chang in "The Direction of Rural Economic Statistics Should Be Changed," *Chung-kuo nung-ts'un*, 1.6: 711–15 (1935).

14. Notably, Chi-ming Hou, *Foreign Investment and Economic Development in China, 1840–1937* (Cambridge, Mass., 1965), pp. 173–77.

15. Ramon H. Myers, "Cotton Textile Handicrafts and the Development of the Cotton Textile Industry in Modern China," *Economic History Review*, 18.3: 614–32 (Dec. 1965); Kraus, pp. 8–12, 119–25; Albert Feuerwerker, "Handicraft and Manufactured Cotton Textiles in China, 1871–1910," *Journal of Economic History*, 30.2: 371–78 (June 1970).

16. *SKYS*, 3: 763.

17. Yen Chung-p'ing, *Mien-fang-chih shih*, p. 256.

18. Feuerwerker, p. 374.

19. Kraus, pp. 119–25.

20. *Ibid.*, p. 125.

21. Imperial Maritime Customs, *Trade Report*, 1876 (Shanghai), pp. 5–6.

22. Great Britain, Foreign Office, *Report on the Native Cloths in Use in the Amoy Consular District*, 1886 (London), misc. series, no. 19, p. 4.

23. Great Britain, Foreign Office, *Diplomatic and Consular Reports on Trade and Finance*, 1892 (London), vol. 81: Hankow, p. 3.

24. *Annual Report of the Board of Directors of the Chamber of Commerce and Manufactures*, 1853 (Manchester, Eng.), p. 20; *ibid.*, 1855, p. 10.

25. Imperial Maritime Customs, *Decennial Reports, 1922–1931* (Shanghai, 1933), 1: 113, 182.

26. *Ibid.*

27. *Ibid., 1882–1891* (Shanghai, 1893), appendix.

28. According to an official survey, only nine of the 49 hsien in Kwangsi province that engaged in handicraft textile production used any locally produced hand yarn. See Rural Reconstruction Commission, *A Survey of the Rural Areas in Kwangsi* (Shanghai, 1935), p. 174. In the cotton-growing province of Hopei, where handspinning was relatively extensive, 89 of the 129 hsien in 1929 engaged in some weaving activities and 68 of these reported the use of handspun yarn. But the value of cloth woven with hand yarn accounted for only 25.9 percent of the total value of handicraft weaving in that province. See Li Fung, "The Development of Commercial Capital in the Handicraft Cotton Textile Industry in the Rural Areas in Hopei in the Past 50 Years," in *Chung-kuo nung-ts'un*, 1.3: 309 (1934).

29. Wu Chih, *Hsiang-ts'un chih-pu kung-yeh ti i-ko yen-chiu* (A study of the rural weaving industry) (Shanghai, 1936), pp. 122, 198.

30. Fong, *Chung-kuo chih mien-fang chih-yen*, p. 327.

31. National Agricultural Research Bureau, *Crop Reports*, 4.11: 292–93 (Nov. 1936).

32. Chang Shih-wen, *Ting-hsien nung-ts'un kung-yeh tiao-ch'a* (Survey of the rural industry in Ting hsien (Ting hsien, Hopei, 1936), pp. 423, 426, 431, 440, 441, 444, 452, 457.

33. South Manchuria Railway Shanghai Office, *Survey Research Material*, no. 38 (1941), appendix table 11.

34. Wu Chih, p. 81; *SKYS*, 3: 785.

35. *SKYS*, 3: 785.

36. Chang Shih-wen, p. 79; Yen Chung-p'ing, "The Problems of Handicraft Textile Industries," *Chung-shan wen-hua chiao-yü kuan chi-kan*, 4.3: 1040 (1937).

37. Pi Hsiang-hui, "The Operational Pattern of Commercial Capital in the Rural Domestic Handicrafts," in *Chung-kuo nung-ts'un*, 1.8: 42 (1935).

38. Yen Chung-p'ing, "Problems," p. 1047.

39. Yen Chung-p'ing, *Mien-fang-chih shih*, p. 254.

40. *SKYS*, 3: 682.

41. *Ibid.*, p. 684.

42. *Ibid.*, p. 683.

43. See note 28, above.

44. Chang Shih-wen, *Ting-hsien*, p. 79.

45. Imperial Maritime Customs, *Returns of Trade and Trade Reports*, 1887 (Chefoo), p. 42.

46. Chang Shih-wen, p. 79.

47. *Ibid.*, p. 72.

48. *Ta kung pao* (Impartial daily), Tientsin, Oct. 17, 1934.

49. Yen Chung-p'ing, *Mien-fang-chih shih*, pp. 243, 294.

50. Kraus, pp. 83, 86.

51. *Chung-wai ching-chi chou-k'an*, 109: 42 (Apr. 25, 1925).

52. Ralph M. Odell, *Cotton Goods in China* (Washington, D.C., 1916), p. 186.

53. *SKYS*, 3: 69.

54. Wang Tzu-chien, *Chung-kuo t'u-pu-yeh tzu chien-tu* (The future of China's native cloth production; Shanghai, 1936), p. 131.
55. On Kiangsu, *SKYS*, 3: 107, 444, 787; on Shantung and Hopei, Wang Tzu-chien, p. 131.
56. H. D. Fong, *Tien-ching chih-pu kung-yeh* (The weaving industry in Tientsin; Tientsin, 1930), p. 18.
57. *SKYS*, 3: 21, 107, 690.
58. Yen Chung-p'ing, *Mien-fang-chih shih*, p. 253.
59. Chang Shih-wen, *Ting-hsien*, p. 427.
60. Wu Chih, *Hsiang-ts'un chih-pu-yeh*, pp. 122–29 and 198–224.
61. *Ibid.*, p. 6.
62. H. D. Fong, *The Growth and Decline of Rural Industrial Enterprise in North China* (Tientsin, 1936), p. 5; Lung Chiu, "Rural Subsidiary Production in Wei hsien, Shantung," in Ch'ien Chia-chü, ed., *Chung-kuo nung-ts'un ching-chi lun-wen chi* (Collected essays on China's rural economy; Shanghai, 1936), p 537.
63. Lung Chiu, p. 537.
64. Chang Shih-wen, p. 113.
65. Fong, *Growth and Decline*, p. 10.
66. *Ibid.*, p. 17.
67. Su Cheng-hsiang, "The Native Cloth of Pao-ti," *Shang-hsüeh hui-pao*, 1: 38–40 (July 1935).
68. Wu Chih, *Hsiang-ts'un chih-pu-yeh*, pp. 9–30.
69. *Ibid.*, p 196.
70. Yen Chung-p'ing, *Mien-fang-chih shih*, p. 41.
71. For instance, Fong, *Growth and Decline*, pp. 13, 23–24, 31–36, 67–68; Wu Chih, pp. 12 27, 31, 77–85, 96, 227–40; and *SKYS*, 3: 212–14, 217, 456–58, 627–46, 703.
72. Fong, *Growth and Decline*, p. 13.
73. *SKYS*, 3: 461.
74. See Fong, *Growth and Decline*, p. 65; and Wu Chih, pp. 222, 267.
75. *SKYS*, 3: 261; Lung Chiu, "Rural Subsidiary Production," p. 541; and Wang Tzu-chien, *Chung-kuo t'u-pu yeh*, p. 131.
76. Wu Chih, *Hsiang-ts'un chih-pu-kung-yeh*, p. 29.
77. Fong, *Growth and Decline*, p. 14.
78. Wu Chih, pp. 27–30.
79. *SKYS*, 3: 454.
80. *Ibid.*, p. 24.
81. National Agricultural Research Bureau, *Crop Reports*, 4. 11: 292–93 (Nov. 1936).
82. Chi Pin, "A Prosperous Village in South Hopei Amidst the Bankrupting Rural Sector," in Ch'ien Chia-chü, *Chung-kuo nung-ts'un ching-chi lun-wen chi*, pp. 502–13; *SKYS*, 3: 176–77.
83. The declined purchasing power in the rural sector is confirmed by John Lossing Buck, *Land Utilization in China* (Nanking, 1937), pp. 345–47.
84. *SKYS*, 3: 397.
85. *Ibid.*, p. 765.
86. Fong, *Growth and Decline*, p. 54.

87. *Ibid; SKYS,* 3: 454.
88. Odell, *Cotton Goods in China,* p. 185.
89. *Ibid.*
90. Freda Utley, *Lancashire and the Far East* (London, 1931), p. 237.
91. Fong, *Chung-kuo chih mien-fang chih-yen,* p. 275.
92. Ou Pao-san, *Chung-kuo kuo min so-te, 1933 nien* (China's national income; Shanghai, 1937), 1: 64–69.
93. Yen Chung-p'ing, *Mien-fang-chih shih,* p. 251.
94. Kraus, "Cotton and Cotton Goods," p. 114.
95. See Table 7.
96. *Chin-hsi,* p. 157, 167.
97. *Ibid.,* p. 180.
98. *Ibid.,* p. 181.
99. Yen Chung-p'ing, *Mien-fang-chih shih,* p. 281.
100. See Fessenden S. Blanchard, *The Textile Industries of China and Japan* (New York, 1944), p. 23; A. S. Becker, "Economics of the Cotton Textile Industry of the USSR, 1938–1955," Ph.D. diss., Columbia University, 1959, pp. 3–4.

The Growth of Producer Industries, 1900–1971

Chinese-language article titles are given in English only. The journals *Chi-hua ching-chi, Chi-hsieh kung-yeh,* and *Hua-hsüeh kung-yeh* are abbreviated as *CHCC, CHKY,* and *HHKY* in the Notes.

1. Wang Hu-sheng, "Several Problems of Classifying Heavy and Light Industry," *Ching-chi yen-chiu,* 4: 18 (1963).
2. For data on output and exports of coal, see Tezuka Masao, *Shina jūkōgyō hattatsu-shi* (History of the development of China's heavy industries; Tokyo, 1944), pp. 124–25, 140, 172; and Yen Chung-p'ing et al., *Chung-kuo chin-tai ching-chi shih t'ung-chi tzu-liao hsüan-chi* (Selected statistical materials of modern Chinese economic history; Peking, 1955), p. 80; on iron ore and other minerals, *ibid.,* pp. 139–40; on pig iron, Ch'en Chen, ed., *Chung-kuo chin-tai kung-yeh shih tzu-liao* (Collected material on modern Chinese industrial history; reprint ed., Tokyo, 1966), collection 4, vol. 2 p. 754 (hereafter 4.2: 754.)
3. Lists of products appear in Ch'en Chen, 4.2: 801; and Ku Yü-hsien, "Thirty Years of Machine-Building," in Chou K'ai-ch'ing, ed., *San-shih-nien lai chih Chung-kuo kung-ch'eng* (Thirty years of Chinese engineering; reprint ed., Taipei, 1967), 2: 8–17.
4. Nathan Rosenberg has described this process in a number of articles dealing with United States industrial history.
5. These hypotheses were suggested by John C. H. Fei.
6. Chung-kuo k'o-hsüeh yuan Shang-hai ching-chi yen-chiu so and Shang-hai she-hui k'o-hsüeh yuan ching-chi yen-chiu so, comps., *Ta-lung chi-ch'i-ch'ang ti fa-sheng fa-chan yü kai-tsao* (Birth, development, and reform of the Ta-lung Machinery Works; Shanghai, 1959), pp. 2–3.
7. Ch'en Chen and Yao Lo, eds., *Chung-kuo chin-tai kung-yeh shih tzu-liao* (Collected material on modern Chinese industrial history; reprint ed., Tokyo, 1966), collection 1, p. 597 (1: 597).
8. *Ibid.,* p. 618.
9. *Chung-kuo kuo-huo kung-ch'ang shih-lüeh* (Capsule histories of Chinese

factories; Shanghai, 1935), pp. 143, 213–14; Ch'en Chen and Yao Lo, 1: 593. Fan Hsü-tung, founder of the important Yung-li Chemical Company, studied chemistry at Tokyo Imperial University (Ch'en Chen and Yao Lo, 1: 513).

10. The sample includes plants described in Ch'en Chen and Yao Lo, 1: 593–631; and in *Chung-kuo kuo-huo.*

11. *Ta-lung,* pp. 16, 32, 35, 39.

12. Ch'en Chen and Yao Lo, 1: 606, 608.

13. *Ta-lung,* pp. 6–7, 10.

14. *Ibid.,* p. 7.

15. Large price increases for cotton products are shown in *Nung-shang t'ung-chi piao,* pp. 304–5. Nan-k'ai ta-hsüeh ching-chi yen-chiu so, comp., *Nan-k'ai chih-shu tzu-liao hui-pien* (Collected Nankai index number materials; Peking, 1958), p. 74, shows the Tientsin wholesale price of 16-count yarn rising from 103.77 to 216.96 yuan per *pao* between 1914 and 1918. The base spindle price charged by the largest American textile machinery maker, which exported its products to China, rose from $2.00 to $6.75 between 1913 and 1920 (George S. Gibb, *The Saco-Lowell Shops,* Cambridge, Mass., 1950, p. 470). The lack of response by Chinese machinery producers is evident from the stagnation of the national spindle stock during 1914–18 (Yen Chung-p'ing, *T'ung-chi tzu-liao hsüan-chi,* pp. 134–35).

16. *Ta-lung,* p. 20.

17. *Ibid.,* pp. 23, 32.

18. The marketing organization of British textile machinery plants is described for an earlier period in S. B. Saul, "The Market and the Development of the Mechanical Engineering Industries in Britain, 1860–1914," in S. B. Saul, ed., *Technological Change: The United States and Britain in the 19th Century* (London, 1970), p. 153.

19. *Ta-lung,* pp. 33–35, 51–54.

20. *Ibid.,* pp. 22, 65.

21. *Ibid.,* pp. 45, 52.

22. *Ibid.,* pp. 46–48.

23. *Ibid.,* chaps. 3, 4.

24. *Nung-shang t'ung-chi piao,* pp. 240–46, lists only 35 enterprises with 1,297 workers in Kiangsu's machinery and tool industry in 1919; over one-third of the firms and one-fourth of the workers listed were in the jewelry trade.

25. Food-processing was the most capital-intensive major industry in Tientsin as well as Shanghai; machinery accounted for about 7 percent of Tientsin's factories, but only 2.5 percent of the industrial workers and 0.2 percent of the industrial capital (Fang Hsien-t'ing, "Industrialization and Labor of Hopei Province," *Ching-chi t'ung-chi chi-k'an,* 1.2: 281 [1932]).

26. Shang-hai she-hui chü, comp., *Shang-hai chih chi-chih kung-yeh* (Factory industry in Shanghai; Shanghai, 1933), p. 26.

27. Match imports from John K. Chang, *Industrial Development in Pre-Communist China* (Chicago, 1969), p. 46. Output rose from below 600,000 chests in 1929 to 810,000 chests in 1936, and the number of plants increased by 40 percent during 1930–33 (Ch'en Chen and Yao Lo, *Kung-yeh shih tzu-liao,* 1: 66–68). Tezuka, *Shina jūkōgyō hattatsu-shi,* p. 5, puts the value of annual imports of match-making equipment for 1933–36 at 253,000 yuan, 331,000 yuan, and 113,000 yuan. Two of several domestic producers of match

machinery are listed in Shang-hai she-hui chü, comp., *Shang-hai chih kung-yeh* (Shanghai's industry; Shanghai, 1930), p. 116.

28. Other Shanghai textile-machinery producers are mentioned in *Shang-hai chih kung-yeh*, p. 115, which includes a discussion of import substitution in machinery for silk production; and in Ōtsuka Reizō, *Shina kōgyō sōkan* (Comprehensive survey of Chinese industry; Tokyo, 1942), 2: 12.

29. Ta-lung's experience as subcontractor for a British firm and its later dealings with Chinese subcontractors are discussed in *Ta-lung*, pp. 8, 12.

30. On Chinese blundering, see Albert Feuerwerker, "China's Nineteenth-Century Industrialization: The Case of the Hanyehping Coal and Iron Company, Limited," in C. D. Cowan ed., *The Economic Development of China and Japan* (London, 1964), pp. 79–110. Anshan's early history is described in M. Gardner Clark, *The Development of China's Steel Industry and Soviet Technical Aid* (Ithaca, N.Y., 1973), pp. 1–2; and in Manshū kaihatsu yonjūnenshi kankō kai, comp., *Manshū kaihatsu yonjūnenshi* (Forty years of development in Manchuria; Tokyo, 1964–65), 1: 233–35.

31. Hollis B. Chenery and Lance Taylor, "Development Patterns Among Countries and Over Time," *Review of Economics and Statistics*, 50.4: 412 (1968), state that the basic metals sector appears to be the only one with important scale economies in every branch.

32. Feuerwerker, p. 90; Tezuka, p. 207.

33. Clark, p. 46, referring to blending coal.

34. *Ibid.*, pp. 45–48, 52–53; *Manshū kaihatsu*, 2: 462.

35. Clark, p. 1.

36. *Manshū kaihatsu*, 2: 461.

37. Outlay data from *ibid.*, 1: 297; output from Ch'en Chen, *Kung-yeh shih tzu-liao*, 4.1: 746.

38. *Manshū kaihatsu*, 2: 461.

39. Anshan capital figure from *ibid.*, 2: 461. Manchukuo yen were worth slightly less than Shanghai yuan during 1932–37 (*Manchoukuo Yearbook, 1942*, Hsinking, 1941, pp. 254–55). Ch'en Chen and Yao Lo, *Kung-yeh shih tzu-liao*, 1: 649–55, present 177 capital and profit figures compiled from annual reports of 98 firms for 1933–37; five firms reported capital in excess of ten million yuan, and only the Shen-hsin Textile Plant had assets larger than Anshan's. Annual profits in excess of one million yuan appear in nine instances, with only one figure surpassing two million yuan.

40. Application of one test indicates that China experienced "marked improvement" in financial effectiveness during the 1930's because the ratio of bank deposits to national product rose more than five percentage points in ten years. However, the terminal position (1936) barely escapes the boundary (15 percent ratio of currency plus deposits to GNP) separating financial networks with "negligible" and those with "some" contribution to financing industry and agriculture. For the test, see Irma Adelman and Cynthia T. Morris, *Society, Politics and Economic Development* (Baltimore, 1967), pp. 120–22. Data on national product, currency, and deposits from K. C. Yeh, "Capital Formation," in Alexander Eckstein, Walter Galenson, and T. C. Liu, eds., *Economic Trends in Communist China* (Chicago, 1968), p. 510; Arthur N. Young, *China's Nation-Building Effort, 1927–1937* (Stanford, Calif., 1971), pp. 170–71, 486–89; and Leonard G. Ting, "Chinese Modern Banks and the

Finance of Government and Industry," *Nankai Social and Economic Quarterly*, 8.3: 580 (1935).

41. Ting, p. 596, provides data showing that the annual yield calculated from average monthly prices of actively traded domestic securities averaged 17.3 percent per annum between 1928 and June 1935, surpassing 20 percent in 21 of 87 months and dropping below 11 percent only once.

42. Mishina Yoritata, *Hokushi minzoku kōgyō no hattatsu* (Development of native industry in North China; Tokyo, 1942), pp. 79–84, gives data on the low shares of commercial bank loans offered to industry. Data for large commercial banks show over three-fourths of industrial loans going to textiles and flour milling and virtually none extended to producer industries (Ting, p. 605; Mishina, p. 80).

43. "State Plans for Industrial Development, I: The Steelworks Project," *Chinese Economic Journal*, 15.2: 204–27 (1934), describes one set of state plans.

44. Feuerwerker, "China's Nineteenth-Century Industrialization," pp. 106–8; Ku Yüan-t'ien, "China's Iron and Steel Industry," *Ching-chi t'ung-chi chi-k'an*, 2.3: 706 (1933).

45. Ku Yüan-t'ien, p. 709; Fang Hsien-t'ing and Ku Yüan-t'ien, "A Bird's Eye View of China's Iron and Steel Industry," in Fang Hsien-t'ing, ed., *Chung-kuo ching-chi yen-chiu* (Studies of China's economy; Changsha, 1938), p. 650.

46. Ch'en Chen, *Kung-yeh shih tzu-liao*, 4.2: 746.

47. The development of these enterprises is a major theme of *Manshū kaihatsu*, particularly vol. 2.

48. *Ibid.*, 2: 488, discusses Japanese reluctance to promote Manchuria's machinery industry prior to the 1930's.

49. Ancillary engineering works are mentioned in *ibid.*, 2: 487–510; and Elizabeth B. Schumpeter, "Mineral Resources of Japan and Manchukuo," in Schumpeter, ed., *The Industrialization of Japan and Manchukuo* (New York, 1940), p. 407. The South Manchurian Railway Company's work force grew from 11,000 in 1906 to a wartime peak of 398,000 (*Manshū kaihatsu*, 1: 152).

50. South Manchurian Railway, sōmubu chōsaka, comp., *Shina kōjō jijō* (Conditions in China's factories; Darien, 1928), pp. 67–68, 169ff.

51. *Ibid.*, pp. 43–44. Its activities included the repair and manufacture of locomotives, rolling stock, radiators, boilers, railway and bridge girders, and woodworking equipment.

52. Manchukuo's machinery imports rose by 86 percent in 1932–33 and by 46 percent in 1933–34 (Yu-kwei Cheng, *Foreign Trade and Industrial Development of China*, Washington, D.C., 1956), p. 202

53. South Manchurian Railway, chōsaka, comp., *Manshū gokanen keikaku gaiyō* (Outline of the Five-Year Plan for Manchukuo; Dairen, 1937), pp. 136–37; *Manshū kaihatsu*, 2: 499.

54. *Manshū kaihatsu*, 2: 378, 500.

55. Paid-up capital for corporations newly formed in 1937–41 in the machinery sector was 294 million yen, 4.9 times the figure for 1932–36 (Ch'en Chen, Yao Lo, and Feng Hsien-chih, eds., *Chung-kuo chin-tai kung-yeh shih tzu-liao*, Collected material on modern Chinese industrial history; reprint ed., Tokyo, 1966, collection 2, p. 472 [2: 472]).

56. *Manshū kaihatsu*, 2: 508, states that machinery output rose by 600 percent between 1932 and 1939.

57. Indices of Hsinking and Tokyo wholesale prices appear in Elizabeth B. Schumpeter, "Conclusion: Industrial Development and Government Policy, 1936–1940," in Schumpeter, *Industrialization*, p. 826; and in *Manshū kaihatsu*, 2: 882.

58. Anshan sales prices calculated from Kantōkyoku kambō bunshoka, comp., *Manshū kōjō tōkei sokuhō* (Bulletin of Manchurian factory statistics; Lushun, 1940 and 1941), 1939 ed., p. 3, and 1940 ed., pp. 2–3.

59. *Manshū kaihatsu*, 2: 504, states that 1939 machine-tool output advanced to 13 million yen, but this is inconsistent with other data giving 1940 output as only 378 machine tools (*ibid.*, 2: 378).

60. Nai-ruenn Chen, ed., *Chinese Economic Statistics* (Chicago, 1967), pp. 28–29, and Wang Hu-sheng, "Several Problems," summarize the Chinese literature on industrial classification. Reports giving the FFYP investment shares of "heavy" and "producer" industries at 87.4 and 85.6 percent respectively indicate the near identity of the two groups (Nai-ruenn Chen, p. 169). The official output data in Table 5 cover "modern industry," which includes "modern factories" and "handicraft factories" but excludes "individual handicrafts," a category consisting of handicraft operations employing less than four hired workers (*ibid.*, p. 29). The extent to which statistical practice observed these definitions is not known.

61. "The Problem of Classifying Producer and Consumer Goods," *T'ung-chi kung-tso*, 3: 3 (1957), states that "in the past, we classified military industry (*chün-shih kung-yeh*) entirely within producer goods (*sheng-ch'an tzu-liao*)," and outlines arguments for alternative classifications. Li Hui-hung, Sung Ch'i-jen, and Wang Hua-hsin, "Opinions on the Problem of Classifying Light and Heavy Industry," *ibid.*, 18: 13 (1957), specifically exclude defense industries from the producer sector. In an earlier work, Ching Lin, an official of the State Planning Commission, included tanks, military aircraft, and warships within the machinery industry in the FFYP (*Ti-i-ko wu-nien chi-hua-chung ti chi-ch'i chih tsao yeh* (Machine-building in the First Five-Year Plan; Peking, 1955), pp. 2, 3, 7–11, 18.

62. Thomas G. Rawski, "Chinese Industrial Production, 1952–1971," *Review of Economics and Statistics*, 55.2: 169–81 (1973).

63. This is one of the combinations used in Ta-chung Liu, "Quantitative Trends in the Economy," in Eckstein et al., eds., *Economic Trends*, p. 136; and in Simon Kuznets, "A Comparative Appraisal," in Abram Bergson and Simon Kuznets, eds., *Economic Trends in the Soviet Union* (Cambridge, Mass., 1963), p. 355. The similarity among productivity series based on various input weights allows us to disregard the issue of whether or not industrial wages accurately reflect marginal labor productivity.

64. Machinery output in 1957 was 6.177 billion 1952 yuan (Shigeru Ishikawa, *National Income and Capital Formation in Mainland China*, Tokyo, 1965, p. 60); the planned figure of 3.47 billion yuan appears in *Chūgoku no tekkōgyō to kikai kōgyō* (China's steel and machinery industries; Tokyo, 1964), p. 75. This is a partial translation of *Wo-kuo kang-t'ieh tien-li mei-t'an chi-hsieh fang-chih tsao-chih kung-yeh ti chin-hsi* (The present and past of our iron and steel, power, coal, machinery, textile, and paper manufacturing industries; Peking, 1958).

65. Thomas G. Rawski, "The Economics of Chinese Machine-Building, 1931–1967," Ph.D. diss., Harvard University, 1972, p. 123a, estimates that total factor productivity in machine-building rose by 14.1–15.8 percent annually between 1952 and 1957.

66. Clark, *Development of China's Steel Industry*, chap. 2.

67. *Chūgoku no tekkōgyō to kikai kōgyō*, p. 76, shows wide discrepancies between planned and actual average capacity for several machinery products. For examples of complaints by commerce officials and their generally unsuccessful efforts to force concessions from industrial ministries, see Su Lin, *T'an-t'an wo-kuo kuo-tu shih-ch'i ti chia-ko cheng-ts'e* (Talks on China's price policy in the transition period; Shanghai, 1956), p. 47; and *Survey of the China Mainland Press*, 690: 19–20.

68. Audrey G. Donnithorne, *China's Economic System* (London, 1967), pp. 418–33, 436–39, 449–53, discusses financial laxity and average cost pricing.

69. Output and capacity of enterprises for 1957 under the First Ministry from Chang Kuang-en, "Big-Letter Poster," *CHCC*, 4: 25 (1958); and Ching Lin, "On the Proportional Relation Between Steel and Machine-Building," *CHCC*, 9: 14 (1957). Idle capacity specifically affected agricultural and textile machinery, prospecting equipment, machine tools, and diesel engines (Ching Lin, p. 14); and the "First Ministry of Machine-Building Directive for 1957," *CHKY*, 9: 2–5 (1957), stated that "the majority" of enterprises would operate below full capacity.

70. General discussions of reduced investments such as Yü Chien t'ing, "The Problem of Proportional Relation Between Our Steel and Machinery Industries," *Ching-chi yen-chiu*, 6: 24 (1957), were supplemented by plans to suspend or delay specific projects, including the Peking Lathe Works, the Tientsin and Loyang tractor plants, the Wuhan Boiler Plant, and the Wuhan Heavy Machinery Works (Rawski, "Economics of Chinese Machine-Building," p. 146).

71. Estimated fixed capital available for productive use in the machinery sector rose by less than two-thirds between 1952 and 1957 (Rawski, "Economics of Chinese Machine-Building," p. 109).

72. The Pauley report cited in Onoe Etsuzō, *Chūgoku no sangyō ritchi ni kansuru kenkyū* (Studies in the location of Chinese industry; Tokyo, 1971), pp. 228–29, indicates a larger rate of destruction for Japanese investments in machine-building (80 percent) than for any other industrial sector. A report that output of metal products fell 80 percent in Shanghai during 1940–42 (Ch'en Chen and Yao Lo, *Kung-yeh shih Tzu-liao*, 1: 126) suggests an absence of wartime investment in Shanghai's machinery industry.

73. Overall industrial output, by contrast, exceeded the 1957 target of 53.56 billion yuan (*Chūgoku no tekkōgyō to kikai kōgyō*, p. 75) by only 21 percent.

74. Calculated from the supplement to this essay (available from the author).

75. *Survey of the China Mainland Press*, 1534: 9–12 .

76. Ajia tsūshinsha, comp., *Chūgoku sangyō bōeki sōran* (Tokyo, 1963), pp. 25, 27; "Concentration of Production of Standard Parts Is Economically Rational," *CHKY*, 22: 18 (1957).

77. Lin I-fu, "Take Active Steps for Full Utilization of Latent Productive

Capacity of Existing Industries," *CHCC*, 3: 7 (1958); Wang Te-yuan, "Perceive the Conditions of Steel Supply, Dig Up Latent Sources of Domestic Supply," *CHKY* 9: 29 (1957); Hsiang Lin, "How to Implement the Principle of Frugal National Construction in Basic Construction," *CHCC*, 11: 21 (1957).

78. Jan S. Prybyla, *The Political Economy of Communist China* (Scranton, Pa., 1970), chap. 7, provides a general description.

79. Clark, *Development of China's Steel Industry*, pp. 9–10, describes the Leap's impact at Anshan.

80. "Fifteen Years of Great Results," *Lao-tung*, 10:14 (1964); employment in the Shih-ching-shan plant had risen from 12,000 in 1958 to 52,000 in 1960 (Clark, p. 17); Lu Yün-ho and Ch'en Kuo-t'ai, "Find Ways to Save Labor," *Lao-tung*, 4: 19 (1962); Li Yü-heng and Ch'ang Pao-yü, "T'ai-yüan Saves Labor to Assist Agriculture," *ibid.*, 9: 15 (1962).

81. "Personnel Down, Efficiency Up," *ibid.*, 7: 9 (1964).

82. See the 1961–65 issues of *CHKY*, *HHKY*, and *Lao-tung* held by the Library of Congress.

83. Hu Pu-chou, "Establish Revolutionary Ambitions, Progress and Advance," *CHKY*, 15: 21 (1964); Liu Yao-ming, "With Politics Leading, Results Are Great," *CHKY*, 7: 17 (1966).

84. Hu Pu-chou, p. 20; "Be Conscientious, Small Things Are Important," *CHKY*, 23: 10–16 (1964).

85. Christopher Howe, *Wage Patterns and Wage Policy in Modern China, 1919–1972* (Cambridge, Eng., 1973), p. 77, describes new banking controls.

86. Kung Shih, "Study the Advanced, Uncover Idle Capacity," *Lao-tung*, 8: 17 (1963); Liang Ta, "Enforce Economy, Reform Management, Advance Production," *CHKY*, 9: 11 (1964).

87. For instance, Wang Shu-hui, "Management of Circulating Capital," *CHKY*, 6: 14 (1963), reports a 42 percent decline in inventory value at the Shanghai Machine Tool Plant; "The Experience of the Wan Hsien Ironworks in Reducing Casting Costs," *CHKY*, 23: 14–16 (1963), reports reduced transport costs; raw material savings are cited in *HHKY*, 9: 26–27 (1964).

88. "Strengthen Economic Control, Lower Product Costs," *CHKY*, 19: 14–16 (1963), describing the Shanghai Construction Machinery Plant, is one of many such articles.

89. Chu Hsi-ken et al., "Further Develop Specialized Production of Hardware," *CHKY*, 8: 29–32 (1963); Teng Chan-ming, "Problems of Developing Economic Cooperation Among Industries and Firms," *Ching-chi yen-chiu*, 3: 19–23 (1965); Rawski, "Economics of Chinese Machine-Building," pp. 187–93.

90. Thomas G. Rawski, "Recent Trends in the Chinese Economy," *China Quarterly*, 53: 24–26 (1973).

91. *Ibid.*, p. 25; "Continuously Raise the Technical Level of Old Workers," *Chung-kuo nung-yeh chi-hsieh*, 3: 29 (1962).

92. A typical description is in Hu Kuang, "The Developing Petroleum Equipment Manufacturing Industry," *CHKY*, 20: 14–15 (1964).

93. Ezra F. Vogel, *Canton Under Communism* (Cambridge, Mass., 1969), p. 312.

94. Such comparisons appear in Ku Min, "The Experience of Shanghai Ma-

chine Tool Plant in Starting a Production and Economy Campaign," *CHKY*, 9: 6–8 (1963); "Our Casting Shop's Method in Starting a Production and Economy Campaign," *CHKY*, 7: 11–12 (1963); Hu Pu-chou, "Establish Revolutionary Ambitions"; and Kung Shih, "Study the Advanced."

95. The Lanchow plant was begun with Soviet aid in 1957. Institute for the Study of Chinese Communist Problems, comp., *1967 Fei-ch'ing nien pao* (1967 yearbook of Chinese Communism; Taipei, 1967), p. 852; Ajia kenkyūjo, comp., *Chūgoku kōgyō kōjō sōran* (Handbook of China's industrial plants; Tokyo, 1970), 2: 603; "Some Ideas for Organizing to Complete Basic Construction and Engineering Plans," *CHKY*, 19: 17–18 (1963).

96. The author is Hu Kuang, who reports an output increase of 60 percent for 1962–63 and of 100 percent for the first eight months of 1963–64.

97. Hsiang Wen, "The Usefulness of Old Plants as Seen from Ta-lung's Transformation," *CHKY*, 20: 18–20 (1964).

98. Jon Sigurdson, "Rural Industry: A Traveller's View," *China Quarterly*, 50: 317–18 (1972).

99. *Chūgoku no tekkōgyō to kikai kōgyō*, p. 94.

100. Hsü P'ing, "Seek Weaknesses, Uncover Latent Strength, Lower Product Costs," *CHKY*, 8: 6–9 (1963); Hu Pu-chou, "Establish Revolutionary Ambitions."

101. Machinery import shares from Chu-yuan Cheng, *The Machine-Building Industry in Communist China* (Chicago, 1971), p. 55; and Rawski, "Recent Trends," p. 11.

102. "Advance Down the Road Toward Overtaking Advanced World Levels," *HHKY*, 2: 14–16 (1966).

103. Statement by a member of a Chinese economic mission to Japan, *Japan Times*, Oct. 11, 1973, p. 10.

Cooperation in Traditional Agriculture and Its Implications for Team Farming

The work *Chūgoku nōson kankō chōsa* (Studies on rural customs in China; Tokyo, 1952), comp. Chūgoku nōson kankō chōsa kankō, is abbreviated as *CNKC* in the Notes.

1. Kung-chuan Hsiao, *Rural China: Imperial Control in the Nineteenth Century* (Seattle, 1960), p. 36.

2. Mantetsu Hokushi jimukyoku chōsabu, *Hōtō fukin nōson jittai chōsa hōkoku* (A report on village conditions in the vicinity of Paotow; Peking, 1939), pp. 4–5.

3. Mantetsu Hokushi jimukyoku chōsabu, *Santōshō ichi nōson (Chō-yō ton) ni okeru shakai keizai jijō* (Social and economic conditions in Chang yao t'un village, Shantung; Tsingtao, 1936), p. 10.

4. C. K. Yang, *A Chinese Village in Early Communist Transition* (Cambridge, Mass., 1959), p. 103.

5. This assertion is based on a general reading of materials for the early 1960's. Since many villages were combined and production teams reorganized, particularly outside the large cities in vegetable-producing areas, team size must have varied enormously.

David L. Denny has made available to me data he has collected in his research on the range of size of production teams and brigades, and I cite them below.

Unit		Number of Households				
Brigade (approximates one or more villages)	less than 100	100–199	200–299	300–399	400–499	500 and over
	11	10	18	8	3	7
Teams	less than 10	10–19	20–39	40–59	60–69	70 and over
	0	7	19	7	3	8

6. Kung-chuan Hsiao, chap. 2.

7. Ramon H. Myers, *The Chinese Peasant Economy* (Cambridge, Mass., 1970), pp. 59–62, 82–85, 97–102, 116–20, 259–63.

8. A study of the Sheng-li agricultural producers' cooperative has a map showing that certain areas of village land are to be farmed by teams of households that generally reside in the same village neighborhood. Fan Hung, *Hsi-shan nung-yeh sheng-ch'an ho-tso she ti ch'eng-chang* (The development of Hsi-shan agricultural producers' cooperative; Peking, 1957), pp. 44–45.

9. Myers, *Chinese Peasant Economy*, pp. 59–62, 82–85, 97–102, 116–20, 259–63.

10. Sidney D. Gamble, "Hsin Chuang: A Study of Chinese Village Finance," *Harvard Journal of Asiatic Studies*, 8: 6–7 (1944–45); Mark Selden, *The Yenan Way in Revolutionary China* (Cambridge, Mass., 1971), p. 243.

11. See Myers, *Chinese Peasant Economy*, pp. 264–65, for a description of the *t'an-k'uan* tax levy imposed on villages.

12. Union Research Institute, *Documents of Chinese Communist Party Central Committee Sept. 1956–Apr. 1969* (Hong Kong, 1971), 1: 695–725. For an account of how such reorganization affected one commune in Lien-chiang hsien, Fukien, see C. S. Chen, ed., *Rural People's Communes in Lien-chiang* (Stanford, Calif., 1969); for a case in Kwangtung province, see John C. Pelzel, "Economic Management of a Production Brigade in Post-Leap China," in W. E. Willmott, ed., *Economic Organiaztion in Chinese Society* (Stanford, Calif., 1972), pp. 387–414.

13. A good example of how teams and brigades used labor during the idle farming season of winter can be found in Shan-tung sheng ching-chi yen-chiu suo nung-yeh ching-chi tsu, "Tung-k'uo ta-tui chien-she she-hui chu-i hsin nung-ts'un ti tiao-ch'a" (A survey of the Tung-k'uo brigade building socialism and a new rural community), *Ching-chi yen-chiu*, 2: 16 (1966).

14. Evidence of the size variation in private plots can be found in Kenneth R. Walker, *Planning in Chinese Agriculture* (Chicago, 1965), pp. 42–56.

15. Any prewar rural survey that stratified households according to land owned or farmed or by size of household according to family size or work force showed this imbalance between land and labor. The study containing the most informative data demonstrating this imbalance is John L. Buck, *Land Utilization in China: Statistics* (Chicago, 1937), chap. 7.

16. Numerous rural surveys show that cotton required more labor input than wheat and that millet needed more labor per unit of land than sorghum. For one particularly good detailed survey of Sung village in Ch'ang-te hsien,

Honan, showing the labor inputs according to crop and their rotations, see Minami Manshū tetsudō kabushiki kaisha, *Hoku shi nōson gaikyō chōsa hōkoku* (A survey report of village conditions in North China; Tokyo, 1940), pp. 118–19. See also Sidney D. Gamble, *Ting Hsien: A North China Rural Community* (Stanford, Calif., 1968), p. 243.

17. See C. K. Yang, *A Chinese Village*, p. 38, on the renting of buffalo, pp. 47–50 on land tenure contracts, and pp. 51–52 on the hiring of farm workers.

18. These village surveys can be found in Kanton dai Nihon teikoku sōryō-jikan, comp., *Kantonshō nōson chōsa hōkoku* (A report on villages of Kwangtung province; Canton, 1942).

19. Daniel Harrison Kulp II, *Country Life in South China* (Taipei, 1966).

20. Fei Hsiao-t'ung, *Peasant Life in China* (London, 1962), p. 162.

21. Martin C. Yang, *A Chinese Village* (London, 1947). The only aspect of rural cooperation that Yang discusses relates to the possibility that cooperatives could be formed in small market-town complexes (see pp. 246-47).

22. *CNKC*, 1: 105.

23. *Ibid.*, p. 106.

24. *Ibid.*

25. Examples of similar cooperation in farming can be found in *ibid.*, 3: 53, reporting that households of the same clan in Ssu pei ch'ai village, Hopei, helped one another build homes and even cooperated to purchase fertilizer.

26. Imahori Seiji, "Shindai ni okeru nōson kikō kindaika ni tsuite" (The modernization of rural institutions in the Ch'ing period), *Rekishigaku kenkyū*, 191.1: 8 (Jan. 1955).

27. Rinji Taiwan kyūkan chōsakai, *Taiwan tōgyō kyūkan ippan* (An overview of traditional customs in the Taiwan sugar industry; n.p., 1910), pp. 1–125.

28. Both practices are cited in Imahori Seiji, "Shindai no suiri dantai to seiji kenryoku" (Irrigation associations and political power in the Ch'ing period), *Ajiya kenkyū*, 10.3: 1–23 (Oct. 1963).

29. See *CNKC*, 6: 97–121, for evidence of household organization for irrigation management. This volume provides numerous examples like the one described in the text for other counties in North China.

30. See Maedo Shotarō, "Kahoku ni okeru suiri kikō" (Irrigation associations in North China villages), in *Gendai Ajiya no kakumei to hō—Niida Noboru kinen kōza* (Revolution and law in modern Asia—A memorial to Professor Niida Noboru; Tokyo, 1966) 1: 43–79.

31. See Morita Akira, "Kantonshō Nankaiken sōeni no chisui kikō ni tsuite" (The irrigation system in Sang-yüan-wei of Nan-hai hsien, Kwangtung), *Tōyō Gakuhō*, 47.2: 73–74 (Sept. 1964). The discussion in the text is based entirely on this study, which covers pp. 65–88.

32. Morita Akira, "Shindai no kosui kanri ni tsuite" (Lake management in the Ch'ing period), *Tōhōgaku*, 40: 99–100 (Sept. 1970).

33. *Ibid.*, pp. 103–4. Households were assessed in the same way in P'u-t'ien hsien, Fukien, where irrigation was managed on a cooperative basis during the Ch'ing period. Morita Akira, "Fukkenshō ni okeru suiri kyōdōtai ni tsuite" (Water utilization associations in Fukien), *Rekishigaku kenkyū*, 261: 19–28 (Nov. 1962).

34. Morita, "Shindai no kosui kanri ni tsuite," pp. 111–12.

35. Fei Hsiao-t'ung, p. 173.
36. *Ibid.*, p. 173.
37. Shinjō Toshiaki, "Hōtō no soengei nōgyō ni okeru kangai" (Irrigation vegetable farming in Paotow), *Mantetsu chōsa geppō*, 21.9 (Sept. 1941).
38. Fei Hsiao-t'ung, p. 27.
39. Irene B. Taeuber, "The Families of Chinese Farmers," in Maurice Freedman, ed., *Family and Kinship in Chinese Society* (Stanford, Calif., 1970), pp. 81–82.
40. *CNKC*, 1: 232. In Sha-ching village the peasants said of the transfer of chia-chang leadership when the household head died and only a sister survived: "Women have no right to become the household head. The brother of the deceased can select someone to assume this role. If a male is adopted from another family, permission from the clan must be obtained. This procedure is called *kuo-chi.*"
41. *CNKC*, 1: 236.
42. Francis L. K. Hsu, *Under the Ancestor's Shadow: Kinship, Personality, and Social Mobility in China* (Stanford, Calif., 1971), chaps. 9 and 10.
43. *Ibid.*, p. 247. Martin Yang too stresses that "a great part of the household activities are regulated by the invisible power of the ancestors" (*A Chinese Village*, p. 45).
44. Taeuber, p. 69.
45. According to Martin Yang, p. 50, most families in his village considered farming a dependable and socially desirable means of earning a living. A family expressed keen satisfaction and pride if it owned enough land for its sons to work.
46. These data can be found in a table in Kokumuin jigyōbu rinji chōsakyoku, comp., *Kōtoku gannendo nōson jittai chōsa* (Survey of village conditions in 1934; Hsinkyo, 1935), p. 1017. A similar table for another village showing the same mobility pattern over time can be found in Ramon H. Myers, "Economic Development in Manchuria Under Japanese Imperialism: A Dissenting View," *China Quarterly*, 55: 551 (July-Sept. 1973).
47. Burton Pasternak, *Kinship and Community in Two Chinese Villages* (Stanford, Calif., 1972).
48. C. K. Yang, *A Chinese Village*, p. 26.
49. *CNKC*, 6: 99.
50. A brief, useful description of rural cooperative development between 1920 and 1936 can be found in Mantetsu Shanhai jimusho, *Shina ni okeru nōson gosakusha no kentō* (Survey of rural cooperatives in China; Shanghai, 1939).
51. Sidney D. Gamble, *North China Villages* (Berkeley, Calif., 1963), chap. 5. Also Hatada Takashi, "Kyū Chūgoku sonraku no kyōdōtaiteki seikaku ni tsuite no kentō: Mura no tochi to mura no hito" (Study of the cooperative nature of traditional Chinese villages: Village land and villagers), *Jimbun gakuhō*, 51: 1–152 (Feb. 1966). According to Hatada, crop watching first evolved on a private contractual basis when households employed workers to guard their fields. Only when the theft of crops became a serious "village" problem did the peasants begin to take steps to form an organization to guard the fields at night.

On the Yenan Origins of Current Economic Policies

1. Jan Myrdal, *Report from a Chinese Village* (New York, 1965), p. xxvii.
2. V. Vyatsky and G. Dmitriev, "The Anti-Scientific, Voluntaristic Character of Mao Tse-tung's Economic Policy," *Voprosy Ekonomiki*, 11 (1968), as translated in *Reprints from the Soviet Press*, 8.4: 3–25 (1969), express this criticism.
3. Correspondents, "The Spirit of Yenan," *Peking Review*, 15.43: 10–13 (Oct. 27, 1972).
4. This section paraphrases and expands part of the introductory chapter of my book *Guerrilla Economy, 1937–1945: The Development of the Shensi-Kansu-Ninghsia Border Region* (forthcoming).
5. *Selected Works of Mao Tse-tung* (Peking, 1965), 1: 69–70.
6. Richard C. Thornton, *The Comintern and the Chinese Communists, 1928–1931* (Seattle, 1060), pp. 56–57
7. The more important items have been published in the *Fundamental Laws of the Chinese Soviet Republic* (New York, 1934).
8. *Selected Works of Mao Tse-tung*, 3: 196.
9. For an interpretation of these events, see John E. Rue, *Mao Tse-tung in Opposition, 1927–1935* (Stanford, Calif., 1966), pp. 262–63.
10. *Selected Works of Mao Tse-tung*, 1: 147–48.
11. Hsiao Tso-liang, *Power Relations Within the Chinese Communist Movement, 1930–1934* (Seattle, 1961), 2: 741–44.
12. For a discussion of the early history, see Mark Selden, "The Guerrilla Movement in Northwest China: The Origins of the Shensi-Kansu-Ninghsia Border Region," *China Quarterly*, 28: 63–81 (1966); 29: 61–81 (1967).
13. Edgar Snow, *Red Star over China* (New York, 1961), pp. 474, 476–77.
14. Chung-kuo k'o-hsüeh yüan, li-shih yen-chiu so, ti-san so, *Shan-Kan-Ning pien ch'ü ts-an-i hui wen-hsien hui-chi* (Collection of records of the Assemblies of Representatives of the Shensi-Kansu-Ninghsia Border Region; Peking, 1958), p. 37.
15. For the main themes of this struggle, see Rue, p. 279.
16. For most of the written materials on the rectification movement, see Boyd Compton, *Mao's China: Party Reform Documents, 1942–1944* (Seattle, 1952). On the early development of the movement, see Mark Selden, *The Yenan Way in Revolutionary China* (Cambridge, Mass., 1971), pp. 188ff.
17. *Selected Works of Mao Tse-tung*, 1: 291.
18. *Ibid.*, 2: 203.
19. For a summary presentation of the statistical evidence, see Schran, *Guerrilla Economy*, Table 4.5. There were no progress reports for 1944 and 1945, which suggests that the expansion of cooperation during the final years of the period was not great.
20. See *ibid.*, chap. 5, especially Table 5.2.
21. See *ibid.*, Table 6.1.
22. See *ibid.*, Table 7.6. The land cultivated by the rear army units in 1944 accounted for about 15 percent of all the land reclaimed in 1937–44.
23. See *ibid.*, Table 6.1. The irrigated land accounted for 0.3 percent of the cultivated land in 1944, according to official statistics. Much of this mar-

ginal land may have developed only surface fertility due to. fallow, with the result that the fields would have quickly become exhausted.

24. See *ibid.*, Tables 6.3, 6.4, 8.5, 8.6.

25. See *ibid.*, Tables 6.1, 6.3.

26. See *ibid.*, Tables 6.3, 6.10.

27. See *ibid.*, Table 6.5.

28. See *ibid.*, Tables 8.1, 8.2.

29. See *ibid.*, Table 7.2.

30. On the redistributive effects of taxation, see *ibid.*, Table 9.10; and *Ching-chi yen-chiu*, 2: 105–12 (1956).

31. Chung-kuo k'o-hsüeh yüan, p. 287.

32. For repeated statements to this effect, see *Selected Works of Mao Tse-tung*, 4.

33. For an illuminating discussion of the critical issues, see Franz Schurmann, *Ideology and Organization in Communist China*, new ed. (Berkeley, Calif., 1970), especially parts 4 and 5.

34. Selden stresses this consequence in *Yenan Way*.

35. Kang Chao, *Agricultural Production in Communist China, 1949–1965* (Madison, Wis., 1970), chap. 1, brings out this change in perspective.

36. *Ibid.*, p. 24, indicates that the agricultural development program was formulated by Mao in consultation with provincial Party secretaries, most of whom may be presumed to have experienced the production campaigns in the base areas.

37. See *Selected Works of Mao Tse-tung*, 3: 243–44, 326, for the expression of this view with respect to production by the institutional households in the base areas.

38. Schurmann. For a summary of the contrasting features, see Peter Schran, "Economic Management," in John M. H. Lindbeck, ed., *China: Management of a Revolutionary Society* (Seattle, 1971), especially pp. 205ff.

39. For a detailed description of the movement, see Selden, *Yenan Way*, pp. 224–29. For indications of limited success in the transfer of superfluous personnel, see Schran, *Guerrilla Economy*, Table 5.2.

40. For a detailed discussion, see Rensselaer W. Lee, III, "The *Hsia Fang* System: Marxism and Modernization," *China Quarterly*, 28: 40–62 (1966).

41. I have omitted, for instance, the efforts in educational reform. On this point, see Peter J. Seybolt, "The Yenan Revolution in Mass Education," *China Quarterly*, 48: 641–69 (1971); and Robert D. Barendsen, "The Agricultural Middle School in Communist China," *ibid.*, 8: 106–34 (1961).

42. Dwight H. Perkins, "Economic Growth in China and the Cultural Revolution (1960–April 1967)," *China Quarterly*, 30: 33–48 (1967), illuminates the development of this opposition to Mao—without reference to Yenan.

43. See Alexander Eckstein, "Economic Fluctuations in Communist China's Domestic Development," in Ping-ti Ho and Tang Tsou, eds., *China in Crisis* (Chicago, 1968), 1.2: 710–12, for an interpretation of this response.

44. Note again in particular the omission of correspondences in educational reform, which was a critical concern during the Cultural Revolution. See Seybolt; and Marianne Bastid, "Economic Necessity and Political Ideals in Educational Reform During the Cultural Revolution," *China Quarterly*, 52: 605–19 (1972).

45. For citations of official references to this precedent, see Chalmers Johnson, "Chinese Communist Leadership and Mass Response: The Yenan Period and the Socialist Education Campaign Period," in Ho and Tsou, 1.1: 433–34.

46. *Ibid.*; Jack Gray and Patrick Cavendish, *Chinese Communism in Crisis* (New York, 1968), pp. 223–38.

47. *Peking Review*, 15.43: 13 (Oct. 27, 1972).

48. See Edgar Snow, "Talks with Chou En-lai—The Open Door," *The New Republic*, Mar. 27, 1971, p. 21.

Index

Africa, 6n, 7f, 145
agrarian revolution, 281, 287–88, 297.
  See also Land
Agricola, G., 106
agriculture: commercialization of, 3–4,
  26, 34; status of, 12–13, 271–72, 334;
  traditional cooperation in, 17, 265–70,
  274–77; and equilibrium trap, 24–26;
  input to, 24–26, 69, 112, 243; growth
  of, 62n, 145, 147; and industry, 62–63;
  surplus in, 65–70; technology for,
  86, 91–96, 101–2, 104, 112, 227; in
  national product, 116, 138–44, 146f,
  161f; government expenditure on,
  143–45, 147, 164; under Communists,
  143–44, 145n, 149–55, 164, 229f, 285,
  288, 290, 294–302; agrarian dualism, 235, 238, 241–46, 253; labor
  productivity in, 244–47, 249–50
—output of, 3–4, 24–25, 69–70, 79–80,
  116–18, 120–22, 127, 129–30, 137n,
  150–51, 155; per capita, 63n–64;
  Soviet compared, 131, 319; under
  Communists, 143–44, 145n, 149–55,
  164, 295, 301–2
Amoy, China, 32, 176
Anshan ironworks, 213, 215f, 219
Archimedean water-screw, 104–7
artisans, *see* Handicraft industry
Asia, *see by individual country name*

Bangkok, 10, 257
banking and finance: native, 4, 31, 42,
  45, 288, 291; foreign, 11n, 37, 42, 45;
  development of, 119, 160, 215–16,
  288; loans to industry, 215–16, 226
Baran, Paul A., 50–55, 59, 309
beancake manufacture, 108–9, 112
Besson, J., 111
blockade, Nationalist, 282, 285f,
  289f, 292
Böckler, G. A., 111
Boxer Rebellion, 15

brigade, production, 262, 264, 331–32
Buck, John Lossing, 57, 61, 69, 80,
  236, 310
Burki, Shahid, 149
Burma, 8

cadres, 263, 287, 293, 296–97, 300ff
Canton, 32, 262
capital, 40, 45, 83, 103; inflow of Chinese, 11, 35; formation of, 16, 133–38,
  163–65, 234; as input in equilibrium
  trap, 24–26; use of, 58, 204, 234;
  shortage of, 213–16, 290, 296. *See
  also* Foreign investment
capital-intensive production, 9, 45,
  56, 325
cement, 9, 120, 158, 232, 308
cereals, 34–35, 92, 150. *See also
  individual products by name*
ceremonial expenses, 57, 69n
Chahar, 188
Chambers of Commerce, Chinese, 42
Chang, Chung-li, 82
Chang, John, 32, 78
Chang Tso-lin, 218
Chao, Kang, 16, 121
Chao Lei-sheng, 106
Chekiang province, 88, 92–98 *passim*,
  102–3, 112, 153n, 171, 269, 276
chemicals, 35, 41, 121, 158, 163, 203,
  221, 232–33
Chen Han-seng, 22, 57
Ch'en Ch'i-yüan, 108
Ch'en Yüan-lung, 88
Ch'en Yun-kung, 96
Chenery, Hollis B., 34f, 139–43, 146–47
Cheng, Chu-yuan, 159
Ch'eng T'ing-tso, 110–11
Chi Ch'i-kuang, 112
Ch'i Chung, 94
Ch'i Yen-huai, 101–2, 104, 107
chia, 262ff, 270f, 273, 276
China: as less-developed country, 1, 3,

129441

DATE			
FEB 8 1979			
FEB 3 1 1979			
~~			
NOV 2 7 1984			